The Theatre Experience

TWELFTH EDITION

EDWIN WILSON

Professor Emeritus
Graduate School and University Center
The City University of New York

McGraw Hill

Connect
Learn
Succeed™

THE THEATRE EXPERIENCE

Published by McGraw-Hill, an imprint of The McGraw-Hill Companies, Inc., 1221 Avenue of the Americas, New York, NY 10020. Copyright © 2011 by Edwin Wilson. All rights reserved. No part of this publication may be reproduced or distributed in any form or by any means, or stored in a database or retrieval system, without the prior written consent of The McGraw-Hill Companies, Inc., including, but not limited to, in any network or other electronic storage or transmission, or broadcast for distance learning.

This book is printed on acid-free paper.

2 3 4 5 6 7 8 9 0 DOW/DOW 9 8 7 6 5 4 3 2 1

ISBN: 978-0-07-338219-7
MHID: 0-07-338219-1

Vice President, Editorial: *Michael Ryan*
Publisher: *Christopher Freitag*
Sponsoring Editor: *Betty Chen*
Editorial Coordinator: *Sarah Remington*
Marketing Manager: *Pamela Cooper*
Director of Development: *Nancy Crochiere*
Developmental Editor: *Laura Wilk*
Production Editor: *Jasmin Tokatlian*
Media Project Manager: *Shannon Gattens*
Manuscript Editor: *Susan Gamer*
Design Manager: *Laurie Entringer*
Cover Designer: *Brad Norr*
Photo Research Coordinator: *Natalia Peschiera*
Photo Editor: *Inge King*
Buyer II: *Tandra Jorgensen*
Composition: *10.5/13 Garamond by Thompson Type*
Printing: *45# New Era Matte, RR Donnelley*

Front cover: Event tickets. © Kacey Baxter/Acorn Studios/istockphoto.com.
Back cover: Ghost light at the Floyd and Delores Jones Playhouse, University of Washington School of Drama. © Paul Butzi Photography.

Library of Congress Cataloging-in-Publication Data
Wilson, Edwin.
      The theater experience / Edwin Wilson.—12th ed.
      p. cm.
      ISBN 978-0-07-338219-7 ISBN 0-07-338219-1
      1.   Theater. I. Title.

      PN1655.W57 2010
      792-dc22

                                                    2010029394

The Internet addresses listed in the text were accurate at the time of publication. The inclusion of a Web site does not indicate an endorsement by the authors or McGraw-Hill, and McGraw-Hill does not guarantee the accuracy of the information presented at these sites.

www.mhhe.com

About the Author

Teacher, author, and critic, Edwin Wilson has worked in many aspects of theatre. Educated at Vanderbilt University, the University of Edinburgh, and Yale University, he received an MFA from the Yale Drama School, as well as the first Doctor of Fine Arts degree awarded by Yale. He has taught at Yale, Hofstra, Vanderbilt, Hunter College, and the CUNY Graduate Center. At Hunter he served as chair of the Department of Theatre and Film and head of the graduate theatre program. At CUNY he founded and was Executive Director of the Martin E. Segal Theatre Center.

Edwin Wilson was the theatre critic of *The Wall Street Journal* for 22 years. In addition to *The Theatre Experience*, he is coauthor with Alvin Goldfarb of *Living Theatre: A History*, *Theatre: The Lively Art*, and the *Anthology of Living Theatre*, also published by McGraw-Hill. He was also responsible for the volume *Shaw on Shakespeare*. He was the president of the New York Drama Critics Circle and served several times on the Tony Nominating Committee and the Pulitzer Prize Drama Jury. He is on the boards of the John Golden Fund and the Susan Smith Blackburn Prize. He served for many years on the board of the Theatre Development Fund, of which he was also president.

Before turning to teaching and writing, Edwin Wilson was assistant to the producer for the film *Lord of the Flies*, directed by Peter Brook, and the Broadway play *Big Fish, Little Fish*, directed by John Gielgud. He produced several off-Broadway shows and coproduced a Broadway play directed by George Abbott. He also directed in summer and regional theatre, serving one season as resident director of the Barter Theatre in Virginia. He was Executive Producer of the film *The Nashville Sound*. As a playwright he has had successful stage readings or productions of a farce, a history play, a musical revue, and a musical version of Dickens' *Great Expectations*, for which he wrote book and lyrics.

The Theatre Experience encourages students to attend and respond to productions, and take an active role as an audience participant.

Understanding Today's Introduction to Theatre Course

New focused 15-chapter organization fits within a semester's schedule without sacrificing key substance and context. New ideas and concepts, such as postmodernism, deconstruction, and non-text-based theatre, are introduced and expanded.

Bringing Theatre to Life

Photo Essays and the text's dynamic art program allow students to visualize the core theatrical concepts introduced in each chapter.

Responding to Theatrical Productions

The Audience's Response feature engages students in their role as audience participants by asking them to apply key chapter concepts to their own experiences through critical-thinking questions.

Appreciating the World of Theatre

The new introduction takes students around the world to visit the origins of theatre, preparing them for the global content presented throughout the text. In addition, Chapter14: Global Theatre Today and the Global Crosscurrents features, found throughout the text, present the global reach and influences of theatre from various cultures.

To my wife, Catherine

Contents in Brief

Contents

Chapter 3   **Background and Expectations of the Audience   45**

PART 2

The Performers and the Director   88

PART 3

Setting the Stage: The Playwright and the Play 150

Features

Photo Essays

Global Crosscurrents

Dynamics of Drama

Historical Perspectives

The Audience's Response

Letter from the Author

I felt strongly that the time had come to undertake the most extensive revision to *The Theatre Experience* in the book's history. In developing the twelfth edition, I wanted to accomplish two things at once. On the one hand, I wanted to retain and reinvigorate the hallmark features that have gained such wide acceptance for the book. First and foremost among those is the book's focus on the audience's active role. On the other hand, I wanted to re-envision the content and structure for today's students.

As instructors, we always hope that a few talented students will eventually become theatre artists and professionals. We know, however, that most students in introductory or theatre appreciation courses are future audience members. In that sense, the "experience" referred to in the title of the book has always been very much aimed at them. I have not only continued this emphasis on the audience, I have enhanced it, not only in the crucial Part One devoted to the audience, but with many additional features, including a new critical-thinking feature, "The Audience's Response."

Those aspects of the text that have always set it apart remain vital, indispensible components. One example is the book's vivid, exciting illustration program, in which each photograph is tied directly to the text. Another is the book's clear, direct writing style. This includes references throughout to students' everyday experiences, such as sports analogies and role playing in daily life. In short, the essence and substance of the book remain what they have always been.

At the same time, I have made a number of significant improvements in the book. Perhaps most importantly, it has been reduced from 19 chapters to 15 chapters. This has been accomplished not by losing insights or information but by careful, judicious editing, in which each chapter, each paragraph has been examined with a with a fresh, critical eye. Correspondingly, important new ideas and concepts have been introduced or expanded. Postmodernism, deconstruction and non-text-based theatre, for instance, are discussed not only earlier in the book, but at length in Chapter 15.

Another crucial enhancement is expanded coverage of global theatre. In the previous edition, a new chapter was devoted to this subject and "Global Crosscurrents" features were introduced. In this edition, additional global profiles were added, and the global chapter was thoroughly revised. Most importantly, I created an entirely new opening section for Chapter 1, in which students are taken to four ancient sites on four different continents—Egypt, Athens, Japan, and the Mayan civilization—to experience first-hand early theatre events. This introduction underscores the universal impulse toward theatre, and of course the importance of the audience.

Wherever students see performances, whether in a large formal theatre or an intimate black box, the new insights and features in this edition of *The Theatre Experience* will prepare them for their role as audience participants. In doing so, the twelfth edition is not just a revival of the previous edition—it's the début of a brand new show.

NEW CONTENT IN THE TWELFTH EDITION

In addition to restructuring the table of contents to better accommodate semester-long courses, the twelfth edition includes the following changes and improvements:

Chapter 1, Experiencing Theatre: Past and Present. Fully revised with a new introduction, this chapter introduces students to the universal appeal of theatre throughout history. Global content is introduced in this chapter to bring the multicultural world of theatre to the forefront of the book. In doing so, students are prepared for the international influences integral to the study of theatre.

Chapter 3, Background and Expectations of the Audience. This chapter is restructured to include special audience members—the critic and the dramaturg—previously discussed in separate chapters. By incorporating these important figures into the overarching conversation on the roles of audience members, students get a comprehensive look at the active role all people play when attending a theatre performance.

Chapter 5, Acting. This chapter combines the content from the eleventh edition's chapters on "Acting: Offstage and in the Past" and "Stage Acting Today" into one chapter. Students get a more focused introduction to the training, development, and collaboration that goes into the final productions they observe as audience members.

Chapter 6, The Director and the Producer. New content on postmodern directors provides a comprehensive look at the responsibilities of these key figures. By providing additional examples of the director's role as a surrogate spectator throughout each play's development, students get a better understanding of how performances are shaped with the audience in mind.

Chapter 9, Tragedy, Comedy, and Tragicomedy. By combining the content from the previous edition's chapters on "Tragedy and Other Serious Drama" and "Comedy and Tragicomedy," students receive a thorough introduction to thinking about plays in terms of genre.

Chapter 14, Global Theatre Today. This chapter was a new addition to the eleventh edition. In the twelfth edition it has been fully revised to include new information on theatre in Africa, Asia, Latin America, the Middle East, Australia, North America, and Europe. It includes a brief historical background on all the theatrical centers of the world, and discusses how these different regions have influenced theatre in other areas.

ONLINE LEARNING CENTER: WWW.MHHE.COM/WILSONTE12E

The Theatre Experience offers a wealth of learning and teaching resources. Student and instructor materials include:

- Chapter-by-chapter quizzes for testing students.
- Correlation Guide for *The Anthology of Living Theatre.*
- Weblinks and Internet Exercises for each chapter, including links to play synopses.
- Instructor's Manual and Test Bank.
- EZ Test Computerized Test Bank: McGraw-Hill's EZ Test is a flexible, easy-to-use electronic testing program that allows instructors to create tests from

specific items in the text. It accommodates a wide range of question types, and instructors may add their own questions. Multiple versions of the test can be created, and any test can be exported for use with course management systems. The program is available for Windows and Macintosh.

- Detailed explanations and examples of Major Theatrical Forms and Movements (previously Appendix B in the Eleventh Edition).
- Synopses of Plays (Previously Appendix A in Eleventh Edition).
- Select Bibliography.

COURSESMART E-TEXTBOOK

This text is available as an eTextbook at www.CourseSmart.com. At CourseSmart, students can take advantage of significant savings off the cost of a print textbook, reduce their impact on the environment, and gain access to powerful Web tools for student learning. You can view CourseSmart eTextbooks online or download them to a computer. CourseSmart eTextbooks allow students to do full text searches, add highlighting and notes, and share notes with classmates. Visit www.CourseSmart .com to learn more and try a sample chapter.

ACKNOWLEDGMENTS

I first developed many of the ideas in this book while teaching a course in Introduction to Theatre at Hunter College of the City University of New York. To my former students and colleagues at Hunter, I express my continuing appreciation.

This edition of *The Theatre Experience* builds on editions of the past, and to those professors and other experts who contributed to prior versions, I express my deep appreciation. For this particular edition I wish to especially thank Alexis Greene, Naomi Stubbs, Susan Tenneriello, Marina Volok, Donny Levit, and Frank Episale for their important contributions, including research and the special sections they have written. In addition, I express my gratitude to Professor Jeff Entwistle for his prodigious contribution to the chapters on design—scenic, costume, lighting, and sound—and I also thank Professor Laura Pulio for her helpful suggestions on acting. To Professor Oliver W. Gerland and his fellow teachers at the University of Colorado I express my appreciation for bringing me into the twenty-first century.

Additionally, a number of professors submitted reviews of the text, which helped to shape our revision. I am grateful for their suggestions and hope they will find that the twelfth edition has benefitted extensively from their input.

Randal Blades, Jacksonville State University
Emily Becher-McKeever, James Madison University
Sharon Taylor, Edinboro University
Holly E. McDonald, University of Central Florida
Alison E. Stafford, Hinds Community College
Lisa Inzer Coleman, Southwest Tennessee Community College
Cheryl Hall, University of Alabama at Birmingham
Tom Mikotowicz, University of Maine
Jeff Entwistle, University of Wisconsin Green Bay

Tammis Doyle, Bellevue College
Paula Pierson Heitman, San Diego State University
John Eby, Parkland College

Through twenty-five editions of my three textbooks published by McGraw-Hill, Inge King, the astonishing photography expert, has discovered every photograph that has appeared in every edition of every text, including this edition of *The Theatre Experience.* Inge is a nonpareil and irreplaceable colleague. As I pointed out in the last edition, through the years Inge has discovered and shown me and my editors nearly 35,000 photographs from which to select the ones that make up our extraordinary illustration program. There is no way to adequately acknowledge her amazing taste, her persistence, her abiding loyalty to the project, and her creativity. Also with us on the previous ten editions of *The Theatre Experience,* as well as our other two texts, is the industrious, incomparable and ever-accurate copy editor, Susan Gamer, to whom I am always grateful.

At McGraw-Hill I express my gratitude to my vigilant editors, Betty Chen, Laura Wilk, and Nancy Crochiere for their insight, their foresight, and their dedication.

The Theatre Experience

Experiencing Theatre: Past and Present

The time is around 1875 BCE, nearly 4,000 years ago. The location is Abydos, a sacred place near the present-day Luxor in Egypt. A performer named Ikhernofret is participating in a ritual drama that is thought to have been reenacted at this spot every year for 2,000 years, from roughly 2500 to 550 BCE. The thousands of people who have made their way to Abydos have come to see the mythic story of the god Osiris, a ruler of Egypt who married his sister Isis. The brother of Osiris, jealous of him, killed him and scattered parts of his body throughout the kingdom. Later, the wife, Isis, was able to recover these remains and bring Osiris back to life. He could not remain on earth, however, so his spirit went to dwell in the underworld, where he became a favorite among the Egyptian gods.

We know about Ikhernofret's participation in this ritual drama because we have a document written by him about it. Though fragmentary, this document shows clearly that the ceremony at Abydos incorporated many theatrical elements. For example, there were performers like Ikhernofret, whose different roles he describes. There was a scenario of some kind depicting the sequence of events; there were also costumes, and possibly dance; and, of course, there was an audience.

From Abydos and the continent of Africa, we move north across the Mediterranean Sea to a different continent—specifically, to Athens, Greece. The year is 441 BCE, about 100 years after the Abydos ritual in Egypt had ended its 2,000-year span. It is a morning in late March in Athens and the citizens of the city are up early, making their way to the Theatre of Dionysus, an open-air theatre on the south side of the Acropolis, the highest hill in Athens. Semicircular seating has been built into the slope of the

◀ **TODAY'S GLOBAL, DIVERSE THEATRE**

Theatre today is truly global, with exchanges among theatre artists from all parts of the world. Many western nations, for instance, have become extremely familiar with the theatre of Asia. An excellent example, seen here, is Haruhiko Jo as an ancient former beauty in a drama in "modern nō" style: Yukio Mishima's Sotoba Komachi, *with an all-male cast, directed by Yukio Ninagawa, and presented at a Lincoln Center Festival. (© Michael Kim/Corbis)*

hill, and at the foot is a flat, circular space where the actors will perform. It is at this time, the fifth century BCE, and in this place, Athens, that western theatre began.

The performance the spectators are to see today is part of the City Dionysia festival, an annual series of dramas dedicated to the god of wine and fertility. So important is the festival that while it is on, all business in Athens—both commercial and governmental—comes to a halt. The play about to begin is *Antigone* by Sophocles. Based on a myth, it tells the story of the daughter of King Oedipus, Antigone, who is determined to defy the king, her uncle Creon. After her father's death, her two brothers, Eteocles and Polynices, fought a war against each other during which they killed one another. Creon blames Polynices for the conflict and issues an edict that Polynices is not to be given an honorable burial.

Antigone, however, feels compelled to give her dead brother a proper burial. She tells her sister that she intends to disobey the king, knowing that she will be put to death if she is caught. During the play, when Antigone does attempt to bury Polynices, she is caught and brought before the king. In their confrontation, Antigone defies Creon, and as a result she is sentenced to death and put into a cave to die. By the end of the play, not only is Antigone dead; so too are Creon's wife and son, who have killed themselves.

The time is nearly 1,000 years later, 1413 CE. We have moved half a world away from Athens, to the Kitano temple, a religious site in Kitano, Japan, near the present-day town of Nagoya. At the Kitano temple, a platform stage, with a floor of polished wood, has been set up. The actor performing today is named Zeami. He is 50 years old and has been under the patronage of the shogun of Japan since he was 12. Zeami's father, Kan'ami, was a renowned actor before him, and Zeami has carried his father's art to even greater heights, having studied different acting styles, perfected his own technique, trained other actors, and written plays. The theatre he has fashioned from all this is called nō; it has elements of opera, pantomime, and formal, stylized dance. In nō theatre, the main character, who wears striking costumes and a beautifully carved, hand-painted wooden mask, recites his character's adventures to the constant accompaniment of several onstage musicians.

The audience gathered at Kitano is awaiting Zeami's performance in *Sotoba Komachi*, in which he will portray the leading character, a beautiful woman named Komachi. In the play Komachi is pursued by a man named Shii no Shōshō. Komachi tells Shōshō that he must call on her for 100 nights in a row, and for ninety-nine nights he comes, in all kinds of weather. But on the hundredth night, a snowstorm is raging and he falls exhausted, and dies on her doorstep.

During the play, the audience watches Zeami's performance with rapt attention. At one point, his character becomes possessed: the spirit of Shōshō takes over and Zeami acts this out in pantomime, to a musical accompaniment. At another point, Komachi is dressed as Shōshō and becomes him, feeling his death agony, which he performs as a mesmerizing, frightening dance. At the end of the play, the spirit of Shōshō leaves Komachi, and prays to Buddha for guidance and for a peaceful life in the hereafter.

In the same time period as Zeami's performance—that is, the early 1400s CE—on the other side of the Pacific Ocean, in the continent now known as South America, another theatrical event takes place. The location is Rabinal in the central mountains of present-day Guatemala. (The people of Rabinal know nothing of the people of Japan, or of any other area, for that matter. It will be more than 100 years before the Spanish conquistadors invade their territory.)

The occasion of which we are speaking is a ceremonial drama presented each year at this site. From miles around, hundreds, perhaps thousands, of people gather to witness a remarkable presentation: *Rabinal Achi,* which means "Man of Rabinal." We are in the land of the Mayan people, a culture rich in history and tradition. The so-called classic period in Mayan history, during which the culture reached an exceedingly high level of civilization in architecture, art, science, and religion, ran from the fourth through the tenth centuries CE. At some point, a catastrophe struck the Maya, but enough of the traditions and accomplishments survived for the people to rebuild; and by the time we are discussing, the early fifteenth century, an impressive degree of maturity had been achieved.

Rabinal Achi, an annual event in the city for which it is named, is striking evidence of the Maya's achievement. Artifacts make clear that this ceremonial drama involved elaborate costumes and masks, as well as sophisticated dance, choreography,

THEATRICAL CEREMONIES AND RITUALS

Many ceremonies—including present-day rituals but also many ancient ones—have extensive theatrical elements. A particularly intriguing ceremony is known as *Rabinal Achi.* It has been performed for many centuries, at least since the early fifteenth century, at a place called Rabinal in central Guatemala. It was originally a Mayan ritual celebrating the victory of the prince of Rabinal, who defeated a villain attempting to overthrow him and capture his children. The sacred ritual, a scene from which is shown here, is still celebrated each year, in a form close to the original. (Roman Catholic authorities some years ago modified it for religious reasons.) (Rodrigo Abd/AP Images)

poetry, and music. The story resonates with aspects of Mayan history and religion. The title character in the narrative is a warrior who serves the ruler of Rabinal. Guarding the lord of the kingdom are two characters named Eagle and Jaguar. In the court of the lord are a wife, a daughter, and a slave. The chief villain of the piece is Cawek, a renegade warrior from a neighboring nation, the Forest People. At the end of the story Rabinal is able to capture Cawek and bring him to justice.

The music, poetry, dialogue, dances, costumes, and masks were passed down over generations in an oral tradition. So colorful, so dramatic, so remarkable was this ceremonial drama of the Maya that when the Spanish later conquered the area and saw a performance, they were awestruck and, after introducing several Catholic elements, allowed it to continue each year, as it has done to the present day.

THEATRE: GLOBAL AND UNIVERSAL

The four theatrical presentations just cited tell us a number of things about the nature of theatre. One is that theatre is global; another is that the impulse to create theatre is universal. These four events—at Abydos, Athens, Kitano, and Rabinal—took place over a span of nearly 4,000 years, and they occurred on four continents, in most cases widely separated by oceans and huge landmasses. The people involved had no contact with one another and knew nothing of each other, and yet they all came up with rituals, ceremonies, and dramatic performances that were highly theatrical and endured for hundreds of years.

THE IMPULSE TOWARD THEATRE IS UNIVERSAL
Throughout the world, cultures have rituals, ceremonies, and dances that include theatrical elements such as masks, costumes, and impersonations not only of people but sometimes of animals or spirits. Here, in Mali, west Africa, teetering on stilts high above a crowd of villagers, masked Dogon dancers imitate a long-legged waterbird. (© Charles and Josette Lenars/Corbis)

In addition to those noted above, one could add further examples of the global, universal nature of theatre. Full-fledged theatre emerged, for example, in India, China, and Indonesia even before it appeared in Japan, and elaborate rituals and ceremonies were a hallmark of numerous cultures in Africa as well as among Native Americans in North America.

The development of theatrical undertakings in so many widely dispersed areas points to the inherent impulse in all cultures to create theatre. Wherever a group of people has developed a civilization and achieved a sense of community, the group invariably seeks fulfillment and expression in the arts: dance, music, painting, architecture, sculpture, and, as we have pointed out, theatre.

Taken in its broadest sense, theatre is everywhere around us. A wedding is theatre; a funeral is theatre. A Thanksgiving Day parade, a Mardi Gras parade, a fireworks display on the Fourth of July—all these are theatre. So, too, is a presidential nominating convention, a Senate hearing, or a White House press conference. Even seemingly spontaneous, unrehearsed events, such as a high-speed automobile chase or a gunman holding hostages in a suburban home, have become a form of theatre by the time they are seen on television. The person holding the television camera has framed the "shots" showing the event; and for the evening news, the people who edit and report a segment on a family tragedy have taken great care to present the story as a brief drama, with an attention-grabbing opening followed by a suspenseful or shocking revelation and then a closing—a quotation, perhaps, from a relative or neighbor. We even encounter drama in seemingly real-life reports on television: not only on the evening news but in documentaries and so-called reality shows. The popularity of music videos on MTV, VH1, and YouTube also reflects the integration of theatrical elements into contemporary music. These videos turn many songs into visual, dramatic narratives.

When we turn from electronic media to live performance, we see that throughout history musicians and performers have appropriated theatrical elements. Beginning with Little Richard and Elvis Presley in the 1950s, and the Beatles in the 1960s, through punk rock, glam rock, rap, hip-hop, and other forms, musical performers have used costumes, lights, props, and makeup to entertain audiences. Recently, the pop singer Lady Gaga incorporated innovative costumes, complex choreography, and multistage sets into two of her tours: *The Fame Ball* and *The Monster Ball*.

THEATRICALITY IN THE POPULAR ARTS
Good examples of the crossover of theatrical elements between the popular arts and traditional theatre are the elaborate, outsize presentations by individual performers and popular rock groups, which use extravagant costumes, spectacular lighting, sound, and full-scale scenic effects. Shown here is the star Lady Gaga performing in a dress made of bubbles. (Yana Paskova/The New York Times/Redux)

PERFORMATIVE ACTIVITIES AND PERFORMATIVE ARTS

This is a good point at which to differentiate among different types of performances. Theatrical events in everyday life—weddings, funerals, graduations, inaugurations—are considered *performative activities.* In addition to formal ceremonies and special occasions, performative activities also include role playing, a subject we will discuss in the section on stage acting. Role playing by individuals involves both professional and private roles: a woman, for example, may be both a physician and a mother.

Performative arts, or *performing arts,* include such ceremonies and presentations as the Abydos and Mayan ritual dramas described above. Throughout history, formal rituals, ceremonies, celebrations, and religious services have emerged all over the globe: among Native Americans, in many parts of Africa, in Australia, and elsewhere. These are formal occasions, repeated over and over again through generations, often at a given time each year or every few years. They generally include many theatrical components, including costumes, performance roles, and dance, which help to tell a story.

The *theatrical arts* constitute a third manifestation of performance. In the east—China, India, Japan, and elsewhere—and in the West, first in Greece, then in Rome, and later in other parts of Europe and the Americas, the type of theatre with which we are most familiar developed. Simply stated, this type of theatre consists of a dramatic presentation by actors on some kind of stage before an audience. Usually it involves such elements as a dramatization of a story, a scenic environment, and costumes.

Obviously, the theatrical arts are closely allied to the performance arts, and in recent years, the two have increasingly overlapped. Dance-drama is just one example. Throughout this volume we will look at the relationship of the theatrical arts and other performing arts. Our primary focus, however, will be on the art form of theatre in the tradition of Sophocles and Zeami, who were discussed above, and especially on the experience of the audience in attending this kind of theatre. We will explore what it means to observe, absorb, appreciate, and understand a theatrical presentation.

THEATRE AS SOURCE AND FOUNDATION

Most of us are likely to have our first theatrical experiences with some form other than actually attending theatre: movies, television, and our computers. In seeing these electronic presentations we may experience a wide range of emotions—suspense, conflict, horror, humor, joy, sometimes even ecstasy—the same emotions that theatre can evoke in us.

What we are probably not aware of is that all these electronic or media events and all these experiences have their roots in live theatre. Live theatre is the forerunner, the foundation, the fountainhead of everything we see, from a gripping, suspenseful movie to a situation comedy on television to a chilling report of a family tragedy on the evening news. For more than 2,000 years—in Europe and Asia, and later in the Americas—theatre was the only form of dramatic art in existence. Over the centuries, live theatre went through various transformations, but the basic formula—performers on a stage enacting a dramatic story—remained unchanged.

Around 1900, the dramatic universe began to change, and it continued to do so throughout the twentieth century as one technological development after another

THEATRE: THE SOURCE OF ALL DRAMA

Theatre is the root of all dramatic forms: not only of live theatre itself, but of film, television, and theatrical presentations on a computer. A good example is the ancient legend of Orpheus and Eurydice, which is the basis of Sarah Ruhl's play *Eurydice*. The drama, a modern interpretation of the story told from Eurydice's point of view, presents a contemporary account of the legend, in which Eurydice dies and goes to the underworld, but can be rescued by her husband Orpheus if he will not look back at her after he travels to find her—but he does look back. Seen here in the foreground are Maria Dizzia as the title character and Charles Shaw Robinson as Orpheus. (Sara Krulwich/The New York Times/Redux)

came on the scene. Silent films, radio, sound films, television, computers, and DVDs appeared in quick succession and transformed the entertainment landscape. Today, these electronic marvels are everywhere around us and, in fact, seem to bombard us from all sides. The question arises: where is live theatre in the midst of this?

The first thing to note is that everything we see in movies, on television, and in computer versions of drama has its roots in theatre. Situation comedies on television are based on Broadway comedies of the 1930s, and before that their lineage can be traced in an almost direct line back to Roman comedy, 2,000 years ago. Daytime soap operas on television are the modern equivalent of nineteenth-century domestic stage melodramas. Any number of types of movies come from nineteenth-century stage plays: westerns from frontier dramas; crime stories from mystery or detective melodramas; swashbuckler or underwater films from nautical stage offerings; animal stories from plays featuring horses onstage. Fantasy films that take place in the future or in outer space have earlier counterparts in such plays as William Shakespeare's *The Tempest*.

Aside from the many types of films and television dramas that trace their origins directly to live theatre, the techniques applied to dramatic works by modern writers, directors, and actors—and the approaches taken—are rooted in theatre. The way a story is translated into a suspenseful dramatic plot, the way characters are created and portrayed, the technique of writing sharp dialogue—these were developed and perfected during the long history of live theatre.

The fact that modern dramatic offerings of all kinds—movies, television, DVDs, video games—are based on and derived from live theatre is one reason why it is important to understand theatre past and present. But there is an even more important reason, which has to do with the nature of live theatre: it is an event that takes place only when the performers are in the presence of an audience, and it alone among dramatic presentations has this element. As we will discuss in more detail in Part One, the fact that theatre is live is the single most important element of its magic and its longevity.

THE ACTOR-AUDIENCE ENCOUNTER

When you think about it, the endurance of theatre in the face of the many challenges of the past 100 years is astonishing. Mechanical and electronic forms of delivering dramatic material are far more economical and convenient than live theatre can ever be. For instance, we can watch a drama on television in our own home virtually free. In the face of such competition, how has live theatre endured—and even thrived?

There are several answers, but most important is the fact that theatre is live—it happens at a given moment before our very eyes. We are there watching it; we are actually participants in the event. The drama critic Walter Kerr (1913–1996) explained what it means for audience and actors to be together:

> It doesn't just mean that we are in the personal presence of performers. It means that they are in *our* presence, conscious of us, speaking to us, working for and with us until a circuit that is not mechanical becomes established between us, a circuit that is fluid, unpredictable, ever-changing in its impulses, crackling, intimate. *Our* presence, the way we respond, flows back to the performer and alters what he does, to some degree and sometimes astonishingly so, every single night. We are contenders, making the play and the evening and the emotion together. We are playmates, building a structure. This never happens at a film because the film is already built, finished, sealed, incapable of responding to us in any way. The actors can't hear us or feel our presence; nothing we do, in our liveness, counts. We could be dead and the film would purr out its appointed course, flawlessly, indifferently.[1]

And, as we shall see in the next section, there is no substitute for that electricity and immediacy.

THEATRE IS TRANSITORY AND IMMEDIATE

A theatre performance changes from moment to moment as the audience encounters a series of shifting impressions and stimuli. It is a kaleidoscopic adventure through which the audience passes, with each instant a direct, immediate experience.

The transitory nature of theatre—a quality it shares with all the performing arts—sets it apart in a significant way from literature and the visual arts. A painting, a piece of sculpture, a novel, or a book of poems is a fixed object. When it leaves the artist's hands (or, in the case of a book, when it leaves the printer's shop), it is complete. In a world of change and uncertainty, these objects remain the same. The Winged

Victory from the island of Samothrace in Greece is today almost the same majestic figure that was fashioned 2,200 years ago. When we see this statue, we are looking at a soaring figure, facing into the wind, which is essentially what the Greeks saw at the time it was created.

The essence of literature and the visual arts is to catch something at a moment in time and freeze it. With the performing arts, however, that is impossible, because the performing arts are not objects but events. Specific objects—costumes, props, scenery, a script—are a part of theatre, but none of these constitutes the art. Bernard Beckerman, Shakespeare scholar and director, explains the difference:

> Theater is nothing if not spontaneous. It occurs. It happens. The novel can be put away, taken up, reread. Not theater. It keeps slipping between one's fingers. Stopping, it stops being theater. Its permanent features, facets of activity, such as scenery, script, stage, people, are no more theater than the two poles of a generator are electricity. Theater is what goes on between the parts.[2]

Plays are often printed in book form, like literature, and many novels and short stories contain extensive passages of dialogue that could easily be scenes in a play. But there is an important difference between the two forms. Unlike a novel, a play is written to be performed. In some respects a script is to a stage production as a musical score is to a concert, or an architectural blueprint is to a building: it is an outline for a performance.

Drama can be studied in a classroom in terms of imagery, character, and theme, but with drama, study of this sort takes place *before* or *after* the event. It is a form of preparation for or follow-up to the experience; the experience is the performance itself. Obviously, we have more opportunities to read plays in book form than to see them produced; but when we read a play, we should always attempt to visualize the other aspects of a production in our mind's eye.

THE PERMANENCE OF THE VISUAL ARTS
If they are preserved, painting and sculpture—unlike performing arts such as theatre, dance, and music—are permanent and unchanging. An example is this sculpture of the Nike of Samothrace, goddess of victory, on display at the Louvre Museum in Paris, France. The torso enfolded in flowing robes and the outstretched wings appear much as they did when the sculpture was first created on the island of Samothrace in Greece around 200 BCE, about 2,200 years ago.
(© Erich Lessing/Art Resource, NY)

HUMAN BEINGS—THE FOCUS OF THEATRE

Books often focus on people, but they can also focus on science or nature; music focuses on sound; abstract painting and sculpture focus on shapes, colors, and forms. Uniquely among the arts, theatre focuses on one thing and one thing only—human

THE FOCUS OF THEATRE: HUMAN CONCERNS
Painting concentrates on colors and shapes, dance on movement, music on sound; but theatre focuses on encounters among human beings. Human characters and their concerns are always at the center of any dramatic presentation. This is true even with an allegorical play such as the medieval drama *Everyman*. A number of characters in the play represent abstract ideas: Good Deeds, Death, and so on. But the main character is Everyman, the embodiment of all human beings. Shown here is a German adaptation by Hugo von Hofmanstahl staged annually outside the cathedral in Salzburg, Austria. In this scene, we see Clemens Schick in the role of Death and Peter Simonischek as Everyman. (Kerstin Joensson/AP Images)

beings. This is true even though different plays emphasize different human concerns, from profound problems in tragedy to pure entertainment in light comedy. And even when the performers play animals, inanimate objects, or abstract ideas, theatre concentrates on human concerns.

In the modern world, human beings have lost the central place they were once believed to occupy in the universe. In the Ptolemaic view of the universe, which prevailed until the sixteenth century—when Copernicus theorized that Earth revolved around the sun—it was assumed that Earth was the center of everything. In science, we have long since given up that notion, particularly in light of recent explorations in outer space. The human being has become seemingly less and less significant, and less and less at the center of things. But not in theatre. Theatre is one area where the preoccupations of men and women are still the core, the center around which other elements orbit.

A THEATRE OF INFINITE VARIETY

A character in William Shakespeare's play *Antony and Cleopatra* describes Cleopatra as a woman of "infinite variety." This is also perhaps the best way to describe the range of options and opportunities available to today's theatergoers. Audiences can choose from old and new works, both classics and cutting-edge. There are productions from all parts of the globe, showcasing diverse multiethnic and multicultural works. There are impassioned political plays, as well as plays that are part of the gay and lesbian theatre movement.

The choices of venue are almost as unlimited as the diversity of productions, from elegant theatres that seat 3,000 spectators and tiny theatres that seat fewer than 100, to makeshift theatre spaces created in lofts, firehouses, churches, and warehouses. Today's commercial, not-for-profit, university, and community theatres provide audiences with a truly global experience. This "infinite variety" of offerings will be introduced here, and then covered extensively throughout the book.

MULTIETHNIC, MULTICULTURAL, GLOBAL, AND GENDER THEATRE

In the late nineteenth century and the early twentieth, the United States was known as a "melting pot," a term that implied that the aim of the many foreign-born people who came here was to become assimilated and integrated into the prevailing white, European culture. In the last few decades, however, many people in our society have urged that, rather than embrace everyone in a common culture, we should recognize and celebrate our differences along with our shared values. This trend toward diversity has been reflected in theatre; many organizations have emerged that present theatrical productions by and for groups with a special interest. These include a number of political, ethnic, gender, and racial groups. There will be a full discussion of multicultural, political, and gender theatre in Chapter 15.

African American Theatre

African American theatre—also referred to as black theatre—is a prime example of a theatre that reflects the diversity of American culture and the contributions of a particular group to that culture. African American theatre is theatre written by and for black Americans or performed by black Americans. During the nineteenth century, there was an active, though segregated, African American theatre. At the beginning of the twentieth century, several successful musicals written by and starring African Americans appeared on Broadway.

A significant development for black theatre during the 1930s was the Federal Theatre Project, discussed in Chapter 15. This project, which was meant to help theatre artists through the Depression, formed separate black units in twenty-two cities, and those units mounted plays by black and white authors and employed thousands of African American writers, performers, and technicians. The Federal Theatre Project created a new generation of African American theatre artists who would develop the theatre of the 1940s and 1950s.

The 1950s saw an explosion of black theatre that would continue over the next six decades, much of it reflecting the struggle for civil rights. In 1970 the Black Theater Alliance listed more than 125 producing groups in the United States. Another major change in the 1970s was the presence of a larger black audience at Broadway theatres, which accounted for a significant number of commercial African American productions.

Many people feel that the most important American playwright of the latter part of the last century was the African American dramatist August Wilson (1945–2005), who wrote a ten-play cycle about the black experience in the United States throughout the twentieth century, one play for each decade of that century.

Asian American Theatre

For most of the nineteenth century and the first half of the twentieth century, Asians appeared in dramatic offerings in the United States strictly as stereotypes. With the coming of cultural and ethnic awareness in the 1960s and 1970s, that situation began to change. As a result, during the 1970s and 1980s, a number of plays by Asian American writers were produced, including a memory play by Philip Kan Gotanda (b. 1950) called *Song for a Nisea Fisherman* (1980).

A playwright who came to prominence in the 1980s was David Henry Hwang (b. 1957), son of first-generation Americans who immigrated from China to California. Hwang wrote several plays that won wide recognition. Hwang and the actor B. D. Wong, who played the Chinese opera singer in the original production of *M. Butterfly,* led a movement to have more Asian Americans employed as performers in appropriate roles in professional theatre. The struggle met with success in 1996, when a revival of *The King and I* opened on Broadway with a large proportion of Asian American performers.

Hispanic Theatre

Contemporary Hispanic theatre in the United States can be divided into at least three groups: Chicano, Cuban American, and Puerto Rican or Nuyorican. All three address the experiences of Hispanics living in the United States, and the plays are sometimes written in Spanish but are usually in English. Chicano theatre, which

THEATRE OF DIVERSITY: HISPANIC THEATRE
Theatre of all kinds has emerged in recent decades, representing many cultures, ethnic groups, gender orientations, and the like. A good example is *In the Heights,* a Broadway production. It tells the story of a Hispanic community in Manhattan's Washington Heights—a place of the corner bodega and the rhythm of three generations of music—a community on the brink of change, full of hopes, dreams, and pressures. *In the Heights* was conceived by Lin-Manuel Miranda, who also starred in the play, with Andrea Burns (center stage, in the red dress). (© Joan Marcus)

originated primarily in the west and southwest, came to prominence during the civil rights movements of the 1960s. Cuban American theatre developed chiefly in Florida. The Federal Theatre Project of the 1930s resulted in fourteen Cuban American productions in 1936 and 1937. A highly regarded Cuban American dramatist who began to be produced in the 1970s is Maria Irene Fornés (b. 1930). *Nuyorican* is a term that refers to Puerto Rican culture, mostly in New York, but elsewhere as well. Works by playwrights with a Puerto Rican orientation began to be produced in the 1960s and 1970s, originally by groups based in New York City.

Native American Theatre

Strictly speaking, there was no Native American theatre tradition; rather, there were spiritual and social traditions that had theatrical elements. These were found primarily in ancient rituals and communal celebrations, which were often infused with cosmic significance. Also, in these celebrations, unlike traditional western theatre, there

NATIVE AMERICAN THEATRE

An important theatre in the United States today is the Native American Theatre or the American Indian Theatre as some Native Americans prefer to call it. Whether basing their material on the heritage of Native Americans or dealing with their life today, American Indian playwrights give this significant segment of the country a strong artistic voice. Shown here are Patty Victor, Elizabeth King, Zeke Reedy, and Adoesha Bennett in a scene from a play called *Rough Face Girl* by Marcie R. Rendon, who is a member of the White Earth Anishnabe Nation. The play is a story about unhealed grief and one young woman's ability to see beauty in the face of fear, loneliness, and pain. (© Dianne Yeahquo Reyner/American Indian Repertory Theatre)

was no audience as such: those observing were considered participants just as much as the principal performers. Many of these ceremonies and the like were outlawed by the American government in the nineteenth century. Thus, the traditional rituals and ceremonies, which had strong theatrical components—not to mention important spiritual and cultural value—were forced to go "underground" if they continued at all. The American Indian Religious Freedom Act of 1972 made it legal once again for certain ceremonies, such as the sun dance, to resume.

What is important to note about Native American theatre today is that it is not primarily historical or ceremonial. Rather, the playwrights and producers emphasize contemporary work, fusing the problems and aspirations of today's Native Americans with their heritage.

Today's Global Theatre

When we speak of global theatre today, we mean not only separate national or cultural developments, but also the international exchanges and influences in theatre—the way one geographical area is conscious as never before of theatre in other areas. This movement began at the end of the nineteenth century, accelerated in the twentieth century, and has become even more pronounced at the beginning of the twenty-first century.

Similarly, a director from one country is likely to be strongly influenced by the work of a director in another country. An American director might travel to Japan to observe the work of the avant-garde director Tadashi Suzuki (b. 1939); another director would learn from seeing the productions of Peter Stein (b. 1937) in Germany. Festivals are particularly fertile ground for the international exchange of theatre groups; such festivals include Avignon in France, the Fringe Festival in Edinburgh, Scotland, and the International Festival each summer at Lincoln Center in New York City.

Political Theatre

Political theatre can be a measured drama pitting a character with a conservative point of view against a character with a liberal viewpoint. It can also be a polemic, that is, passionate advocacy of one political idea and an ardent attack on anyone who opposes that idea. And, of course, it can be a drama that falls anywhere between these two types.

Political theatre has been around since the comedies of Aristophanes in ancient Greece, when the playwright took on issues of the day. In the twentieth century and the twenty-first, political theatre has become increasingly urgent, and in some cases, strident. The German playwright Bertolt Brecht brought political theatre to the forefront in the mid-twentieth century. He was a socialist, and he wanted his plays to present his socialist arguments in the strongest possible terms.

In more recent years the wars in Vietnam, Iraq, and Afghanistan have sharpened political debates about the course the United States should follow in pursuing foreign wars; and political drama has played a lively, and sometimes vital, role in that debate. In another sense, many of the plays described below—about gay and lesbian matters; about the AIDS crisis—are political dramas. Good examples of political theatre are documentaries by Erik Jensen and Jessica Blank: *Exonerated* (2002), about people who were released from death row; and *Aftermath* (2009), based on interviews with refugees from the Iraq war who were living in Jordan.

POLITICAL THEATRE

Political theatre uses the stage to present a point of view about some urgent concern, either national or international. *Aftermath* is a documentary drama based on interviews with Iraqi victims forced by the war to live in exile in Jordan. Their stories are both harrowing and haunting. Shown here is Demosthenes Chrysan as one of the refugees. *Aftermath* was developed by Jessica Blank and Erik Jensen. (Sara Krulwich/The New York Times/Redux)

Feminist Theatre

In the United States, many female playwrights have questioned traditional gender roles and the traditional place of women in American society; and feminist theatre companies have urged audiences to reexamine their own gender biases and those of their society. Some scholars estimate that more than 100 feminist companies have been founded in the United States. Feminist theatre has roots in the past. One significant forerunner, for example, was the American playwright Rachel Crothers (1878–1958). Crothers wrote and directed many successful plays from 1906 to 1937; all of them dealt with women's moral and social concerns.

Gay and Lesbian Theatre

Lesbian theatre groups can be part of feminist theatre, but gay and lesbian theatre is also a distinct movement. A number of plays and performers introduced gay and lesbian themes before the 1960s. One example is Lillian Hellman's *The Children's Hour* (1934), in which a presumed lesbian relationship between two schoolteachers was presented.

GAY THEATRE

Among the many alternative theatres that emerged in the last part of the twentieth century was theatre centering on the gay and lesbian experience. Shown here is a scene from *Next Fall* by Geoffrey Nauffts, a play that chronicles the five-year relationship of a gay couple, Adam and Luke, as they grapple with their respective demons. The play examines what it means to "believe" in this day and age, and what it might cost us not to. The actors are Patrick Heusinger, left, as Luke, and Patrick Breen as Adam. (Sara Krulwich/The New York Times/Redux)

However, the play that first brought gay life to the forefront was *The Boys in the Band* (1968), by Mart Crowley (b. 1935). In the years that followed, in the 1970s and 1980s, complex gay characters were presented unapologetically. In these dramas, not only was the lifestyle of gays and lesbians presented forthrightly, but frequently a gay or lesbian agenda was also put forward. In addition to a general concern for gay and lesbian issues, there was a sense of urgency engendered by the AIDS crisis and gay rights issues, which led to a number of significant dramas. "Gender-bender" groups in San Francisco and in New York were an offshoot of gay and lesbian theatre.

Performance Art

In the past three decades, a number of artists have experimented with forms that compel audiences to confront certain issues: What is performance? What is theatre? What is the subject of theatrical representation? Some of these artists are also political-minded; some are not. Performance art is one recent form that poses these questions and then some. What is considered performance art has undergone several transformations in recent decades, but today it often means a single artist who presents material that is autobiographical, sometimes in an environment that is innovative or unusual.

Avant-Garde and Experimental Theatre

Theatre that breaks away from the mainstream tradition—avant-garde and experimental theatre—has been a part of the theatre landscape for most of the past 100 years. Movements such as expressionism, surrealism, absurdism, and theatre of cruelty appeared during the first three-quarters of the century; their descendants continue into the present. Among theatre movements of this kind is multimedia theatre, which

AVANT-GARDE AND EXPERIMENTAL THEATRE
Aside from large professional theatres, there are many smaller theatres off-off-Broadway and in cities across the United States. Some of these are minority theatres or theatres by and for special groups: gays, lesbians, or others. Alternative theatre also includes avant-garde and experimental productions. Shown here is Willem Dafoe in a scene from *Idiot Savant,* written, designed, and directed by Richard Foreman, a well-known auteur director. It was presented at the Public Theater in New York City. (Sara Krulwich/The New York Times/Redux)

incorporates theatre, dance, painting, and video into a single art form. Performance art may also fall into this category.

There are times when the groups described above overlap; political theatre, for instance, might intersect with feminist theatre. One example of the convergence of several movements is a theatre piece created by the performance artist Karen Finley (b. 1956). In this presentation, Finley, who was nude, covered parts of her body with chocolate, which was supposed to represent human feces. The performance made a highly feminist and bold political statement, as well as striking theatre.

A form of postmodern theatre, theatre that is non-text-based, in which individual directors or acting ensembles "deconstruct" texts, that is, take them apart and re-create them, has also become a significant example of today's avant-garde theatre.

Crossover Theatre

Plays or productions from groups with a special perspective have often crossed over into a wider arena of American theatre. The plays of the African American dramatist August Wilson are regularly produced on Broadway, as was the Asian American drama *M. Butterfly,* written by David Henry Hwang. Gay theatre has been represented by such works as *Torch Song Trilogy* by Harvey Fierstein (b. 1954) and two musicals: *La Cage aux Folles* and *Falsettos. Angels in America,* a Broadway play by Tony Kushner (b. 1956) that won the Pulitzer Prize, has both political and homosexual components.

Today there is theatre for almost everyone, in many kinds of places, under widely varying conditions, and for very different purposes. With theatre taking so many forms, it is important in approaching the subject not to have a preconceived or rigidly fixed notion of what it is.

In the following chapters we will look at this immense variety of theatre experiences. At the same time, we will look at the people who create theatre—actors; directors; producers; playwrights; scenic, costume, and lighting designers—and the ways they work together to produce the magic and excitement of theatre. We will begin, however, with another group that is the largest component, and an indispensable component, in creating theatre—the audience.

SUMMARY

1. A range of early theatre events—at Abydos, Egypt, for 2,000 years BCE; in Athens, Greece, in the fifth century BCE; in Kyoto, Japan, and Rabinal in what is now Guatemala, in the early fifteenth century CE—attest to the fact that theatre is global and that the impulse to create theatre is universal.

2. Theatre is all around us: in weddings, religious ceremonies, parades, and films, and on television. The theatrical element of many activities derives from theatre itself.

3. Theatre is a transitory art that occurs through time. A theatre performance changes from moment to moment, and a theatre event is created by cumulative sights, sounds, and impressions. One special quality of theatre is its immediacy.

4. The focus—the subject matter—of theatre is always human beings.

5. The impulse toward theatre is universal and has appeared wherever human society has developed. Rituals, religious ceremonies, and celebrations have certain elements of theatre, including a performance in front of an audience, costumes, and storytelling.

6. Today's theatre is global. Theatre from one country or culture influences theatre in other countries. Also, theatre from around the world is available to audiences in all active theatre cultures.

7. Theatre is diversified. There is wide diversity in theatre today: multicultural theatre, multi-ethnic theatre, gender theatre, political theatre.

8. Theatre of all kinds—serious, comic, farcical, political, escapist—can be found in a multitude of venues: indoors and outdoors, large theatres and small, traditional spaces and improvised spaces.

9. In the past, theatre experiences were relatively uniform within any one society, but in contemporary society their time, place, content, and purpose are far more varied. Theatre groups today produce works expressing the viewpoints of people of all political, ethnic, gender, and racial perspectives: African Americans, Asian Americans, Hispanics, Native Americans, feminists, gays, lesbians, and others. Added to this is global theatre, around the world.

1

The Audience

THE AUDIENCE ▶

The basic encounter in theatre is the exchange between the audience and everything that happens onstage. The presence of the audience sets live theatre apart from all other forms of dramatic entertainment. Here the audience is waiting for Shakespeare's *Romeo and Juliet* to begin at the American Repertory Theatre. Note the audience seated on two sides of the stage.

(© T Charles Erickson)

Part One

The Audience

In theatre, spectators are essential. To be complete, each one of the performing arts—opera, ballet, and symphony concerts as well as theatre—requires an audience. Most people first encounter a dramatic work on television or at the movies. Whether the work is a classic like *Romeo and Juliet,* or a modern family play, it is likely that a young person's initial exposure to a theatrical event is on film or television. It must be remembered, however, that this experience is quite different from attending theatre. In watching a movie or television, the viewer is looking at a screen on which there are no live people but only pictures of people. And the experience of being in the presence of a living, breathing person makes all the difference. Another way of putting this is to say that the audience is not an incidental factor in a theatrical performance; it is a key, indispensable, essential element.

At a theatrical performance, spectators are keenly aware of the actors onstage. What the audience may not realize is that the actors are just as keenly aware of its presence. Laughter at a comedy or a deep silence at a tense moment in a serious drama is communicated directly to the actors and has a very real effect on their performance.

In a number of events other than the performing arts, spectators often play a key role. For example, most sports contests—football, baseball, basketball, soccer, tennis, NASCAR races—elicit huge interest from fans. This is true whether the sports event is at the high school, college, or profes-

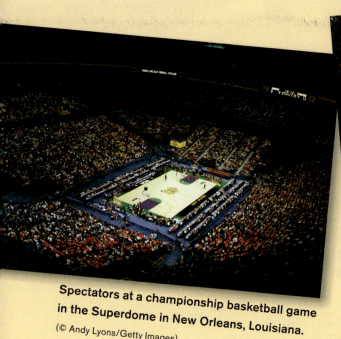

Spectators at a championship basketball game in the Superdome in New Orleans, Louisiana.
(© Andy Lyons/Getty Images)

Barack Obama accepting the nomination for president at the 2008 Democratic national convention in Denver.
(Ted S. Warren/AP Images)

sional level. In other spheres as well, the participation of viewers is considered crucial. Political conventions and political rallies depend on large, supportive crowds to be considered successful. A good example is a national nominating convention. The hall where the event takes place becomes a giant stage set, with a stagelike platform, backdrops, and carefully arranged positions for entrances and exits. The programs are carefully scripted to build to a climax, with a finale consisting of stirring music and literally thousands of balloons dropping from the ceiling.

It should be pointed out that despite the similarity between theatre events and sports events, there is one unmistakable difference. Theoretically, a sports contest could take place in an empty stadium and still be considered complete: though the thrill, the excitement, and the sense of participation would be missing, the results would be entered in the record book, and the won-lost statistics would be just as valid as if the game had taken place before an overflowing crowd.

This is not true for the performing arts. Each theatre, ballet, or opera performance, and each musical concert, is intended specifically to be presented in the presence of an audience, which is an absolutely essential part of the event. Of course, any of these can be recorded on a CD or DVD, but listening to or viewing one of these is not the same as attending a live event. In a very real sense, a theatre performance at which no audience is present is actually *not* a performance. It may be a rehearsal of some kind, but the performance occurs only when the actors perform in the presence of an audience.

In Part One we will explore who makes up the audience, how audiences are created, how they differ from one another, how they respond to what is happening onstage, and how they interact with performers.

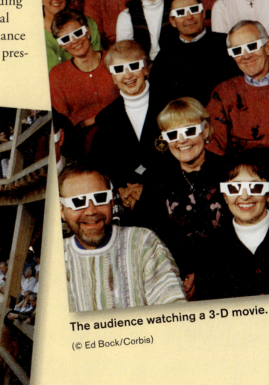

The audience watching a 3-D movie.

(© Ed Bock/Corbis)

e audience at a performance of *The Two Gentlemen of Verona* at Shake-
eare's Globe in London. (© Gideon Mendel/Corbis)

The Audience:
Its Role and Imagination

2

Today we are accustomed to seeing theatrical presentations in many forms in addition to live performances. How has theatre been able not only to compete with these convenient forms, but to emerge in some ways stronger than ever? There are several answers, but perhaps the most important has to do with the "live" nature of theatre.

THE SPECIAL NATURE OF THEATRE:
A CONTRAST WITH FILM

The special nature of theatre will be more apparent if we contrast a drama seen in a theatre with one shown on film or television. Both present a story told in dramatic form—an enactment of scenes by performers who speak and act as if they were the people they represent. The same actress can play Juliet in *Romeo and Juliet* by William Shakespeare (1564–1616) on both stage and screen. Not only the dramatization and the acting but also other elements, such as scenery and costumes, are often similar on stage and screen. In fact, many films and television specials have been based on stage productions: *A Chorus Line, The Piano Lesson, The Phantom of the Opera, The Importance of Being Earnest,* and numerous plays by Shakespeare—including Kenneth Branagh's productions of *Much Ado about Nothing, Hamlet,* and *Henry V;* Baz Luhrmann's *Romeo and Juliet; The Merchant of Venice,* with Al Pacino; and *Ten Things I Hate about You,* a modern version of *The Taming of the Shrew,* with Julia Stiles and

◀ **THE IMAGINATION OF THE AUDIENCE**

The audience and the performers are the two essential elements of theatre: both are required for theatre to occur. The presence of the audience sets theatre apart from the experience of watching a theatrical presentation on film, on television, or in any other electronic medium. One aspect of the audience's participation is the use of its imagination. For a production of War Horse, *which originated at the National Theatre in London, the audience was called on to imagine that a large puppet operated by actors was actually a real horse. The horses were created by the Handspring Puppet Company. (© Marilyn Kingwill/ArenaPAL)*

chapter two

Heath Ledger. Also, unquestionably, one can learn a great deal about theatre from watching a play on film or television. And film and television can give us many of the same feelings and experiences that we have when watching a theatre performance. Moreover, the accessibility of film and television means that they play a crucial role in our overall exposure to the depiction of dramatic events and dramatic characters.

As important as the similarities are, however, there is a crucial difference between experiencing live theatre and watching it on television or on film. I am not speaking here of the technical capabilities of film or television, the ability to show outdoor shots taken from helicopters, cut instantaneously from one scene to another, or create special effects such as those in *Star Trek, Watchmen,* or *2012.* No, the most significant—in fact, the overriding—difference between films and theatre is the *performer-audience relationship.* The experience of being in the presence of the performer is more important to theatre than anything else. With a film or with television, we are always in the presence of an *image,* never a person.

The American playwright Jean-Claude van Itallie (b. 1936) has explained the importance of the actor-audience relationship in theatre, and how theatre differs from films and television:

> Theater is not electronic. Unlike movies and unlike television, it does require the live presence of both audience and actors in a single space. This is the theater's uniquely important advantage and function, its original religious function of bringing people together in a community ceremony where the actors are in some sense priests or celebrants, and the audience is drawn to participate with the actors in a kind of eucharist.[1]

TELEVISION: A DIFFERENT EXPERIENCE FROM THEATRE
When audiences see films or television shows, they see images of people on a screen rather than the people themselves. In this photograph we see teenagers watching an episode of *Gossip Girl,* but they are looking at a screen, not the living performers, and this fact makes a tremendous difference in the nature of the experience. (Joe Fornabaio for The New York Times/Redux)

THE CHEMISTRY OF PERFORMER-AUDIENCE CONTACT

Like films, television seems very close to theatre; sometimes it seems even closer than film. Popular television talk shows, award shows, and even dramas often purport to be *live;* however, the word *live* must be qualified. Before television, *live* in the entertainment world meant "in person": not only was the event taking place at that moment; it was taking place in the presence of the spectator. Today, although the term *live television* may still mean that an event is taking place at this moment, many so-called live events are actually taped and rebroadcast on one or more subsequent occasions. Also, "live" television does not take place in the presence of the viewer. In fact, it is generally far removed from the television audience, possibly half a world away. With television we see an image on a relatively small screen; we are free to look or not look, or even to leave the room.

The fascination of being in the presence of a famous person is difficult to explain but not difficult to verify. No matter how often fans have seen a favorite star in the movies or heard a singer on a CD or on television, they will go to any lengths to see him or her in person. Probably, at one time or another each of us has braved bad weather and shoving crowds to see celebrities at a parade, a political rally, or a concert. Even a severe rainstorm will not deter fans from seeing their favorite star at an outdoor concert. The same pull of personal contact draws us to the theatre.

At the heart of the theatre experience, therefore, is the performer-audience relationship: the immediate, personal encounter whose chemistry and magic give theatre its special quality. During a stage performance the actresses and actors can hear laughter, can sense silence, and can feel tension in the audience. In short, the audience can affect, and in subtle ways change, the performance. At the same time, members of the audience watch the performers closely, consciously or unconsciously asking themselves questions: Are the performers convincing in their roles? Will they do something surprising? Will they make a mistake? At each moment, in every stage performance, the audience is looking for answers to questions like these.

Actually two experiences are occurring almost simultaneously: the individual experience, which is highly personal; and the group experience, which will be discussed below.

THEATRE AS A GROUP EXPERIENCE

Certain arts—such as painting, sculpture, and literature—provide solitary experiences. The viewer or reader contemplates the work alone, at her or his own pace. This is true even in a museum: although many people may flock to look at a single painting and are with each other, they respond as individuals, one by one. In the performing arts, however, including theatre, the group experience is indispensable. The performing arts share this trait with other communal events such as religious services, spectator sports, and celebrations. Before the event can take place, a group must assemble, at one time and in one place. When people are gathered together in this way, something mysterious happens to them. Though still individuals, with their own personalities and backgrounds, they take on other qualities as well, qualities which often overshadow their independent responses.

Psychology of Groups

Not all crowds are alike. Some are aggressive, such as an angry mob that decides to riot or

THEATRE AS A GROUP EXPERIENCE
In theatre, the size, attitude, and makeup of the audience affect the overall experience. The theatre can be large or small, indoors or outdoors, and the audience can be people of similar tastes and background or a collection of quite varied individuals. Depicted here is the audience at a performance of Shakespeare's *Love's Labour's Lost* at a 1,200-seat theatre with an Elizabethan stage, the Allen Pavilion at the Oregon Shakespeare Festival. The works of Shakespeare and his contemporaries are presented here each summer to a diverse audience. (© T Charles Erickson)

a gang that terrorizes a neighborhood. Others are docile—a group of spectators on a sidewalk observing a juggler, for example. A crowd at a football game is different from a congregation at a religious observance; and a theatre crowd is distinct from any of these. In spite of being different, however, the theatre audience shares with all such groups the special characteristics of the *collective mind.*

Becoming part of a group is a crucial element of the theatre experience. For a time, we share a common undertaking, focused on one activity—the performance of a play. Not only do we laugh or cry in a way we might not otherwise; we also sense an intangible communion with those around us.

When a collection of individuals respond more or less in unison to what is occurring onstage, their relationship to one another is reaffirmed. If there is a display of cruelty at which we shudder, or sorrow by which we are moved, or pomposity at which we laugh, it is reassuring to have others respond as we do. For a moment we are part of a group sharing an experience; and our sorrow or joy, which we thought might be ours alone, is found to be part of a broad human response.

How Audience Makeup Affects the Theatre Experience

Although being part of a group is an essential element of theatre, groups vary, and the makeup of a group will alter a theatrical event. Some audiences are general—for instance, the thousands who attend outdoor productions such as the Shakespeare festival in Ashland, Oregon, and *Unto These Hills,* which is a play about the Cherokee Indians presented each summer on a Cherokee reservation in western North Carolina. General audiences include people of all ages, from all parts of the country, and from all socioeconomic levels. Other audiences are more homogeneous, such as spectators at a high school play, a children's theatre production, a Broadway opening night, a political play, or a performance in a prison.

Another factor affecting our experience in the theatre is our relationship to the other members of the audience. If we are among friends or people of like mind, we feel comfortable and relaxed, and we readily become part of the group experience. On the other hand, if we feel alien—for example, a young person with an older group or a radical with conservatives—we will be estranged from the group as a whole. The people with whom we attend theatre—their relative homogeneity and our relation to them—strongly influence our response to the total event.

THE SEPARATE ROLES OF PERFORMERS AND SPECTATORS

It is important to note the difference between *observed* theatre and *participatory* theatre. In observed theatre, the audience participates vicariously or empathetically with what is happening onstage. Empathy is the experience of mentally or emotionally entering into the feelings or spirit of another person—in this case, a character onstage. Sometimes an audience will not be in tune with the characters onstage but will react vehemently against them. In either situation, though, members of the audience are participating empathetically. They might shed tears, laugh, pass judgment, sit frozen, or literally tremble with fear. But they participate through their imagination while separated from the action.

There are also times when the audience participates in a theatre event. In rituals and ceremonies in parts of Africa and among certain tribes of Native Americans, those attending have in effect become participants, joining in the singing and dancing, for instance. At a number of contemporary theatre events spectators have also been urged to take part. For example, one of the chief aims of the Theatre of the Oppressed created by Augusto Boal was to eliminate the distinction between audience members and performers. In Boal's philosophy, every spectator could be and should be an actor, and he developed a number of strategies to bring this about.

How Should the Audience Be Involved?

The attempt to involve audience members directly springs from a desire to make theatre more immediate and intense, and such work can be innovative and exciting. It remains, however, an exception to the kinds of theatre people are likely to encounter. The theatre most people will experience requires a degree of distancing, in the same way that all art requires a certain perspective.

Imagine trying to get the full effect of a large landscape painting when standing a few inches from the canvas: one would see only the brushstrokes of a single tree or a small patch of blue sky. To perceive and appreciate a work of art, we need distance. This separation, which is called *aesthetic distance,* is as necessary in theatre as in any other art.

In the same way that a viewer must stand back from a painting to get its full effect, so in theatre spectators must be separated from the performance in order to see and hear what is happening onstage and thus absorb the experience. If an audience member becomes involved in the proceedings or goes onstage and takes part in the action, as often occurred in a Boal production, he or she reverses roles and becomes a performer, not a spectator. The separation between performers and spectators remains.

Audience Participation through Direct Action

It should be noted that today a range of activities employ theatrical techniques when the aim is not a performance viewed by an audience, but rather is educational and therapeutic. Those who take part in such activities are not performers in the usual sense, and there is no attempt to follow a written script. Rather, the emphasis is on education, personal development, or therapy—fields in which theatre techniques have opened up new possibilities. In schools, for example, creative dramatics, theatre games, and group improvisations have proved invaluable for self-discovery and the development of healthy group attitudes. By acting out hypothetical situations or giving free rein to their imagination, children can build self-confidence, discover their creative potential, and overcome their inhibitions. In some situations, creative dramatics can teach lessons that are difficult to teach by conventional means. Playwriting, too, has often proved to be an invaluable educational tool. Students who write scenes, whether autobiographical or fictional, find the experience not only fulfilling but enlightening.

In addition to creative dramatics, a wide range of other activities—*sociodrama, psychodrama,* and *drama therapy*—incorporate theatrical techniques. For adults as well as children, these activities have come to the forefront as educational and therapeutic methods. In sociodrama, the members of participating groups—such as parents

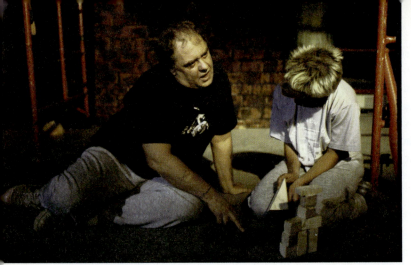

DRAMA THERAPY

Theatre techniques can be used for educational and therapeutic purposes. A group called the Geese Company, for example, visits prisons and has convicts reenact scenes from their own lives. Here, the actress Pamela Daryl (right) is listening to a prisoner unburdening himself of painful memories of childhood. (© Steve Liss/Time Life Pictures/Getty Images)

and children, students and teachers, or legal authorities and ordinary citizens—explore their own attitudes and prejudices. One successful approach is *role reversal*. A group of young people, for instance, may take the part of their parents while the adults assume the roles of the children; or members of a street gang will take the roles of the police, and the police will take the roles of the street gang. In such role playing, both groups become aware of deep-seated feelings and arrive at a better understanding of one another.

Psychodrama uses some of the same techniques as sociodrama but is more private and interpersonal; in fact, it can become so intense that it should be carried out only under the supervision of a trained therapist. In psychodrama, individual fears, anxieties, and frustrations are explored. A person might reenact a particularly traumatic scene from childhood, for example.

In participatory drama, theatre is a means to another end: education, therapy, group development, or the like. Its aim is not public performance, and there is little emphasis on a carefully prepared, expertly performed presentation before an audience; in fact, just the opposite is true. In observed drama, on the other hand, the aim is a professional performance for spectators, and this requires a separation between the performers and the audience—the "aesthetic distance" described earlier.

THE IMAGINATION OF THE AUDIENCE

For those who create it, theatre is a direct experience: an actress walks onstage and impersonates a character; a carpenter builds scenery; a scene designer paints it. For these people the experience is like cutting a finger or being held in an embrace: the pain or the warmth is felt directly and physically.

Members of a theatre audience experience a different kind of pain or warmth. As spectators in a theatre, we sense the presence of other audience members; we observe the movements and gestures of performers and hear the words they speak; and we see costumes, scenery, and lighting. From these we form mental images or make imaginative connections that provoke joy, laughter, anger, sorrow, or pain. All this occurs, however, without our moving from our seats.

We naturally assume that those who create theatre are highly imaginative people and that their minds are full of vivid, exciting ideas that might not occur to the rest of us. If we conclude, however, that we in the audience have only a limited theatrical imagination, we do ourselves a great injustice. As we saw earlier, theatre is a two-way street—an exchange between performers and audience—and this is nowhere more evident than in the creation of *illusion*. Illusion may be initiated by the creators of theatre, but it is completed by the audience.

GLOBAL CROSSCURRENTS

AUGUSTO BOAL: THE THEATRE OF THE OPPRESSED

If ever there was an international theatre figure in recent times, it was Augusto Boal (1931–2009). Born in Brazil, Boal (pronounced Bo-AHL) attended Columbia University in the United States. Returning to Brazil, he began working in the Arena Theatre in São Paulo. At first he directed conventional dramatic works, but Boal was a man with a powerful social conscience. During his early years he began to develop his philosophy of theatre. He concluded, for example, that mainstream theatre was used by the ruling class as a soporific, a means of sedating the audience and inoculating it against any impulse to act or revolt. In other words, conventional theatre oppressed ordinary citizens, especially the underprivileged.

Boal also became fascinated with the relationship of actors to audience members. He establish a partnership between them, and he felt strongly that spectators should participate in any theatre event, that a way must be found for them to become performers, and a part of the action. In putting these theories into practice, he began to present agitprop plays, that is, plays with a strong political and social message. He experimented with several versions of such plays. One was the Invisible Theatre, in which actors, seemingly spontaneously, presented a prepared scene in a public space such as a town square or a restaurant. Another was his Forum Theatre, in which a play about a social problem became the basis of a discussion with audience members about solutions to the problem.

Considered an enemy of the authoritarian government in Brazil for his work in the 1960s, he was jailed in 1971 and tortured. Released after a few months, he was exiled from his native land. Following that he lived in various countries: Argentina, Portugal, and France. He decided along the way that his approach should be less didactic than it had been, that he would be more effective if he engaged audiences in the theatrical process rather than confronting them. This was the basis of his Theatre of the Oppressed, which became the cornerstone of his lifework from then on. He wrote a book by that title, which appeared in 1974.

Augusto Boal (Sucheta Das/AP Images)

In 1985 Boal returned to Brazil. From that point until his death, for the next quarter century, he traveled all over the world, directing, lecturing, and establishing centers furthering the Theatre of the Oppressed. He also wrote other books, which were widely read. His approach to theatre found adherents in more than forty countries. Wherever the Theatre of the Oppressed was established, its productions challenged injustice, especially in poor and disenfranchised communities where citizens are often without a voice or an advocate. In his later years he was looked upon by many as the most inspirational person of his time in propagating socially oriented theatre.

THE AUDIENCE USES ITS IMAGINATION

In theatre, the audience is called on to use its imagination in order to accept many things: ghosts, spirits, witches, and imaginary objects and actions. In Ibsen's *Peer Gynt* the title character, an irresponsible, self-involved adventurer, meets a number of otherworldly figures: a Troll King, an amorphous blob known as the Boyg, and others. The audience accepts these fantastical creatures as part of the fantasy of theatre. Here we see Barret O'Brien as Peer Gynt in a production by the Yale School of Drama. (© T Charles Erickson)

In the eerie world of William Shakespeare's *Macbeth,* when three witches appear out of the mist or when Banquo's ghost interrupts the banquet, we know it is fantasy; witches and ghosts like those in *Macbeth* do not appear in everyday life. In the theatre, however, we take such fantasy at face value. In Shakespeare's own day, for instance, a convention readily accepted by audiences was that women's parts were played by boy actors. Shakespeare's heroines—Juliet, Desdemona, Lady Macbeth—were not acted by women, as they are today, but played by boys. Everyone in the audience at an Elizabethan theatre knew that the boys were not actually women but accepted without question the notion that a boy actor was presenting an impression or an imitation of a woman. The film *Shakespeare in Love* afforded a fascinating glimpse of this: the actress Gwyneth Paltrow plays a young woman portraying a boy actor (in secret), while her acting partner is a young man playing a young woman portrayed by a boy (in the open).

Along with fantasy, theatre audiences accept drastic shifts in time and space. Someone onstage dressed in a Revolutionary uniform says, "It is the winter of 1778, at Valley Forge," and we do not question it. What is more, we accept rapid movements back and forth in time. ***Flashbacks***—abrupt movements from the present to the past and back again—are a familiar technique in films such as *Babel, The Departed,* and *Notes on a Scandal;* but they are also commonplace in modern drama.

A similar device often used in drama is *anachronism.* An anachronism involves placing some character or event outside its proper time sequence: for example, having people from the past speak and act as if they were living today. Medieval mystery and morality plays frequently contained anachronisms. The medieval play *Abraham and Isaac,* for instance, is set in the time of the Old Testament, but it makes several references to the Christian trinity—a religious concept that was not developed until centuries later. The medieval audience accepted this shift in time as a matter of course, just as we do in theatre today.

In his play *Angels in America,* Tony Kushner includes a number of bizarre and fantastic characters or events. For example, a character in the play called Mr. Lies is an imaginary person created in the mind of Harper, a housewife who is addicted to pills. Near the end of part 1, Mr. Lies takes Harper on a fantasy trip to the Antarctic. At the very end of part 1, an angel crashes through the ceiling and speaks to Prior, a man ill with AIDS.

In the theatre, then, our imagination allows us to conceive of people and events we have never seen or experienced and to transcend our physical circumstances to the point where we forget who we are, where we are, or what time it is. How is this possible? It happens because in the theatre our imagination works for us just as it does in everyday life.

Tools of the Imagination: Symbol and Metaphor

We can understand this process better if we look closely at two tools of our imagination: symbol and metaphor.

Functions of Symbols
In general terms, a *symbol* is a sign, token, or emblem that signifies something else. A simple form of symbol is a sign. Some signs stand for a single, uncomplicated idea or action. In everyday life we are surrounded by them: road signs, such as an S-shaped curve; audible signals, like sirens and foghorns; and a host of mathematical and typographical symbols: $, 1/4, @, &. We sometimes forget that language itself is symbolic; the letters of the alphabet are only lines and curves on a page. Words are arrangements of letters that by common agreement represent something else. The same four letters mean different things depending on the order in which they are placed: *pear, reap, rape.* These three words set different imaginative wheels in motion and signal responses that vary greatly from word to word.

In commerce, the power of the symbol is acknowledged in the value placed on a trademark or a logo. The term *status symbol* is a frank recognition of the importance of personal possessions in conferring status on the owner. What cars people drive, how they dress, how they furnish their homes: these indicate what kind of people they are—at least, that is the theory.

At times, symbols exert incredible emotional power; a good example is a flag, embodying a nation's passions, fears, and ambitions. Flags are symbols: lines, shapes, and colors that in certain combinations become immediately recognizable.

Like flags, some symbols signify ideas or emotions that are far more complex and profound than the symbol itself. The cross, for

THE POWER OF SYMBOLS

Symbols and metaphors, though not real in a literal sense, have enormous power to influence our lives; in that respect, they become "realer than real." A forceful symbol of the bravery, tragedy, and losses of the Vietnam War is the wall designed by Maya Lin in Washington, where the names of those who died are etched into the side of the memorial. (© R. Morley/PhotoLink/Getty Images)

example, is a symbol of Christ and, beyond that, of Christianity as a whole. Whatever form a symbol takes—language, a flag, or a religious emblem—it can embody the total meaning of a religion, a nation, or an idea.

Functions of Metaphors

A similar transformation takes place with metaphor, another form of imaginative substitution. With metaphor we announce that one thing is another, in order to describe it or point up its meaning more clearly. (In poetry, you will remember, a simile says that one thing is like another; metaphor simply states directly that one thing is another.) The Bible is filled with metaphors. The psalmist who says, "The Lord is my shepherd," or who says of God, "Thou art my rock and my fortress," is speaking metaphorically. He does not mean literally that God is a shepherd, a rock, or a fortress; he is saying that God is like these things.

Like symbols, metaphors are part of the fabric of life, as the following common expressions suggest:

"How gross."

"He's off the wall."

"It's a slam dunk."

"Give me the bottom line."

"That's cool."

We are saying one thing but describing another. When someone describes a person or event as "cool," the reference is not to a low temperature but to an admirable quality. The term "slam dunk" comes from basketball, but in everyday parlance is applied to a wide range of activities that have nothing to do with sports. We can see from these examples that metaphors, like symbols, are part of daily life.

The "Reality" of the Imagination

Our use of symbol and metaphor shows how large a part imagination plays in our lives. Millions of automobiles in the United States can be brought to a halt, not by a concrete wall, but by a small colored light changing from green to red. Imagine attempting to control traffic, or virtually any type of human activity, without symbols. Beyond being a matter of convenience, symbols are necessary to our survival.

The same holds true for metaphor. Frequently we find that we cannot express fear, anxiety, hope, or joy—any of the deep human feelings—in descriptive language. That is why we sometimes scream. It is also why we have poetry and use metaphors. Even scientists, the men and women we are most likely to consider realists, turn to metaphor at crucial times. They discuss the "big bang" theory of the origin of the universe and talk of "black holes" in outer space. Neither term is "scientific," but both terms communicate what scientists have in mind in a way that an equation or a more logical phrase could not.

Dreams provide another example of the power of the imagination. You dream that you are falling off a cliff; then, suddenly, you wake up and find that you are not flying through the air but lying in bed. Significantly, however, the dream of falling means more to you than the objective fact of lying in bed.

Although people have long recognized the importance of dreams in human life, in the modern period interest in dreams has been intensified as a result of the work of

THE AUDIENCE'S RESPONSE

- During a performance you may observe a puppet or group of puppets who appear as real as people we deal with every day. Or you may see on a bare stage two or three props (a tree, for example, or a throne) and assume you are in a forest or a royal palace. Why do you think during a performance we are able to let our imaginations take over? Is this something we also do in everyday life?

- While watching a performance you may dissolve into laughter or cry real tears. The whole time, on some level, you know what you are observing is not "real." But does this matter? In some sense is the experience real? What is the relationship between a theatre experience such as this and an experience in daily life?

- Imagine two friends viewing the same theatre production. One friend is captivated, feeling that what he or she saw was genuine and moving, a deeply affecting experience. The other friend was not moved and felt that the performance was artificial and inauthentic. Why do you think the same performance can elicit two such different reactions?

Sigmund Freud (1856–1939) on the subconscious. Despite variations and corrections of his theories, no one today disputes Freud's notion of the importance and "reality" of dreams, nightmares, and symbols in the human mind.

Theatre functions in somewhat the same way. Though not real in a literal sense, it can be completely—even painfully—real in an emotional or intellectual sense. The critic and director Harold Clurman (1901–1980) gave one of his books on theatre the title *Lies Like Truth*. Theatre—like dreams or fantasies—can sometimes be more truthful about life than a mundane, objective description. This is a paradox of dreams, fantasies, and art, including theatre: by probing deep into the psyche to reveal inner truths, they can be more real than outward reality.

THE IMAGINARY WORLDS OF THEATRE

Realism and Nonrealism

An audience in a theatre is asked to accept many kinds of imaginary worlds. One way to classify these imaginary realms is as ***realism*** and ***nonrealism.*** At the outset, it is essential to know that in theatre the term *realistic* denotes a special application of what we consider "genuine" or "real." A realistic element is not necessarily more truthful than a nonrealistic element. Rather, in theatre, *realistic* and *nonrealistic* denote different ways of presenting reality.

Realistic Elements of Theatre   In theatre, a realistic element is one that resembles *observable* reality. It is a kind of photographic truth. We apply the term *realistic* to those elements of theatre that conform to our own observations of people, places, and events. Realistic theatre follows the predictable logic of everyday life: the law of gravity, the time it takes a person to travel from one place to another, the way a room in a house looks, the way a person dresses. With a realistic approach, these conform to our normal expectations. In realistic theatre, the act of imagination demanded of the audience is acceptance of the notion that what is seen onstage is not make-believe but real.

REALISTIC AND NONREALISTIC THEATRE CONTRASTED

These scenes illustrate some of the differences between two approaches to the make-believe of theatre. At the top we see Yvette Freeman and Lizan Mitchell in the fully functioning kitchen on the set of *Having Our Say: The Delany Sisters' First 100 Years* at the McCarter Theatre, where they prepare a complete meal onstage. In contrast, the scene below is from an avant-garde production, *Black Rider: The Casting of the Magic Bullets,* directed and designed by Robert Wilson. Note the abstract setting, the eerie lighting, the symbolic characters. This kind of theatre contrasts sharply with realism. (Top: © T Charles Erickson; Bottom: © Craig Schwartz/Center Theatre Group, Ahmanson Theatre)

We are quite familiar with realism in films and television. Part of the reason is mechanical. The camera records what the lens "sees." Whether it is a bedroom in a house, a crowded city street, or the Grand Canyon, film captures the scene as the eye sees it.

Theatre too has always had realistic elements. Every type of theatre that is not pure fantasy has realistic aspects. For example, characters who are supposed to represent real people must be rooted in a human truth that audiences can recognize. When we are so readily able to verify what we see before us from our own experience, it is easy to identify with it and to accept its authenticity. For this reason, realistic theatre has become firmly established in modern times, and it seems likely to remain so.

Nonrealistic Elements of Theatre   Nonrealistic elements of theatre include everything that does not conform to our observations of surface reality: poetry instead of prose, ghosts rather than flesh-and-blood people, abstract forms for scenery, and so forth. Again, we find a counterpart in films and television. Movies like *District 9* and *Harry Potter* and television shows like *Heroes* and *Lost* use special effects to give us otherworldly creatures, rides through outer space, or encounters with prehistoric monsters. The *Star Wars* trilogy had computer-generated characters, which became famous but also created controversy over questions of ethnic identity.

In theatre, the argument for nonrealism is that the surface of life—a real conversation, for instance, or a real room in a house—can never convey the whole truth, because so much of life occurs in our minds and imagination. If we are depressed and tell a friend that we feel "lousy" or "awful," we do not even begin to communicate the depth of our feelings. It is because of the inadequacy of ordinary words that people turn to poetry, and because of the inadequacy of other forms of daily communication that they turn to music, dance, art, sculpture, and the entire range of symbols and metaphors discussed earlier.

A wide range of theatrical techniques and devices fall into the category of nonrealism. One example is the *soliloquy,* in which a solitary character speaks to the audience, expressing in words a hidden thought. In real life, we might confess some of our inner fears or hopes to a priest, a psychiatrist, or our best friend; but we do not announce such fears out loud for the world to hear as Hamlet does when he says, "To be, or not to be . . ." Another example is *pantomime,* in which performers pretend to be using objects that are not actually present, such as

NONREALISTIC ELEMENTS
Realism has been a major approach to theatre since the late nineteenth century, but for hundreds of years before that, theatre incorporated many unrealistic elements. One example is Shakespeare's use of ghosts and various otherworldly creatures. Shown here in a Royal Shakespeare Company production of *Hamlet* is Vaneshran Arumugam in the title role (right background) encountering the ghost of his dead father, played by John Kani (left foreground). (© Geraint Lewis)

DYNAMICS OF DRAMA

REALISM AND NONREALISM: A CONTRAST

The distinction between realistic and nonrealistic techniques in theatre becomes clearer when the two approaches are examined side by side. This distinction is present in all aspects of theatre.

Realistic Techniques	Nonrealistic Techniques

STORY

Events that the audience knows have happened or might happen in everyday life: Blanche DuBois in Tennessee Williams's *A Streetcar Named Desire* goes to New Orleans to visit her sister and brother-in-law.	Events that do not take place in real life but occur only in the imagination: in Kushner's *Angels in America,* a character in a housewife's mind takes her on an imaginary trip to the Antarctic.

STRUCTURE

Action is confined to real places; time passes normally, as it does in everyday life: the hospital room setting in Margaret Edson's *Wit* is an example.	Arbitrary use of time and place: in August Strindberg's *The Dream Play,* walls dissolve and characters are transformed, as in a dream.

CHARACTERS

Recognizable human beings, such as the priest and the nun in John Patrick Shanley's *Doubt.*	Unreal figures like the ghost of Hamlet's father in William Shakespeare's *Hamlet* or the three witches in *Macbeth.*

ACTING

Performers portray people as they behave in daily life: the men on a summer holiday in the country house in Terrence McNally's *Love! Valor! Compassion!*	Performers portray animals in the musical *The Lion King;* they also engage in singing, dancing, and acrobatics in musical comedy or performance art.

LANGUAGE

Ordinary dialogue or conversation: the two brothers trying to get ahead in Suzan-Lori Parks's *Topdog/Underdog.*	Poetry such as Romeo speaks to Juliet in Shakespeare's play; or the song "Tonight" in the musical *West Side Story.*

SCENERY

Rooms of a real house, as in Edward Albee's *Who's Afraid of Virginia Woolf?*	Abstract forms and shapes on a bare stage—for example, for a Greek play such as Sophocles's *Electra.*

LIGHTING

Light onstage appears to come from natural sources—a lamp in a room, or sunlight, as in Ibsen's *Ghosts,* where the sunrise comes through a window in the final scene.	Shafts of light fall at odd angles; also, colors in light are used arbitrarily. Example: a single blue spotlight on a singer in a musical comedy.

COSTUMES

Ordinary street clothes, like those worn by the characters in August Wilson's *The Piano Lesson.*	The bright costumes of a chorus in a musical comedy; the strange outfit worn by Caliban, the half-man, half-beast in Shakespeare's *The Tempest.*

MAKEUP

The natural look of characters in a domestic play such as Lorraine Hansberry's *A Raisin in the Sun.*	Masks worn by characters in a Greek tragedy or in a modern play like the musical *Beauty and the Beast.*

drinking from a cup or opening an umbrella. Many aspects of musical comedy are nonrealistic. People in the streets or in an office building do not break into song or dance as they do in musicals like *Guys and Dolls, West Side Story, Billy Elliot, Mary Poppins,* or *Wicked.* One could say that any activity or scenic device that transcends or symbolizes reality tends to be nonrealistic.

Combining the Realistic and the Nonrealistic   In discussing realistic and nonrealistic elements of theatre, we must not assume that these two approaches are mutually exclusive. The terms *realistic* and *nonrealistic* are simply a convenient way of separating those parts of theatre that correspond to our observations and experiences of everyday life from those that do not.

Most performances and theatre events contain a mixture of realistic and nonrealistic elements. In acting, for example, a Shakespearean play calls for a number of nonrealistic qualities or techniques. At the same time, any performer playing a Shakespearean character must convince the audience that he or she represents a real human being. To take a more modern example, in *The Glass Menagerie* by Tennessee Williams (1911–1983), and in *Our Town* by Thornton Wilder (1897–1975), one of the performers serves as a narrator and also participates in the action. When the performer playing this part is speaking directly to the audience, his actions are nonrealistic; when he is taking part in a scene with other characters, they are realistic.

Distinguishing Stage Reality from Fact

Whether theatre is realistic or nonrealistic, it is different from the physical reality of everyday life. In recent years there have been attempts to make theatre less remote from our daily lives. For example, plays have been presented that were largely transcripts of court trials or congressional hearings. This was part of a movement called **theatre of fact,** which involved reenactments of material gathered from actual events. Partly as a result of this trend, theatre and life have become intertwined. Television has added to this with *docudramas,* dramatizing the lives, for example, of rape victims, convicts, and ordinary people who become heroic. There has also been a vogue for what is called "reality television," in which real people are put in stressful situations with a presumably unplanned outcome.

This kind of interaction—and sometimes confusion—between life and art has been heightened, of course, by the emergence of television and film documentaries, which cover real events but are also edited. In addition, today we have "staged" political demonstrations and hear of "staged news." In politics staged events have become commonplace: a presidential or senatorial candidate visits a flag factory, an aircraft carrier, or an elementary school for what is called a "photo opportunity." When news becomes "staged" and theatre becomes "fact," it is difficult to separate the two.

These developments point up the close relationship between theatre and life; nevertheless, when we see a performance, even a re-creation of events that have actually occurred, we are always aware, on some level, of being in a theatre. No matter how authentic a reenactment may be, we know that it is a replay and not the original event. Most of us have seen plays with a stage setting so real we marvel at its authenticity: a kitchen, for instance, in which the appliances actually work, with running water in the faucets, ice in the refrigerator, and a stove on which an actor or actress can cook. What

FACT-BASED THEATRE

A popular form that has emerged in the past half century is theatre based on facts. This includes documentary theatre taken from court trials, congressional hearings, and interviews. Shown here is Forrest McClendon, center, as a New York lawyer in a Kander and Ebb musical *The Scottsboro Boys,* choreographed and directed by Susan Stroman. *The Scottsboro Boys* is based on the 1930s trials of nine young black men falsely accused and convicted of raping two white women in Alabama. (© Richard Termine)

we stand in awe of, though, is that the room *appears* so real when we know, in truth, that it is not. We admire the fact that, not being a real kitchen, it looks as if it were.

We are abruptly reminded of the distinction between stage reality and physical reality when the two lines cross. If an actor unintentionally trips and falls onstage, we suddenly shift our attention from the character to the person playing the part. Has he hurt himself? Will he be able to continue? A similar reaction occurs when a performer forgets lines, or a sword falls accidentally during a duel, or a dancer slips during a musical number.

We remember the distinction, also, at the moment when someone else *fails* to remember it. Children frequently mistake actions onstage for the real thing, warning the heroine of the villain's plan or assuming that blows on the head of a puppet actually hurt. There is a famous story about a production of *Othello* in which a spectator ran onstage to prevent the actor playing Othello from strangling Desdemona.

Most people, however, are always aware of the difference; our minds manage two seemingly contradictory feats simultaneously: on the one hand, we know that an imagined event is not objectively real, but at the same time we accept it completely as fantasy. This is possible because of what the poet and critic Samuel Taylor Coleridge

(1772–1834) called the "willing suspension of disbelief." Having separated the reality of art from the reality of everyday life, the mind is prepared to go along unreservedly with the reality of art.

In this chapter we have been concerned with the role the audience plays and the imagination it uses to enter into a theatre event. But there are other factors surrounding our attendance at the theatre that also have a bearing on how we view the experience and how well we understand it. These include the circumstances under which a play was created and the expectations we have when we attend a performance; and they are the subject to which we turn next, in Chapter 3.

SUMMARY

1. During the past 100 years, theatre has been challenged by a succession of technological developments: silent movies, radio, talking movies, television, and so on. It has survived these challenges partly because of the special nature of the performer-audience relationship.

2. The relationship between performer and audience is "live": each is in the other's presence, in the same place at the same time. It is the exchange between the two that gives theatre its unique quality.

3. Theatre—like the other performing arts—is a group experience. The makeup of the audience has a direct bearing on the effect of the experience.

4. Participants and spectators play different roles in the theatre experience; the role of spectators is to observe and respond.

5. There is a difference between participating in theatre by direct action and by observation. In the former situation, nonactors take part, usually for the purpose of personal growth and self-development. In the latter, a presentation is made by one group to another, and the spectators do not participate physically in the experience.

6. For the observer, theatre is an experience of the imagination and the mind. The mind seems capable of accepting almost any illusion as to what is taking place, who the characters are, and when and where the action occurs.

7. Our minds are capable of leaps of the imagination, not just in the theatre but in our everyday lives, where we use symbol and metaphor to communicate with one another and to explain the world around us.

8. The world of the imagination—symbols, metaphors, dreams, fantasies, and various expressions of art—is "real," even though it is intangible and has no objective reality. Frequently it tells us more than any form of logical discourse about our true feelings.

9. Theatre makes frequent use of symbols and metaphors—in writing, acting, design, etc.—and theatre itself can be considered a metaphor.

10. In theatre, audiences are called on to imagine two kinds of worlds: realistic and nonrealistic. Realistic theatre depicts things onstage that conform to observable reality; nonrealistic theatre includes the realm of dreams, fantasy, symbol, and metaphor. In theatre, realism and nonrealism are frequently mixed.

11. In order to take part in theatre as an observer, it is important to keep the "reality" of fantasies and dreams separate from the real world. By making this separation, we open our imagination to the full range of possibilities in theatre.

Background and Expectations of the Audience

When audiences attend a theatre event, they bring more than their mere presence; they bring a background of personal knowledge and a set of expectations that shape the experience. Several important factors are involved:

1. The knowledge and personal memories of individual members of the audience.
2. Their awareness of the social, political, and philosophical world in which the play was written or produced—the link between theatre and society.
3. Their specific information about the play and playwright.
4. Their individual expectations concerning the event: what each person anticipates will happen at a performance. As we will see, misconceptions about what the theatre experience is or should be can lead to confusion and disappointment.

BACKGROUND OF INDIVIDUAL SPECTATORS

A background element that every member of the audience brings to a theatre performance is his or her own individual memories and experiences. Each of us has a personal catalog of childhood memories, emotional scars, and private fantasies. Anything we see onstage that reminds us of this personal world will have a strong impact on us.

When we see a play that has been written in our own day, we bring with us a deep awareness of the world from which the play comes, because we come from the same world. Through the books we read, through newspapers and television, through discussions with friends, we have a background of common information and beliefs.

◀ **THE AFRICAN AMERICAN EXPERIENCE**

Members of a theatre audience come to a performance with individual, personal backgrounds, as well as with certain cultural assumptions and other information. It is helpful to an audience to have as much knowledge as possible about an event. An example would be the play Fences *by August Wilson, about an African American family. Any African American would have special knowledge that would make the experience meaningful, and others would appreciate the performance more if they were familiar with the challenges and life history of African Americans. The production shown here, at the Hartford Stage Company, featured Rob Riley as Cory and Wandachristine as Rose. (© T Charles Erickson)*

Our shared knowledge and experience are much larger than most of us realize, and they form a crucial ingredient in our theatre experience.

The play *A Raisin in the Sun* by Lorraine Hansberry (1930–1965) tells the story of an African American family in Chicago in the late 1950s whose members want to improve their lives by finding better jobs and moving to a new neighborhood. But they face a number of obstacles put in their way by society. Any African American—or, for that matter, any person who belongs to a minority or to a group that has lacked opportunities—can readily identify with this situation. Such a person will know from personal experience what the characters are going through. A more recent play that evokes similar emotions is the Pulitzer Prize–winning *Topdog/Underdog* (2002) by Suzan-Lori Parks (b. 1964), about two brothers trying to make their way in life but meeting a series of obstacles.

BACKGROUND OF THE PERIOD

Even when we identify closely with the characters or situation in a play, in drama from the past there is much that we cannot understand unless we are familiar with the history, culture, psychology, and philosophy of the period when it was created. This is because there is a close connection between any art form and the society in which it is produced.

Theatre and Society

Art does not occur in a vacuum. All art, including theatre, is related to the society in which it is produced. Artists are sometimes charged with being "antisocial," "subver-

TOPDOG/UNDERDOG
The personal background of audience members will affect the experience of seeing theatre. For example, an African American or anyone who grew up in a similar environment or situation will have a deeper understanding of a play such as *Topdog/Underdog* by Suzan-Lori Parks. The play, which won the Pulitzer Prize, is about two African American brothers trying to make their way in life but meeting a series of obstacles. The actors shown here are Don Cheadle and Jeffrey Wright. The production originated at the Joseph Papp Public Theater in New York and was directed by George C. Wolfe. (© Michal Daniel)

sive," or "enemies of the state," and such accusations carry the strong suggestion that artists are outsiders or invaders rather than true members of a culture. To be sure, art frequently challenges society and is sometimes on the leading edge of history, appearing to forecast the future. More often than not, however, such art simply recognizes what is already present in society but has not yet surfaced. A good example is the abstract painting that developed in Europe in the early twentieth century. At first it was considered a freakish aberration: an unattractive jumble of jagged lines and patches of color with no relation to nature, truth, or anything human. In time, however, abstract art came to be recognized as a genuine movement, and the disjointed and fragmentary lines of abstract art seem to reflect the quality of much of modern life.

Art grows in the soil of a specific society. With very few exceptions—and those are soon forgotten—art is a mirror of its age, revealing the prevailing attitudes, underlying assumptions, and deep-seated beliefs of a particular group of people. Art may question society's views or reaffirm them, but it cannot escape them; the two are as indissolubly linked as a person and his or her shadow. When we speak of art as "universal," we mean that the art of one age has so defined the characteristics of human beings that it can speak eloquently to another age; but we should never forget that every work of art first emerges at a given time and place and can never be adequately understood unless the conditions surrounding its birth are also understood.

Greek Theatre and Culture

A study of theatre in significant periods of history confirms the close link between art and society. In ancient Greece, for example, civilization reached a high point in Athens during the time of Pericles, the latter part of the fifth century BCE. This was the golden

THE SYMMETRY OF A GREEK TEMPLE
The formalism and sense of order of Greece in the fifth century BCE are reflected in the Parthenon, on the acropolis in Athens. All art, including theatre, reflects the attitudes and values of the society in which it is created. (© Adam Crowley/Getty Images)

age of Greece—when politics, art, architecture, and theatre thrived as they never had before, and rarely have since. As the Athenians of that period gained control over the world around them and took new pride in human achievements, they developed ideals of beauty, order, symmetry, and moderation that permeated their entire culture, including theatre.

By the fifth century BCE, standard forms of drama had emerged in Greece, both for tragedies and for comedies. One convention limited the number of scenes in a play: usually, there were only five scenes, interspersed with choral sections. In addition, the drama took place in one locale—often in front of a palace—and within a short span of time. Another convention reflected this society's sense of balance and order. Though bloody deeds occurred often in the myths on which most Greek plays were based, in the plays that have survived these deeds almost never took place in sight of the audience—murders, suicides, and other acts of violence usually occurred offstage. The Greek concept of moderation is reflected in another convention of most Greek tragedies: any character in a play who acted in an excess of passion was generally punished or pursued by avenging furies.

Elizabethan Theatre and Culture

Another example of the strong link between theatre and society—an example that stands in contrast to the classical Greek period—is the Elizabethan age in England. Named after Queen Elizabeth I, who reigned from 1558 to 1603, this period saw England become a dominant force in the world. Under Elizabeth's rule, England became a unified country; trade and commerce flourished, and with the defeat of the Spanish Armada in 1588, an age of exploration for England was under way. England was expanding confidently on all fronts, and these characteristics were reflected in the drama of the period.

From medieval drama the Elizabethans had inherited stage practices that made it possible to shift rapidly in a play from place to place and from one time period to another. Using these techniques, as well as others they perfected, Shakespeare, Christopher Marlowe (1564–1593), and their contemporaries wrote plays that are quite different from the more formal drama of the Greeks. A single play might move to a number of locations and cover a period of many years. Rather than being restrictive, Elizabethan plays are expansive in terms of numbers of characters and in terms of action, and there is no hesitancy whatsoever about showing murder and bloodshed onstage. At the end of an Elizabethan play, corpses frequently cover the stage in full view of the audience. This expansiveness and this sense of adventure mirror the temper of the age in which the plays were written.

HISTORICAL PERSPECTIVES

WOMEN IN GREEK AND ELIZABETHAN THEATRES

Did women attend theatre in ancient Greece? In Elizabethan England, why were women forbidden to appear onstage? These are only two of many significant and intriguing questions that arise when one examines the role of women at various times in theatre history. And of course, they are inextricably linked to larger questions about the treatment of women in society in every age.

In Athenian society of ancient Greece, only male citizens had the right to participate in politics. Although women counted as citizens, they were generally excluded from the institutions of government. They were thus also excluded from appearing onstage in the annual spring theatre festival called the City Dionysia. The plays were written and acted by men, even though many feature important female characters. A broader social question is whether women were allowed to attend the dramatic festivals as spectators. There appears to be no conclusive answer, and the question continues to perplex classical scholars. Even if a select number of women were at performances—after all, men brought their male slaves to the theatre—the plays primarily address a large male audience. Contemporary sources supporting the view that women attended theatre are fragmentary and inconclusive; for instance, a character in the *The Frogs* by Aristophanes (c. 447–388 BCE) remarks ironically that all decent women committed suicide after seeing one of Euripides's plays. Later commentaries, such as an often-repeated story that a few women who saw the chorus of Furies in *The Eumenides* by Aeschylus (525–456 BCE) had miscarriages, are discounted because women did attend theatre after the classical period. One argument for the attendance of women is the important role women often played in other aspects of the cultural life of the city-state. They contributed to civic life, for example, by playing leading roles in religious ceremonies, celebrations, and other ritual activities. In fact, they were creatively involved in theatre at other festivals. Because the public activities of women were regulated in order to protect their reputation, female entertainers came to be associated with indecent behavior. Even so, popular entertainments included female performers as singers, dancers, acrobats, and musicians.

In the sixteenth century, actresses appeared onstage in continental Europe. Also, women had appeared in medieval theatre productions in England, but in the English public theatres in the time of Elizabeth I (r. 1558–1603), women were forbidden by law to appear on the stage. Although some actors rose to become celebrities, actresses were often associated with "public women" or prostitutes—particularly by Puritans who viewed theatre as an immoral profession. Female roles therefore were played by boys, notable for their ability to imitate feminine beauty and grace. An exception to the prohibition of actresses was the appearance of Italian singers and French actresses who performed in England for both the nobility and commoners. Outside the public theatres, historians identify a vast, hidden tradition of female performance gleaned from private documents, such as letters and diaries. At court and in manor houses aristocratic women took part in extravagant spectacles called masques; parish dramas and pageants included female members of the community; other women worked as traveling entertainers. The disapproval of women performing in public changed with the restoration of the monarchy in 1660, when actresses were finally permitted to appear in licensed theatres.

Prepared by Susan Tenneriello, Baruch College, CUNY.

Modern Theatre and Culture

Moving to the contemporary period, we find once again a link between theatre and society. Modern society, especially in the United States, is heterogeneous. We have people of many races, religions, and national backgrounds living side by side. Moreover, the twentieth century was marked by increasingly swift global communication. By means of radio, television, computers, and the Internet, an event occurring in one place can be flashed instantaneously to the rest of the world. By these means, too, people are continually made aware of cultures other than their own.

When cultures and societies are brought together, we are reminded of the many things people have in common but also of the differences among us. At the same time that we are brought together by global communications, other aspects of life have become increasingly fragmented. A number of institutions that held fairly constant through many centuries—organized religion, the family, marriage—have been seriously challenged in the century and a half preceding our own day.

Discoveries by Charles Darwin (1809–1882) about evolution raised fundamental questions about views of creation held at that time: were human beings created specially by God, or were they subject to the same process of evolution as other forms of life? People of the nineteenth century feared that if human beings had evolved, they might not occupy the unique place in the universe that had always been assumed for them. Shortly after Darwin published his findings, Karl Marx (1818–1883) put forward revolutionary ideas on economics that challenged long-held beliefs about capitalism. At the end of the nineteenth century, Sigmund Freud cast doubt on the ability of human beings to exercise total rational control over their activities. Later, Albert Einstein (1879–1955) formulated theories about relativity that questioned long-established views of the universe.

Similar changes and discoveries continued throughout the twentieth century. The cumulative effect of these discoveries was to make human beings much less certain of their place in the cosmos and their mastery of events. Today, in the early twenty-first century, life appears much less unified and less ordered than it once seemed.

We must add to these two developments—the bringing together of cultures by population shifts and communication, and the challenges to long-held beliefs—a third factor, which is the series of horrific events that have occurred over the past 100 years: two world wars, the second of which saw the Holocaust, the extermination of millions of Jews and others by the Nazi regime; the highly controversial Vietnam War; the equally controversial Iraq War; and natural disasters like the deadly tsunami in the Indian Ocean on December 26, 2004, in which 185,000 people were killed.

All these developments—communications, changes in society, human-made and natural disasters—are reflected in today's theatre. It is a theatre of fragmentation and of *eclecticism*—the embracing of different strains, and also global theatre, that is, theatre from around the world. And it can hardly be a totally lighthearted theatre devoted only to fluff and escapism. A typical theatre company today performs a wide range of plays. In a single season, the same company may present a tragedy by Shakespeare, a farce by the French dramatist Molière (1622–1673), a modern drama by the Spanish writer Federico García Lorca (1898–1936), and a play like *Eurydice,* by Sarah Ruhl (b. 1974), a young American playwright. Moreover, the dramatists of today write on many subjects and in many styles.

The three periods we have looked at—the Greek, the Elizabethan, and the modern—are examples of the close relationship between a society and the art and theatre it produces. One could find comparable links in every culture. It is important to remember, therefore, that whatever the period in which it was first produced, drama is woven into the fabric of its time.

BACKGROUND INFORMATION ON THE PLAY OR PLAYWRIGHT

Sometimes, we need additional knowledge not only about the historical period of a play but also about the play itself. For instance, a play may contain difficult passages or obscure references, which it is helpful to know about before we see a performance.

As an example, we can take a segment from Shakespeare's *King Lear:* the scene in the third act when Lear appears on the heath in the midst of a terrible storm. Earlier in the play, Lear divided his kingdom between two of his daughters, Goneril and Regan, who he thought loved him but who, he discovers, have actually deceived him.

BACKGROUND INFORMATION ON THE PLAY OR PLAYWRIGHT
When we see a play from another time or culture, or a play on a subject with which we are not familiar, the experience will be greatly enhanced if we have some knowledge of what the playwright was trying to do and of the context in which the play was written. Knowledge of the themes, the language, and the conventions of Elizabethan theatre production will enhance and enrich our experience of seeing a play such as *King Lear*. A scene from *King Lear* is shown here, with Ian McKellen, left, as Lear, and William Gaunt as Gloucester, directed by Trevor Nunn at the Royal Shakespeare Company. (© Manuel Harlan/Royal Shakespeare Company)

Gradually, they have stripped him of everything: his possessions, his soldiers, his dignity. Finally, they send him out from their homes to face the wind and rain in open country. As the storm begins, Lear speaks the following lines:

> Blow, winds, and crack your cheeks! Rage! Blow!
> You cataracts and hurricanoes, spout
> Till you have drenched our steeples, drowned the cocks!

In the first line, the expression "crack your cheeks" refers to pictures in the corners of old maps showing a face puffed out at the cheeks, blowing the wind.[1] Shakespeare is saying that the face of the wind should blow so hard that its cheeks will crack. In the second line, "cataracts and hurricanoes" refers to water from both the heavens and the seas. In the third line, "cocks" refers to weathercocks on the tops of steeples; Lear wants so much rain to fall that even the weathercocks on the steepletops will be submerged. If we are aware of these meanings, we can join them with the sounds of the words—and with the rage the actor expresses in his voice and gestures—to get the full impact of the scene.

In contemporary theatre, playwrights frequently use special techniques that will confuse us if we do not understand them. The German playwright Bertolt Brecht (1898–1956), who lived and wrote in the United States during the 1940s, wanted to provoke his audiences into thinking about what they were seeing. To do this, he would interrupt a story with a song or a speech by a narrator. His theory was that when a story is stopped in this manner, audience members have an opportunity to consider more carefully what they are seeing and to relate the drama onstage to other aspects of life.

If one is not aware that this is Brecht's purpose in interrupting the action, one might conclude that he was simply a careless or inferior playwright. Here, as in similar cases, knowledge of the play or playwright is indispensable to a complete theatre experience.

EXPECTATIONS: THE VARIETY OF EXPERIENCES IN MODERN THEATRE

People who have not often been to the theatre sometimes expect that all theatre experiences will be alike. In fact, audiences go to the theatre for different purposes. Some spectators, like those who enjoy the escape offered by movies and television, are interested primarily in light entertainment. Audiences at dinner theatres or Broadway musicals do not want to be faced with troublesome problems or serious moral issues. They look for something that will be amusing and perhaps include music, dancing, and beautiful scenery and costumes. On the other hand, some people want to be stimulated and challenged, both intellectually and emotionally. To these audiences, a situation comedy or a light musical will seem frivolous or sentimental. It must be remembered, too, that many people like both kinds of theatre. At times a person may seek light entertainment; at other times, meaningful drama.

Not only do performances vary in terms of the type of theatre they offer; they also take place in a variety of settings, and this too has an effect on the nature of the experience. In the mid-twentieth century in the United States "the theatre" was synonymous with one kind of experience: Broadway. In the last several decades this has changed radically—further evidence of how diversity in theatre reflects the overall

BROADWAY THEATRE
Productions in the major theatres in New York City—collectively known as Broadway—are usually characterized by elaborate scenic elements, first-rate acting, and scripts with wide appeal: either new works or revivals. Shown here is a scene from the award-winning *Billy Elliot, the Musical,* directed by Stephen Daldry, with David Alvarez, one of three young actors alternating in the title role on Broadway. (Sara Krulwich/The New York Times/Redux)

diversity in contemporary life. To see the changed circumstances in which theatre is presented, it will be helpful to look at developments in this area in the United States over the past half century.

Broadway and Touring Theatre

Broadway is the name of the oldest professional theatre in New York City: it refers specifically to plays performed in the large theatres in the district near Times Square. From 1920 until the early 1950s, most new plays written in the United States originated there, and productions in other areas were usually copies of Broadway productions. The thirty or more theatres located in these few blocks are about the same size, seating between 700 and 1,400 people, and have the same style of architecture as well as the same type of stage: a picture-frame stage (discussed in Chapter 4).

Productions sent on tour from Broadway to the rest of the country are exact replicas of the original. Scenery is duplicated down to the last detail, and performers from New York often play roles they had played on Broadway. Nonprofessional theatres have copied Broadway as well; acting versions of successful plays are published for colleges, schools, and community theatres, providing precise instructions for the movements of the performers and the placement of scenery onstage.

Because our society is diverse and complex, and because theatre reflects society, no one form of theatre today can speak equally to all of us. As if in response to the complexity of the modern world, in the second half of the twentieth century people began searching for new forms in theatre, and for alternative locations in which to present theatre.

Resident Professional Theatre

One significant development, which began in a few cities in the 1950s and has since spread across the country, is resident professional theatre, sometimes known as *regional theatre*. Theatre companies have been formed, and theatre facilities built, for the continuing presentation of high-quality professional productions to local residents. The performers, directors, and designers are generally high-caliber artists who make theatre their full-time profession.

A few of these theatres are **repertory** companies that perform several plays on alternate nights, rather than presenting a single play night after night for the length of its run. For reasons of economy, very few theatres in the United States find it feasible to offer true repertory. Most cities have developed theatres that present a series of plays over a given time, with each play being performed for about 4 to 12 weeks.

Among the best-known of these theatres are the Arena Stage in Washington, D.C., the Long Wharf in New Haven, the American Repertory Theatre in Boston, the Actors Theatre of Louisville, the Alley Theatre in Houston, the Goodman Theatre in Chicago, the Milwaukee Repertory Theater, the Guthrie Theater in Minneapolis, the Seattle Repertory Theatre, and the Mark Taper Forum in Los Angeles. Among African American theatres, examples are Towne Street Theatre of Los Angeles, the North Carolina Black Repertory, and the Black Repertory Company of St. Louis. A season of plays in these theatres will usually include both new plays and classics, and theatergoers are encouraged to buy a season subscription.

In addition to resident companies, there are now a number of permanent summer theatre festivals and Shakespeare festivals throughout the United States and Canada. Among the best-known are the Shakespeare festivals at Stratford, Ontario; San Diego, California; and Ashland, Oregon.

Alternative Theatre: Off-Broadway and Elsewhere

In New York City *off-Broadway theatre* began in the 1950s as an alternative to Broadway, which was becoming increasingly costly. Off-Broadway theatres were smaller than Broadway theatres—most of them had fewer than 200 seats—and were located outside the Times Square area in places like Greenwich Village. Because off-Broadway was less expensive than Broadway, it offered more opportunity for producing serious classics and experimental works.

Off-Broadway itself, however, became expensive and institutionalized in the 1960s and 1970s. Consequently, small independent groups had to develop another forum for producing plays. The result was *off-off-Broadway*. Off-off-Broadway shows are produced wherever inexpensive space is available—churches, lofts, warehouses, large basements—and are characterized by low-priced productions and a wide variety of offerings.

An important development in American theatre is that counterparts to off-off-Broadway have been established in other major cities across the United States—Washington, Atlanta, Chicago, Minneapolis, Los Angeles, San Francisco, Seattle—where small theatre groups perform as alternatives to large organizations. It is in these

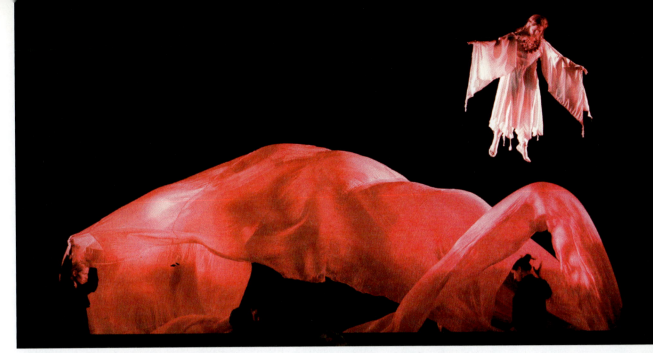

THEATRE AWAY FROM THE MAINSTREAM
In addition to traditional mainstream theatre, there is an important active theatre such as off-Broadway, off-off-Broadway, and avant-garde, not only in major cities but in many other places around the world. An example of such an experimental theatre is Mabou Mines. Typical of its work was *Red Beads,* described as a combination fairy tale, puppet play, and chamber opera. *Red Beads* mixes music, dance, puppetry by Basil Twist, and other theatrical elements to tell the story of a 13-year-old girl coming of age. With a strong Asian influence, the story is presented in fragments, and features such elements as characters suspended in the air and billowing silk fabric, as seen here. (© Beatriz Schiller)

smaller theatres, in New York and across the country, that most experimental and new works are performed. In addition, all across the country there are cabaret and dinner theatres in which the atmosphere of a nightclub or restaurant is combined with that of a theatre. In these informal settings, guests eat and drink before watching a performance.

Young People's and Children's Theatre

A branch of theatre that has earned an important place in the overall picture is children's theatre, sometimes called *theatre for youth.* These theatres include a wide spectrum from the most sophisticated professional organizations to semiprofessionals to improvisational groups to undertakings that are predominately amateur or educational. The aim in all cases, however, is to provide a theatrical experience for young people. In some cases it is to offer school-age children an opportunity to see first-class productions of plays dealing with people and subjects in which they might be personally interested. In other cases, the emphasis is on dramatizing the lives of significant figures in history—Abraham Lincoln; Martin Luther King, Jr.; Eleanor Roosevelt— or giving dramatic life to literary classics such as *Tom Sawyer* or *Huckleberry Finn.*

Other types of children's theatre strive to give young people experiences in creating and presenting theatre. The participants take part as actors, designers, lighting technicians, stage managers, and the like.

A number of young people's or children's theatre organizations across North America have a long history and feature first-class theatre spaces and production facilities. Moreover, the caliber of those responsible for their productions—performers, designers, directors, etc.—is excellent and the equal of any professional regional or not-for-profit theatre. Among those in this category are the Children's Theatre Company of Minneapolis, the Children's Theatre of Charlotte, the Orange County Children's Theater, the Nashville Children's Theatre, and TheatreworksUSA in New York City.

COLLEGE AND UNIVERSITY THEATRE

A vital segment of theatre in the United States is the many productions mounted by theatre departments in colleges and universities, which often achieve a high degree of professionalism. They also provide excellent training for theatre practitioners, as well as affording audiences excellent, first-rate productions. Seen here are Gianfranco Aparicio as Protagonist (P) and Patricia Piñeiro as Assistant (A) in the Colorado State University Theatre production of Samuel Beckett's *Catastrophe,* translated into Spanish by Professor Jose Luis Suarez-Garcia and presented in English and in Spanish, directed by Professor Eric Prince. (© William A. Cotton/Colorado State University)

College and University Theatre

In the last few decades, *college* and *university theatre* departments have also become increasingly important, not only in teaching theatre arts but also in presenting plays. In some localities, college productions are virtually the only form of theatre offered. In other areas, they are a significant supplement to professional theatre.

The theatre facilities in many colleges are excellent. Most large colleges and universities have two or three theatre spaces—a full-size theatre, a medium-size theatre, and a smaller space for experimental drama—as well as extensive scene shops, costume rooms, dressing rooms, and rehearsal halls. Productions are usually scheduled throughout the school year.

The quality and complexity of these productions vary. In some places, productions are extremely elaborate, with full-scale scenery, costumes, lighting, and sound. Colleges vary, too, in the level of professionalism in acting. Many colleges use only performers from the undergraduate theatre program. If a college has a master's degree program, it will use both graduate and undergraduate performers. Colleges or universities may also bring in outside professionals to perform along with students. Most college and university theatres offer a variety of plays, including classics and experimental plays rarely done by professional theatres.

Community and Amateur Theatre

In addition to the many forms of professional theatre, and to college and university theatre, another area in which theatre activity thrives is community and amateur theatre. In hundreds of locations throughout the United States and Canada, and in many parts of the world, one finds semiprofessional or nonprofessional theatres serving local communities. In some cases, those involved—actors, directors, designers, crew members—have had professional training and experience but have chosen not to pursue a full-time career, for a number of reasons. These could include jobs, families, financial considerations, and the like.

Along with the part-time professionals, community theatres include amateurs who also love the theatre. In a fully amateur theatre, all the participants are nonprofessionals. Many of these theatres approach their productions—the selection of plays, rehearsals, the building of scenery, advertising, and ticket sales—in much the same way as their professional counterparts. Some of these groups produce in their own theatres, but many use alternative spaces such as town halls, high school theatres, and churches. In a number of cases, also, the level of work is surprisingly good, and overall, the work of community and amateur theatres adds immeasurably to the total mix of theatrical activity. In many parts of the country, community and amateur theatres afford the only live theatre available to audiences.

SPECIAL AUDIENCE MEMBERS: THE CRITIC AND THE DRAMATURG

Most people who go to the theatre or the movies, or who watch a television show, are amateur critics. When a person says about a performance, "It started off great, but it fizzled," or "The star was terrific, just like someone in real life," or "The woman was OK, but the man overacted," or "The acting was good, but the story was too downbeat for me," he or she is making a critical judgment. The difference between a critic and an ordinary spectator is that the critic presumably is better informed about the event and has developed a set of critical standards by which to judge it.

THE CRITIC

A *critic,* loosely defined, is someone who observes theatre and then analyzes and comments on it. Ideally, the critic serves as a knowledgeable and highly sensitive audience member. Audiences can learn from critics not only because critics impart information and judgments but also because a critic shares with an audience the point of view of the spectator. Unlike those who create theatre—writers, performers, designers—critics sit out front and watch a performance just as other members of the audience do. Critics generally write serious articles that appear in newspapers, magazines, and books.

A familiar type of critic is the reviewer. A *reviewer,* who usually works for a television station, a newspaper, or a magazine, reports on what has occurred at the theatre. He or she will tell briefly what a theatre event is about, explaining whether it is a musical, a comedy, or a serious play and perhaps describing its plot. The reviewer might also offer an opinion about whether or not the event is worth seeing. The reviewer is usually restricted by time, space, or both. A television reviewer, for instance, will have only a minute or two on the air to describe a play and offer a reaction. A newspaper reviewer, similarly, is restricted by the space available in the newspaper and by the newspaper's deadline.

Today, in addition to critics and reviewers whose opinions appear in print or on television, we have a new source of theatre criticism: blogs, YouTube, and popular Web sites like Theatremania.com. Many of these sites have their own theatre reviewers;

other sites may have amateur critics who send in their unsolicited opinions. At times these assessments of a production can be helpful and informative, but a word of caution is in order here. A number of these self-appointed reviewers may have little or no background in theatre criticism, or, in fact, in theatre itself. They enjoy being part of the wider world of theatre criticism, but may not have the credentials to do so. In other words, these volunteer critics may not have the preparation for criticism described in the pages that follow.

What Is Criticism?

When a new movie opens, or a new television series begins, daily papers run reviews of it. The person writing a review often spells out the plot and makes a value judgment about the story, the acting, and the direction. The reviewer may be astute and may write a well-reasoned and informative review, which can be helpful to those planning to see a movie, or a play onstage.

These reviews become distorted, however, when the producer of the film or television production takes a review and extracts sensational "quotes"—statements that praise the show to the skies—and features these in newspaper ads. Some of the ads are downright dishonest. The producers will take a sentence such as "Up to the point where the hero entered, it was a great show," and put in the ads: "It was a great show." Still, most people who see the ads realize that this is not serious criticism; it is not even criticism at all. We are concerned here with the serious critic—one who has the background and judgment to assist audience members in understanding and appreciating what they see onstage.

One popular image of a theatre critic is a caustic writer who makes sharp, rapier-like thrusts at performers and playwrights. Some epithets of critics have become legendary. John Mason Brown described the actress Tallulah Bankhead in a production of Shakespeare's *Antony and Cleopatra* by saying, "Tallulah Bankhead barged down the Nile last night as Cleopatra and sank." When Katharine Hepburn, who was a stage actress before she went into films, appeared in a play called *The Lake,* the critic Dorothy Parker wrote that Hepburn "runs the gamut of emotions from A to B." Before he became a playwright, George Bernard Shaw (1856–1950) was a critic, and he had harsh things to say about a number of people, including Shakespeare. Shaw wrote that Shakespeare's *Cymbeline* was "for the most part stagy trash of the lowest melodramatic order." About Shakespeare himself Shaw said:

GEORGE BERNARD SHAW: CRITIC AND PLAYWRIGHT
Most people know Shaw (1856–1950) as one of the best British dramatists of the past 100 years, but he was also one of the finest critics of modern times. Though opinionated and often caustic, Shaw had many admirable attributes as a critic: a wide knowledge of theatre, both past and present, as well as of the other arts, politics, and social affairs; a clear set of criteria for plays and performances; and a writing style that was strong, fluid, and lively. (Culver Pictures)

"With the single exception of Homer, there is no eminent writer, not even Sir Walter Scott, whom I can despise so entirely as I despise Shakespeare when I measure my mind against his."

The word *criticize* has at least two meanings. One is "to find fault," and that is what we see in the comments above. But *criticize* also means "to understand and appraise," and this meaning is much more important for a theatre critic.

Preparation for Criticism

In order to make criticism more meaningful to audiences, the theatre critic ideally should have a thorough theatre background of the kind discussed in Chapter 2. It would consist of a full knowledge of theatre history, as well as other aspects of theatre, such as acting, directing, and design. The critic must be familiar with plays written in various styles and modes and should know the body of work of individual writers. Also, the critic ought to be able to relate what is happening in theatre to what is happening in the other arts and, beyond that, to events in society generally.

In addition, the theatre critic should understand the production elements discussed later in this book—directing, acting, and design. The critic must know what a director does and what constitutes good and bad direction. The critic should also understand acting and should be able to judge whether a performer has the skills and the talent to be convincing in a role and whether the role has been interpreted appropriately. In addition, the critic should be familiar with the principles and practices of design—scenery, costumes, and lighting. He or she ought to have some idea of what is called for in each area and be able to judge whether the design elements measure up in a given production.

"What part of Noh don't you understand?"

(© The New Yorker Collection 2001 Pat Byrnes from cartoonbank.com)

Admittedly, this is asking a great deal of critics, and very few acquire the broad range of knowledge required; but it is an ideal to which all critics should aspire and which audiences have a right to expect of first-rate critics.

Critical Criteria

Along with a strong background, a good critic should develop criteria by which to judge a play and a production. These criteria should take the form of a set of questions to be asked each time she or he attends a performance.

What Is Being Attempted?

One of the first questions is, *What is the play, and the production, attempting to do?* This question must be raised both about the script and about the production. The critic should make clear what the playwright is trying to accomplish. Is the play a tragedy meant to raise significant questions and stir deep emotions? Is it a light comedy intended to entertain and provide escape? Is it a political drama arguing for a point of view?

Have the Intentions Been Achieved?

A second question a critic must address is, *How well have the intentions of the playwright been carried out?* If a theatre piece originates with an acting ensemble, or with a director, the question is, *How well have the intentions of the original creators been realized?* A theatre company may be producing an acknowledged masterpiece such as *Hamlet* or *Macbeth,* in which case the question becomes how well the play has been acted, directed, and designed. Have the performers brought Shakespeare's characters to life convincingly and excitingly? Or has the director—perhaps by striving to be too original or by updating the play and putting the characters into modern dress—distorted Shakespeare's intentions beyond recognition?

In the case of a new script, the critic must also ask how well the playwright has realized his or her own intentions. If the play is intended to probe deeper into family relationships—parents and children, or husbands and wives—how convincingly and how insightfully has the dramatist accomplished this? If the intention is to entertain, to make the audience laugh, the question must be asked: Just how funny is the play? Did it succeed in providing entertainment? Was it clever, witty, and full of amusing situations, or did it fall flat?

Was the Attempt Worthwhile?

A third question for the critic falls more into the realm of personal taste and evaluation: *Is the play or production worth doing?* Many critics think that anything that succeeds at giving pleasure and providing entertainment is as worthwhile in its own way as a more serious undertaking. Others, however, do not. In cases like this, readers must make up their own minds.

If audience members are aware of these criteria, they not only can note whether critics—in print or on television—address these questions but also can ask the questions for themselves.

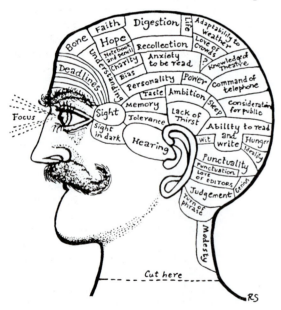

THE IDEAL CRITIC

In this drawing, the artist Ronald Searle humorously suggests the many qualities a person must have in order to be a good theatre critic—everything from knowledge of the theatre to adaptability to weather, from punctuality to punctuation. (© Ronald Searle, 1952)

Descriptive and Prescriptive Criticism

In judging a play or another theatre event, critics frequently take one of two different approaches. The first approach could be called *descriptive;* that is, it attempts to describe as clearly and accurately as possible what is happening in a play or a performance. The second could be called *prescriptive,* meaning that the critic not only describes what has been done but also offers advice or comments about how it *should* be done.

Fact and Opinion in Criticism

In reading the commentary of critics, it is important to distinguish between *fact* and *opinion.* Opinion should be carefully weighed. On the other hand, facts or insights presented by a critic can be extremely helpful. Critics can often make us aware of information we might not otherwise have known—for example, by explaining a point that was confusing to the audience or noting how a particular scene in a play relates to an earlier scene. A critic might also offer background material about the playwright, the subject matter of the play, or the style of the production. Such information can broaden the audience's understanding and appreciation of theatre. The more we know about what a playwright is attempting to do and why a playwright arranges scenes in a certain way, the better we will be able to judge the value of a theatre event.

A good example would be an explanation by a critic of the intentions and techniques of the playwright Maria Irene Fornés in *Fefu and Her Friends.* The first act of

CRITICS PROVIDE BACKGROUND
Certain plays, both past and present, can prove difficult for an audience to understand fully, especially when first seen. Included in this group are avant-garde or experimental plays. A good example of the latter is *Fefu and Her Friends* by Maria Irene Fornés, which focuses on eight women. During the course of the action, the audience is divided into four groups and taken to four separate locations to see different scenes. Without the proper orientation, this unusual arrangement might at first prove confusing. Shown here are Julianna Margulies as Emma and Joyce Lynn O'Connor as Fefu in a production at the Yale Repertory Theatre. (© Gerry Goodstein/Yale Repertory Theatre)

this play takes place in the living room of Fefu's New England home, which was once a farmhouse. The audience sits in one location watching the action in the living room. The second act, however, is presented differently and has an unusual structure. There are four different locations, which must be spaces in the theatre other than the stage, such as backstage, offstage, in the lobby, or in a rehearsal hall. One of these locations represents a lawn outside the house, a second a bedroom, a third the study, and the fourth the kitchen. The characters in the play split up and perform separate scenes in each of the four locations. The scenes are supposed to be occurring simultaneously: all at the same time. The audience is divided into four groups as well; audience members move from one location to the next until they have seen all four; the scenes in the separate locations are repeated four times so that each group of audience members can see what has happened. For the third act of the play, the audience reassembles in the main auditorium to watch a scene that takes place once again in the living room, onstage.

Among other things, Fornés uses the second act to break out of the usual theatre setting. She also wants to show the fragmentation of life as well as its simultaneity. She wants the audience to get a sense of life overlapping and continuing in different places in addition to those on which we usually focus. A critic can explain Fornés's purpose and techniques so that when audience members attend a performance they will be better prepared for what they are experiencing.

THE DRAMATURG OR LITERARY MANAGER

A person who often serves a theatre company as a resident or in-house critic is the dramaturg. The term *dramaturg* comes from a German word for "dramatic adviser." In Europe, the practice of having a dramaturg, or *literary manager,* attached to a theatre goes back well over a century. In the United States, the role of the dramaturg is relatively new; in recent years, however, many regional professional groups and other not-for-profit theatres have engaged full-time dramaturgs. Among the duties frequently undertaken by dramaturgs are discovering and reading promising new plays, working with playwrights on the development of new scripts, identifying significant plays from the past that may have been overlooked, conducting research on previous productions of classic plays, preparing reports on the history of plays, researching criticism and interpretations of plays from the past, and writing articles for the programs that are distributed when plays are produced.

Just as a good critic can be helpful to audience members, so too can a perceptive dramaturg. He or she is usually the person who prepares educational material for students and teachers who attend performances. And if there is a discussion with audiences and members of the artistic team before or after a performance, the dramaturg often leads such a discussion.

THE AUDIENCE'S RELATIONSHIP TO CRITICISM

As suggested earlier, when the audience combines awareness of criticism with the theatre event itself, the experience can be greatly enhanced: background information and critical appraisals are added to one's own firsthand reactions. There are cautionary notes, however, of which audience members should be aware.

The Audience's Independent Judgment

Quite often critics state unequivocally that a certain play is extremely well written or badly written, beautifully performed or atrociously performed, and so on. Because critics often speak so confidently and because their opinions appear on television or in print, their words have the ring of authority. But theatergoers should not be intimidated by this. In New York City, Chicago, or Los Angeles, where a number of critics and reviewers in various media comment on each production, there is a wide range of opinion. It is not unusual for some critics to find a certain play admirable, others to find the same play highly objectionable, and still others to find a mixture of good and bad. This implies that there is no absolute authority among critics, and that audience members should make up their own minds. If a critic, for example, dislikes a certain play because he or she finds it too sentimental and you happen to like that kind of sentiment, you should not be dissuaded from your own preferences.

THE AUDIENCE'S JUDGMENT
Critics and reviewers can be enormously helpful to theatre audiences in providing background material, critical criteria, and other information. In the end, though, audiences should make up their own minds. A good example is the Broadway musical *The Addams Family,* which opened to mixed and negative reviews but has been a hit on Broadway. In this scene we see Nathan Lane with the Company, directed by Jerry Zaks. (Sara Krulwich/The New York Times/Redux)

Analysis and Overanalysis

Is there a risk in a critic's being very analytical about a theatre performance? There can be, of course. Some people are so preoccupied with trying to determine what is wrong with a play or performance that they lose all sense of immediacy; the spontaneity and joy of the experience are sacrificed. Most critics, however, find that their alertness to what is happening during a performance helps rather than hinders their emotional response to the event. After all, human beings have an enormous capacity for receiving information on several levels simultaneously. We do it all the time in our daily lives. With a little practice, the same thing can happen in theatergoing, both for audience members and for professional critics. We develop standards for theatre events—a sense of what makes good theatre—and we judge a performance by those standards at the same time that we lose ourselves in the overall experience.

In Chapters 2 and 3 we have examined the role of the audience and of two special audience members: the critic and the dramaturg. Those who watch a theatre performance are a necessary part of theatre. In Chapter 4 we turn to another aspect of theatre with which the audience is intimately, even physically, related—the actual space in which a performance occurs.

SUMMARY

1. Each individual attending a theatre event brings to it a personal background of experience that becomes a vital ingredient in his or her response.

2. Theatre—like other arts—is closely linked to the society in which it is produced; it mirrors and reflects the attitudes, philosophy, and basic assumptions of its time.

3. Spectators attending a play written in their own day bring to it an awareness of their society's values and beliefs, and this background information forms an important part of the overall experience.

4. A play from the past can be understood better if the spectator is aware of the culture from which it came.

5. For any play that presents difficulties in language, style, or meaning, familiarity with the work itself can add immeasurably to a spectator's understanding and appreciation of a performance.

6. With an unfamiliar work, it is also helpful to learn about the playwright and his or her approach to theatre.

7. Expectations about the nature of the theatre experience affect our reaction to it. The various experiences in theatre today in the United States include Broadway and touring theatre; resident professional theatre; alternative theatre; young people's and children's theatre; college and university theatre; community and amateur theatre; and multiethnic, multicultural, global, and gender theatre.

8. Most people who attend theatre events are amateur critics, making judgments and drawing conclusions about what they see.

9. The professional critic has several tasks: to understand exactly what is being presented, including the intentions of the playwright and the director; to analyze the play, the acting, and the direction, as well as other elements such as scenery and lighting; to evaluate the presentation—was this worth doing? does it serve a purpose? and so forth.

10. People commenting on theatre can be divided into *reviewers,* who report briefly on a theatre event in newspapers, in magazines, or on television; and *critics,* who write longer articles analyzing in depth a performance or the work of a playwright.

11. The dramaturg or literary manager is a position that originated in Europe and is now found in many theatres in the United States, particularly not-for-profit theatres. The dramaturg analyzes scripts, advises directors, and works with playwrights on new dramas.

12. Audience members must realize that critics, too, have their limitations and prejudices and that ultimately each individual spectator must arrive at his or her own judgment regarding a theatre event.

The Audience Views the Stage: Theatre Spaces

For those who create theatre, the experience begins long before the actual event. The dramatist spends weeks, months, or perhaps years writing the play; the director and designers plan the production well ahead of time; and the actors and actresses rehearse intensively for several weeks before the first public performance.

For the spectator, too, the experience begins ahead of time. Members of the audience read or hear reports of the play; they anticipate seeing a particular actress or actor; they buy tickets and make plans with friends to attend; and before the performance, they gather outside the theatre auditorium with other members of the audience.

CREATING THE ENVIRONMENT

When spectators arrive at a theatre for a performance, they immediately take in the environment in which the event will occur. The atmosphere of the theatre building has a great deal to do with the audience's mood in approaching a performance, not only creating expectations about the event but conditioning the experience once it gets under way.

Spectators have one feeling if they come into a formal setting, such as a picture-frame stage surrounded by carved gilt figures, with crystal chandeliers and red plush seats in the auditorium. They have quite a different feeling if they come into an old warehouse converted into a theatre, with bare brick walls, and a stage in the middle of the floor surrounded by folding chairs.

For many years people took the physical arrangement of theatres for granted. This was particularly true in the period when all houses were facsimiles of the Broadway theatre, with its proscenium, or picture-frame, stage. In the past half century,

◄ **STAGE SPACES: AN OUTDOOR THRUST STAGE**

The Mary Rippon outdoor theatre, home of the Colorado Shakespeare Festival at Boulder, is a Greek-style amphitheatre with capacity for 1,000 spectators. With a thrust stage and the audience on three sides, it is one of the oldest and most popular configurations for a theatre space. The production shown here is Shakespeare's The Comedy of Errors, *directed by Stephanie Shine, with Jake Hart as Angelo.*

(Lou Costy, Photography, © Regents of the University of Colorado)

however, not only have people been exposed to other types of theatres; they have also become more aware of the importance of environment. Many experimental groups have deliberately made awareness of the environment a part of the experience.

An avant-garde production of Euripides's *The Bacchae,* called *Dionysus in 69,* by the Performance Group in New York, introduced the audience to the performance in a controlled manner. Spectators were not allowed into the theatre when they arrived but were made to line up on the street outside. The procedure is outlined by Victoria Strang in a book describing the production.

> The audience begins to assemble at around 7:45 P.M. They line up on Wooster Street below Greenwich Village. Sometimes the line goes up the block almost to the corner of Broome. On rainy nights, or during the coldest parts of the winter, the audience waits upstairs over the theater. The theater is a large space, some 50 by 40 and 20 feet high. At 8:15 the performance begins for the audience when the stage manager, Vickie May Strang, makes the following announcement. Inside the performers begin warming up their voices and bodies at 7:45.
>
> VICKIE: Ladies and gentlemen! May I have your attention, please. We are going to start letting you in now. You will be admitted to the theater one at a time, and if you're with someone you may be split up. But you can find each other again once you're inside. Take your time to explore the environment. It's a very interesting space, and there are all different kinds of places you can sit. We recommend going up high on the towers and platforms, or down underneath them. The password is "Go high or take cover." There is no smoking inside and no cameras. Thank you.[1]

In an interview included in the book, Strang gave her own view of this procedure.

> We let the public in one at a time. People on the queue outside the theater ask me why. I explain that this is a rite of initiation, a chance for each person to confront the environment alone, without comparing notes with friends. People are skeptical. Some few are angry. Many think it's a put-on. I must confess to a perverse pleasure in teasing people on a line. Many will come up and ask anxiously, "Has it already begun?" I say, "It begins before we let anybody in, but it begins when everybody is in, and really it begins when you go in." True.[2]

By having spectators enter the theatre in an unconventional way, or by rearranging the theatre space itself, some contemporary groups deliberately make the audience conscious of the theatre environment. But the feeling we have about the atmosphere of a theatre building as we enter it has always been an important element in the experience. In the past, spectators may not have been conscious of it, but they were affected by it nevertheless. Today, with the many varieties of theatre experience available to us, the first thing we should become aware of is the environment in which an event takes place. Whether it is large or small, indoors or outdoors, formal or informal, familiar or unfamiliar, it will inevitably play a part in our response to the performance.

At times scenic designers are able to alter the architecture of a theatre space to create a new arrangement or configuration. If the auditorium space is too large for a specific production, balconies might be blocked off, or the rear of the orchestra might be closed in some manner. Also, the decor can be altered: bright colors, banners, and bright lighting could create a festive atmosphere in a space that is ordinarily formal and subdued. The first things for audience members to note are general characteristics: Is the space formal or informal? Is it large or small? Next is the question of the configuration of stage and audience seating.

THEATRE SPACES

A consideration of environment leads directly to an examination of the various forms and styles of theatre buildings, including the arrangements of audience seating. Throughout theatre history, there have been five basic stage arrangements, each with its own advantages and disadvantages, each suited to certain types of plays and certain types of productions, and each providing the audience with a somewhat different experience. The five are (1) the **proscenium,** or picture-frame, stage; (2) the **arena,** or circle, stage; (3) the **thrust** stage with three-quarters seating;[3] (4) *created* and *found* stage spaces; and (5) all-purpose and **"black box"** theatre spaces, out of which a version of any one of the other four can be created.

Proscenium Stage

Perhaps the most familiar type of stage is the proscenium, or picture-frame, stage. Broadway-style theatres, which for many years were models for theatres throughout the country, have proscenium stages.

The term *proscenium* comes from *proscenium arch,* the frame that separates the stage from the auditorium and that was first introduced in Italy during the Renaissance. Although it was an arch in the past, today this frame is usually a rectangle, which forms an outline for the stage itself. As the term *picture-frame stage* suggests, it resembles a large picture frame through which the audience looks at the stage. Another term for this type of stage is **fourth wall,** from the idea of the proscenium opening as a transparent glass wall through which the audience looks at the other three walls of a room.

Because the action takes place largely behind the proscenium opening, or frame, the seats in the auditorium all face in the same direction, toward the stage, just as seats in a movie theatre face the screen. The auditorium itself—the **house,** or **front of the house,** as it is called—is slanted downward from the back to the stage. (In theatre usage, the slant of an auditorium or stage floor is called a **rake.**) The stage itself is raised several feet above the auditorium floor, to aid visibility. There is usually a balcony (sometimes there are two balconies) protruding about halfway over the main floor. The main floor, incidentally, is called (in American usage) the **orchestra.** (In ancient Greek theatre, the

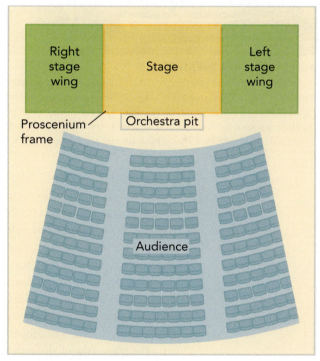

PROSCENIUM THEATRE
The audience faces in one direction, toward an enclosed stage encased by a picture-frame opening. Scene changes and performers' entrances and exits are made behind the proscenium opening, out of sight of the audience.

THE PROSCENIUM THEATRE

The traditional proscenium theatre resembles a movie theatre in terms of audience seating: all the seats face in one direction, toward the stage. The frame of the stage is like a picture frame, and behind the frame are all the elements of the visual production such as scenery, painted drops, pieces that move across the stage, platforms, steps, perhaps the interior of a room or several rooms. The theatre shown here, the Bolton Theatre at the Cleveland Play House, is an excellent example of a proscenium theatre. It was redesigned by the architect Philip Johnson and renovated in 1983. (Photo by Paul Tepley, courtesy of The Cleveland PlayHouse)

orchestra was the circular acting area at the base of the hillside amphitheatre, but in modern usage it is the main floor of the theatre, where the audience sits.) In certain theatres, as well as concert halls and opera houses that have the proscenium arrangement, there are horseshoe-shaped tiers, or *boxes,* which ring the auditorium for several floors above the orchestra.

The popularity of the proscenium stage on Broadway and throughout the United States in the nineteenth century and the early twentieth century was partly due to its wide acceptance throughout Europe. Beginning in the late seventeenth century, the proscenium theatre was adopted in every European country.

The stage area of these theatres was usually deep, allowing for elaborate scenery, including scene shifts, with a tall *fly loft* above the stage to hold scenery. The loft had to be more than twice as high as the proscenium opening so that scenery could be concealed when it was raised, or "flown." (When pieces of scenery are raised out of sight, they are said to *fly* into the loft.) Scenery was usually hung by rope or cable on a series of parallel pipes running from side to side across the stage. Hanging the pieces

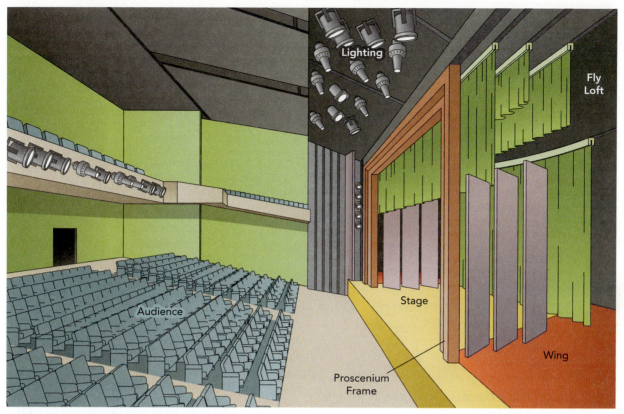

A MODERN PROSCENIUM-STAGE THEATRE
In this cutaway drawing we see the audience seating at the left, all facing in the one direction, toward the stage. Behind the orchestra pit in the center is the apron on the stage; and then the proscenium frame, behind which are the flats and other scenic elements. Overhead, scenery can be raised into the fly loft above the stage area.

straight across, one behind the other, allowed many pieces of scenery to be stored and raised and lowered as necessary.

Several mechanisms for raising and lowering scenery were developed during the period when the proscenium stage itself was being adopted. An Italian, Giacomo Torelli (1608–1678), devised a ***counterweight*** system in which weights hung on a series of ropes and pulleys balanced the scenery, allowing heavy scenery to be moved easily by a few stagehands. Torelli's system also allowed side pieces, known as ***wings,*** to be moved into and out of the stage picture. By connecting both the hanging pieces and the side pieces to a central drum below the stage, Torelli made it possible for everything to move simultaneously, and in this way a complete stage set could be changed at one time.

Shortly after Torelli, a dynasty of scenic artists emerged who carried scene painting to a degree of perfection rarely equaled before or since. Their family name was Bibiena, and for over a century, beginning with Ferdinando (1657–1743) and continuing through several generations to Carlo (1728–1787), they dominated the art of scene painting. Their sets usually consisted of vast halls, palaces, or gardens. Towering columns and arches framed spacious corridors or hallways, which disappeared into an

A BIBIENA SET FOR A FORMAL PROSCENIUM THEATRE
The standard theatre throughout Europe and the United States from the eighteenth century to the early twentieth century was a formal proscenium space. The audience sat in a downstairs orchestra, in balconies, and in side boxes facing an ornate picture-frame stage. Impressive scenery and other visual effects were created and changed behind the curtain that covers the proscenium opening. In the eighteenth century, the Bibiena family from Italy created scene designs on a grand scale for such theatres throughout Europe. They painted backdrops with vistas that seemed to disappear into the far distance. This scene is by Giuseppe di Bibiena (1696–1757). (Victoria and Albert Museum, London)

endless series of vistas as far as the eye could see. Throughout this period, audiences, as well as scene designers and technicians, became so carried away with spectacle that at times the visual aspects were emphasized to the exclusion of everything else, including the script and the acting.

Although there have been many changes in theatre production, and today we have a wide variety of production approaches, audiences are still attracted to ingenious displays of visual effects in proscenium theatres. This is especially true of large musicals such as *The Phantom of the Opera, The Lion King, Mary Poppins,* and *Wicked.* Because the machinery and the workings of scene changes can be concealed behind a proscenium opening, this type of stage offers a perfect arrangement for spectacle.

There are other advantages to the proscenium stage. Realistic scenery—a living room, an office, a kitchen—looks good behind a proscenium frame; the scene designer can create the illusion of a genuine, complete room more easily with a proscenium stage than with any other. Also, the strong central focus provided by the frame rivets the attention of the audience. There are times, too, when members of the audience want the detachment, the distancing, that a proscenium provides.

THE PROSCENIUM THEATRE: IDEAL FOR SPECTACLE
For large-scale musicals the proscenium theatre is ideal. The scenery and other elements can be hidden above, behind, and around the stage, and then moved into the main stage area, as if by magic. In addition, the scale of the scenic effects can be extensive and sometimes electrifying. The scene shown here is from *Mary Poppins,* a musical based on the Walt Disney film and directed by Richard Eyre, with Laura Michelle Kelly and Gavin Lee. (© Geraint Lewis)

Arena Stage

To some people, proscenium theatres, decorated in gold and red plush, look more like temples of art than theatres. These audience members prefer a more informal, intimate theatre environment. A movement in this direction began in the United States just after World War II, when a number of theatre practitioners decided to break away from the formality that proscenium theatres tend to create. This was part of an overall desire to bring many aspects of theatre closer to everyday life: acting styles, the subject matter of plays, the manner of presentation, and the shape of the theatre space. One form this reaction took was the *arena stage*—a return to one of the most ancient stage arrangements.

From as far back as we have records, we know that tribal ceremonies and rituals, in all parts of the world, have been held in some form of circle theatre. Many scholars believe that the ancient Greek theatre evolved from an arena form. According to this theory, Greek tribes beat down a circle in a field of threshed grain; an altar was placed

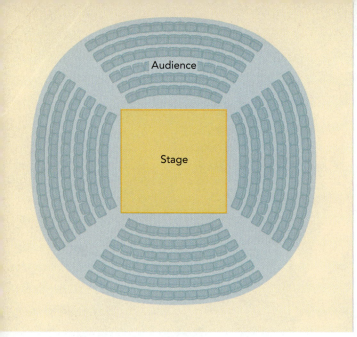

PLAN OF AN ARENA STAGE

The audience sits on four sides or in a circle surrounding the stage. Entrances and exits are made through the aisles or through tunnels underneath the aisles. A feeling of intimacy is achieved because the audience is close to the action and encloses it.

in the center, and ceremonies were performed around the altar while members of the tribe stood on the edge of the circle. This arrangement was later made more permanent, when ceremonies, festivals, and Dionysian revels—forerunners of Greek theatre—were held in such spaces.

The arena stage (also called *circle theater* or *theatre-in-the-round*) has a playing space in the center of a square or circle, with seats for spectators all around it. The arrangement is similar to that in sports arenas featuring boxing or basketball. The stage may be a raised area a few feet off the main floor, with seats rising from the floor level; or it may be on the floor itself, with seats raised on levels around it. When seating is close to the stage, there is usually some kind of demarcation indicating the boundaries of the playing area.

One advantage of the arena theatre is that it offers more intimacy than the ordinary proscenium. With the performers in the center, even in a larger theatre, the audience can be closer to them. If the same number of people attend an arena event and a proscenium event, at least half of those at the arena will be nearer the action: someone who would have been in the twelfth row in a proscenium theatre will be in the sixth row in an arena theatre. Besides, with this proximity to the stage, the arena theatre has another advantage: there is no frame or barrier to separate the performers from the audience.

Beyond these considerations, in the arena arrangement there is an unconscious communion, basic to human behavior, which comes when people form a circle—from

THE STAGE AND SEATING IN AN ARENA THEATRE

The arena theatre attempts to capture the immediacy of primitive theatre. It uses the barest essentials of stage scenery but the full resources of contemporary stage lighting.

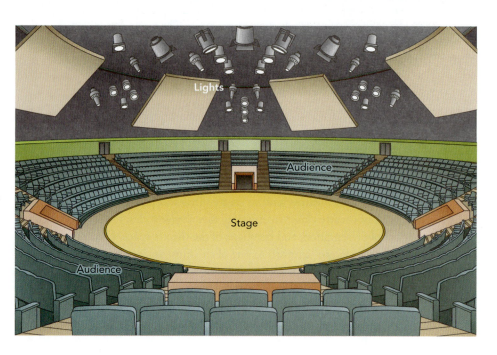

the embrace of two people to a circle for children's games to a larger gathering where people form an enclosure around a fire or an altar. It is no coincidence that virtually all primitive forms of theatre were "in the round."

A practical advantage of the arena theatre is economy. All you need for this kind of theatre is a large room: you designate a playing space, arrange rows of seats around the sides, and hang lights on pipes above, and you have a theatre. Elaborate scenery is impossible because it would block the view of large parts of the audience. A few pieces of furniture, with perhaps a lamp or sign hung from the ceiling, are all you need to indicate where a scene takes place. Many low-budget groups have found that they can build a workable and even attractive theatre-in-the-round when a proscenium theatre would be out of the question.

These two factors—intimacy and economy— no doubt explain why arena theatre is one of the oldest stage forms, as well as one still very much in use today. In spite of its long history, however, and its resurgence in recent years, the arena stage has often been eclipsed by other forms. One reason is that its design, while allowing for intimacy, also dictates a certain austerity. As I said before, it is impossible to have elaborate scenery because that would block the view of many spectators. Also, the performers must make all their entrances and exits along aisles that run through the audience, and they can sometimes be seen before and after they are supposed to appear onstage. The arena's lack of adaptability in this respect may explain why some of the circle theatres that opened twenty or thirty years ago have since closed. A number survive, however, and continue to do well. One of the best-known is the Arena Stage in Washington, D.C. In addition, throughout this country there are a number of *tent theatres* in arena form where musical revivals and concerts are given.

A CONTEMPORARY ARENA THEATRE
The arena stage shown above is built inside a larger, more formal space. It creates the closeness and the contact provided when the audience surrounds the action. It is a much more intimate version of spectators at a sporting event. The arena stage pictured here is at A Contemporary Theatre in Seattle, Washington. (Steve Keating for Callison Architecture/Courtesy of A Contemporary Theatre, Seattle)

Thrust Stage

Falling between the proscenium and the arena is a third type of theatre: the *thrust stage* with three-quarters seating. In one form or another, this U-shape arrangement has been the most widely used of all stage spaces. In the basic arrangement for this type of theatre, the audience sits on three sides, or in a semicircle, enclosing a stage, which protrudes into the center. At the back of the playing area is some form of **stage house** providing for the entrances and exits of the performers as well as for scene changes.

AN ORIGINAL THRUST STAGE: THE GREEK AMPHITHEATRE
An original prototype of the thrust stage was the amphitheatre in ancient Greece. Shown here is the theatre at Epidauros, Greece. The seating surrounds the playing area on three sides. Acting took place on the raised platform at the back, but also in the circular area that is thrust into the audience. Among many other remarkable traits of these theatres are the incredible view of the mountains in the distance and the amazing acoustics of the theatre. A person in the back, top row can hear an actor speaking without any artificial amplification. (© Jose Fuste Raga/Corbis)

The thrust stage combines some of the best features of the other two stage types: the sense of intimacy and the "wraparound" feeling of the arena, and the focused stage placed against a single background found in the proscenium.

The thrust stage was developed by the Greeks for their tragedies and comedies. They adapted the circle used for tribal rituals and other ceremonies—this circle was called the *orchestra*—by locating it at the base of a curving hillside. The slope of the

THRUST STAGE WITH THREE-QUARTERS SEATING

The stage is surrounded on three sides by the audience. Sometimes seating is a semicircle. Entrances and exits are made from the sides and backstage. Spectators surround the action, but scene changes and other stage effects are still possible.

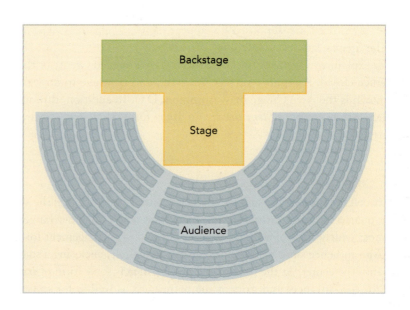

A MODERN THRUST STAGE

The thrust stage, with a stage area extending into audience seating that surrounds it on three sides, is one of the oldest arrangements, having been used by the Greeks and by the Elizabethans in the time of Shakespeare. It has been revived successfully in the modern period and is widely used in Europe and the United States. A good example is the recently renovated Mark Taper Forum in Los Angeles. (© Craig Schwartz)

hill formed a natural amphitheatre for the spectators. At the rear of the orchestra circle, opposite the hillside, they placed a stage house, or **skene.** The skene had formal doors through which characters made their entrances and exits and served as a background for the action. It also provided a place for the actors to change their costumes.

The largest Greek theatres seated 15,000 or more spectators, and their design was duplicated all over Greece, particularly in the years following the conquests of Alexander the Great (356–323 BCE) in what is known as the *Hellenistic* period. Remnants of these Hellenistic theatres remain today throughout that part of the world, in such places as Epidaurus, Priene, Ephesus, Delphi, and Corinth, to name a few.

The Romans, who took the Greek form and built it as a complete structure, had a theatre that was not strictly a thrust stage but a forerunner of the proscenium. Instead of using the natural amphitheatre of a hillside, they constructed a freestanding stone building, joining the stage house to the seating area and making the orchestra a semicircle. In front of the stage house, which was decorated with arches and statues, they erected a long platform stage where most of the action occurred.

Another example of the thrust stage is found in the medieval period, when short religious plays began to be presented in churches and cathedrals in England and parts of continental Europe. Around 1200 CE, performances of these religious plays were moved outdoors. One popular arrangement for these outdoor performances was the **platform stage.** A simple platform was set on trestles (it was sometimes called a *trestle stage*), with a curtain at the back which the performers used for entrances and costume

THE CLASSIC SPANISH STAGE

A variation on the thrust stage used in Elizabethan England is the Spanish *corral.* A version of this stage, uncovered by accident in 1953, is shown here in Almagro, Spain, where a theatre festival is held each year. Not strictly speaking a thrust stage, it has all the other components of a Renaissance outdoor theatre, with the platform stage and audience seating in boxes or a balcony around three sides. (Courtesy Festival d'Almagro)

changes. The area underneath the stage was closed off and provided, among other things, a space from which devils and other characters could appear, sometimes in a cloud of smoke. In some places the platform was on wheels (a **wagon stage**) and was moved from place to place through a town. The audience stood on three sides of the platform, making it an improvised thrust stage. This type of stage was widely used from the thirteenth to the fifteenth centuries in England and various parts of Europe.

The next step following the wagon stage was a thrust stage that appeared in England in the sixteenth century, just before Shakespeare began writing for the theatre. A platform stage would be set up at one end of the open courtyard of an inn. The inns of this period were three or four stories high, and the rooms facing the inner courtyard served as boxes from which spectators could watch the performance. On the ground level, spectators stood on three sides of the stage. The fourth side of the courtyard, behind the platform, served as the stage house.

An interesting coincidence is that an almost identical theatre took shape in Spain at the same time. The inns in Spain were called **corrales,** and this name was given to the theatres that developed there. (Another coincidence is that a talented and prolific dramatist, Lope de Vega, was born within two years of Shakespeare and emerged as his Spanish counterpart.)

The formal English theatres of Shakespeare's day, such as the Globe and the Fortune, were similar to the inn theatres: the audience stood in an open area around a platform stage, and three levels of spectators sat in closed galleries at the back and sides. A roof covered part of the stage; at the back of the stage, some form of raised area served for balcony scenes (as in *Romeo and Juliet*). At the rear of the stage, also, scenes could be concealed and then "discovered." On each side at the rear was a door used for entrances and exits.

These theatres were fascinating combinations of diverse elements: they were both indoors and outdoors; some spectators stood while others sat; and the audience was composed of almost all levels of society. The physical environment must have been stimulating: performers standing at the front of the thrust stage were in the center of a hemisphere of spectators, on three sides around them as well as above and below. These theatres held 2,000 to 3,000 spectators, but no one in the audience was more than 60 feet or so from the stage, and most people were much closer. Being in the midst of so many people, enclosed on all sides but with the open sky above, must have instilled a feeling of great communion among audiences and performers. Something of the same feeling can be recaptured when one visits the recently reconstructed Globe Theatre in London.

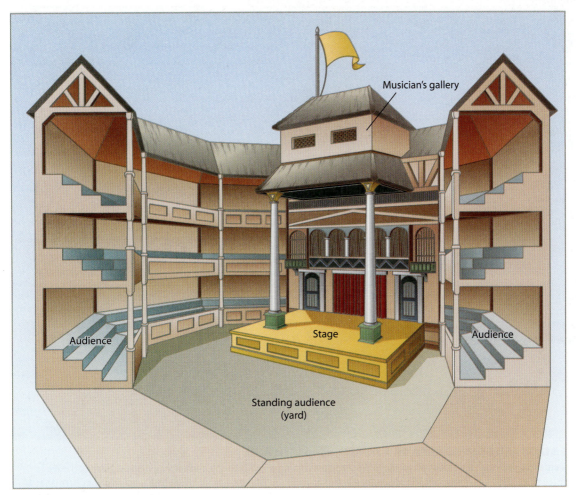

AN ELIZABETHAN PLAYHOUSE
This drawing shows the kind of stage on which the plays of Shakespeare and his contemporaries were first presented. A platform stage juts into an open courtyard, with spectators standing on three sides. Three levels of enclosed seats rise above the courtyard. There are doors at the rear of the stage for entrances and exits and an upper level for balcony scenes.

Shortly after Shakespeare's day, in the latter part of the seventeenth century, there were two significant theatrical developments in England, in Spain, and throughout Europe: (1) the theatre moved completely indoors; and (2) the stage began a slow but steady retreat behind the proscenium opening, partly because performances were indoors, but more because the style of theatres changed. For more than two centuries the thrust stage was in eclipse, not to reappear until about 1900, when a few theatres in England began using a version of the thrust stage to produce Shakespeare.

The return of the thrust stage resulted from a growing realization that Elizabethan plays could be done best on a stage similar to the one for which they had been written. In the United States and Canada, though, it was not until the mid-twentieth century that the thrust stage came to the fore again. Since then a number of fine theatres of this type have been built, including the Guthrie in Minneapolis; the Shakespeare Theater

THE STAGE AND SEATING AREA OF A THRUST-STAGE THEATRE

This cutaway drawing of a thrust stage shows how the playing area juts into the audience, which surrounds the stage on three sides. This configuration affords intimacy, but at the back (shown here at the right) is an area that furnishes a natural backdrop for the action.

in Stratford, Ontario; the Mark Taper Forum in Los Angeles; and the Long Wharf in New Haven.

The basic stage of traditional Chinese and Japanese drama (including nō theatre in Japan) is a form of thrust stage: a raised, open platform stage, frequently covered by a roof, with the audience sitting on two or three sides around the platform. Entrances and exits are made from doors or ramps at the rear of the stage.

The obvious advantages of the thrust stage—the intimacy of three-quarters seating and the close audience-performer relationship, together with the fact that so many of the world's great dramatic works were written for it—give it a significant place alongside the other major forms.

Created and Found Spaces

After World War II a number of avant-garde theatre artists, such as the Polish director Jerzy Grotowski (1933–1999), undertook to reform theatre at every level. Since the various elements of theatre are inextricably bound together, their search for a more

THE AUDIENCE'S RESPONSE

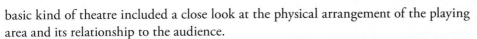

- As discussed in this chapter, there are five major types of stage spaces: proscenium, thrust, arena, created or found space, and the "black box." What do you think are the advantages and disadvantages of each? On which type of stage space would you prefer to watch a performance?

- Using information from this chapter, explain which type of stage space you feel is best suited to the following productions: a large-scale musical, an intimate personal drama, a Shakespearean drama, and a play of political protest.

- The capacity of theatre spaces can range from more than 3,000 spectators to fewer than 100. What do you consider an ideal size for a theatre? How many seats, and how large a stage space?

basic kind of theatre included a close look at the physical arrangement of the playing area and its relationship to the audience.

The Performance Group, which led spectators one at a time into the production of *Dionysus in 69* (as described earlier in this chapter), is typical in this regard. It presented its productions in a large garage converted into an open theatre space. At various places in the garage, scaffolding and ledges were built for audience seating.

The Performance Group, like other modern avant-garde companies, owed a great debt to a Frenchman, Antonin Artaud (1896–1948), one of the first theatre people to examine in depth the questions raised by the avant-garde. An actor and director who wrote a series of articles and essays about theatre, Artaud was brilliant but inconsistent (he spent several periods of his life in mental institutions). Many of Artaud's ideas, however, were to prove prophetic: notions he put forward in the 1920s and 1930s, considered impossible or impractical at the time, have since become common practice among experimental theatre groups. Among his proposals was one on the physical theatre:

> We abolish the stage and auditorium and replace them by a single site, without partition or barrier of any kind, which will become the theater of the action. A direct communication will be reestablished between the spectator and the spectacle, between the actor and the spectator, from the fact that the spectator, placed in the middle of the action, is engulfed and physically affected by it. This envelopment results, in part, from the very configuration of the room itself.
>
> Thus, abandoning the architecture of present-day theaters, we shall take some hangar or barn which we shall have reconstructed according to processes which have culminated in the architecture of certain churches or holy places, and of certain temples in Tibet.[4]

Some of Artaud's ideas were put into practice when the movement to explore new concepts became widespread. In the generation after Artaud, Jerzy Grotowski included the physical arrangements of stage space in his experiments. Not only Grotowski but others in the avant-garde movement developed theatre space in a variety of ways.

Nontheatre Buildings Artaud mentioned a barn or hangar for performances. In recent years virtually all kinds of structures have been used: lofts, warehouses, fire stations, basements, churches, breweries, and gymnasiums. This practice should not be confused with the conversion of unusual spaces to full-scale theatres, which has numerous precedents in the past; historically, indoor tennis courts, palace ballrooms, and monastery dining halls have been converted into theatres. I am speaking here of using unusual structures as they are, with their original architectural elements intact, and carving out special areas for acting and viewing—as with the garage used by the Performance Group.

Adapted Spaces   One frequent practice was using a space to fit a play, rather than (as is normally the case) making the play fit the space. Grotowski, in particular, pursued the notion of finding a different, appropriate configuration for each production. In Grotowski's production of the Doctor Faustus story, for example, the theatre was filled with two long tables at which spectators sat as if they were guests at a banquet hosted by Faustus. The action took place at the heads of the tables and even on the tabletops. For his production of *The Constant Prince,* a fence was built around the playing area, and the audience sat behind the fence, looking over it like spectators at a bullfight. In recent decades there have been similar attempts to deal with theatre spaces in many parts of Europe and the United States.

Street Theatre   One development—which was actually a return to practices in medieval Europe—is theatre held outdoors in nontraditional settings. A good example is *street theatre.* Generally, street theatre is of three types: (1) plays from the standard repertoire presented in the streets; (2) *neighborhood theatre,* in which an original play deals with problems and aspirations of a specific population of a city, such as Puerto Ricans, African Americans, or Italians; and (3) *guerrilla theatre,* aggressive, politically oriented theatre produced by an activist group in the streets in an attempt to persuade audiences to become more politically involved. Whatever the form, the important point for our purposes is that these productions take place not in theatre buildings but in places like parks, hospitals, jails, and bus stations.

In these productions, theatre is brought to people who might not otherwise see it. Also, audiences in such unusual settings are challenged to rethink what theatre is all about. On the other hand, there are inherent disadvantages to impromptu productions in the streets or other "found spaces": the audience must be caught on the run, and there is rarely time for more than a

CREATED OR FOUND SPACE: STREET THEATRE

The Polish theatre company Biuro Podrozy interprets Shakespeare's *Macbeth* using its trademark stilts near the Royal Mile at the Edinburgh Festival Fringe in Edinburgh, Scotland. The company's 1995 Fringe debut performance of *Carmen Funebre,* a portrayal of the Bosnian war, led to repeat performances in subsequent years and the Fringe First award. (© Jeff J Mitchell/Getty Images)

AN ISLAND FOR SITE-SPECIFIC THEATRE

In the Netherlands there is a festival, known as the Oerol Festival, in which for ten days in June an entire island, Terschelling, is used by a variety of theatre companies to present their pieces. Groups set up in all kinds of places on the island—taverns, barns, tents, and garages, and on beaches—to offer their productions. Shown here on a beach is a production entitled *Salted,* written and directed by Judith de Rijke and produced by Tryater of Holland, which brought together young artists from various regions to celebrate the linguistic diversity of Europe. (Photo courtesy of Sake Elzinga)

SITE-SPECIFIC PERFORMANCE IN NEW ORLEANS

A fascinating site-specific performance was held in the areas of New Orleans almost destroyed by hurricane Katrina and still devastated. An artist, Paul Chan, invited the Classical Theatre of Harlem to come to the city and stage Beckett's *Waiting for Godot.* The emptiness in the landscape and in the lives of Beckett's characters found a striking parallel in the desolate neighborhoods of New Orleans. Seen here as the two main characters, in front of an abandoned house, are J. Kyle Manzay (right) and Wendell Pierce. (Lee Celano/The New York Times/Redux)

sketch or vignette. Nor are there facilities for presenting a fully developed work—but often that is not the purpose of these undertakings in the first place.

Multifocus Environments   An approach that sometimes accompanies these unusual arrangements is *multifocus theatre.* In simple terms, this means not only that there is more than one playing area, such as the four corners of the room (as Artaud suggested in one article), but also that something is going on in several of them simultaneously. This is somewhat like a three-ring circus, where the spectator sees an activity in each ring and must either concentrate on one or divide his or her attention among two or three.

There are several theories behind the idea of multifocus theatre. One is that a multifocus event is more like everyday life; if you stand on a street corner, there is activity all around you—in the four directions of the streets, in the buildings above—not just in one spot. You select which area you will observe, or perhaps you watch several areas at one time. The argument is that in theatre, you should have the same choice.

In multifocus productions no single space or activity is supposed to be more important than any other. The spectator either takes in several impressions at once and synthesizes them in his or her own mind or selects one item as most arresting and concentrates on that. There is no such thing as the "best seat in the house"; all seats are equally good, because the activity in all parts of the theatre is equally important. Sometimes multifocus theatre is joined with *multimedia theatre*—presentations that offer some combination of acting, films, video, dance, music, slides, and light shows.

All-Purpose Theatre Spaces: The Black Box

Because of the interest in a variety of spaces in modern theatre production, and the requirements of many different kinds of productions, a number of theatre complexes, including many college theatre departments, have built spaces that can be adapted to an almost infinite variety of configurations. Seats, lights, platforms, levels—every aspect of such a theatre is flexible and movable.

In this kind of space the designers can create a proscenium, a thrust, an arena, or some combination of these, but the designers can also create corner stages, island stages, and multifocus arrangements with playing areas in several parts of the studio. This space is sometimes referred to as a *black box* because it is often an empty rectangular space into which various audience seating and stage arrangements can be introduced.

SPECIAL REQUIREMENTS OF THEATRE ENVIRONMENTS

Simply assigning a theatre to a category does not adequately describe the environment; we must also take into account a number of other variables. Two theatres may be of the same type and still be quite different in size, atmosphere, and setting. The experience in a small off-off-Broadway-type thrust theatre will be far different from that in a thrust theatre several times larger, such as the Guthrie in Minneapolis. Also, one theatre may be indoors and another of the same type outdoors.

There are other factors that architects, producers, and designers must take into account, one of which is the human scale. No matter what the configuration, the per-

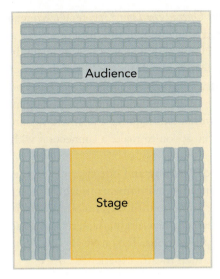
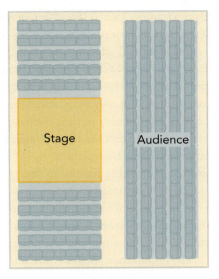
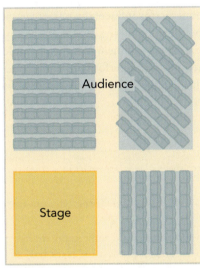
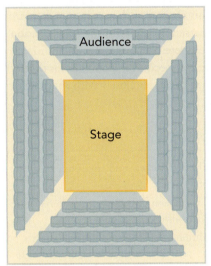

THE MULTIPURPOSE OR "BLACK BOX" THEATRE

A popular type of modern theatre is the multipurpose space, sometimes called a "black box." It consists of an open space with perhaps a pipe grid on the ceiling from which lighting and sound instruments can be suspended. A stage platform can be positioned at any place in the space, and movable chairs for spectators can be placed around the playing area. The diagrams suggest some of the possibilities of stage arrangements in a multipurpose theatre.

former is the basic scale by which everything is measured in theatre. Theatre architects as well as scenic and lighting designers must always keep this in mind, and audience members should be aware of it as well. When the theatre environment and the stage space violate this human scale in some way, problems are created for performers and spectators.

There are also questions of appropriateness and aesthetic distance. By *appropriateness* I mean the relationship of a stage space to a play or production. *Aesthetic distance* is the principle discussed in Chapter 2 with regard to the performer-audience relationship. A large-scale musical such as *The Phantom of the Opera, The Lion King,* or *Wicked* requires a full stage—usually a proscenium stage—and a large auditorium from which the audience can get the full effect of the spectacle. However, the effect of an intimate drama such as *A Number* by Caryl Churchill would be greatly diminished in a large space. In this play a father (played in New York by Sam Shepard) confronts three sons who are cloned children. Not only are issues of cloning raised, but troubling family relationships are probed. The intensity of the personal confrontations requires a small playing area so that audience members are close enough to the action to make a connection with the characters onstage.

Rather than being limited to one type of building and one type of stage, audiences today are fortunate in having a full range of environments in which to experience theatre. Taken all in all, whether single-focus or multifocus, indoors or outdoors, the recent innovations in theatre milieus have added new alternatives, rich in possibilities, to the traditional settings for theatrical productions. They have also called attention to the importance of environment in the total theatre experience.

In this chapter we have examined environmental factors influencing our experience at a theatrical event, including the location of the theatre building, its size, its setting, its atmosphere, and its layout. In addition to a general environment in a theatre building, there is a specific environment for the performer. It is to the performer—and the person who works most closely with the performer, the director—that we turn in Part Two.

SUMMARY

1. The atmosphere and environment of the theatre space play a large part in setting the tone of an event.

2. Experimental theatre groups in recent years have deliberately made spectators aware of the environment.

3. Throughout theatre history there have been five basic stage and auditorium arrangements: proscenium, arena, thrust, created or found space, and all-purpose or "black box" spaces.

4. The proscenium theatre features a picture-frame stage, in which the audience faces directly toward the stage and looks through the proscenium opening at the "picture." The proscenium stage aids illusion: placing a room of a house behind the proscenium, for example, allows the scene designer to create an extremely realistic set. This type of stage also allows elaborate scene shifts and visual displays because it generally has a large backstage area and a fly loft. It also creates a distancing effect, which works to the advantage of certain types of drama. At the same time, however, the proscenium frame sets up a barrier between the performers and the audience.

5. The arena or circle stage places the playing area in the center with the audience seated in a circle or square around it. This offers an economical way to produce theatre and an opportunity for great intimacy between performers and spectators, but it cannot offer full visual displays in terms of scenery and scene changes.

6. The thrust stage with three-quarters seating is a platform stage with seating on three sides. Entrances and exits are made at the rear, and there is an opportunity for a certain amount of scenery. This form combines some of the scenic features of the proscenium theatre with the intimacy of the arena stage.

7. Created or found space takes several forms: use of nontheatre buildings, adaptation of a given space to fit individual productions, use of outdoor settings, street theatre, multi-focus environments, and all-purpose spaces.

8. The theatre space referred to as a *black box* is an open, adaptable space that can be configured into a variety of stage-audience arrangements, providing for maximum flexibility and economy.

9. Size and location (indoors or outdoors, etc.), along with the shape and character of a theatre building, affect the environment.

2

The Performers and the Director

THE PERFORMERS TAKE THE STAGE

Actors and actresses are at the heart of theatre. They embody the characters as well as projecting the story and language of the play. Seen here is a scene from Chekhov's *The Cherry Orchard* directed by Nicholas Martin in a new translation by Richard Nelson at the Huntington Theatre, with Kate Burton leading the cast in the role of Madame Ranevskaya.

(© T Charles Erickson)

The Performers and the Director

Performers, by their presence, set theatre apart from films, television, and the visual arts; they serve as the direct, immediate contact that members of the audience have with theatre. More than that, performers embody the heart and soul of theatre. The words of a script, the characters created by a dramatist, and the scenery and costumes come to life only when an actor or actress steps onto a stage.

Acting, however, is not confined to theatre. Of course, there is acting on film and television. But there are also many forms of "acting" in our daily lives. Most of us might be surprised to learn that acting is almost as old as the human race. From the earliest days of civilization, people have mimicked other people and have told stories, imitating the voices and gestures of the characters in those stories. There have also been rituals and ceremonies in which

the celebrants wore costumes and performed assigned roles—one example is the person officiating in a religious service.

Children are among the best imitators in the world, and we are frequently amused by a child who imitates a parent or some other grown-up: a four-year-old girl, for instance, who puts on a long dress, makeup, and high heels. As we grow older, imitation continues to be a part of our experience: in

Religious celebrations, such as the Jewish bar mitzvah—shown here at the Western Wall in Jerusalem—have many things in common with theatre. (© Richard T. Nowitz/Corbis)

Virtually all types of ceremonies and performance worldwide—ancient and modern, religious and secular—have theatrical elements. Here we see a masked actor performing in a Tibetan opera in China. (© Chris Lisle/Corbis)

every class in school, from elementary school through college, there is usually one person—a clever mimic—who imitates the teacher or the principal with great humor, and sometimes with cruelty. One familiar type of imitation is an attempt to copy the lifestyle of a hero—a singer, a film actor, or some other well-known personality. The imitator adopts the same wardrobe, the same stance, the same physical movements, and the same hairstyle as the hero or heroine.

A second type of "acting" prevalent in our daily lives is role playing. Much has been written about role playing in recent years, and a currently popular term is *role model,* referring to people whose lives, or "roles," serve as models or guides for others.

On the less admirable side, how often have we had a behind-the-scenes glimpse

at a politician, a movie star, or a corporate executive just before the person is to appear at a press conference? Sometimes the person is scowling, peppering his or her language with profanity and invective, speaking sharply to assistants. Then, suddenly, when the person moves before the television cameras, he or she breaks into a smile and takes on the persona of someone who is affable, pleasant, and charming. In a public appearance, the person is playing a "role." Looked at from a different perspective, in the age of the Internet, of Facebook, Twitter, and YouTube, a certain kind of acting in everyday life has become commonplace. As George Vecsey, a columnist for the *New York Times,* has written, "In the YouTube era, everybody under a certain age is a performer."

We have been speaking of "acting" in everyday life. When we turn to acting for the stage, we will observe that for all the similarities, there are significant, even crucial, differences between imitation or role playing in daily life and the acting that takes place onstage. For one thing, everyone concerned—audiences as well as those onstage—will recognize that it is a performance. It is a conscious act that requires not only talent but a tremendous amount of training and discipline. In Part Two, we will look at the art and craft of theatrical performance. We will also look at the role of a person who works most closely with actors: the director.

Imitation and role playing are two types of acting in which everyone participates, even the very young. (© Myrleen Ferguson/PhotoEdit)

PERFORMING IN EVERYDAY LIFE
Many activities not usually thought of as theatre are theatrical in nature. Here, drum major Bill Pierpont, in costume, leads a Memorial Day parade at Shelton, Connecticut. (© Peter Hvizdak/The Image Works)

Acting

Throughout theatre history, the performer has been the center of attention. For an audience at a performance, the actress or actor provides the connection and the electricity that are at the heart of the theatre experience. Today, as in the past, because performers are the focus of all eyes, it is assumed that acting is a glamorous profession—and it can be.

Successful performers are interviewed on television or written up in newspapers or magazines. Some even have books written about them. The publicity, however, is deceptive: it disguises the fact that acting for the stage is a difficult, disciplined profession. In addition to talent and ability, it requires years of arduous training.

Before turning to acting for the stage, however, we will look a bit more at what we have called "acting in everyday life."

EXAMPLES OF ACTING IN EVERYDAY LIFE

In the introduction to Part Two, I mentioned two examples of acting in daily life: imitation and role playing. The second of these, role playing, can generally be divided into two categories: social and personal.

Social Roles

Social roles are general roles recognized by society: father, mother, child, police officer, store clerk, teacher, student, business executive, physician, and so on. Every culture expects definite types of behavior from people who assume social roles. For many

◀ **STAGE ACTING**

To play a character convincingly, an actor must develop both outer techniques and inner emotional resources. This is true whether performing in a modern, realistic play, or a classical play such as Shakespeare. In addition, classic plays often require unusual physical and vocal skills to adequately portray characters. John Douglas Thompson is a widely praised actor who has distinguished himself in the title roles of both modern and classic plays, including The Emperor Jones *and* Othello. *Here he is seen in the title role of Shakespeare's* Richard III *in a production by Shakespeare & Company in Lenox, Massachusetts. (© Kevin Sprague/Shakespeare & Company)*

years in western culture, for example, the roles of women as secretaries or housewives were considered subordinate to the roles of men. Even when women held positions similar to those of men in business and the professions, they frequently received a lower salary for the same job. The women's movement challenged the notion of subservient roles for women. So entrenched was the idea, however, that it took an entire movement to call it into question. (One aspect of this movement was *consciousness-raising:* making people aware of social attitudes toward women.) Before changes could begin to be made in the subordinate roles women played, everyone had to understand that these *were* roles.

Personal Roles

Aside from social roles, we develop personal roles with our family and friends. For example, some people become braggarts, boasting of their (sometimes imaginary) feats and accomplishments and embellishing the truth to appear more impressive than they are. Others become martyrs, constantly sacrificing for others and letting the world know about it. Still others are conspirators, people who pull their friends aside to establish an air of secrecy whenever they talk. Frequently, two people fall into complementary roles: one dominant and the other submissive, one active and the other passive.

ACTING IN LIFE VERSUS ACTING ONSTAGE

In a scene in *Death of a Salesman* by Arthur Miller, a young man, Happy, is waiting in a restaurant for his brother, Biff, and his father, Willy Loman. Happy should be concerned only about his father, who is at the low point in his life, having just lost his job.

ROLE PLAYING ILLUSTRATED IN DRAMA

In Arthur Miller's *Death of a Salesman,* the character of Happy plays the "role" of a big shot, and invents exaggerated stories to make himself seem more important than he is. Left to right, Stephanie March as Miss Forsythe, Ted Koch as Happy Loman, and Shannon McCastland as Letta in the Goodman Theatre's production.

(© Eric Y. Exit)

Part 2   The Performers and the Director

But Happy sees two young women at a nearby table and turns his attention to them; he cannot resist trying to impress them. He tells the waiter to bring them champagne, explaining to the young women that he sells champagne. He goes on to boast that he graduated from West Point. When he finds out that the women know nothing about football, he tells them that his brother is the quarterback for the New York Giants.

The champagne, West Point, the football hero: none of this is true. Happy is just a would-be hotshot, a man who has to play the role of a wheeler-dealer, a smooth operator, a "winner," even if he is not. In other words, he is a good example of "acting in everyday life." For all the similarities, however, between the kind of acting illustrated in this scene from *Death of a Salesman* and acting for the stage, the differences between the two are crucial—and these differences reveal a great deal about the nature of stage acting.

Some of the differences between stage acting and acting in daily life are obvious. For one thing, actors and actresses onstage are always being observed. In real life there may be observers, but their presence is not essential to an event. Bystanders on a street corner where an accident has occurred form a kind of audience, but their presence is incidental and unrelated to the accident itself. Onstage, however, the performer is always on display and often in the spotlight.

Acting onstage, too, requires a performer to play roles he or she does not play in life. A scene between a father and his son arguing about money, or between a young husband and wife discussing whether or not to have children, is one thing when it is actually occurring in our lives, but something quite different onstage. Generally, the roles we play in life are genuine. A father who accepts his responsibilities toward his children does not just play a father; he *is* a father. A woman who writes novels does not just play a novelist; she *is* one.

REAL-LIFE ROLES SEEN ONSTAGE

Roles onstage are often similar to roles people are called on to play in real life. Workers in a diner or restaurant are a good example. Here we see two familiar, everyday occupations: the proprietor of a doughnut shop (Michael McKean) and his employee (Jon Michael Hill) in the play *Superior Donuts* by Tracy Letts, which originated at Steppenwolf Theatre in Chicago and then moved to Broadway. (© Robert J. Saferstein)

In real life, a lawyer knows the law; but onstage, an actor playing the role of a lawyer may not know the difference between jurisprudence and habeas corpus and probably has never been inside a law school. Playing widely divergent parts or parts outside their personal experience requires actors and actresses to stretch their imagination and ability. For example, a young actress at one time or another might be called on to play parts as dissimilar as the fiery, independent heroine in Sophocles's *Antigone;* the vulnerable, love-struck heroine in Shakespeare's *Romeo and Juliet;* and the neurotic, obsessed heroine in Strindberg's *Miss Julie.*

At times performers even have to *double,* that is, perform several parts in one play. In Greek theatre it was customary for a play to have only three principal actors, all male; each of them had to play several parts, putting on different masks and costumes to assume the various roles. The German dramatist Bertolt Brecht wrote many plays with large casts that call for doubling. His play *The Caucasian Chalk Circle* has forty-seven speaking parts, but it can be produced with only twenty-five performers. A fascinating situation calling for doubling is written into another play by Brecht, *The Good Woman of Setzuan:* the actress playing the lead character, who becomes pregnant during the course of the play, must also play the part of her cousin—a man.

Another important distinction between acting onstage and acting in real life is that a theatrical performance is always *conscious.* Performers and audience are aware that the presentation has been planned ahead of time.

This underscores still another significant difference between acting for the stage and "acting" in life: that dramatic characters are not real people. Any stage character— Joan of Arc, Antigone, Oedipus, Hamlet, Willy Loman—is a symbol or an image of a person. Stage characters are fictions created by dramatists and performers to represent people. They remind us of people—in many cases they seem to *be* these people, but they are not.

The task of the performer in attempting to make the characters onstage *appear* to be real requires not only talent but training and discipline as well. Before we examine the training of performers in today's theatre, it will be helpful to look at what was required of performers in the past.

STAGE ACTING: A HISTORICAL PERSPECTIVE

Before the modern era, the challenges of acting were dictated by the very specific demands of the type of theatre in which performers appeared.

Physical Demands of Classical Acting

Both ancient Greek theatre and traditional Asian theatre stressed formal movement and stylized gestures similar to classical ballet. The chorus in Greek drama sang and danced its odes, and Asian theatre has always had a significant component of singing and dancing. In addition, Greek performers wore masks and Asian performers often wore richly textured makeup.

In western theatre, from the Renaissance through the nineteenth century, actions onstage were not intended to replicate the movements or gestures of everyday life. For example, performers would often speak not to the character they were addressing but directly to the audience. This approach to acting was expected and accepted as perfectly normal, but it could also lead to excess and exaggeration, a tendency that

Habillement d'Athalie au théâtre de la Comédie françoise. On l'a prise ici au moment où su
desespoir du couronnet de Joas elle l'écrie avec violence, Dieu des Juifs....tu l'emportes.

MACBETH.   Scene I.

Mrs SIDDONS as LADY MACBETH.

L. Macb.—hark!—I laid their daggers ready,

ACTING IN THE PAST

Acting requirements in the past were often different from those of today. Forceful, sometimes exaggerated movements and a powerful voice were two essentials for successful performers. Actors were expected to declaim their lines and strike impressive poses, while wearing elaborate costumes. Two examples from the late eighteenth century and early nineteenth century are shown here. The first is an actress in the costume for a character in *Athalie* by Jean Racine; the second is a famous English performer, Sarah Siddons, portraying Lady Macbeth. (*Athalie,* Historical Picture Archive/Corbis; Siddons, Bridgeman Art Library)

more than one writer or commentator cautioned against. In Shakespeare's *Hamlet,* for instance, Hamlet's speech to the players is a good example of such a warning:

> Speak the speech, I pray you, as I pronounced it to you, trippingly on the tongue; but if you mouth it, as many of your players do, I had as lief the towncrier spoke my lines. Nor do not saw the air too much with your hand, thus, but use all gently; for in the very torrent, tempest, and, as I may say, the whirlwind of your passion, you must acquire and beget a temperance that may give it smoothness. Oh, it offends me to the soul to hear a robustious periwig-pated fellow tear a passion to tatters, to very rags. . . . Be not too tame neither, but let your discretion be your tutor: suit the action to the word, the word to the action; with this special observance, that you o'erstep not the modesty of nature: for anything so overdone is from the purpose of playing, whose end, both at the first and now, was and is, to hold, as't were, the mirror up to nature.

HISTORICAL PERSPECTIVES

THE STATUS OF THE PERFORMER

Through the centuries there has been a wide fluctuation in the social and political position of performers. First, it must be noted that in several key periods of theatre history, women were prohibited from performing at all. Two prime examples are the theatre of ancient Greece—the era of the playwrights Aeschylus, Sophocles, and Euripides—and the Elizabethan age, during which Shakespeare and his contemporaries wrote. In both periods women could not even appear onstage.

The next point to be noted is that frequently in the history of acting, performers were regarded as quite low on the social scale. An early exception was the classical period in Greece. Because theatre presentations were part of a religious festival, actors were treated with dignity. At the time, the most prominent figures in theatre production were those who wrote the plays and those who produced them, but performers were highly respected. In the Hellenistic period, which began in 336 BCE, actors came even more to the forefront, so much so that by 277 BCE they had established their own union, the Artists of Dionysus.

In Roman theatre, women were allowed to perform, but only in a lower form of theatre known as *mime.* Unlike their Greek predecessors, Roman actors, even those in more formal theatre, were sometimes looked at as little better than itinerant entertainers and vagabonds. Some actors, however—such as Roscius, who performed in the first century BCE—became renowned and highly regarded.

In medieval drama, especially religious drama, most performers were amateurs, drawn in many cases from craft guilds. Though most actors were men and boys, women did occasionally participate as performers. During the Renaissance in Europe, acting became more professional, but the social position of actors was still problematic. Women began to appear with acting troupes in Italy and Spain; but in Spain, for instance, it was required that any actress in a company be a relative (wife, mother, sister) of one of the leaders of the troupe.

An example of the problems faced by actors in being fully accepted is the fate of the Frenchman Molière. Though he was one of the most renowned actors and playwrights of his day, France at that time had laws preventing actors from receiving a Christian burial, and thus Molière was buried secretly at night.

When women began to appear on the English stage in the Restoration period, after 1660, they were regarded by some as on a par with courtesans or prostitutes. Others, however, accepted them into high society, and one actress, Nell Gwynn, was a mistress of the king. During the eighteenth and nineteenth centuries there were a number of famous and celebrated actors and actresses on the European continent, in England, and in the United States. In England, when the actor Henry Irving was knighted in 1895, it was felt that actors had finally arrived socially.

In the twentieth century, with the advent of television, and following the great popularity of film, performers became full-fledged celebrities. Every blip on the radar screen of their lives was featured in fan magazines, on television, and on Web sites.

In Asian theatre, performers for many centuries were primarily men, though a curious phenomenon occurred at the beginning of kabuki in Japan. This form of theatre began in the early seventeenth century with all-women troupes. Social disruptions arose, however, because of feuds over the sexual services of the women, and in 1629 the shogun forbade performances of women's kabuki. Thereafter the performers were all boys, but eventually it was felt that these young men were becoming the sexual targets of older men in the audience; and so in 1652, boys' kabuki was banned as well. From that point on, kabuki was adult and all-male, as were nō theatre and puppet theatre, bunraku.

Shakespeare himself was an actor, and no doubt he had seen performers "saw the air" with their hands and "tear a passion to tatters"; here he is using the character of Hamlet to express his own desire for reasonable, convincing acting by those who performed in his plays.

In France in the seventeenth century, Molière spoke out in his short play *The Impromptu of Versailles* against excessive, absurd practices among performers. He mocked actors in a rival company who ended each phrase with a flourish in order to get applause. (The term *claptrap,* incidentally, comes from a habit of performers of that period who would punctuate a speech or an action with some final inflection or gesture to set a "clap trap"—that is, to provoke applause.) Molière criticized actresses who preserved a silly smile even in a tragic scene; he pointed out how ridiculous it was for two performers in an intimate scene (two young lovers together, for instance, or a king alone with his captain) to declaim as if they were addressing the multitudes.

In England during the eighteenth and nineteenth centuries, acting alternated between exaggerated and more natural styles. Throughout this period, every generation or so a performer would emerge who was praised for acting in a less exaggerated, more down-to-earth way. A good example is the eighteenth-century actor David Garrick (1717–1779), who was famous for his convincing style. One scholar has described the contrast between Garrick and his predecessors in playing Shakespeare's character Richard III:

> Instead of declaiming the verse in a thunderous, measured chant, this actor [Garrick] spoke it with swift and "natural" changes of tone and emphasis. Instead of patrolling the boards with solemn pomp, treading heavily from pose to traditional pose, he moved quickly and gracefully. Instead of standing on his dignity and marbling his face into a tragedian's mask, his mobile features illustrated Richard's whole range of turbulent feelings. He seemed, indeed, to identify himself with the part. It was all so real.[1]

Still, all performers before the twentieth century moved in a more formal, stylized manner than we are accustomed to onstage, in films, or on television.

Vocal Demands of Classical Acting

Vocal requirements in the past were also different from those of modern times. The language of plays was most often poetry, which, with its demanding rhythms, sustained phrases, and exacting meters, required intensive training in order for the performer to speak the lines intelligently and distinctly. There were problems of projection, too. Greek amphitheatres were marvels of acoustics, but they seated as many as 15,000 spectators in the open air, and throwing the voice to every part of these theatres was no small task.

In the Elizabethan period in England, Christopher Marlowe, a contemporary of Shakespeare's, wrote superb blank verse that made severe demands on performers' vocal abilities. An example is a speech in Marlowe's *Doctor Faustus,* addressed by Faustus to Helen of Troy, who has been called back from the dead to be with him. In the speech Faustus says to Helen:

> O, thou art fairer than the evening's air
> Clad in the beauty of a thousand stars;
> Brighter art thou than flaming Jupiter
> When he appear'd to hapless Semele;
> More lovely than the monarch of the sky
> In wanton Arethusa's azured arms;
> And none but thou shalt be my paramour!

These seven lines of verse are a single sentence and, when spoken properly, should be delivered as one overall unit, with the meaning carried from one line to the next. How many of us could manage that? A fine classical actor can speak the entire passage at one time, giving it the necessary resonance and inflection as well. Beyond that, he can stand onstage for 2 or 3 hours delivering such lines.

PERFORMING IN CLASSICS TODAY

No one would expect an actress or actor today to perform a classical role as it was originally presented. Although we don't know exactly how such a performance would have looked or sounded, it seems clear from what we do know that the effect today would be ludicrous. At the same time, it should also be clear that any modern performer who is appearing in a play from the past must develop a special set of skills and must be able to respond successfully to a number of challenges.

Consider an actor undertaking the role of Hamlet. To begin with, the actor must have a sense of the physical and vocal qualities that a character like Hamlet would have. How would Hamlet walk? How would he handle a sword? How would he greet a friend like Horatio? What movements and gestures would he use? And how would he speak? What vocal range and speech patterns would he use?

The actor must have athletic ability and control of his body. If the stage setting has ramps and platforms, he must be able to navigate these with ease; and in a scene near the end of the play, he must engage in a sword fight with Laertes, which requires that he must have mastered certain techniques of fencing.

Moreover, an actor playing Hamlet must be able to speak Shakespeare's lines clearly and intelligently. This is particularly true of Hamlet's soliloquies—the speeches he delivers while alone onstage. Because much of the language of Shakespeare's plays is poetry, the actor must have breath control and an ability to project his voice. To achieve beauty of sound, he should also have a resonant voice; and to convey the meaning of a speech, he must have a full understanding of the words.

In addition to all this, the actor must be able to convey the numerous and often contradictory emotions the character is experiencing: that Hamlet is aware of the betrayal and treachery taking place around him; that he is saddened by the recent

PERFORMING IN CLASSICS TODAY

Contemporary performers in classic plays must have vocal training to be able to speak and project poetry properly; they must have the physical training necessary to engage in sword fights and other activities; and they must be familiar with the historical eras of the playwrights and of the texts they are to perform. Here, Jude Law recites a soliloquy in his role as Hamlet in the Donmar West End production directed by Michael Grandage. (© Geraint Lewis)

death of his father and the hasty marriage of his mother to his uncle; that he wants to murder his uncle once he learns that his uncle has murdered his father, but has difficulty bringing himself to do so; that he berates himself for not being more decisive; that he loves Ophelia but is repelled by the web of circumstances of which she, perhaps unwittingly, is a part.

In preparing for a role like Hamlet, one of the actor's first tasks is to study the script carefully and analyze the role. Many choices must be made regarding interpretation, emphasis, and the like. It will be impossible for the actor to make these choices intelligently unless he has a firm understanding of the play and his part.

THE DEVELOPMENT OF REALISTIC ACTING

Any actor today has a double challenge. On the one hand, he or she must meet the requirements of performing in the classics: the mastery of voice and body techniques described above. On the other hand, the performer must learn the techniques and skills called for in realistic acting.

A believable, realistic approach to acting became more important than ever at the end of the nineteenth century, when drama began to depict characters and situations close to everyday life. Three playwrights—Henrik Ibsen (1828–1906) of Norway, August Strindberg (1849–1912) of Sweden, and Anton Chekhov (1860–1904) of Russia—perfected the type of drama that came to be known as *realism*. This drama

GLOBAL CROSSCURRENTS

PUPPETRY AROUND THE WORLD

Puppetry in its various forms (puppets, marionettes, shadow puppets) has a long and honorable history. Remarkably, it emerged independently in widely separated parts of the world: Indonesia, Japan, sections of Europe, and among Native Americans in the far northwest of what is now the United States.

In whatever form, the puppet figure is the image, the reflection, the embodiment of a theatrical character, and therefore a replacement for the actor. Puppets can run the gamut of emotions. They can be evil, demonic personages; they can be eerie, otherworldly creatures; they can be wildly comic, as in Punch and Judy shows, when they biff each other across the head and knock each other down; they can be intensely human, as in the suffering characters in Japanese bunraku. In short, when they are onstage, the audience usually experiences these silent, nonhuman characters as real people.

It should be noted as well that while puppet or marionette characters are often either comic or tragic figures, they are also frequently employed as advocates for a political point of view. The Bread and Puppet Theatre of San Francisco, founded by Peter Schuman (b. 1934), features larger-than-life, exaggerated figures made of papier-mâché. The theatre began with protests against the Vietnam War but has continued, often with the figures processing down city streets, in protests against all wars, including the Iraq War.

Puppet characters are created and manipulated in various ways. In Indonesia and other parts of southeast Asia, two kinds of puppets were developed. One type was rod puppets, so-called because the movements of the puppets are controlled by rods attached to the head and limbs and operated by one or more persons, from either above or below. (Though they are most often associated with southeast Asia, rod puppets, nearly life-size, were developed as well in the island of Sicily in the Mediterranean.) The other type of puppet popular in southeast Asia—in Java and Bali as well as Indonesia—is the shadow puppet. In this case, silhouette figures, often made of leather, are highlighted on a screen that is lit from behind.

Marionettes are puppets controlled by strings attached to the head, arms, and legs, and operated from above. A unique type of puppet is the bunraku puppet from Japan, which will be discussed in more detail in Chapter 14. Originating in the late seventeenth century, it was firmly established by the eighteenth century and has continued to this day. In the early eighteenth century, one of the most famous playwrights of all time, Chikamatsu Monzaemon, wrote masterful plays for bunraku theater. In the case of bunraku figures, which today are roughly two-thirds life-size, one man operates the feet; another, the left hand; and a third, the face, head, and right hand.

Probably the puppet figures most familiar to western audiences are hand puppets, operated by a person who has one or two hands inside the puppet itself. Among the immediately recognizable hand puppets are the Muppets, featuring such popular and enduring characters as Kermit the Frog and Miss Piggy.

Puppetry remains, and will continue to be, a vital art form in its own right, and an important adjunct to live theatre.

Quanzhou Marionette Theater, from China. (James Estrin/The New York Times/Redux)

was called *realistic* because it closely resembled what people could identify with and verify from their own experience. In performing plays by these dramatists, not only the spirit of the individual dramatic characters but also the details of their behavior had to conform to what people saw of life around them. This placed great demands on actors and actresses to avoid any hint of fakery or superficiality.

The Stanislavsky System: A Technique for Realistic Acting

Before the realistic drama of the late 1800s, no one had devised a method for achieving the kind of believability these plays required. Through their own talent and genius, individual actresses and actors had achieved it, but no one had developed a system whereby it could be taught to others and passed on to future generations. The person who eventually did this most successfully was the Russian actor and director Konstantin Stanislavsky (1863–1938).

A cofounder of the Moscow Art Theatre in Russia and the director of Anton Chekhov's most important plays, Stanislavsky was also an actor. He was involved in both traditional theatre—using stylized, nonrealistic techniques—and the emergence of the modern realistic approach. By closely observing the work of great performers of his day, and by drawing on his own acting experience, Stanislavsky identified and described what these gifted performers did naturally and intuitively. From his observations he compiled and then codified a series of principles and techniques, which today are regarded as fundamental to both the training and the performance of actors who want to create believable characters onstage.

We might assume that believable acting is simply a matter of being natural; but Stanislavsky discovered first of all that acting realistically onstage is extremely difficult. He wrote:

> All of our acts, even the simplest, which are so familiar to us in everyday life, become strained when we appear behind the foot lights [*sic*] before a public of a thousand people. That is why it is necessary to correct ourselves and learn again how to walk, sit, or lie down. It is essential to reeducate ourselves to look and see, on the stage, to listen and to hear.[2]

To achieve this "reeducation," Stanislavsky said, "the actor must first of all believe in everything that takes place onstage, and most of all, he must believe what he himself is doing. And one can only believe in the truth." On some level the performer must believe wholeheartedly and completely in the character and what the character is doing. In other words, the portrayal must be "true." To give substance to his ideas, Stanislavsky studied how people acted in everyday life and how they communicated feelings and emotions; and then he found ways to accomplish the same things onstage. These observations resulted in a series of exercises and techniques for the actor, which had the following broad aims:

1. To make the outward behavior of the performer—gestures, voice, and rhythm of movements—natural and convincing.
2. To have the actor or actress convey the goals and objectives—the inner needs—of a character. Even if all the visible manifestations of a character are mastered, a performance will appear superficial and mechanical without a deep sense of conviction and belief.

3. To make the life of the character onstage not only dynamic but continuous. Some performers tend to emphasize only the high points of a part; in between, the life of the character stops. In real life, however, people do not stop living.

4. To develop a strong sense of *ensemble* playing with other performers in a scene.

Let us now look in some detail at Stanislavsky's techniques.

Relaxation When he observed the great actors and actresses of his day, Stanislavsky noticed how fluid and lifelike their movements were. They seemed to be in a state of complete freedom and relaxation, letting the behavior of the character come through effortlessly. He concluded that unwanted tension has to be eliminated and that the performer must at all times attain a state of physical and vocal *relaxation*.

Concentration and Observation Stanislavsky also discovered that gifted performers always appeared fully concentrated on some object, person, or event while onstage. Stanislavsky referred to the extent or range of concentration as a *circle of attention*. This circle of attention can be compared to a circle of light on a darkened stage. The performer should begin with the idea that it is a small, tight circle including only himself or herself and perhaps one other person or one piece of furniture. When the performer has established a strong circle of attention, he or she can enlarge the circle outward to include the entire stage area. In this way performers will stop worrying about the audience and lose their self-consciousness.

Importance of Specifics One of Stanislavsky's techniques was an emphasis on concrete details. A performer should never try to act *in general,* he said, and should never try to convey a feeling such as fear or love in some vague, amorphous way. In life, Stanislavsky said, we express emotions in terms of specifics: an anxious woman twists a handkerchief, an angry boy throws a rock at a trash can, a nervous businessman jangles his keys. Performers must find similar *concrete* activities. Stanislavsky points out how Shakespeare has Lady Macbeth in her sleepwalking scene—at the height of her guilt and emotional upheaval—try to rub blood off her hands.

The performer must also conceive of the situation in which a character exists—what Stanislav-

TECHNIQUES OF ACTING: THE IMPORTANCE OF SPECIFICS
Konstantin Stanislavsky believed that performers should concentrate on specifics. In *The Glass Menagerie,* the playwright Tennessee Williams has provided the character Laura with a collection of glass animals with which she is preoccupied. Shown here is Keira Keeley as Laura, with Josh Charles as the Gentleman Caller, in a production at the Long Wharf Theatre. (© T Charles Erickson)

sky referred to as the *given circumstances*—in terms of specifics. In what kind of space does an event take place: formal, informal, public, domestic? How does it feel? What is the temperature? The lighting? What has gone on just before? What is expected in the moments ahead? Again, these questions must be answered in concrete terms.

Inner Truth   An innovative aspect of Stanislavsky's work has to do with *inner truth,* which deals with the internal or subjective world of characters—that is, their thoughts and emotions. The early phases of Stanislavsky's research took place while he was also directing the major dramas of Anton Chekhov. Plays like *The Three Sisters* and *The Cherry Orchard* have less to do with external action or what the characters say than with what the characters are feeling and thinking but often do not verbalize. It becomes apparent that Stanislavsky's approach would be very beneficial in realizing the inner life of such characters.

Stanislavsky had several ideas about how to achieve a sense of inner truth, one being the **"magic if."** The word *if* can transform our thoughts in such a way that we can imagine ourselves in virtually any situation. "*If* I suddenly became wealthy . . ." "*If* I were vacationing on a Caribbean island . . ." "*If* I had great talent . . ." "*If* that person who insulted me comes near me again . . ." The word *if* becomes a powerful lever for the mind; it can lift us out of ourselves and give us a sense of absolute certainty about imaginary circumstances.

Action Onstage: What? Why? How?   Another important principle of Stanislavsky's system is that every action onstage must have a purpose. This means that the performer's attention must always be focused on a series of physical actions (also called *psychophysical actions*) linked by the circumstances of the play. Stanislavsky determined these actions by asking three essential questions: What? Why? How? An action is performed, such as opening a letter *(what)*. The letter is opened because someone has said that it contains extremely damaging information about the character *(why)*. The letter is opened anxiously, fearfully *(how)*, because of the calamitous effect it might have on the character. These physical actions, which occur from moment to moment in a performance, are in turn governed by the character's overall objective in the play.

Rather than seeing emotions as leading to action, as he had thought earlier in his career, Stanislavsky came to believe that it was the other way around: purposeful action undertaken to fulfill a character's goals is the most direct route to the emotions. When an action is performed as a result of the given circumstances in a play to bring about a change in the dramatic situation, emotion will follow. Because psychophysical or purposeful action is the key, a well-trained, well-developed, responsive body and voice are indispensable.

Through Line of a Role   According to Stanislavsky, in order to develop continuity in a part, the actor or actress should find the character's *superobjective.* What is it, above all else, that the character wants during the course of the play? What is the character's driving force? If a goal can be established toward which the character strives, it will give the performer an overall objective. From this objective can be developed a *through line,* which can be grasped, as a skier on a ski lift grabs a towline and is carried to the top. Another term for *through line* is **spine.**

ENSEMBLE PLAYING

Good actors are aware of the importance of ensemble playing. Performers coordinate their work by listening carefully to each other, sensing each other's actions and moods, and responding alertly. Ensemble playing is especially important in plays where interaction between characters is crucial. Anton Chekhov's plays call for an emphasis on ensemble acting. One example is *The Seagull,* shown here at the Yale School of Drama, 2009. (© T Charles Erickson)

To help develop the through line, Stanislavsky urged performers to divide scenes into units (sometimes called *beats*). In each unit there is an objective, and the intermediate objectives running through a play lead ultimately to the overall objective.

Ensemble Playing   Except in one-person shows, performers do not act alone; they interact with other people. Stanislavsky was aware that many performers tend to "stop acting," or lose their concentration, when they are not the main characters in a scene or when someone else is talking. This tendency destroys the through line and causes the performer to move into and out of a role. That, in turn, weakens the sense of ensemble—the playing together of all the performers.

Later Interpretations of Stanislavsky's Approach   Stanislavsky had a profound influence on the training of performers throughout the twentieth century.

An actor who began working with Stanislavsky but then broke away to develop his own approach to training actors was Michael Chekhov (1891–1955), a nephew of the playwright Anton Chekhov. Michael Chekhov is best-known for the *psychological gesture*—the notion that character can be successfully projected by the creation of notable, telling gestures that sum up inner feelings, desires, and emotions. For example, a character facing death wants to confess to another man that he has cheated this man. In playing this role, Chekhov kept digging his hands into the area of the other man's heart, as though he wanted to become one with the other man.

In the United States, several people who were performers or directors with the Group Theater in the 1930s went on to become important teachers of acting. These included Sanford Meisner, Stella Adler, Robert Lewis, Lee Strasberg, and Uta Hagen. Strasberg for many years headed the Actors Studio in New York, where a number of prominent film and stage stars studied, including Marlon Brando, James Dean, Paul Newman, Marilyn Monroe, and Al Pacino. Uta Hagen, a well-known actress as well as a teacher, wrote two books, *Respect for Acting* and *A Challenge for the Actor,* which are required reading in many actor training programs.

The interpretation of Stanislavsky's approach in the United States has been a cause of considerable controversy. A number of experts, for example, feel that Strasberg mistakenly emphasized only the inner or emotional side of Stanislavsky's technique—the early work—and neglected the importance of physical action, the voice, and the body. Strasberg particularly emphasized a technique that Stanislavsky in his earlier writings called ***emotional recall.*** This is a tool intended to help the performer achieve a sense of emotional truth onstage; it consists of remembering a past experience in the performer's life that is similar to one in a play. By recalling sensory impressions of an experience in the past (such as what a room looked like, any prevalent odors, and any contact with objects), the actor arouses emotions associated with the experience that can be used as the basis of feelings called for in the play.

This technique has a place in actors' training, but as we have seen, Stanislavsky himself moved away from an emphasis on inner, emotional qualities toward the psychophysical; and teachers like Adler, Lewis, and Meisner, mentioned above, felt that Strasberg's approach was too one-sided.

Various Approaches

Just as Adler, Lewis, and Meisner developed their own individual approaches to the teaching of acting, subsequent teachers have done the same. (Most of their methods, it should be pointed out, are in some way based on or influenced by Stanislavsky.) The following three examples indicate similarities and differences in current approaches to actors' training.

Uta Hagen, in her book *Respect for Acting,* strongly emphasizes emotional and memory recall. She provides a number of exercises that enable the students to pull past experiences from their own lives as a means of reaching required emotion within the context of any given role. Hagen's idea is not to allow the student to become overwhelmed by past emotion, but to use it as a springboard into the action of the play.

In *Acting One,* Robert Cohen encourages students to use the text as an instrument of action. In his "Contentless Scene" exercise he has students memorize the same text. He then asks them to perform the scene but changes the given circumstances of the scene each time. The outcome is the obvious realization that the words are not nearly as important as the meaning behind them. And, clearly, without solid given circumstances actors are simply saying lines instead of using those lines to further the action of the play.

Another teacher, Robert Benedetti, in *The Actor at Work* focuses on the actor's body and how it can be used to help shape character. Using a variety of movement exercises Benedetti encourages students to explore elements of rhythm, time, weight, intensity, and space through improvisational work. These exercises allow the students to start with the "outside" (physical) aspects of defining a character. Once the physical form is found, they can then use it to define the inner life (emotions) of the character.

The important thing for students of acting is to explore different methods and approaches to acting, such as those outlined above, and to decide which techniques and types of training—or which combination of these—works best for them. Ultimately each individual actor must develop his or her own methodology.

Performers' Training Today

Body and Voice Training
One aspect of contemporary training of performers is developing skills in the areas Stanislavsky articulated: relaxation; concentration; inner truth; given circumstances; and attention to specifics, goals, and objectives. As we have seen, however, to meet the requirements of acting in the classics—such as the plays of Shakespeare and Molière, and Greek tragedies—body and voice training are also indispensable.

Let us consider the voice, for example. A primary requirement for performers is to make certain that the lines they speak are heard clearly by the audience. To be heard throughout a theatre seating 1,000 or more people, a performer must *project,* that is, throw the voice into the audience so that it penetrates to the uttermost reaches of the theatre. In modern realistic plays this task is made more difficult by the necessity of maintaining believability. For example, in real life the words of a man and a woman in an intimate love scene would be barely audible even to people only a few feet away; in a theatre, however, every word must be heard by the entire audience. A performer needs to strike a balance, therefore, between credibility and the necessity of being heard.

In order to develop projection and achieve the kind of balance just described, performers must train and rehearse extensively. For example, an actor or actress might use breathing exercises, controlling the breath from the diaphragm rather than the throat so that vocal reproduction will have power and can be sustained. These exercises are often quite similar to those used by opera singers. Also, head, neck, and shoulder exercises can be used to relax the muscles in those areas, thus freeing the throat for ease of projection.

For the development of the body and the voice, series of exercises and programs have been created. The box on page 109 shows a set of warm-up exercises. It should be emphasized, though, that these exercises represent only a small fraction of the kinds of exercises performers must undertake in developing acting skills. There are more specific, advanced exercises for such things as fencing, dancing, and rapid movements up and down stairs or platforms. Also, there are specific vocal exercises for the delivery of poetry, for vocal projection, and so forth.

Beyond exercises, there are other areas of training. For example, vocal training includes learning to coordinate the meaning and understanding of lines of poetry with their proper delivery. Physical training includes developing the skills necessary to deal with the peculiarities of a given historical period, such as the curtsy and bow for plays involving kings and queens.

As a part of body and voice training, many acting teachers emphasize *centering.* This is a way of bringing everything together and allowing the performer to eliminate

DYNAMICS OF DRAMA

WARM-UP EXERCISES FOR VOICE AND BODY

To get a sense of the types of exercises performers must undertake during their years of training—and during their careers as professionals—it is interesting to look at some samples of warm-up exercises. The exercises here are designed to relax the body and the voice.

The following are typical warm-up *exercises for body movement:*

1. Lie on your back; beginning with the feet, tense and relax each part of the body—knees, thighs, abdomen, chest, neck—moving up to the face. Note the difference in the relaxation of various muscles and of the body generally after the exercise is completed.
2. Stand with feet parallel, approximately as far apart as the width of the shoulders. Lift one foot off the ground and loosen all the joints in the foot, ankle, and knee. Repeat with the other foot off the ground. Put the feet down and move to the hip, spine, arms, neck, etc., loosening all joints.
3. Stand with feet parallel. Allow all tension to drain out of the body through the feet. In the process, bend the knees, straighten the pelvis, and release the lower back.
4. Begin walking in a circle; walk on the outside of the feet, then on the inside, then on the toes, and then on the heels. Notice what this does to the rest of the body. Try changing other parts of the body in a similar fashion and observe the effect on feelings and reactions.
5. Imagine the body filled with either helium or lead. Notice the effect of each of these sensations, both while standing in place and while walking. Do the same with one body part at a time—each arm, each leg, the head, etc.

The following *vocal exercises* free the throat and vocal cords:

1. Standing, begin a lazy, unhurried stretch. Reach with your arms to the ceiling, meanwhile lengthening and widening the whole of your back. Yawn as you take in a deep breath and hum on an exhalation. Release your torso so that it rests down toward your legs. Yawn on another deep breath and hum on an exhalation. On an inhalation, roll up the spine until you are standing with your arms at your sides. Look at something on the ceiling and then at something on the floor; then let your head return to a balance point, so that the neck and shoulder muscles are relaxed.
2. Put your hands on your ribs, take a deep breath, and hum a short tune. Repeat several times. Hum an *m* or *n* up and down the scale. Drop your arms; lift the shoulders an inch and drop them, releasing all tension.
3. Take a deep breath, and with the palm of your hand push gently down on your stomach as you exhale. Do this several times. Exhale on sighs and then on vowels.
4. Standing, yawn with your throat and mouth open and be aware of vibrations in the front of your mouth, just behind your front teeth, as you vocalize on the vowels *ee, ei,* and *o.* Take these up and down the scales. Sing a simple song and then say it, and see if you have just as much vibration in your mouth when you are speaking as when you are singing.
5. Using a light, quick tempo, shift to a tongue twister (such as *Peter Piper picked a peck of pickled peppers*). Feel a lively touch of the tongue on the gum ridge on the *t*'s and *d*'s, and a bounce of the back of the tongue on the *k*'s and *g*'s. Feel the bouncing action on the lips on the *p*'s and *b*'s.

Source: Provided by Professor John Sipes of the Oregon Shakespeare Festival and Professor Barbara F. Acker of Arizona State University.

any blocks that could impede either the body or the voice. Centering involves locating the place—roughly in the middle of the torso—where all the lines of force of the body come together. It is the "point of convergence of the muscular, emotional and intellectual impulses within our bodies."[3] When performers are able to "center" themselves, they achieve a balance, a freedom, and a flexibility they could rarely find otherwise.

Training Techniques from Other Disciplines   In modern training of actors and actresses, teachers borrow from other disciplines. A good example is Asian theatre. Stylization and symbolism characterize the acting of the classical theatres of India, China, and Japan. To achieve the absolute control, the concentration, and the mastery of body and nerves necessary to carry out stylized movements, performers in the various classical Asian theatres train for years under the supervision of master teachers. Every movement of these performers is prescribed and carefully controlled, combining elements of formal ballet, pantomime, and sign language. Each gesture tells a story and means something quite specific—a true symbolism of physical movement.

One Asian discipline, not from theatre but from martial arts, which modern acting teachers have found helpful is *tai chi chuan,* commonly called *tai chi.* Unlike some martial arts, tai chi is not aggressive: it is a graceful, gentle exercise regimen performed widely by men, women, and children in China. It has spread to other countries, where it is sometimes practiced in conjunction with meditation or body awareness. The movements

DYNAMICS OF DRAMA

FINGER LANGUAGE: A PART OF INDIAN ACTING AND DANCING

The precise gestures of this Indian art—the graceful, symbolic movements—require extensive training and discipline to perfect. In the finger language shown here, the numbers indicate the following states or emotions: (1) separation or death, (2) meditation, (3) determination, (4) joy, (5) concentration, (6) rejection, (7) veneration, (8) proposal, (9) vexation, and (10) love.

Source: From Margaret Berthold, *A History of World Theater,* copyright 1972 by Frederick Ungar Publishing Co., Inc.

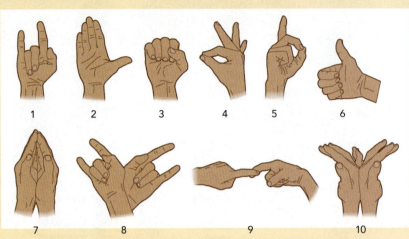

ACTING TRAINING FROM OTHER DISCIPLINES
Actors' training today often involves exercises and other activities from related disciplines such as circus routines, juggling, acrobatics, and Asian martial arts. A good example is tai chi, a refined form of martial arts from China, here being practiced in a park. (© Inge King)

of tai chi are stylized and often seem to be carried out in slow motion. Among other things, tai chi requires concentration and control—valuable qualities for a performer.

Another field to which people involved in training actors and actresses have turned is the circus. Juggling, for instance, teaches both coordination and concentration; tightrope walking calls for fierce concentration; acrobatics make the body limber; and other activities call for teamwork of a very high order.

Training for Special Forms of Theatre

Certain types of theatre and theatre events require special discipline or training. For example, musical theatre obviously requires talent in singing and dancing. Coordination is also important in musical theatre: the members of a chorus must frequently sing and dance in unison.

Pantomime is another demanding category of performance: without words or props, a performer must indicate everything by physical suggestion, convincingly lifting an imaginary box or walking against an imaginary wind.

Various forms of modern avant-garde and experimental theatre also require special techniques. A good example is Samuel Beckett's *Happy Days,* in which an actress is

TRAINING FOR MUSICAL THEATRE
Along with the classics and various types of theatre from other nations, the American musical with its physical and vocal demands requires extensive training. A prime example is the exuberant dancing by the men in *West Side Story* performing "Cool," one of the show's most technically demanding numbers. The 2009 Broadway revival was directed by Arthur Laurents, with choreography based on that of Jerome Robbins. Music by Leonard Bernstein; lyrics by Stephen Sondheim. (Sara Krulwich/The New York Times/Redux)

buried onstage in a mound of earth up to her waist in the first act, and up to her neck in the second. She must perform through the entire play while virtually immobile.

In some types of avant-garde theatre, the performers become acrobats, make human pyramids, or are used like pieces of furniture. In *Suitcase,* by the Japanese playwright Kobo Abe (1924–1993), the actor who plays the suitcase must move as if he is being carried like a piece of luggage. In another play by Abe, *The Man Who Turned into a Stick,* an actor must play the part of a stick.

In the theatre of Robert Wilson (b. 1944) and of Mabou Mines and similar groups, story, character, and text are minimized or even eliminated. The stress, rather than being on a narrative or on exploring recognizable characters, is on the visual and ritualistic aspects of theatre. The overall effect is sometimes like a series of tableaux or a moving collage. Because of the emphasis on the visual picture formed onstage, there is an affinity between this kind of theatre and painting. Stage movement in performance art is often closely related to dance; thus the performers must have the same discipline, training, and control as dancers.

THE SPECIAL DEMANDS OF ACTING

At times performing makes exceedingly strong demands, requiring performers to convey a range and depth of emotions, or to transform themselves in terms of age, mood, and the like. A good example is Samuel Beckett's *Happy Days,* in which the actress playing Winnie—in this case, Fiona Shaw—must perform while buried in a mound of sand up to her waist, and later up to her neck. This production was directed by Deborah Warner at the National Theatre in London in 2006. (© Robbie Jack/Corbis)

UNIQUE ACTING DEMANDS OF AVANT-GARDE THEATRE

Avant-garde theatre often requires special training and techniques—acrobatics, tumbling, mime, and special control of voice and body. Here we see Ruth Amarante and Jorge Puerta Armenta in *Nefés,* a theatre-dance piece by the German experimental director Pina Bausch, whose troupe goes by the name Tanztheater Wuppertal. (© Stephanie Berger)

In Wilson's work, performers are frequently called on either to move ceaselessly or to remain perfectly still. In an early piece by Wilson, *A Letter to Queen Victoria*, two performers turn continuously in circles like dervishes for long periods of time—perhaps 30 or 40 minutes. In other works by Wilson, performers must remain frozen like statues.

The demands made on performers by experimental and avant-garde theatre are only the most recent example of the rigorous, intensive training that acting generally requires. The goal of all this training—both internal and external—is to create for the performer an instrument that is flexible, resourceful, and disciplined.

Moving from Preparation to Performance

At this point it is important to make a distinction between *preparation* and *performance*. The various techniques, exercises, and the like that we have been discussing—the approaches of teachers such as Hagen, Cohen, or Benedetti, and vocal and body training—these must be brought together. After being exposed to these various aspects of training, the next step toward maturity for an actor or actress is to synthesize and integrate everything that has been learned. The performer creates a single, powerful instrument that encompasses the mind, the body, the voice, and the imagination.

At this point the actor is ready to play a role in a performance, and his or her concentration must move from training to developing and preparing a specific role in a specific play.

When a performer is approaching a role in a play, the first task is to read and analyze the script. The actress or actor must discover the superobjective of the character she or he is playing and put together not only the spine of the role but the many smaller moments, each with its own objective and given circumstances.

The next challenge is to begin specific work on the role. In taking this step, some performers begin with the outer aspects of the character—with a walk, or posture, or a peculiar vocal delivery. They get a sense of how the character looks in terms of makeup and other characteristics, such as a mustache or a hairstyle. They consider the clothes the character wears and any idiosyncrasies of speech or movement, such as a limp or a swagger. Only then will they move on to the inner aspects of the character: how the character feels; how the character reacts to people and events; what disturbs the character's emotional equilibrium; what fears, hopes, and dreams the character has.

Other performers, by contrast, begin with the internal aspects: with the feelings and emotions of the character. These performers delve deeply into the psyche of the character to try to understand and duplicate what the character feels inside. Only after that will they go on to develop the outer characteristics. Still other actors work on both aspects—inner and outer—simultaneously.

What is important to remember is that whatever the starting point, the end result must be a synthesis of these two aspects. The various aspects of the craft of acting must be blended into a seamless whole to create the total persona of a character, so that the inner emotions and feelings and the outer physical and vocal characteristics become one. Only then will the character be forcefully and convincingly portrayed. This process is called *integration*.

Finally, we must realize that although a competent, well-trained performer may become a successful actress or actor, another ingredient is required in order to electrify an audience, as truly memorable stage artists do. This results from intangibles—qualities that cannot be taught in acting schools—which distinguish an acceptable, accomplished actor or actress from one who ignites the stage. *Presence, charisma, personality, star quality:* these are among the terms used to describe a performer who communicates directly and kinetically with the audience. Whatever term one uses, the electricity and excitement of theatre are enhanced immeasurably by performers who possess this indefinable attribute.

THE ACTING EXPERIENCE

In this chapter we have looked at three types of training for actors: (1) preparation for performing in the classics; (2) approaches to realistic acting; (3) special techniques such as acrobatics and the unique requirements of avant-garde theatre. We move now from training to the experience of a young performer when she or he undertakes appearing onstage in a production at a college or university, or in professional theatre.

Let us look, for example, at a typical sequence that begins before a performer is cast in a role and continues to his or her opening-night performance before an audience. We'll imagine that our performer is an actress named Jennifer.

The first step for Jennifer is hearing about a forthcoming production. This might be a presentation by a theatre department at a college or university, or by an amateur community theatre, or by a professional regional theatre; it might even be a large-scale Broadway production. In each case, the procedure will be similar. Jennifer must ***audition.*** This means that she must appear before the director, the stage manager, and others (perhaps the producer, and in the case of a new play, the playwright) to be interviewed and probably to present one or more scenes she has prepared. These may be scenes from the play being presented, or scenes she has prepared from other plays to demonstrate her abilities. After a first audition, Jennifer may be called back to read again by herself, or perhaps with other performers who are being considered for parts with which her character would interact.

Auditions, like almost every aspect of performing, can be nerve-racking. Each of us wants to be approved of by others, and each of us fears rejection, even in the most casual relationships. In an audition—as in performance before an audience— the reaction is public and pronounced. A performer who does not get a part has been openly turned down, just as a performer attacked by a critic in print has been publicly judged. Those who wish to enter theatre as a career must learn to deal with the disappointment of being turned down for a role or being criticized publicly.

Let us assume, though, that this time Jennifer is one of the fortunate ones: she is selected for the production. The next step will be several weeks of intensive rehearsal. If Jennifer has had previous experience in performing, she will know that there is a difference between her work at an audition and her work in rehearsal for a production. In an audition, she must work for *results:* that is, in a short period of time she must project her personality and the skills that she hopes will get her the part. In the rehearsal period, on the other hand, she will be *exploring* a character, searching for specifics and an overall curve to her performance; she will be interacting with other performers. The emphasis will be on *process,* rather than immediate results.

During this period, she must memorize her part in the script, which could be difficult. Her role may be long, or her lines may be poetry, or she may have to speak in dialect—a British or southern accent, for instance. During the rehearsal period, Jennifer must work closely with the director, learning, among other things, where, when, and how to move onstage. Her movements might come from a combination of ideas from the director and her own ideas—such as an impulse she may have to sit, stand, or cross the stage at a certain moment.

Also, Jennifer must work closely with the other performers, learning to adjust to their rhythms, reacting to the dynamics of their characterizations, and the like. Inevitably there will be difficult moments. For example, she and another performer may not be clicking, or she may not be able to summon up an emotion that is called for—such as different levels of anger, joy, or frustration. She may have to bend every effort to find and portray the required emotion. After working first on individual scenes and sections of the script, she will discover when the play is put together that she must make further adjustments. She may be too emotional in an early segment, leaving herself no room to reach a higher pitch later on; or perhaps the pace is too slow and the play drags, so that she and the other performers must find ways to accelerate the action without losing sincerity and conviction.

Just before the public performances, during the first technical rehearsals, new ingredients are added. The performers are in costume for the first time; the lights are changing; scenery is shifted; and the actresses and actors are temporarily in a foreign land. Away from the safe, protected rehearsal hall with which they have become comfortable, they must now contend with stagehands, lighting technicians, real furniture, doors that open differently—in short, a host of new conditions.

After overcoming the initial shock of these new elements, the production will settle into the level of a complete, full presentation, but soon another component is added: the audience. For the first time, usually at a preview or dress rehearsal, strange people are sitting out front watching and listening. Does a scene that must be emotionally gripping actually hold the audience's attention? Does a comic scene evoke laughter? For Jennifer and her fellow performers, such uncertainties can be terrifying. The other side of the coin, of course, is that if they succeed, they will have the thrill not only of a great accomplishment, but of a kind of contact with the public that most people rarely experience.

One objective of a performance is to look natural and easy—to suggest to the audience that playing the role is effortless, just as a juggler attempts to look as casual and carefree as possible. One reason why it is important for acting to look effortless is to relax the audience members and let them believe in the character rather than concentrate on the performer's lengthy and arduous preparation.

During the first few performances before an audience, adjustments are made in the acting and in other elements, such as lighting and sound. Rough spots are made smoother; the pace is speeded up or slowed down; awkward moments are dealt with. Finally, opening night comes: the night when the production is ready to be seen and judged by audiences and critics. This is another potentially traumatic moment for Jennifer and her fellow performers. Will they forget their lines? Will a lighting miscue leave them in the dark?

A thousand and one fears come to the surface, but once Jennifer is onstage, she is carried along with the moment. All her preparation has given her enough knowledge, experience, and command of the stage to instill security and confidence. When she hears laughter in the audience, or when a hush falls, she knows that she and her colleagues have succeeded, and their many hours of hard work, uncertainty, and fear of failure are washed away in a sense of accomplishment and in the satisfaction of bringing to reality their dream of performing onstage.

photo essay

Performers Play Different Parts

(Sarah Krulwich/The New York Times/Redux)

In theatre—more than in life— performers are called on to play diverse parts. Frequently, too, actors portray people unlike themselves. Many performers welcome this challenge. An American actress who has demonstrated tremendous versatility is Laura Linney, shown here in six contrasting roles.

Laura Linney as Linda in *Holiday* (1995), with Tony Goldwyn.

Laura Linney as Claudia in *Honour* (1998) by Joanna Murray-Smith, directed by Gerald Gutierrez, with Robert Foxworth as Gus.

Laura Linney as Yelena Andreyevna with Derek Jacobi as Vanya in *Uncle Vanya* (2000).

(Sarah Krulwich/The New York Times/Redux)

(Sarah Krulwich/The New York Times/Redux)

Laura Linney and Liam Neeson in Arthur Miller's *The Crucible,* 2002.

Ben Daniels and Laura Linney play former lovers in *Les Liaisons Dangereuses.*

In *Time Stands Still* by Donald Margulies, Laura Linney plays Sara Goodwin, a photojournalist who has been injured in the Iraq War.

THE AUDIENCE'S RESPONSE

- What is the most convincing performance you've seen—the performance in which you felt the actor onstage was really the person being portrayed? What was it about the performance that made it believable?

- In Shakespeare's plays and other classic plays, the actors often speak verse. How important do you think the various vocal techniques described in this chapter are to the actors' preparation and ultimate execution of such roles?

- When two, three, or four actors are performing in a scene where the characters are locked in conflict, what can the actors do to hold the attention of the audience and make their actions and feelings convincing? How do you think these actors can best prepare for conflict scenes?

THE AUDIENCE: JUDGING PERFORMANCES

As observers, we study the techniques and problems of acting so that we will be able to understand and judge the performances we see. If a performer is unconvincing in a part, we know that he or she has not mastered a technique for truthful acting, such as the system developed by Stanislavsky and his successors. We recognize that a performer who moves awkwardly or cannot be heard clearly has not been properly trained in body movement or vocal projection. We learn to notice how well performers play together: whether they listen to one another and respond appropriately. We also observe how well performers establish and maintain contact with the audience.

Earlier, we saw that a performer must project his or her voice into the audience. In fact, the performer must project his or her total personality, because (as has frequently been noted) it is the contact between performer and audience which forms the basic encounter of theatre. This is true even in the many types of theatre where performers appear to act as if the audience did not exist. From the audience's standpoint, the performer-audience relationship is very intense, because audience members focus exclusively on the stage. The performers are also conscious of this relationship. They may concentrate on an object onstage, or on one another, but a part of them constantly senses the audience and monitors its reaction. Their involvement is so intense that a cough or whisper, which would be unnoticed in an ordinary room, is magnified a hundredfold. This is why an announcement frequently is made before the beginning of a performance asking audience members to turn off their cell phones.

In short, when we consider all the aspects of acting, we see that there is great variation in the intensity and honesty of performers. If they are absorbed in a life-and-death struggle onstage, the audience will be absorbed too, like bystanders at a street fight. If they are listless and uninvolved, the audience will lose interest.

Before leaving the subject of the performer, we should note that actors and actresses have always fascinated audiences. In some cases this is because they portray larger-than-life characters; it can also result from the exceptional talent they bring to their performances. Also, of course, some performers have personal charisma or appeal. Theatre audiences have often responded to stars onstage in the same way that people tend to respond to a musician or a film star. There is something in these personalities that audiences find immensely attractive or intriguing. Moreover, the personal lives of actors are often of great interest to the public, and some people find it difficult to separate a stage character from the offstage woman or man.

In Chapter 6, we turn to the person who works most closely with actresses and actors and who helps them shape their performances—the director.

SUMMARY

1. All human beings engage in certain forms of acting; imitation and role playing are excellent examples of acting in everyday life.

2. Acting onstage differs from acting in everyday life, for several reasons—including the fact that a stage actor or actress is always being observed by an audience, and the fact that acting for the stage involves playing roles with which the performer may have no direct experience in life.

3. Historically, stage performances have required exceptional physical and vocal skills: the ability to move with agility and grace and to engage in such actions as sword fights and death scenes; the ability to deal with poetic devices (meter, imagery, alliteration, etc.); the skill to project the voice to the farthest reaches of the theatre space.

4. Acting is a difficult, demanding profession. Despite its glamour, it calls for arduous training and preparation. Looking at what is called for in a role like Hamlet gives some idea of the challenges involved.

5. From the end of the nineteenth century to the present day, many plays have been written in a very realistic, lifelike style. The characters in these plays resemble ordinary people in their dialogue, behavior, etc. Presenting them requires that performers make the characters they portray believable and convincing.

6. A Russian director, Konstantin Stanislavsky, developed a system or method of acting to enable performers to believe in the "truth" of what they say and do. His suggestions included applying techniques of relaxation and concentration; dealing with specific objects and feelings (a handkerchief, a glass of water, etc.); using the power of fantasy or imagination (the "magic if") to achieve a sense of inner truth in a role; using psychophysical action; developing a *spine,* or *through line,* which runs through a role from the beginning to the end of a play; and playing together as an ensemble.

7. In the later stages of his work on actor training, Stanislavsky moved from an emphasis on internal elements to more external ones—to what he called *psychological action.* Rather than emotion leading to action, he suggested that action leads to emotion.

8. Exercises and tasks have been developed to train performers. These include numerous physical and vocal exercises and techniques taken from other disciplines such as tai chi and the circus. "Centering" is often emphasized as a part of body and voice training.

9. Avant-garde theatre and some other theatres make additional demands on the performer with regard to voice and body training. The voice is sometimes used to emit odd sounds—screams, grunts, and the like. The body must perform feats of acrobatics and gymnastics.

10. The end result must be a synthesis or integration of the inner and outer aspects of acting.

11. Audience members should familiarize themselves with the problems and techniques of acting in order to judge performances properly.

The Director and the Producer

When we see a theatre performance, our most immediate connection is with the actresses and actors onstage. We begin to identify with the characters they play and absorb the situations in which they find themselves. Behind the performances, however, is the work of another creative person—the *director.* He or she, with the support of the stage manager, rehearses the performers and coordinates their work with that of others, such as the designers, to make certain the event is performed appropriately, intelligently, and excitingly. In this chapter, we will look at the role of the director, and also at the role of the producer or manager—the person who is responsible for the management and business aspects of theatre.

THE THEATRE DIRECTOR

The director works most closely with performers in the theatre, guiding them in shaping their performances. When a new play is being presented, the director also works closely with the playwright. The director is responsible, as well, for coordinating other aspects of the production, such as the work of the scene, costume, lighting, and sound designers. The stage manager communicates the breadth of the director's conceptual vision daily with every production area to clarify ongoing production and rehearsal choices.

For many audience members, the director's work on a production is one of the least obvious components. Other elements, such as performers, scenery, and costumes, are onstage and immediately visible to spectators, and the words of the playwright are heard throughout the performance. But audiences are often not aware that the way

◄ **THE DIRECTOR SHAPES A PRODUCTION**

The director of a production works closely with the cast and the designers (scenic, costumes, lighting, sound). If the production is a new play or musical, the director also collaborates with the writers and composers. The director gives shape to the arc of the play or musical, and determines its style, its pace during the production, and the way the actors create their characters and interact with one another. Joe Dowling is shown here directing actors on the set for a production of Shakespeare's A Midsummer Night's Dream *at the Guthrie Theater in Minneapolis. (© T Charles Erickson)*

photo essay

The Director at Work

(© Michael Kim/Corbis)

The director does most of his or her work in rehearsals with performers and in conferences with designers and technical personnel. Shown on these two pages are five directors rehearsing with actors and collaborating with designers and others.

Yukio Ninagawa directs actors at a dress rehearsal of one in a series of Yukio Mishima's all-male "modern nō" dramas, *Sotoba Komachi,* presented at the Lincoln Center Festival in 2005.

Mark Lamos (center) directed *Edgardo Mine,* by Alfred Uhry, at the Guthrie Theater.

(© T Charles Erickson)

Choreographer-director Bill T. Jones during a rehearsal with Sahr Ngaujah, who plays the title role in the musical *Fela!*

(© Richard Termine)

Director Emily Mann, center, with Yvette Freeman and Lizan Mitchell, stars of *Having Our Say: The Delany Sisters' First 100 Years,* at the McCarter Theatre in Princeton, New Jersey.

(© T Charles Erickson)

Director Mark Brokaw with *Pop*'s creators, Maggie-Kate Coleman and Anna K. Jacobs, at the Yale Repertory Theatre.

(Sara Krulwich/The New York Times/Redux)

HISTORICAL PERSPECTIVES

THE EVOLUTION OF THE DIRECTOR

It is sometimes argued that the theatre director did not exist before 1874, when a German nobleman, George II (1826–1914), duke of Saxe-Meiningen, began to supervise every element of the productions in the theatre in his realm. This supervision included rehearsals, scenic elements, and other aspects—which he coordinated into an integrated whole. It is true that beginning with Saxe-Meiningen, the director emerged as a full-fledged, indispensable member of the theatrical team, taking a place alongside the playwright, the performers, and the designers. Although the title may have been new, however, the *function* of the director had always been present in one way or another.

We know, for example, that the Greek playwright Aeschylus directed his own plays and that the chorus in a Greek play would rehearse under the supervision of a leader for many weeks before a performance. At various times in theatre history, the leading performer or playwright of a company served as a director, though without the title. The French dramatist Molière, for instance, not only was the playwright and the chief actor of his company but also functioned as the director. We know from Molière's short play *The Impromptu of Versailles* that he had definite ideas about the way actors and actresses should perform; no doubt the same advice he offered in that play was frequently given to his performers in rehearsal. When Hamlet gives instructions and advice to the players who perform the play-within-the-play in *Hamlet,* he is functioning as a director. In England after the time of Shakespeare—from the seventeenth century through the nineteenth—there was a long line of *actor-managers* who gave strong leadership to individual theatre companies and performed many of the functions of a director, although they were still not given that title. Among the most famous were Thomas Betterton (1635–1710), David Garrick (1717–1779), Charles Kemble (1775–1854), William Charles Macready (1793–1873), and Henry Irving (1838–1905).

Toward the end of the nineteenth century the term *director* came into common usage and the clearly defined role of the director was fully recognized. Perhaps significantly, the emergence of the director as a separate creative figure coincided with important changes which began to take place in society during the nineteenth century. First, there was a breakdown in established social, religious, and political concepts, resulting in part from the influence of Freud, Darwin, and Marx. Second, there was a marked increase in communication. With the advent of the telegraph, the telephone, photography, motion pictures, and—later—television, various cultures that had remained remote from or unknown to one another were suddenly made aware of each other. The effect of these two changes was to alter the monolithic, ordered view of the world that individual societies had maintained earlier.

Before these developments, consistency of style in theatre had been easier to achieve. Within a given society, writers, performers, and spectators were on common ground. For example, the comedies of the English playwrights William Wycherley (1640–1716) and William Congreve (1670–1729), written at the end of the seventeenth century, were aimed at a specific audience—the elite upper class, which relished gossip, clever remarks, and well-turned phrases. The code of social behavior was well understood by performers and audiences alike; and questions of style in a production hardly arose, because a common approach to style was already present in the fabric of society. The way a man took a pinch of snuff or a lady flung open her fan was so clearly delineated in daily behavior that performers had only to refine and perfect these actions for the stage. Today, however, because style, unity, and a cohesive view of society are so elusive, the director's task is more important.

performers speak and move, the way the scenery looks, and the way the lights change colors and intensity often originate with the director.

After the playwright, the director is usually the first person to become involved in the creative process of a production, and the choices made by the director at every step along the way have a great deal to do with determining whether the ultimate experience will be satisfactory for the spectators.

In Chapter 9, we will see that the playwright incorporates in his or her script a point of view toward the material being dramatized. It may be a tragedy, for example, a melodrama, or a comedy. It is crucial for the director to understand this point of view and translate it into terms relevant to the production, making it clear to the performers, designers, and other artists and technicians involved. Although they work together, these artists and technicians must out of necessity work on segments of the production rather than the entire enterprise. During rehearsals, for instance, the performers are much too busy working on their own roles and their interactions with each other to worry much about scenery. To take another example, a performer who appears only in the first act of a three-act play has no control over what happens in the second and third acts. The one person who does have an overall perspective is the director, and it is essential that this perspective is continually communicated by the production stage manager to everyone concerned, as he or she is the only other member of the production team to experience the entire rehearsal process with the director.

Directors get their training in a variety of ways. Many of them begin as actors and actresses and find that they have a talent for working with other people and for coordinating the work of designers as well as performers. Others train in the many academic institutions that have specific programs for directors. These include large universities with theatre as part of a liberal arts focus as well as special conservatories and institutes.

THE TRADITIONAL DIRECTOR

In this chapter we will look at three approaches to directing: traditional, auteur, and postmodern. We begin with the traditional approach, which might also be called a text-based method. In this approach the starting point, or the foundation, of the director's work is the script. It might be a well-known play by Shakespeare, Ibsen, or Strindberg, or a more recent work, such as one by Lorraine Hansberry or August Wilson. The play might also be a new script by a younger or emerging playwright.

The Director and the Script

For the most part, spectators experience theatre as a unified event. But, as pointed out before, theatre is a complex art involving not one or two elements but many simultaneously: script, performance, costumes, scenery, lighting, and point of view. These diverse elements—a mixture of the tangible and intangible—must be brought together into an organic whole, and that is the responsibility of the director.

Choosing a Script   Frequently, the director chooses the script to be produced. Generally it is a play to which the director is attracted or for which he or she feels a special affinity. If the director does not actually choose the script but is asked to direct it by a playwright or a producer, he or she must still understand and appreciate the material. The director's attraction to the script and basic understanding of it are important in launching a production. Once the script is chosen, the actual work on the production begins.

If the play is new and has never been tested in production, the director may see problems in the script, which must be corrected before rehearsals begin. The director will have a series of meetings with the playwright to iron out the difficulties ahead of time. The director may feel, for example, that the leading character is not clearly defined, or that a clash of personalities between two characters never reaches a climax. If the playwright agrees with the director's assessment, he or she will revise the manuscript. Generally there is considerable give-and-take between the director and the playwright in these preliminary sessions, as well as during the rehearsal period. The stage manager must maintain well-organized rehearsal documentation of possible script revisions for the playwright and director to discuss outside rehearsals. Ideally, there should be a spirit of cooperation, compromise, and mutual respect in this relationship.

Once the script is selected, the director begins analyzing it and preparing a production. There is no one way a director should go about this: individual directors adopt their own personal approach. One method of undertaking this task was suggested by the work of the Russian director Konstantin Stanislavsky. In this case, an initial step is to determine the *spine* of the play.

The "Spine" of the Play
The spine of the drama, also referred to as the *main action,* is determined by the goal, or the primary objective, of the scenes in the play, both collectively and individually. There is nothing magical about the spine: it is a working hypothesis that gives directors a foundation and a through-line on which to base their analysis and their work with the actors.

To illustrate how this takes place, let us consider Tennessee Williams's play *The Glass Menagerie,* in which the three main characters are a mother and her son and daughter. The mother is a faded southern belle who longs for the life she led as a young debutante in Mississippi. The son is an aspiring poet, now working in a shoe warehouse in St. Louis, trapped by the poverty of the family. The daughter is a shy girl with a bad limp who takes refuge in playing with her collection of glass animals. A possible spine for the play would be "realizing one's dream." Each character has a dream: the mother to return to her glory days, courted by "gentlemen callers"; the son to escape from his present life, in which he feels imprisoned; and the daughter to be left alone by her perpetually nagging mother.

Finding a spine for a play allows the director to understand the action and provides a nerve center from which to develop it. Different directors may find different spines for the same play. With *Hamlet,* for instance, several spines are possible: much will depend on the period in which the play is produced and on the point of view of the individual director. One spine could be simple revenge; another could be Hamlet's attempt to resolve his inner conflicts; still another could be Hamlet's attempt to locate and expose the duplicity and corruption he senses in Denmark. Such varied interpretations are to be expected and are acceptable as long as the spine chosen remains true to the spirit and action of the play. Whatever spine or main action is chosen by the director, the essential point to remember is that it must remain true to the script and to the intentions of the playwright.

The Style of the Production   Once a spine has been found, a second task for a director is to find the *style* in which the play is to be presented. The concept of style in a theatrical production is difficult to explain. It means the *way* a play is presented. When we speak of a "casual style" of clothing, we mean that the clothing is loose and informal; when we speak of a "1960s" style, we mean that it has the look and feel of clothing worn in the 1960s. In theatre, one way to consider style is in terms of realism and nonrealism. The differences between these two types were discussed in Chapter 2, but they can be further subdivided.

For example, there are several types of realism. At one extreme is **naturalism,** a kind of superrealism. The term *naturalism* was originated by several nineteenth-century French writers who wanted a theatre that would show human beings—often in wretched circumstances—as products of heredity and environment. In addition to this special use, the term *naturalism* refers more broadly to attempts to put onstage as exact a copy of life as possible, down to the smallest detail. In a naturalistic stage set of a kitchen, for instance, a performer can actually cook a meal on the stove, the toaster makes toast, the faucet produces water, and the light in the refrigerator goes on

THE DIRECTOR DETERMINES STYLE

One of the crucial decisions for a director is the style of a production, based largely on the script, but at times on other considerations as well. Once a style is chosen, the director must see to it that all the elements of a production—acting, movement, design—conform to that style. The avant-garde director Anne Bogart decided to present Sophocles's *Antigone* in a stark modern style at the Dance Theatre Workshop/SITI Company. Shown here are Makela Spielman, in the title role, with Leon Ingulsrud, and members of the chorus in the background. (Nicole Bengiveno/The New York Times/Redux)

when the door opens. Characters speak and act as if they had been caught unobserved by a sound camera. In this sense, naturalism is supposed to resemble an undoctored documentary film. Naturalism is sometimes called *slice-of-life* drama, suggesting that a section has been taken from life and transferred to the stage.

At the other extreme of realism is *heightened realism,* sometimes referred to as *selective realism.* Here the characters and their activities are intended to resemble life, but a certain license is allowed. The scenery, for example, might be skeletal—that is, incomplete and in outline—although the words and actions of the characters are realistic. Or perhaps a character is allowed a modern version of a soliloquy in an otherwise realistic play.

All art calls for selectivity, and heightened realism recognizes the necessity for the artist to make choices and to inject creativity into the process.

Realism itself occupies the middle ground between naturalism and heightened, or selective, realism; but when it is used as a broad umbrella term, it includes the extremes at each end.

Nonrealism can also be divided into types, which might include such forms as fantasy, poetic drama, musical theatre, absurdist theatre, and symbolism. Examples of two well-known types of nonrealism are *allegory* and *expressionism.*

Allegory is the representation of an abstract theme or subject through symbolic characters, actions, or other elements of a production, such as scenery. Good examples are the medieval morality plays, in which characters personify ideas in order to teach an intellectual or moral lesson. In *Everyman,* performers play the parts of Good Deeds, Fellowship, Worldly Goods, and so on. In less direct forms of allegory, a relatively realistic story serves as a parable or lesson. *The Crucible* by Arthur Miller is about the witch hunts in Salem, Massachusetts, in the late seventeenth century; but it can also be regarded as dealing with specific investigations by the United States Congress in the early 1950s that Miller and others considered modern "witch hunts."

Expressionism was at its height in art, literature, and theatre during the first quarter of the twentieth century, but traces of it are still found today, and contemporary plays using its techniques are called *expressionistic.* In simple terms, expressionism gives outward expression to inner feelings. In Elmer Rice's *The Adding Machine,* when the main character, Mr. Zero, is fired from his job, his feelings are conveyed by having the room spin around in a circle amid a cacophony of shrill sounds, such as loud sirens and whistles.

Deciding on a directorial style for a production involves giving a signature and an imprint to the entire production: the look of the scenery and lights, and the way performers speak and handle their costumes and props. It also involves the rhythm and pace at which the play moves, a subject that is taken up below.

When a director arrives at a style for a production, two things are essential: (1) the style should be appropriate for the play, and (2) it should be consistent throughout every aspect of the production.

The Directorial Concept One way for the director to embody the spine in a production and to implement style is to develop a *directorial concept.* Such a concept derives from a controlling idea, vision, or point of view that the director feels is appropriate to the play. The concept should also create a unified theatrical experience for the spectators.

GLOBAL CROSSCURRENTS

PETER BROOK: INTERNATIONAL DIRECTOR

The English director Peter Brook (b. 1925) presented some of the most memorable productions of the late twentieth century, a number of which drew extensively from the theatrical traditions and source materials of many countries. His major productions include Peter Weiss's *Marat/Sade* (1964), Shakespeare's *Midsummer Night's Dream* (1970), and his own adaptation of an Indian epic, *The Mahabharata* (1985). His best-known writings include *The Empty Space* (1968), *The Shifting Point* (1987), and *The Open Door* (1993).

As a means of escaping commercial theatre and allowing himself to address the universality of the theatrical experience, Brook founded the International Center for Theatre Research in Paris in 1970. This company was formed of actors from a variety of countries including Algeria, Japan, England, France, America, Spain, and Portugal, with directors from Armenia, England, and Romania and a designer from Switzerland. There was much sharing of ideas and techniques, with the Japanese actor teaching daily classes in nō, for example. Brook's vision was for the actors to learn from each other and to approach a kind of universal theatrical language. A production entitled *Orghast* (1971) first allowed the company to present its experimentation with language. The text was written by Ted Hughes in an invented language influenced heavily by Latin and ancient Greek, and was performed in Iran.

Peter Brook directing a rehearsal of *The Mahabharata* in Paris.
(© Julio Donoso/Corbis Sygma)

In 1989, Brook's continued interest in identifying a universality of language in theatre was manifest in his production of *The Mahabharata*. The source text for this play was the Indian epic of the same name, which is more than 90,000 verses long, concerns wars between the Pandavas and the Kauravas, and addresses a great number of philosophical questions. Brook's production of this epic text originally took place at the Avignon Festival in France and took a full nine hours to perform. The source text was Indian, the director English, the theatre company French, and the composer Japanese, and the actors were from all over the globe. This production, which toured widely, clearly drew from a large number of different cultures.

Although Brook has been criticized for exploiting some of his source material (such as *The Mahabharata*, which he greatly simplified), his work has shown a creative and continued interest in drawing from many different theatrical traditions. Unlike other directors who have "borrowed" certain aspects of other theatrical traditions, Brook has sought to use them to identify a common language or universality understood by them all.

Prepared by Naomi Stubbs, CUNY Graduate Center.

THE DIRECTORIAL CONCEPT

At times, directors create an overall image or metaphor for interpreting a play. This serves both to illuminate the text and to give the production unity and cohesion. Frequently the director develops an approach that throws new light on the text, or reminds us of past approaches to a play. The director Debbie Allen cast Tennessee Williams's *Cat on a Hot Tin Roof* with African American actors, headed by James Earl Jones and Phylicia Rashād. Because the play is set in Mississippi and had traditionally been performed with a white cast, Allen's approach was highly original. (© Joan Marcus)

Concept and Period   To indicate what is involved for the director in developing a concept, let us begin with period and location. Take, for instance, Shakespeare's play *The Tempest.* It is set on a faraway, remote island, and an air of mystery is present throughout the play. One director might take a traditional approach and present it as she or he believes it was performed in Shakespeare's day, with appropriate costumes and scenery. Another director might wish to set it in modern times on a secluded island in the Caribbean, with scenery and costumes reflecting a decidedly modern, Latin feeling, including calypso and other native music. A third director might take a *Star Wars* approach, placing the action at some future period on a small planet in outer space. In this case, performers arrive and depart by intergalactic rockets and wear futuristic space outfits.

This kind of transposition has been carried out frequently with Greek plays, Elizabethan plays, seventeenth-century French plays, and other dramatic classics.

Concept and Central Image   Another way to implement a directorial concept is to find a *central,* or *controlling, image* or *metaphor* for a theatrical production.

An example would be a production of *Hamlet* that envisioned the play in terms of a vast net or spiderweb in which Hamlet is caught. The motif of a net or spiderweb could be carried out on several levels: in the design of the stage set, in the ways the performers relate to one another, and in a host of details relating to the central image. There might be a huge rope net hanging over the entire stage, for instance, and certain characters could play string games with their fingers. In short, the metaphor of Hamlet's being caught in a net would be emphasized and reinforced on every level.

Concept and Purpose The directorial concept should serve the play. The best concept is one that remains true to the spirit and meaning of the script. A director who can translate that spirit and meaning into stage terms in an inspired way will create an exciting theatre experience; however, a director who is too intent on displaying his or her own originality may distort or violate the integrity of the script. For instance, a director might decide to make *Macbeth* into a cowboy play, with Duncan as a sheriff and Macbeth as a deputy who wants to kill the sheriff in order to take the job himself. In this version, Lady Macbeth would be the deputy's wife, whom he had met in a saloon. *Macbeth* could be done this way, but it might also come across as simply a gimmick—a means of calling attention to the director rather than to the script.

In most instances the best directorial concept is a straightforward one deriving from the play itself, not a scheme superimposed from outside.

The Director and the Dramaturg

A person who can be of great assistance to the director is the dramaturg, or literary manager. In Chapter 3 I pointed out that among the duties of the dramaturg are discovering promising new plays, working with playwrights on developing their scripts, identifying significant plays from the past that may have been overlooked, preparing material for teachers whose students will be attending performances, and writing articles for the programs that are distributed at performances. Of particular importance to directors is the work of dramaturgs in conducting research on previous productions of classic plays, as well as researching past criticism and interpretations of these plays.

It is easy to see how the work of the dramaturg can be of invaluable help to the director. In particular, the dramaturg can let the director know how previous directors have approached specific plays, and can assist the director in arriving at decisions regarding style, approach, and concept.

THE AUTEUR DIRECTOR AND THE POSTMODERN DIRECTOR

In addition to the traditional director, there are two other types of stage directors, who approach their work differently: the auteur director and the postmodern director. There are a number of similarities between the two, but we will look at them one at a time, beginning with the auteur director.

The Auteur Director

Auteur is a French word meaning "author." Just after World War II, French critics began using this term to describe certain film directors, who, they said, were really the authors of the films they made. In these films the point of view and the implementation of that

DYNAMICS OF DRAMA

MODERN VERSUS POSTMODERN PRODUCTION AESTHETICS

Modern	Postmodern
Organic unity	Interdisciplinary
Single view	No single view can predominate
Single viewer approach	Multiperspective, multifocus
Shared values of audience	Multicultural
Metaphorical or representational	Presentational
Linear	Nonlinear, simultaneous
Closeness	Distance
Time is singularly staged	Multiple time frames are presented simultaneously
Space is unified	Space is fragmented and can be simultaneously conceived

(Prepared by Tom Mikotowicz)

point of view came almost entirely from the director, not from a writer. The term has since been applied to a type of stage director as well. I am not speaking here of directors who alter the time or place in which the action occurs but retain the original script—the playwright's words, the sequence of scenes, and so forth. I am speaking rather of directors who make more drastic alterations or transformations in the material, taking responsibility for shaping *every* element in the production, including the script.

Interestingly, one of the first and most important auteur directors began his work with Stanislavsky and then went out on his own. He was the Russian director Vsevolod Meyerhold (1874–1940), and he developed a type of theatre in which he controlled all the elements. The script was only one of many aspects that Meyerhold used for his own purposes. He would rewrite or eliminate text in order to present his own vision of the material. Performers, too, were subject to his overall ideas. Often they were called on to perform like circus acrobats or robots. The finished product was frequently exciting and almost always innovative, but it reflected Meyerhold's point of view, strongly imposed on all the elements, not the viewpoint of a writer or anyone else.

Following in Meyerhold's footsteps, many avant-garde directors, such as Jerzi Grotowski (1933–1999), Richard Foreman, and Robert Wilson, can also be classified as auteur directors in the sense of demanding that a text serve their purposes, not the other way around. In some cases, such as many of Wilson's pieces, the text is only fragmentary and is one of the least important elements. In the former Soviet Union and eastern Europe, before the political changes of the early 1990s, certain directors, who had not been allowed to deal with material that questioned the government hierarchy, drastically reworked established texts in order to make a political comment. These directors, too, imposed their own vision, rather than that of the playwright, on the material. Another recent auteur director is Ivo van Hove, a Flemish director who enjoys reinventing the classics. In his *Streetcar Named Desire,* Blanche DuBois performs a good part of the play naked in a bathtub; and his version of *The Misanthrope* by Molière, which he transfers to the present day, features cell phones, laptops, BlackBerrys, and digital

TWO AUTEUR DIRECTORS

Robert Wilson is one of the foremost auteur directors in today's theatre. Such directors create their own theatre pieces, providing the vision and the interpretation. They serve not only as directors but as authors, taking elements from many sources and melding them into their own version of what we see onstage. The script or scenario is under their control, as are all the elements of the production. Shown in the photo above are (left to right) Rachel Eberhart, Benoît Maréchal, Ariel Garcia Valdès, and Isabelle Huppert in Robert Wilson's adaptation of *Quartett* by Heiner Müller. (© Richard Termine) Mary Zimmerman is another modern director who creates her own theatre pieces, controlling every aspect of a production and making it her own. Below is a scene from *Mirror of the Invisible World*, adapted and directed by Mary Zimmerman from twelfth-century epic Persian tales and presented at the Goodman Theatre in Chicago. (Photo: Liz Lauren)

cameras. Two additional highly regarded contemporary American auteur directors are Julie Taymor (b. 1952) and Mary Zimmerman (b. 1960).

The Postmodern Director

There is a great deal of overlap between the auteur director and the postmodern director. What is postmodernism? Probably the best way to answer the question is historically. The modern period in drama began in the late nineteenth century with plays like those of Ibsen and Strindberg that broke long-held taboos. The subject matter of their plays included explicit sexual content, social diseases, the subjugation of women, and the hypocrisy of religious figures. The twentieth century, therefore, was the period of modern drama.

At mid-century, however, there were people in theatre who felt that as advanced as theatre had become, it remained bound by the strictures of the text. In their minds this state of affairs did not properly reflect the chaos, the confusion, and the alienation of the world around us. Two groups especially advanced these ideas: the theoreticians who propounded the doctrine of postmodernism; and a series of stage directors who embodied postmodernism in their work with a radical, rebellious, free-form approach to theatre production.

What are the hallmarks of postmodern production? One, which began with Meyerhold and continued with Grotowski in his "poor theatre," was a taking apart of the text, often called *deconstruction,* in which portions of a text may be altered, deleted, taken out of context, or reassembled.

A second hallmark is the abandonment of a narrative or linear structure in a theatre piece. In Chapter 8 we will explain how Robert Wilson (b. 1941) and Richard Foreman (b. 1937) in his Ontological Hysteric Theatre both replace traditional structure with the use of segments, tableaux, and other nonsequential devices.

A third hallmark is unfamiliar, cross-gender, multicultural casting. Lee Breuer (b. 1937) in a Mabou Mines production of *King Lear* recast the title role as a female ranch owner in the southern United States who has difficulty leaving her inheritance to her three "good ole boy" sons. *The Emperor Jones* is a play by Eugene O'Neill (1888–1953) about the ruler of a Caribbean island who is gradually stripped of his powers. When the Wooster Group produced this play, an actress, Kate Valk, played the ruler, appearing in blackface. Sometimes the alteration of a script in this way results in a lawsuit. When the director Joanne Akalaitis (b. 1937) of Mabou Mines attempted to present an ethnically altered version of Samuel Beckett's *EndGame* in a New York subway, she was legally prevented from doing so by the Beckett estate.

A fourth hallmark of postmodern productions is the integration of dance, film, video, and computer material into the production.

In addition to those discussed above, other postmodern directors who deserve to be mentioned are Anne Bogart (b. 1951) and her SITI organization and Elizabeth LeCompte (b. 1944) with the Wooster Group.

THE DIRECTOR AND THE PRODUCTION

The Physical Production

While developing his or her approach to the play, the director is also working with the designers on the physical production. At the outset—once the director's concept is established—the director confers with the costume, scene, lighting, and sound designers to give visual shape and substance to the concept. It is the responsibility of designers to provide images and impressions that will carry out the style and ideas of the production. (See Chapters 10, 11, and 12.)

During the preproduction and rehearsal period, the director meets with the designers to make certain that their work is on schedule and keeping pace with the rehearsals. Obviously, the preparation of these elements must begin long before the actual performance, just as rehearsals must, so that everything will be ready by the time the performance itself takes place. Any number of problems can arise with the physical elements of a production. For example, the appropriate props may not be available, a costume may not fit a performer, or scene changes may be too slow. Early planning will allow time to solve these problems.

The Director's Work with the Performers

Casting   Now we come to the director's work with the performers. Along with choosing and developing a script and settling questions of concept, style, and the physical production, the director also casts the play.

In theatre, *casting* means fitting performers into roles; the term *casting* is derived from the phrase "casting a mold." Generally speaking, directors attempt to put performers into the roles for which their personalities and physical characteristics are best suited. A young actress will play Juliet in *Romeo and Juliet,* a middle-aged or elderly actor with a deep voice will play King Lear, and so on. When a performer closely resembles in real life the character to be enacted, this is known as *typecasting.* There are times, however, when a director will deliberately put someone in a role who does not appear to be right for the part. This is frequently done for comic or satiric purposes and is called *casting against type.* For example, a sinister-looking actor might be called on to play an angelic part.

As described in Chapter 5, in modern American theatre, performers frequently *audition* for parts in a play, and the director casts from those performers who audition. In an audition, actors and actresses read scenes from a play or perform portions of the script to give the director an indication of how they talk and move, and how they would interpret a part. From this the director determines whether or not a performer is right for a given role.

Historically, casting was rarely done by audition, because theatrical companies were more permanent. In Shakespeare's time, and in Molière's, certain people in a theatrical troupe always played certain parts: one person would play heroic roles, for example, while another always played clowns. Under these conditions, when a play was selected, casting was simply a matter of assigning roles to the performers who were on hand. Auditioning might take place only when a new member was being chosen for the company. Modern counterparts of these earlier theatrical companies are today's repertory companies in Europe and Great Britain, where theatre organizations like the Royal National Theatre and the Royal Shakespeare Company have a permanent group of actors and actresses. Another example would be a nō or kabuki troupe in Japan.

From the audience's standpoint, it is important to be aware of casting and the difference it can make to the effectiveness of a production. Perhaps an actor or actress is just right for the part he or she is playing. On the other hand, sometimes the wrong performer is chosen for a part: the voice may not be right, or the gestures or facial expressions may be inappropriate for the character. One way to test the appropriateness of casting is to imagine a different kind of actor or actress in a part while watching a performance.

Rehearsals   Once a play is cast, the director supervises all the rehearsals. He or she listens to and watches the performers as they go through their lines and begin to move about the stage.

Different directors work in different ways during the early phases of rehearsal. Some directors *block* a play in advance, giving precise instructions to the performers. (The term **blocking** means deciding when and where performers move and position themselves on the stage.) Other directors let the actors and actresses find their own movements, their own vocal interpretations, and their own relationships. And of course, there are directors who do a bit of both. Also, some directors want the actors to become thoroughly familiar with the script while they remain seated. Others wish to get the play "on its feet" as soon as possible, meaning that the actors are standing and moving about the rehearsal hall early in the process. Regardless of the director's approach to staging, the production stage manager keeps detailed notes of all the actors' movements and actions to help maintain consistency in the rehearsal process.

During the rehearsal process the director often begins with the cast sitting around a table, reading through the script and discussing the play in general, as well as individual scenes and roles. After this, the director may break down the script into segments or scenes, which will be rehearsed separately. Some scenes will involve only a few people; others, as in a Shakespearean play, may be crowd scenes. At a certain point, the actors will be expected to be "off book," meaning that they have memorized their lines. Gradually, scenes are put together, and an entire act is played without stopping. After that, individual scenes are refined, and then there is a run-through, when the play is performed straight through without stopping.

Throughout the rehearsal period, the director must make certain that the actors and actresses are realizing the intention of the playwright—that they are making sense of the script and bringing out its meaning. Also, the director must ensure that the performers are working well together—that they are listening to one another and beginning to play as an ensemble. The director must be aware of performers' needs, knowing when to encourage them and when to challenge or criticize them. The director must understand their personal problems and help them overcome such obstacles as insecurity about a role or fear of failure.

The Director as the Audience's Eye   One could say that there are two people in theatre who stand in for the audience, serving as surrogate or substitute spectators. One, the critic or reviewer (discussed in Chapter 3), does his or her work after the event; the other, the director, does his or her work before it.

In preparing a theatrical production, the director acts as the eye of the audience. During rehearsals, only the director sees the production from the spectator's point of view. For this reason, the director must help the performers to show the audience exactly what they intend to show. If one performer hides another at an important moment, if a crucial gesture is not visible, if an actor makes an awkward movement, if an actress cannot be heard when she delivers an emotional speech, the director points it out.

USING STAGE AREAS PROPERLY

One responsibility of the director is to make appropriate use of stage areas to create balance, emphasis, and striking visual effects. Note how the director Nicholas Martin has arranged the performers in this scene from Shakespeare's *Love's Labour's Lost* at the Huntington Theatre. Set design, Alexander Dodge; costume design, Mariann Verheyen; lighting design, Ben Stanton. (© T Charles Erickson)

Also, the director underscores the meaning of specific scenes through *visual composition* and *stage pictures,* that is, through the physical arrangement of performers onstage. The spatial relationships of performers convey information about characters. For example, important characters are frequently placed on a level above other characters—on a platform, say, or a flight of stairs. Another spatial device is to place an important character alone in one area of the stage while grouping other characters in another area. This causes the spectator's eye to give special attention to the character standing alone. Also, if two characters are opposed to each other, they should be placed in positions of physical confrontation onstage. Visual composition is more crucial in a play with a large cast, such as a Shakespearean production, than in a play with only two or three characters.

Certain areas onstage can assume special significance. A fireplace, with its implication of warmth, can become an area to which a character returns for comfort and reassurance. A door opening onto a garden can serve as a place where characters go

THE AUDIENCE'S RESPONSE

- Imagine that while you are watching a production, one performer is overacting badly, to the point that he or she is quite unbelievable. Another performer is listless and has no energy. In each case, to what extent do you think this is the director's fault, and to what extent the performer's failure?

- If you get bored or impatient when watching a performance, what do you think the director could have done in preparing the production to prevent this from happening?

- Is it fair to say, as some critics do, that when everything "clicks" in a production—that is, when the acting, the scenery and lighting, and the pace of the action all seem to be beautifully coordinated—the director's hand is "invisible"?

when they want to renew their spirits or relieve a hemmed-in feeling. By guiding performers to make the best use of stage space, the director helps them communicate important visual images to the audience—images consistent with the overall meaning of the play.

It is important to note, too, that directors must adjust their notions of blocking and visual composition to different types of stages: the arena stage, the thrust stage, and the proscenium stage (discussed in Chapter 4) call for different approaches to the performers' movements and the audience's sight lines.

Movement, Pace, and Rhythm   The director gives shape and structure to a play in two ways: in *space,* as was just described, and in time. Since a production occurs through time, it is important for the director to see that the *movement, pace,* and *rhythm* of the play are appropriate. If a play moves too quickly, if we miss words and do not understand what is going on, that is usually the director's fault. The director must determine whether there is too little or too much time between speeches or whether a performer moves across the stage too slowly or too quickly. The director must attempt to control the pace and rhythm within a scene and the rhythm between scenes.

One of the most common faults of directors is not establishing a clear rhythm in a production. An audience at a performance is impatient to see what is coming next, and the director must see to it that the movement from moment to moment and scene to scene has enough thrust and drive to maintain our interest. Variety is also important. If a play moves ahead at only one pace, whether slow or fast, the audience will become fatigued simply by the monotony of that pace. Rhythm within scenes and between scenes works on audience members subliminally, but its effects are very real. It enters our psyche as we watch a performance and thus contributes to our overall response.

It must be borne in mind as well that although pace, rhythm, and overall effect are initially the responsibility of the director, ultimately they become the performers' responsibility. Once a performance begins, the actors and actresses are onstage and the director is not. In cinema, pace and rhythm can be determined in the editing room; in theatre, by contrast, they are in the hands of the performers. Then, too, the audience's reaction will vary from night to night, and that will also alter pace and rhythm. The director must therefore instill in the performers such a strong sense of inner rhythm that they develop an internal clock which tells them how they should play.

TECHNICAL REHEARSAL
Before performances begin, a technical rehearsal is held. All the technical aspects—scenery, lighting, sound, costumes, props—are employed in the same sequence and manner as in performance. This is in order to see that everything is in proper working order and is coordinated. Shown here is a rehearsal at the Guthrie Theater in Minneapolis for a production of *When We Are Married* directed by John Miller-Stephany. Note the tables on which computers are being used by sound, light, and scenic designers to check out the running order and the coordination of all the elements. The set was designed by Frank Hallinan. (© T Charles Erickson)

Technical Rehearsal   Just before public performances begin, a *technical rehearsal* is held. The performers are onstage in their costumes with the scenery and lighting for the first time, and there is a *run-through* of the show from beginning to end, with all the props and scene changes. The stagehands move scenery, the crew handles props, and the lighting technicians control the dimming and raising of lights. The backstage crew must coordinate its work with that of the performers.

Let us say that one scene ends in a garden, and the next scene opens in a library. When the performers leave the garden set, the lighting fades, the scenery is removed, and the garden furniture is taken offstage. Then, the scenery for the library must be brought onstage by stagehands and the books and other props put in place. Next, the performers for the new scene in the library take their places as the lighting comes up. Extensive rehearsals are required to ensure that the lighting comes up at just the moment when the scenery is prepared and the performers are in place. Any mishap on the part of the stage crew, lighting crew, prop crew, or performers would affect the illusion and destroy the aesthetic effect of the scene change. The importance of the technical rehearsal is therefore considerable.

Because the technical rehearsal is held primarily to deal with all the mechanical and physical aspects of a production, the performers usually do not attempt to act convincingly or to convey deep emotion. Sometimes they are even told not to say all their lines but simply to jump "from cue to cue."

Dress Rehearsal   Just after the technical rehearsal, but before the first preview or tryout with an audience, the director will hold a ***dress rehearsal.*** The purpose of the dress rehearsal is to put all the elements together: the full involvement of the performers as well as the technical components. The dress rehearsal is a full-scale run-through of the production. It is performed as if an audience were present, with no stops or interruptions and with full lights, scenery, costumes, and sound. Sometimes a few people are invited—friends of the director or cast members—to provide some sense of an audience.

One function of the dress rehearsal is to give everyone concerned—cast, crew, and director—a sense of what the performance will be like. The dress rehearsal also allows for any last-minute changes before the first performance in front of a full audience.

Previews   Once the technical rehearsals and the dress rehearsal are completed and any problems are solved, the next step is a performance in front of an audience. I have stressed from the beginning the importance of performer-audience interaction and the fact that no play is complete until it is actually enacted for an audience. It is crucial, therefore, for a production to be tried out before a group of spectators. What has gone before, in terms of rehearsals and other elements, must now meet the test of combining harmoniously in front of an audience.

For this purpose there is a period of ***previews***—also called *tryouts*—when the director and the performers discover which parts of the play are successful and which are not. Frequently, for example, the director and performers find that one part of the play is moving too slowly; they know this because the audience members become restless and begin to cough or stir. Sometimes, in a comedy, there is a great deal of laughter where little was expected, and the performers and the director must adjust to this. In this preview period the audiences become genuine collaborators in shaping the play. After several performances in front of an audience, the director and the performers get the "feel" of the audience and know whether or not the play is ready. Throughout the final stages of preparing the production, the stage manager continues to give detailed notes to all actors to ensure consistency in dialogue and movement. Once the play has opened and the director is no longer present at every performance, it is the stage manager's responsibility to maintain consistency of the director's vision. In commercial theatre it is important to realize that stage managers and actors are members of the same union, Actors' Equity Association (AEA).

For an idea of the director's full range of responsibilities, see the chart on page 143.

THE DIRECTOR'S POWER AND RESPONSIBILITY

Any artistic event must have a unity not encountered in real life. We expect the parts to be brought together so that the total effect will enlighten us, move us, or amuse us.

In theatre, the director—who has a voice in so many areas of a production—is in a unique position to bring this about. This power, however, is a double-edged sword. If a director gets too carried away with one idea, for example, or lets the scene designer create scenery that overpowers the performers, the experience for the audience will be unsatisfactory or incomplete. If, on the other hand, the director has a strong point of view—one which is appropriate for the theatre piece and illuminates the script— and if all the parts fit and are consistent with one another, the experience will be meaningful and exciting, and at times even unforgettable.

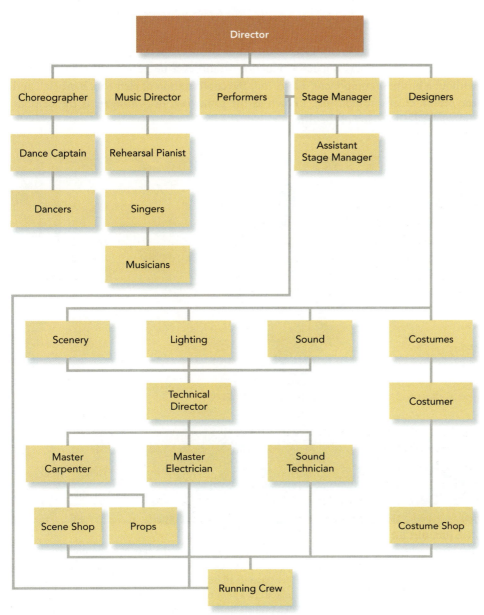

DUTIES OF A DIRECTOR IN A THEATRE PRODUCTION

Once a director has decided on a script (and has worked with the playwright, if it is a new play), he or she must organize the entire artistic side of the production. This chart indicates the many people that the director must work with and the many elements that must be coordinated.

THE AUDIENCE'S VIEW

While watching a production or experiencing a performance, a viewer does not have time to pause and analyze every aspect of the production, from the acting and the script to the visual and aural elements. There is even less time, perhaps, to analyze the work of the director. But the topics covered in this chapter should give audience members some idea of what might or might not be the responsibility of the director: when the director might be at fault for a failure, or, on the other side, when he or she should be given credit for the successful unfolding of a theatrical event.

THE PRODUCER OR MANAGER

A theatre audience naturally focuses on the event onstage rather than on what happens behind the scenes. But no production would ever be performed for the public without a business component. Here, too, the coordination of elements is crucial, and the person chiefly responsible, known as the ***producer,*** or ***manager,*** is the behind-the-scenes counterpart of the director.

THE PRODUCER

The person who puts a production together is the producer or, in the case of a nonprofit company, the artistic director. He or she selects the play or musical to be presented, and then decides who will carry out each function: direction, design, and all other elements. The producer must also see that all elements are properly coordinated. In a commercial production, the producer must in addition raise the necessary funds and determine a number of other factors such as advertising, marketing, and ticket prices. Shown here is Sonia Friedman, one of the busiest producers on both sides of the Atlantic, whose productions have won numerous awards including two Tonys. She is seen in her London office with her dog, Teddy. (Steve Forrest/The New York Times/Redux)

The Commercial Producer

In a commercial theatre venture, the producer has many responsibilities. (See the chart.) In general, the producer oversees the entire business and publicity side of the production and has the following duties:

1. Raising money to finance the production
2. Securing rights to the script
3. Dealing with the agents for the playwright, director, and performers
4. Hiring the director, performers, designers, and stage crews
5. Dealing with theatrical unions
6. Renting the theatre space
7. Supervising the work of those running the theatre: in the box office, auditorium, and business office
8. Supervising the advertising
9. Overseeing the budget and the week-to-week financial management of the production

It is clear that the responsibilities of the commercial producer range far and wide. They require business acumen, organizational ability, aesthetic judgment, marketing

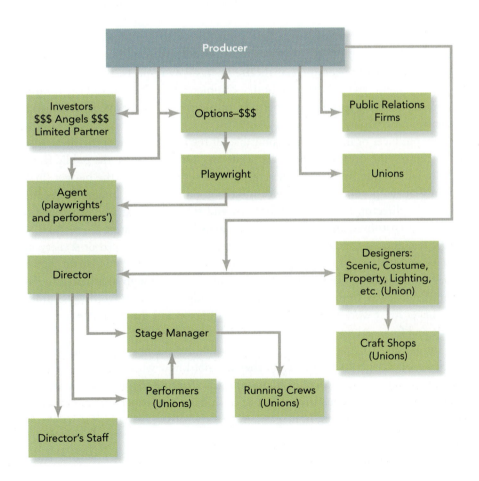

RESPONSIBILITIES OF THE COMMERCIAL THEATRE PRODUCER
When a commercial theatre production is mounted, the person responsible for organizing the full range of non-artistic activities is the producer. This chart shows the producer at the top and indicates the people the producer must deal with and the numerous elements he or she must coordinate.

know-how, and an ability to work with people. The producer in commercial theatre must have the artistic sensibility to choose the right script and hire the right director, but at the same time must be able to raise capital as well as oversee all financial and business operations in a production.

Noncommercial Theatres

In a nonprofit theatre the person with many of the same responsibilities as the producer is called the *executive director,* or *managing director.*

Administrative Organization of a Nonprofit Theatre

Most nonprofit theatres—including theatres in smaller urban centers as well as the large noncommercial theatres in major cities like New York, Chicago, and Los Angeles—are organized with a board of directors, an artistic director, and an executive or managing director. The board is responsible for selecting both the artistic and the managing director. The board is also responsible for overseeing the financial affairs of the theatre, for fundraising, for long-range planning, and the like. To carry out some of these tasks, the board frequently delegates authority to an executive committee.

The artistic director is responsible for all creative and artistic activities. He or she selects the plays that will constitute the season and chooses directors, designers, and other creative personnel. Frequently, the artistic director also directs one or more plays during the season.

Responsibilities of a Noncommercial Producer or Manager

The managing director in a noncommercial theatre is, in many respects, the counterpart of a producer in commercial theatre. In both a commercial production and the running of a nonprofit theatre organization, the tasks of the person in charge of administration are many and complex.

The producer or manager is responsible for the maintenance of the theatre building, including the dressing rooms, the scene and costume shops, the public facilities, and the lobby. The producer or manager is also responsible for the budget, making certain that the production stays within established limits. The budget includes salaries for the director, designers, performers, and stage crews, as well as expenditures for scenery, costumes, and music. Again, an artistic element enters the picture. Some artistic decisions—such as whether a costume needs to be replaced or scenery needs to be altered—affect costs. The producer or manager must find additional sources of money or must determine that a change is important enough artistically to justify taking funds away from another item in the budget. In other words, the producer or manager must work very closely with the director and the designers in balancing artistic and financial needs.

The producer or manager is also responsible for publicity. The audience members would never get to the theatre if they did not know when and where a play was being presented. The producer or manager must advertise the production and decide whether the advertisements should be placed in daily newspapers, on radio, on television, in student newspapers, in magazines, or elsewhere.

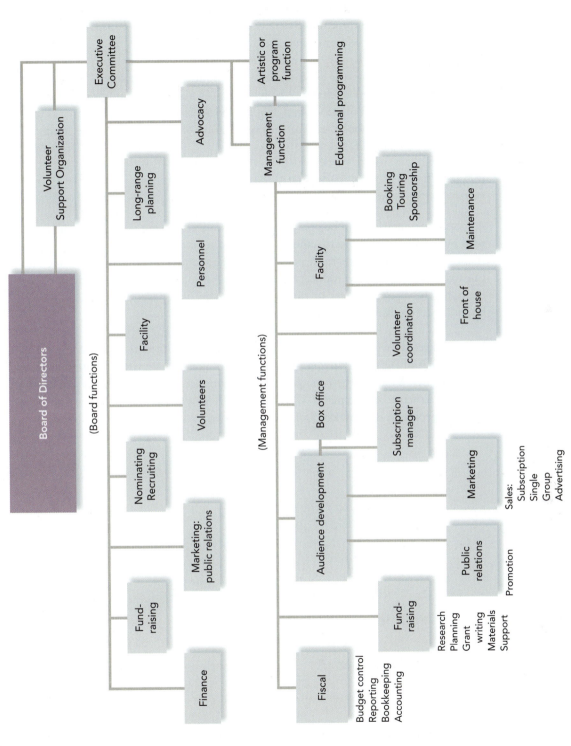

ORGANIZATIONAL STRUCTURE OF A NONPROFIT THEATRE COMPANY

A nonprofit theatre is a complex institution, with many facets. This chart shows the various activities that must be organized for the successful management of such a theatre.

A host of other problems come under the supervision of the producer or manager: tickets must be ordered, the box office must be maintained, and plans must be made ahead of time for how tickets are to be sold. Securing ushers, printing programs, and maintaining the auditorium—usually called the *front of the house*—are also the responsibility of the producer or manager.

Once again, plans must be made well in advance. In many theatre organizations, an entire season—the plays that will be produced, the personnel who will be in charge, and the supplies that will be required—is planned a year ahead of time. It should be clear that coordination and cooperation are as important in this area as they are for the production onstage. (For the organization of a nonprofit theatre company, see the chart on page 147.)

COMPLETING THE PICTURE: PLAYWRIGHT, DIRECTOR, AND PRODUCER

A theatre presentation can be compared to a mosaic consisting of many brightly colored pieces of stone that fit together to form a complete picture. The playwright puts the words and ideas together; the performers bring them to life; the director integrates the artistic elements; the producer or manager coordinates the business side of a production. The separate pieces in the mosaic must become parts of an artistic whole, providing a complete theatre experience.

In Part Three we will turn from the audience and the performers and director to the playwright and the play. How is a dramatic script created? By whom: a dramatist or someone else? What are the various choices a dramatist must make? What will be the dramatic structure of the piece? What point of view will the play reflect: will it be a tragedy, a comedy, or some combination of the two?

SUMMARY

1. The term *director* did not come into general use until the end of the nineteenth century. Certain functions of the director, however—organizing the production, instilling discipline in the performers, and setting a tone for the production—have been carried out since the beginning of theatre by someone in authority.

2. The director's duties became more crucial in the twentieth century. Because of the fragmentation of society and the many styles and cultures that now exist side by side, it is necessary for someone to impose a point of view and a single vision on individual productions.

3. The director has many responsibilities: working with the playwright if the script is a new work; evolving a concept or approach to the script; developing the visual side of the production with the designers; holding auditions and casting roles; working with the performers to develop their individual roles in rehearsals; ensuring that stage action communicates the meaning of the play; establishing appropriate pace and rhythm in the movement of the scenes; establishing the dynamics of the production as a whole; and supervising the technical and preview rehearsals.

4. *Auteur* directors demand that a text serve their own purposes, rather than shaping their purposes to serve the text. *Postmodern* directors often "deconstruct" a text or rearrange elements to create a theatre piece.

5. Because the director has such wide-ranging power and responsibilities, he or she can distort a production and create an imbalance of elements or an inappropriate emphasis. The director is responsible for a sense of proportion and order in the production.

6. The producer or manager of a production is responsible for the business aspects: maintaining the theatre, arranging publicity, handling finances, and managing ticket sales, budgets, ushers, etc.

3

Setting the Stage: The Playwright and the Play

CREATING THE PLAY: THE PLAYWRIGHT

Historically, the tone, shape, and point of view of a play are established by the dramatist. A major playwright of the twentieth century was Tennessee Williams. In his play *A Streetcar Named Desire,* set in New Orleans, Williams not only created a great atmosphere with his language, but put two characters opposite one another who were destined to create dramatic fireworks. Shown here, they are Blanche (Cate Blanchett) and Stanley (Joel Edgerton), in a production from Sydney, Australia, directed by Liv Ullman. (© Sara Krulwich/The New York Times/Redux)

Part Three

Setting the Stage: The Playwright and the Play

It begins with an impulse, a story, an event, an inspiration: a composer has an idea for a song or a symphony, a choreographer conceives of a ballet, a playwright has a story for a drama or a musical, an architect conceives of a building. Following that beginning, the person who envisions the artwork sets about putting the idea into a form that will be recognizable to those with whom he or she will be collaborating. What emerges is the musical score, the script, the blueprint that others can bring alive as an orchestral concert, a theatrical production, an imaginative piece of architecture. The finished script, musical score, or blueprint establishes guidelines that point everyone toward the ultimate realization of the idea.

A theatre production is a collaboration, not only between the audience and the performers but among a whole range of people who work together to make it happen: performers, directors, designers, technicians. All these are essential, but like any enterprise, a theatre production must begin somewhere, and in most cases that starting point is the script. For more than 2,000 years, in both the west and Asia, a script was understood to be the domain of the dramatist. Just like a Native American storyteller who passes down an oral tradition of myth and folklore from one generation to the next, the playwright was the person who chose a story to be told, selected the characters, determined the sequence of dramatic episodes, and wrote the dialogue for the characters to speak.

Like theatre, other forms of art also involve collaboration. For instance, in architecture a team of engineers, designers, and

Choreographer Christopher Wheeldon (right) rehearsing "Carousel (A Dance)" with dancers Kathryn Morgan and Andrew Veyette of the New York City Ballet. (© Paul Kolnik)

An often-repeated story is akin to a drama, with words, characters, and a plot. Here we see a storyteller repeating a folk legend to a group of Native American children on the Barona Indian Reservation. (© Bob Rowan/Corbis)

contractors will work to create the finished structure. It is the vision of the architect, however, that drives the project. In recent years, architects have used computer diagrams to render their plans, allowing the architect to create and be involved in many variations of his or her original idea. In the end, however, one plan is decided on—the equivalent of the blueprint, the script, the score, the scenario.

During the past 100 years, theatre artists other than the playwright have sometimes assumed the work of creating a script. One is the auteur director, who not only conceives and originates the work but also directs and controls what happens onstage. Two other developments in the twentieth century also provided alternative sources of theatre scripts. One was work resulting from ensemble theatre groups. Another was the single-person event: the performance artist.

It is important to understand that these alternative approaches have not eliminated the playwright; rather, in these cases other artists have taken the place of the playwright and have become "dramatists." The creation of a blueprint, a scenario, or script remains an essential element of creating a theatrical event.

Anyone who creates a theatre piece faces the same challenge: how to turn nontheatrical material into a viable work for the stage. At what point in the story does the dramatic action begin? Who are the characters; what actions are they given; what words do they speak? How are interest and excitement developed and maintained? How is suspense created and increased? Will the work be serious or comic, funny or sad? In the process of answering these questions, a script emerges—a script that is both the embodiment of a vision and a blueprint for a production.

Through the centuries, certain principles and strategies have emerged as most effective in creating a dramatic work. In Part Three we look at these principles and strategies, as well as the point of view that is adopted by the creator and that makes the work tragic or comic.

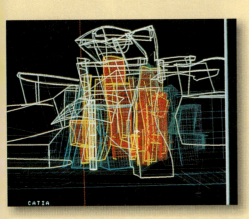

An architect conceives and designs a building in the way that a composer or dramatist creates a composition or a drama. Here is a computer rendering by the architect Frank Gehry to indicate the lines of his Guggenheim Museum in Bilbao, Spain. (© FMGB Guggenheim Bilbao Museoa. Photograph by Erika Barahona Ede. All rights reserved.)

A composer creates a musical score.
(© PhotoLink/Getty Images)

7

Creating the
World of the Play

Every dramatic presentation needs a starting point: a script or scenario on which a production is based. Historically, the person who provides the script is the playwright, though in recent years, others have sometimes assumed the work of creating a dramatic piece. At times it has been a director; at other times it has been a group of performers, or an ensemble, putting together a scenario. Such cases do not mean that the role of the playwright has been eliminated. They simply mean that someone else is fulfilling this role. The important point to remember is that whoever functions as the playwright must make a number of choices and must bear in mind certain principles of theatre that have proved successful through the years.

One of the first choices facing a person or persons creating a theatre piece is to determine the purpose of the work. People go to the theatre for any number of reasons: to be moved, to be entertained, to be challenged, to be inspired, to be amused. The dramatist must ascertain just what dramatic effect he or she wants to accomplish. Is the play intended to recall the past, to take people's minds off their troubles, or to rouse them to political action? The purpose can be any one of these, and many more. Sometimes a play has a combination of purposes: for example, to satirize and to amuse. Whatever the purpose, the dramatist must incorporate in the work a clear message of the intention of the play.

Other questions for the dramatist are what subject matter to present and which characters to include. Will the work be based on history—for example, an episode or incident from the American Civil War, from World War II, from the Vietnamese War,

◀ **THE PLAYWRIGHT CREATES THE TEMPLATE**

In undertaking to write a script, the playwright has a number of options. The intention may be to entertain; to raise timeless questions, as is often the case in tragedy; or to make a political or social comment. In any case, those who create a theatre script, whether playwrights or others, set the tone, the agenda, the approach to be followed by director, actors, designers, and others. An obvious master of achieving these elements is William Shakespeare. Seen here is a scene from Shakespeare's The Tempest, *presented by The Royal Shakespeare Company, directed by Janice Honeyman, with Antony Sher as Prospero and Atandwa Kani as Ariel. (© Geraint Lewis)*

FOCUS AND EMPHASIS

A playwright can choose to emphasize a particular character trait in one play and its opposite in another. Henrik Ibsen in his *Brand,* presents the leading character as a stark, uncompromising figure who will sacrifice everything—family, friends, love—for his principles. The leading character in Ibsen's *Peer Gynt,* however, is always compromising, always running away. In this scene Peer Gynt is played by Mark Rylance (wearing the crown) in a version translated and adapted by Robert Bly, directed by Tim Carroll at the Guthrie Theater in Minneapolis. (© Michal Daniel)

or from the war in Iraq? Perhaps it will be based on biography—on the life of Eleanor Roosevelt or Martin Luther King Jr. Perhaps it will be an exploration of the creator's own life—facing the problems of growing up or facing a personal crisis as an adult. Still another possibility would be an imaginary story, either resembling everyday life or based on a fantasy or a nightmare.

Along with the subject to be dramatized, there is also the question of who and what to focus on. For example, a playwright can emphasize a particular character trait in one play and its opposite in another. This is what Henrik Ibsen often did. In his *Brand,* the leading character is a stark, uncompromising figure who will sacrifice everything— family, friends, love—for his principles. In contrast, the leading character in Ibsen's *Peer Gynt* is just the opposite: always compromising, always running away.

In creating a theatre piece there is great leeway in making a number of decisions. For instance, a playwright can determine the order of events in a play. A good example is the way the myth of Electra was treated by three prominent tragic dramatists in Greece in the fifth century BCE. The story concerns Electra's revenge on her mother, Clytemnestra, and her stepfather, Aegisthus, for having murdered her natural father, Agamemnon. In carrying out her revenge, Electra enlists the help of Orestes, her brother, who has just returned from exile. In the versions by Aeschylus and Euripides, the stepfather is murdered first, and the mother, Clytemnestra, is murdered last. This puts emphasis on the terror of murdering one's own mother. But Sophocles saw the story differently.

He wanted to emphasize that Electra and her brother were acting honorably and to play down the mother's murder. And so he reversed the order of the murders: he had the mother killed first; then he built up to the righteous murder of the stepfather as the final deed. The change made by Sophocles indicates the latitude writers, directors, and performance artists have in altering events to suit their artistic purposes.

Still another choice open to a dramatist is what degree of seriousness to convey, or what point of view to take toward the subject of the drama: will it be comic or tragic, sympathetic or satiric, cynical or celebratory?

THE SUBJECT AND VERB OF DRAMA: PEOPLE AND ACTION

Before turning to the specifics of creating a dramatic work, we should note an important point about the nature of drama. As I previously mentioned, the subject of theatre is always people—their hopes, their joys, their foibles, their fears. In other words, if we were to construct a "grammar of theatre," the *subject* would be people: that is, dramatic characters. In grammar, every subject needs a verb; so, in the grammar of theatre, dramatic characters need some form of action that defines them.

The terms *to act* and *to perform* are used in theatre to denote the impersonation of a character by an actor or an actress, but these words also mean "to do something," or "to be active." The word *drama* derives from a Greek root, the verb *dran,* meaning "to do" or "to act." At its heart, theatre involves action. One way to provide action is to create a test or challenge for the characters. The American dramatist Arthur Miller named one of his plays *The Crucible.* Literally, a *crucible* is a vessel in which metal is tested by being exposed to extreme heat. Figuratively, a crucible has come to stand for

THE CRUCIBLE OF DRAMA
Theatre requires conflict: between people; among family members; between opposing nations, ideologies, or political agendas. Here we see a strong family conflict unfolding in *August: Osage County* by Tracy Letts. The daughter, on the left, is engaging in fierce, volatile combat with her mother, seated on the right. Deanna Dunagan, right, plays Violet Weston, the family matriarch; Amy Morton, left, plays her daughter, Barbara Fordham; Rondi Reed, center, plays Violet's sister, Mattie Fae. (Sara Krulwich/ The New York Times/Redux)

any severe test of human worth and endurance—a trial by fire. In a sense, every play provides a crucible: a test devised by the playwright to show how the characters behave under conditions of stress. Through this test, the meaning of the play is brought out.

STRUCTURAL CONVENTIONS: THE RULES OF THE GAME

Despite the options open to a dramatist with regard to the focus of the drama and the characters involved, there is one thing every dramatist is compelled to do if the work is to succeed as a theatre piece, and that is to transform the raw material of the drama into a viable work for the stage. In order to make certain that the events onstage will be dynamic and that the characters will face a meaningful test, conventions or "ground rules" have evolved for dramatic structure. A good analogy would be the rules in games such as card games, board games, video games, and sports. In each case, rules are developed to ensure a lively contest.

Consider, for example, how theatre can be compared to sports. Theatre is more varied and complex than most sports events, and theatrical rules are not so clearly defined or so consciously imposed as rules in sports. Nevertheless, there are similarities that highlight the ways a play makes its impact.

Limited Space

Most sports have a limited playing area. In some cases this consists of a confined space: a boxing ring, a basketball court, a baseball field. The playing area is clearly defined, and invariably there is some kind of "out of bounds."

LIMITED SPACE

In his play *No Exit,* Jean-Paul Sartre presents three characters involved in an impossible love triangle confined to one room, from which, as the title suggests, there is no escape. Karen MacDonald as Estelle, Will Lebow as Garcin, and Paula Plum as Inez are shown in this scene, directed by Jerry Mouawad at the A.R.T. in Boston. (© T Charles Erickson)

Theatre, of course, is usually limited to a stage; but there is also a limit within the play itself. The action of a play is generally confined to a "world" of its own—that is, to a fictional universe which contains all the characters and events of the play—and none of the characters or actions moves outside the orbit of that world.

Sometimes the world of a play is restricted to a single room. In his play *No Exit*, Jean-Paul Sartre (1905–1980), a French existentialist, confines three characters to one room, from which, as the title suggests, there is no escape. The room is supposed to be hell, and the three characters—a man, Garcin; and two women, Estelle and Inez—are confined there forever. Estelle loves Garcin, Garcin loves Inez, and Inez (a lesbian) loves Estelle. Each one, in short, loves the one who will not reciprocate; and by being confined to a room, they undergo permanent torture. There are numerous modern plays in which the action takes place in a single room, a good example being *'Night, Mother* by Marsha Norman (b. 1947), about a mother and daughter in crisis, which takes place in their rural home.

Limited Time

Sports events put some limit on the duration of action. In football and basketball, there is a definite time limit. In golf, there is a given number of holes; in tennis, there is a limited number of sets. Theoretically, some sports, such as baseball, are open-ended and could go on forever; but spectators tend to become impatient with this arrangement. Tennis, for instance, was originally open-ended but now has a "sudden death" or tiebreaker play-off when a set reaches six-all. A time limit or score limit ensures that the spectators can see a complete event, with a clear winner and loser and no loose ends.

The time limit in theatre can be looked at in two ways: first, as the length of time it takes a performance to be completed; second, as the time limit placed on the characters within the framework of the play itself. These are both examined below.

Most theatrical performances last anywhere from 1 to 3 hours. In the drama festivals of ancient Greece, plays were presented for several days in a row. On a single day there might be a trilogy of three connecting plays followed by a short comic play. Still, even if we count a Greek trilogy as one play, it lasted only the better part of a day.

More important than the actual playing time of a performance is the time limit or deadline *within* the play. This means the time that is supposed to elapse during the events of the play, the time covered by those events—a few hours, a few days, or longer. Frequently, we find in a play a fixed period within which the characters must complete an action. For instance, at the end of the second act of Ibsen's *A Doll's House*, the heroine, Nora, is trying desperately to persuade her husband to put off until the following evening the opening of a letter that she fears will establish her as a forger and will threaten their marriage. When he agrees, Nora says to herself, "Thirty-one hours to live."

Strongly Opposed Forces

Most sports, like many other types of games, involve two opposed teams or individuals. This ensures clear lines of force: the old guard versus the young upstarts, the home team versus the visitors. The musical *West Side Story* (based on Shakespeare's *Romeo and Juliet*) features two opposed gangs, not unlike opposing teams in sports. In the

simplest dramatic situations, one character directly opposes another—the ***protagonist*** against the ***antagonist.***

The man and woman, Julie and Jean, in Strindberg's *Miss Julie* are a perfect example of characters bound to clash. Julie, an aristocrat, is the daughter of the owner of an estate. She has had an unhappy engagement and is deeply suspicious of men, but at the same time sexually attracted to them. Jean is a servant, an aggressive man who dreams of escaping his life of servitude and owning a hotel. These two characters experience strong forces of repulsion and attraction and are drawn together on mid-summer eve in a climactic encounter.

One device frequently used by dramatists to create friction or tension between forces is restricting the characters to the members of one family. Relatives have built-in rivalries and affinities: parents versus children, sisters versus brothers. Being members of the same family, they have no avenue of escape. Mythology, on which so much drama is based, abounds in familial relationships.

Shakespeare frequently set members of one family against one another: Hamlet opposes his mother; Lear opposes his daughters; Othello kills his wife, Desdemona. In modern drama, virtually every writer of note has dealt with close family situations: Ibsen, Strindberg, Chekhov, Williams, Miller, and Edward Albee (b. 1928), to mention a few. The American dramatist Eugene O'Neill wrote what many consider his finest play, *Long Day's Journey into Night,* about the four members of his own family.

A Balance of Forces

In most sports, there are rules designed to ensure that the contest will be as equal as possible without coming to a draw. We all want our team to win, but we would rather see a close, exciting contest than a runaway. And so rules are set up, with handicaps or other devices to equalize the forces. In basketball or football, for instance, as soon as one team scores, the other team gets the ball so that it will have an opportunity to even the score.

In theatre, a hard-fought and relatively equal contest is implicit in what has been said about opposing forces: Jean stands opposite Julie, for example, in *Miss Julie.* Even in the somewhat muted, low-key plays of Anton Chekhov, there is a balance of

MEMBERS OF A FAMILY IN CONFLICT
Shakespeare frequently set members of one family against one another: Hamlet opposes his mother; Lear opposes his daughters; Othello kills his wife, Desdemona. Pictured here are Ian McKellen as King Lear and Monica Dolan as his daughter Regan in a Royal Shakespeare Company production directed by Trevor Nunn. (© Geraint Lewis)

forces among various groups. In *The Cherry Orchard,* the owners of the orchard are set against the man who will acquire it; in *The Three Sisters,* the sisters are opposed in the possession of their home by their acquisitive sister-in-law.

Incentive and Motivation

In sports, as in other kinds of games, a prize is offered to guarantee that the participants will give their best in an intense contest. In professional sports it is money; in amateur sports, a trophy, such as a cup. In addition, there is the glory of winning, as well as the accolades of television and the press and the plaudits of family and friends.

In the same way, good drama never lacks incentive or motivation for its characters: Macbeth wants desperately to be king in *Macbeth,* and Blanche DuBois must find protection and preserve her dignity in *A Streetcar Named Desire.*

CREATING STRUCTURE

Applying the principles and conventions outlined above, the dramatist sets about developing a dramatic structure for the theatre piece. Every work of art has some kind of structure, or framework. It may be loosely connected or tightly knit; the important thing is that the framework exists. In theatre, structure usually takes the form of a *plot,* which is the arrangement of events or the selection and order of scenes in a play. Plot, in turn, is generally based on a *story.*

Plot versus Story

Stories—narrative accounts of what people do—are as old as the human race, and they form the substance of daily conversation, of newspapers and television, of novels and films. But every medium presents a story in a different form. In theatre, the story must be presented in a limited period of time by living actors and actresses on a stage, and this requires selectivity.

It is important to remember that the plot of a play differs from a story. A story is a full account of an event, or series of events, usually told in chronological order. Plot is a selection and arrangement of scenes taken from a story for presentation onstage. It is what actually happens onstage, not what is talked about. The story of Abraham Lincoln, for example, begins with his birth in a log cabin and continues to the day he was shot at Ford's Theater in Washington. To create a play about Lincoln, a playwright would have to make choices. Would the dramatist include scenes in Springfield, Illinois, where Lincoln worked as a lawyer and held his famous debates with Stephen Douglas? Or would everything take place in Washington after Lincoln became president? Would there be scenes with Lincoln's wife, Mary Todd, or would the other characters be only government and military officials? The plot of a play about Abraham Lincoln and Mary Todd would have scenes and characters related primarily to their lives. The plot of a play about the Lincoln-Douglas debates would consist mostly of scenes relating to the debates. Even when a play is based on a fictional story invented by the playwright, the plot must be more restricted and structured than the story itself: characters and scenes must still be selected and the sequence determined.

THE OPENING SCENE

The first scene of a play is crucial, usually setting the location; establishing mood and tone; and introducing characters, themes, and action. A famous opening scene is that in Shakespeare's *Romeo and Juliet,* in which the Capulet and Montague families confront each other in a street fight. Shown here is the opening scene in a production directed by Dominic Dromgoole at Shakespeare's Globe, with Ukweli Roach as Tybalt and Philip Cumbus as Mercutio in the foreground. (© Geraint Lewis)

The Opening Scene

The first scene of a drama starts the action and sets the tone and style for everything that follows. It tells us whether we are going to see a serious or a comic play and whether the play will deal with fantasy or with affairs of everyday life. The opening scene is a clue or signal about what lies ahead. It also sets the wheels of action in motion, giving the characters a shove and hurtling them toward their destination.

The playwright poses an initial problem for the characters, establishing an imbalance of forces or a disturbance in their equilibrium that compels them to respond. Generally, this imbalance has occurred just before the play begins, or it develops immediately after the play opens. In *Antigone,* for example, two brothers have killed each other just before the opening of the play. In *Hamlet,* "something is rotten in the state of Denmark," and early in the play the ghost of Hamlet's father tells Hamlet to seek revenge. At the beginning of *Romeo and Juliet,* the Capulets and the Montagues are at one another's throats in a street fight.

Obstacles and Complications

Having met the initial challenge of the play, the characters then move through a series of steps—alternating between achievement and defeat, between hope and despair. The moment they seem to accomplish one goal, certain factors or events cut across the play to upset the balance and start the characters on another path. In theatre these may be ***obstacles,*** which are impediments put in a character's way; or they may be ***complications***—outside forces or new twists in the plot introduced at an opportune moment.

Shakespeare's *Hamlet* provides numerous examples of obstacles and complications. Hamlet stages a "play within the play" in order to confirm that his uncle Claudius has killed his father. Claudius reacts to the play in a manner that makes his guilt obvious. But when Hamlet first tries to kill Claudius, he discovers him at prayer. An obstacle has been thrown into Hamlet's path: if Claudius dies while praying, he may go to heaven rather than to hell. Since Hamlet does not want Claudius to go to heaven, he does not kill him.

Later, Hamlet is in his mother's bedroom when he hears a noise behind a curtain. Surely Claudius is lurking there, but when Hamlet thrusts his sword through the curtain, he finds that he has killed Polonius. This provides Claudius with an excuse to send Hamlet to England with Rosencrantz and Guildenstern, who carry with them a letter instructing the king of England to murder Hamlet. Hamlet escapes that trap and returns to Denmark. Now, at last, it seems that he can carry out his revenge. But on his return, he discovers that Ophelia has killed herself while he was away, and her brother, Laertes, is seeking revenge on him. This complicates the situation once again, as Hamlet is prevented from meeting

PLOT COMPLICATIONS IN HAMLET
In conventional plot structure, the action is prolonged and tension is increased by a series of problems confronting the characters. The twists and turns in the plot of Shakespeare's *Hamlet* are an example. Shown here is David Tennant as Hamlet, preparing to kill King Claudius (Patrick Stewart), who he thinks has murdered his father. Hamlet hesitates because he does not want to send Claudius to heaven, as he fears might happen if he kills Claudius at prayer. This was a Royal Shakespeare Company production directed by Gregory Doran. (© Geraint Lewis)

Claudius head-on because he must also deal with Laertes. In the end Hamlet does carry out his mission, but only after many interruptions.

Crisis and Climax

As a result of conflicts, obstacles, and complications in a play, the characters become involved in a series of *crises.* A play usually builds from one crisis to another. The first crisis will be resolved only to have the action lead to a subsequent crisis. The final and most significant crisis is referred to as the *climax.* In the final climax the issues of the play are resolved, either happily or, in the case of tragedies, unhappily, often with the death of the hero or heroine.

It should be noted that this notion of a series of crises leading to a climax applies most readily to traditional plays—that is, works created before the modern period. During the past 100 years, a number of variations of classic plot structure have appeared in which the notion of a climax has been either eliminated or minimized. These approaches to structure will be looked at in detail in Chapter 9.

POINT OF VIEW

In addition to structure and character portrayal, the person or persons creating a dramatic work must determine the point of view represented in the work: will it be tragic or comic, humorous or sad, or perhaps a mixture of the two?

People and events can always be interpreted in widely different ways. How we perceive them depends on our point of view. There is a familiar story of two people looking at a bottle that is partly full of wine. The optimist will say that the bottle is half-full, the pessimist that it is half-empty.

Anyone familiar with the presentation of evidence in a courtroom—in a trial involving an automobile accident, for instance—knows that different witnesses, each of whom may be honest and straightforward, will describe the same incident differently. One will say that she saw a minivan go through a stoplight and hit a blue car; another will say that he remembers clearly that the blue car pulled out before the light had changed and blocked the path of the van. The same variation in viewpoint affects our assessment of politicians and other public figures. To some people, a certain politician will be a dedicated, sincere public servant, interested only in what is best for the nation. But to others, the same politician will be a hypocrite and a charlatan.

Point of view is particularly important in the arts. Under ordinary circumstances, those who attempt to influence our point of view, such as advertisers and politicians, frequently disguise their motives. They use subtle, indirect techniques to convince us that they are not trying to impose their views on us, though people who understand the process know that this is exactly what an advertiser or a politician is trying to do. In the arts, on the other hand, the imposition of a point of view is direct and deliberate. The artist makes it clear that he or she is looking at the world from a highly personal and perhaps unusual angle, possibly even turning the world upside down.

In films, for example, we have become familiar with the various points of view, angles of vision, and perspectives that the camera selects for us. In a close-up, we do not see an entire room or even an entire person—we see one small detail: hands on a computer keyboard or a finger on the trigger of a gun. In a medium shot we see more—a couple embracing, perhaps—but still only part of the scene. In an exterior

THE INDIVIDUAL POINT OF VIEW

In addition to the social and cultural climate, the individual artist's outlook also determines whether a work will be serious or comic. Even two people writing in the same country at the same time will view the world differently. In seventeenth-century France, Racine wrote mostly tragedies, such as *Phèdre.* Shown above (left) is a London production at the National Theatre featuring Helen Mirren in the title role with Dominic Cooper as Hippolytus, directed by Nicholas Hytner. (© Geraint Lewis) However, in the same period Racine's countryman and contemporary, Molière, wrote comedies like *The School for Wives.* On the right are Bruce Cromer as Arnolphe and Erin Partin as Agnes in a New Jersey Shakespeare Festival production directed by Brian B. Crowe. (© Gerry Goodstein)

scene we might have a panorama of the Grand Canyon or a military parade. The camera also predetermines the angle from which we see the action. In a scene emphasizing the strength of a figure, the camera might look up from below to show a person looming from the top of a flight of stairs. In another scene we might look down on the action. In still other instances the camera might be tilted so that a scene looks off balance; a scene might be shot out of focus so that it is hazy or blurred, or it might be filmed through a special filter.

Similarly, the viewpoint of the theatre artist tells us how to interpret the words and actions of the characters we see onstage; it provides a key to understanding the entire experience.

DYNAMICS OF DRAMA

STRUCTURE IN WOMEN'S PLAYS

As a result of the women's movement of the 1970s, some feminist theatre critics examined Aristotle's *Poetics* and suggested that his concept of the ideally structured tragedy, which had been the template for western drama for centuries, reflected the west's dominant male culture. Radical feminist theorists, for instance, saw the plot complications, crisis, and denouement in tragedy as a duplication of the male sexual experience of foreplay, arousal, and climax. Other feminist critics viewed traditional linear, cause-and-effect plot development as a reflection of the step-by-step approach that men have traditionally used to empower their lives and control society. The leading figures, or subjects, of these plays, according to feminist critics, were invariably male.

To counter this Aristotelian tradition, feminist theatre critics and practitioners aimed to create what Professor Sue-Ellen Case, in her groundbreaking book *Feminism and Theatre* (1988), called a "new poetics." The idea was to explore a "women's form" of drama, and also to construct new, feminist ways of analyzing and responding to theatrical texts and performance.

Among the pioneers was the French feminist and playwright Hélène Cixous (b. 1937), who, in her famous essay "The Laugh of the Medusa," called for women to create a new language that would be suggestive and ambiguous. Other feminists called for a dramatic form that stressed "contiguity," a form, writes Case, which is "fragmentary rather than whole" and "interrupted rather than complete." This form is often cyclical and without the single climax. It is frequently open-ended and offers woman as subject. One example is *Fefu and Her Friends,* written and directed in 1977 by the Cuban-born American dramatist Maria Irene Fornés (b. 1930). Instead of a plot, there is a cyclical, physical action; and in place of logical cause and effect, Fornés writes each scene as though it were a new event. There is no hero; the subject of the play is a group of educated women sharing thoughts and ideas.

Not all feminists have embraced the new poetics. But increasingly, feminists have experimented with dramatic form and theatrical styles, to confront, expose, and rewrite what they see as centuries of male cultural domination.

Prepared by Alexis Greene.

The Dramatist's Point of View

"There is nothing either good or bad, but thinking makes it so," Shakespeare wrote in *Hamlet.* To this could be added a parallel statement: "There is nothing either funny or sad, but thinking makes it so." One's point of view determines whether one takes a subject seriously or laughs at it, whether it is an object of pity or of ridicule.

Horace Walpole (1717–1797), an English author, wrote: "This world is a comedy to those that think, a tragedy to those that feel." Walpole's epigram underlines the fact that people see the world differently. It is difficult to say just why some people look at the world and weep while others look at it and laugh, but there is no question that they do.

In theatre, point of view begins when a dramatist, a director, or a performance artist takes a strong personal view of a subject, deciding that it is grave, heroic, or humorous. As in other art forms, opportunities for selectivity are greater than in everyday life; hence a point of view can be adopted in drama consciously and deliberately.

In the case of a play, point of view is incorporated by the playwright into the script itself, with characters being given words to speak and actions to perform which convey a certain attitude. In a serious work the writer will choose language and actions suggesting sobriety and sincerity.

Take the lines spoken by Shakespeare's Othello:

> Oh, now for ever
> Farewell the tranquil mind! Farewell content!
> Farewell the plumed troop and the big wars
> that make ambition virtue!

These words express unmistakably Othello's profound sense of loss.

Another writer might take what is ordinarily a serious subject and treat it humorously. A good example is Arthur Kopit (b. 1937), who gave a comic twist to a dead body in his play *Oh, Dad. Poor Dad. Mama's Hung You in the Closet, and I'm Feelin' So Sad.* The title itself, with its mocking tone and its unusual length, makes it clear from the beginning that Kopit wants us to laugh at his subject. Once the playwright's intentions are known, the director and the performers transmit them to the audience.

Society's Point of View

In discussing point of view, we cannot overlook the role that society plays in the viewpoint adopted by an artist such as a playwright. As discussed in Chapter 3, there is a close relationship between theatre and society. This relationship manifests itself particularly in the point of view artists adopt toward their subject matter.

Tragedy, for example, generally occurs in periods when society as a whole assumes a certain attitude toward people and toward the universe. Two periods conducive to the creation of tragedy were the golden age of Greece in the fifth century BCE and the Renaissance in Europe during the fourteenth, fifteenth, and sixteenth centuries CE. Both periods incorporated two ideas essential to tragic drama: on the one hand, a concept of human beings as capable of extraordinary accomplishments; and on the other, the notion that the world is potentially

A CLIMATE FOR TRAGEDY

The worldview of a society is one factor that determines whether it will embrace and encourage tragedy. Some cultures, such as Athens in the fifth century BCE and Elizabethan England, were particularly conducive to the creation of tragic drama. Shakespeare's *Othello* is a good example. Shown here are Othello and Desdemona, played by John Douglas Thompson and Juliet Rylance. (Katie Orlinsky/The New York Times/Redux)

cruel and unjust. A closer look at these two periods will demonstrate how they reflect these two viewpoints.

In both the fifth century BCE in Greece and the Renaissance in continental Europe and England, human beings were exalted above everything else. The gods and nature were given a much less prominent place in the scheme of things. The men and women of those periods considered the horizons of human achievement unlimited. In the fifth century BCE, Greece was enjoying its golden age in commerce, politics, science, and art; nothing seemed impossible in the way of architecture, mathematics, trade, or philosophy. The same was true in Europe and England during the centuries of the Renaissance. Columbus had reached the new world in 1492, and the possibilities for trade and exploration appeared infinite. Science and the arts were on the threshold of a new day as well.

In sculpture during the two periods, the human figure was glorified as it rarely had been before or has been since, and the celebration of the individual was apparent in all the arts as well, including drama. The Greek dramatist Sophocles exclaimed:

> Numberless are the world's wonders, but none
> More wonderful than man.

And in the Renaissance, Shakespeare has Hamlet say:

> What a piece of work is man! How noble in reason! How infinite in faculty! In form, in moving, how express and admirable! In action how like an angel! In apprehension how like a god!

The credo of both ages was expressed by Protagoras, a Greek philosopher of the fifth century BCE:

> Man is the measure of all things.

But there is another side to the tragic coin. Along with this optimistic, humanistic view, there was a faculty for admitting, unflinchingly, that life can be—and frequently is—cruel, unjust, and even meaningless. Shakespeare put it this way in *King Lear:*

> As flies to wanton boys, are we to the gods;
> They kill us for their sport.

In *Macbeth,* he expressed it in these words:

> Out, out brief candle!
> Life's but a walking shadow, a poor player
> That struts and frets his hour upon the stage
> And then is heard no more; it is a tale
> Told by an idiot, full of sound and fury,
> Signifying nothing.

These periods of history—the Greek golden age and the Renaissance—were expansive enough to encompass both strains: the greatness of human beings on the one hand, and the cruelty of life on the other.

To clarify the distinction between the tragic point of view and other points of view, we need only examine periods in history when one or both of the attitudes forming the tragic viewpoint were absent or were expressed quite differently. In continental Europe and Great Britain, the eighteenth century was known as the *age of enlightenment,* and the nineteenth century as the *century of progress.* Enlightenment and progress: together they express the philosophy that men and women can analyze any problem—poverty, violence, disease, injustice—and, by applying their intelligence, solve it. An age of unbounded optimism in which no problem is thought insurmountable, and a sense of moral justice runs strong, is not one in which tragedy can easily emerge.

Before we examine tragedy and comedy in detail, however, we will look at dramatic structure and dramatic characters—the way a playwright moves the action from scene to scene to develop a plot and creates individual stage characters—in Chapter 8.

SUMMARY

1. Drama is written and produced for different purposes: to move us, to involve us, to amuse us, to entertain us, to inform us, to shock us, to raise our awareness, to inspire us. The dramatist must determine which of these purposes the work being created will serve.

2. The action of a play frequently consists of a test, or crucible, for the characters, in which their true nature is defined. This test involves some form of conflict.

3. Dramatic conventions, ensuring a strong plot and continuation of tension, are analogous to rules in sports. In both sports and theatre there are limited spaces or playing areas, time limits imposed on the action, strongly opposing forces, evenly matched contestants, and prizes or goals for the participants.

4. A play generally begins with an imbalance of forces or a loss of equilibrium by one of the characters; this propels the characters to action.

5. As a play progresses, the characters encounter a series of obstacles and complications in attempting to fulfill their objectives or realize their goals. These encounters produce the tension and conflict of drama.

6. Generally, every work of art, including theatre, has some kind of structure. In theatre, structure usually takes the form of a plot.

7. A dramatic plot is not the same as a story. A story is a complete account of an episode or a sequence of events, but a plot is what we see onstage. In a plot the events have been selected from a story and arranged in a certain sequence.

8. Point of view is the way we look at things: the perspective, or angle of vision, from which we view people, places, and events.

9. In the arts, the establishment of a point of view is direct and deliberate; it is an integral part of a performance or work of art, giving the audience a clue about how to interpret and understand what is being seen and heard.

10. Whether a theatre piece is serious, comic, or some combination of the two depends on the point of view of the artists who create it.

11. The viewpoint of society also affects the outlook of individual artists in terms of tragedy, comedy, and so on.

8

Dramatic Structure and Dramatic Characters

DRAMATIC STRUCTURE

Throughout theatre history, we find basic dramatic forms reappearing. In western civilization, a form adopted in Greece in the fifth century BCE emerges, somewhat altered, in France in the seventeenth century. The same form shows up once more in Norway in the late nineteenth century, and is repeated throughout the twentieth century. This form can be referred to as *climactic*. Another, contrasting form, best illustrated by the plays of Shakespeare, can be called *episodic*. Through most of the history of western theatre, one or the other of these two forms—or some combination of the two—has predominated.

In addition, there are other forms. An approach in which dramatic episodes are strung together without any apparent connection has emerged in a new guise in recent times. Structure based on a ritual or pattern is both old and new. And musical theatre has a structure of its own.

The characteristics of the basic types will be clearer when we look at each separately. We will begin with climactic form, go on to examine episodic form, and then take up additional forms.

Characteristics of Climactic Structure

The Plot Begins Late in the Story   The first hallmark of climactic drama is that the plot begins quite late in the story. Ibsen's *Ghosts,* written in 1881, is a clear example.

Before *Ghosts* begins, several events have already occurred: Mrs. Alving has married a dissolute man who fathers an illegitimate child by another woman and contracts

◄ **EPISODIC DRAMATIC STRUCTURE**

In different periods and different countries, various approaches to dramatic structure have been followed. Climactic structure was created by the Greeks and followed by many cultures in the years to come. Another structure is episodic, found in the plays of Shakespeare. A modern German writer employing episodic structure is Bertolt Brecht. Here we see Fiona Shaw as the title character in Brecht's Mother Courage and Her Children, *directed by Deborah Warner at the National Theatre, London.*

(© Robbie Jack/Corbis)

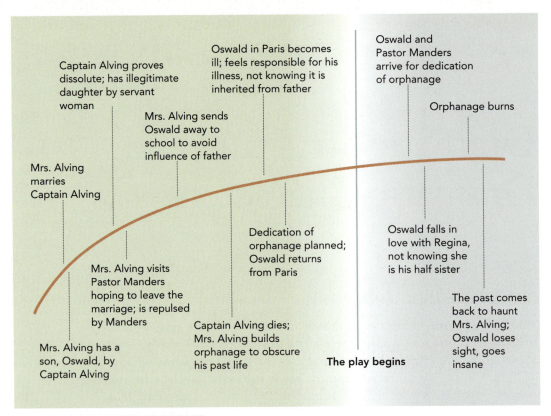

chapter eight

CLIMACTIC STRUCTURE IN GHOSTS

Henrik Ibsen's *Ghosts* follows the climactic form, in which the play begins toward the very end—or climax—of a sequence of events. The parts of the story that occur before the play begins are to the left of the vertical line. Only the events to the right occur in the play; the ones before them must be described in exposition.

a venereal disease. When she discovers her husband's infidelity early in their marriage, Mrs. Alving visits the family minister, Pastor Manders, telling him she wishes to end the marriage. Although Manders is attracted to her and she to him—and although he realizes that she is miserable and has been wronged—for religious reasons, he sends her back to her husband. She stays with her husband out of a sense of duty, though she sends her son, Oswald, away to escape his father's influence. When her husband dies, Mrs. Alving builds an orphanage in his honor to camouflage his true character. At this point—as is typical with climactic plot structure—the play itself has still not begun. It begins later, when the son returns home and the facts of the past are unearthed, precipitating the crisis.

In climactic structure, then, the play begins when all the roads of the past converge at one crucial intersection in the present—in other words, at the climax. The fact that the plot begins so late has at least two important consequences. First, it is frequently necessary to explain what has happened earlier by having one or more characters report the information to others. The technical term for revelation of background information is ***exposition.***

A second consequence of the fact that the plot begins late in the story is that the time span covered within a climactic play is usually brief—in many cases a matter of a

CHARACTERISTICS OF CLIMACTIC DRAMA
A climactic play usually has a minimum number of characters, covers a short space of time, and takes place in a limited space—often one room. A good example is August Strindberg's *Miss Julie,* which takes place in little more than two hours and in one space: the kitchen of an estate in Sweden. In the scene here, we see Johnny Lee Miller and Sienna Miller in *After Miss Julie,* Patrick Marber's adaptation of *Miss Julie,* directed by Mark Brokaw at the Roundabout Theatre. (© Joan Marcus)

few hours, and at the most a few days. Some playwrights, attempting to push events as near the climax as possible, have stage time (the time we imagine is passing when we are watching a play) coincide with real time (that is, clock time). An example is Tennessee Williams's *Cat on a Hot Tin Roof:* the events depicted in the story last the same time as the play itself—2 hours.

Scenes, Locales, and Characters Are Limited
Climactic drama typically has a limited number of long segments, or acts. In Greek plays there are generally five episodes separated by choral interludes. The French neoclassicists invariably used five acts. For much of the nineteenth and twentieth centuries, three acts were standard. Today, the norm is two acts, though the long one-act play performed without intermission is also frequently presented.

Limiting the scenes in a play usually entails restricting the locale as well, sometimes to one room or one house. Along with restriction of locale, there is a restriction of characters. Greek drama generally has four or five principal characters. Many modern plays have no more than a similar number of main characters.

Construction Is Tight
Because it is carefully constructed, a climactic play fits together tightly, with no loose ends. It is like a chain linked in a cause-and-effect relationship. As in a detective story, event A leads to event B; B leads to C, causing D;

D leads in turn to E; and so on. Just as the time frame and the restricted space afford no exit, so the chain of events is locked in. Once the action begins, there is no stopping it.

In this form the aim is always to make events so inevitable that there is no escape—at least not until the very last moment, when a *deus ex machina* may intervene to untangle the knot. Because climactic dramas are so carefully and tightly constructed, they are frequently referred to as **well-made plays.**

Clearly, the method of climactic drama is compression. All the elements—characters, locale, events—are severely restricted. As if by centripetal motion, everything is forced to the center, in a tighter and tighter nucleus, making the ultimate eruption that much more explosive.

Characteristics of Episodic Structure

When we turn to examples of episodic structure, we see a sharp contrast to climactic structure. Episodic drama begins relatively early in the story and does not compress the action but expands it. The forces in episodic drama are centrifugal, moving out to embrace additional elements. Also, unlike climactic drama, episodic plays do not necessarily follow a close cause-and-effect development.

EPISODIC STRUCTURE: MANY CHARACTERS, PLACES, AND EVENTS
A good example of the typically wide-ranging episodic structure is *Julius Caesar* by William Shakespeare. Shown here are Dan Kremer in the title role, with Kryztov Lindquist as the Soothsayer and the cast of the Shakespeare Theatre Company in its production, directed by David Muse. (© Carol Rosegg)

People, Places, and Events Proliferate   In a typical episodic play the action begins relatively early in the story and covers an extensive period of time—sometimes many years. It also ranges over a number of locations. In one play we can go anywhere: to a small antechamber, a large banquet hall, the open countryside, a mountaintop. Short scenes (some only half a page or so in print) alternate with longer ones. Two examples of episodic dramas are Shakespeare's *Antony and Cleopatra,* which has thirty-four characters and forty-plus scenes; and the Spanish playwright Lope de Vega's *The Sheep Well,* which has twenty-six characters and seventeen scenes.

There May Be a Parallel Plot or Subplot   In place of compression, episodic drama offers other techniques. One is the *parallel plot,* or *subplot.* In *King Lear,* by Shakespeare, Lear has three daughters, two evil and one good. The two evil daughters have convinced their father that they are good and that their sister is wicked. In the subplot—a counterpart of this main plot—the Earl of Gloucester has two sons, one loyal and one disloyal, and the disloyal son has deceived his father into thinking he is the loyal one. Both old men have misunderstood their children's true worth, and in the end both are punished for their mistakes: Lear is bereft of his kingdom and his sanity; Gloucester loses his eyes. The Gloucester plot, with complications and developments of its own, is a parallel and reinforcement of the Lear plot.

Juxtaposition and Contrast Occur   Another technique of episodic drama is *juxtaposition* or *contrast.* Rather than moving in linear fashion, the action alternates between elements: Short scenes alternate with longer scenes, public scenes alternate with private scenes, we move from one group to an opposing group, and comic scenes alternate with serious scenes.

An example of this last alternation comes in Shakespeare's *Macbeth.* Just after Macbeth has murdered King Duncan, there is a knock on the door of the castle. This

COMIC SCENES ALTERNATE WITH SERIOUS SCENES
One device possible in episodic drama is the juxtaposition and alternation of serious and comic scenes. Shakespeare often incorporates this technique in his plays. In the grave-digging scene in *Hamlet,* comedy interrupts very serious scenes involving the death of Ophelia and other tragic events. Shown here is David Tennant as Hamlet with the skull of Yorick, in a Royal Shakespeare Company production. (© Geraint Lewis)

King Lear by William Shakespeare

I-1 Lear's Palace. Kent and Gloucester discuss the division of the kingdom and Gloucester's sons. Lear comes. The division of kingdom: first Goneril and then Regan praise Lear. Kent intercedes and is banished. Gloucester enters with Burgundy and France. Burgundy will not have Cordelia without a dowry. France takes her. Goneril and Regan begin plotting. (305 lines)

I-2 Gloucester's Castle. Edmund's soliloquy and scheme. Letter and plan against Edgar begins. Gloucester leaves, Edgar comes, scheme furthered. (173 lines)

I-3 Albany's Palace. Goneril and Oswald scheming. (26 lines)

I-4 The Same. Kent enters disguised; Lear comes, then Oswald, Kent trips him. Fool enters and talks to Lear. Goneril comes, chides Lear. He curses her and leaves. Goneril, Albany, and Oswald conspire further, then leave. (336 lines)

I-5 In Front of Palace. Lear, Kent, Fool. Lear sends letters to Gloucester, starts to Regan. (46 lines)

II-1 A Court in Gloucester's Castle. Edmund and Curan. Edgar comes, then leaves. Edmund stabs himself; Gloucester comes, Edmund blames Edgar, Gloucester finds letter. Cornwall and Regan enter. (The forces of evil join.) (129 lines)

II-2 Before Gloucester's Castle. Kent confronts Oswald, Cornwall comes; Kent put in stocks. (168 lines)

II-3 The Open Country. Edgar's soliloquy: he will disguise and abase himself. (21 lines)

II-4 Before Gloucester's Castle. Lear comes, sees Kent; confronts Regan. She is stubborn too. Goneril comes. He sees a league. Begs; leaves as storm begins. (306 lines)

III-1 A Heath. Kent with a Gentleman. (55 lines)

III-2 Another Part of Heath. Lear comes with Fool. Storm and insanity begin. Kent comes. (95 lines)

III-3 Gloucester's Castle. Gloucester tells Edmund of divisions between dukes and of letter from France. (23 lines)

III-4 The Heath before a Hovel. Lear, Kent, Fool—storm. Lear's madness and beginning self-realization. Edgar joins them, then Gloucester with a torch. (172 lines)

III-6 Gloucester's Castle. Cornwall and Edmund scheming. (22 lines)

III-6 **A Farmhouse Near Gloucester's Castle.** The mock trial for Lear. Kent, Gloucester, Fool, Edgar. All leave but Edgar. (112 lines)

III-7 **Gloucester's Castle.** Cornwall, Regan, Goneril, Edmund. They send for Gloucester (the "traitor"), prepare to blind him. Servant is killed; they pluck out Gloucester's eyes. (106 lines)

IV-1 **The Heath.** Edgar. Enter Gloucester, blind. Edgar prepares cliff scene. (79 lines)

IV-2 **Before Albany's Palace.** Goneril and Edmund. Enter Oswald. Intrigue of Goneril and Edmund. Albany comes; Goneril chides him. Servant comes telling of Cornwall's death. (979 lines)

IV-3 **French Camp Near Dover.** Kent and Gentleman report Lear ashamed to see Cordelia. (55 lines)

IV-4 **French Camp.** Cordelia and Doctor enter; plan to go to England. (29 lines)

IV-5 **Gloucester's Castle.** Regan and Oswald. She says Edmund is for her. (40 lines)

IV-6 **Country Near Dover.** Gloucester and Edgar—jumping scene. Lear comes, mad. The two wronged madmen together. Gentleman comes, then Oswald attacks him. Edgar kills Oswald, finds letters to Edmund—Goneril is plotting Albany's death in order to marry Edmund. (283 lines)

IV-7 **Tent in French Camp.** Cordelia and Kent. Lear brought in. The awakening and reconciliation. (96 lines)

V-1 **British Camp Near Dover.** Edmund, Regan, etc. Goneril comes, also Albany. Edgar enters, leaves. (69 lines)

V-2 **A Field between Camps.** Cordelia and Lear cross. Edgar and Gloucester come. (11 lines)

V-3 **British Camp.** Edmund comes, Lear and Cordelia are prisoners; are sent away. Edmund sends note with guard. Enter Albany, Goneril, and Regan, who quarrel. Edgar comes; challenges Edmund and wounds him. Truth about Goneril's plan comes out; she leaves. Edgar talks. Goneril and Regan are brought in dead. Edmund dies. Lear enters with the dead Cordelia; then he dies. Kent and Albany pronounce the end. (326 lines)

EPISODIC STRUCTURE IN KING LEAR

Shakespeare's play sets up a juxtaposition of scenes. Note how the scenes move from place to place and alternate from one group of characters to another. Note, too, that the scenes move back and forth from intimate scenes to those involving a number of characters (an alternation of public and private scenes) and that the length of the scenes varies, with short scenes followed by longer ones, and so forth. This structure gives the play its dynamics, its rhythm, and its meaning.

DYNAMICS OF DRAMA

COMPARING CLIMACTIC AND EPISODIC FORM

Climactic	Episodic
1. Plot begins late in the story, toward the very end or climax.	1. Plot begins relatively early in the story and moves through a series of episodes.
2. Covers a short space of time, perhaps a few hours or at most a few days.	2. Covers a longer period of time: weeks, months, and sometimes many years.
3. Contains a few solid, extended scenes, such as three acts with each act comprising one long scene.	3. Has many short, fragmented scenes; sometimes an alternation of short and long scenes.
4. Occurs in a restricted locale, such as one room or one house.	4. May range over an entire city or even several countries.
5. Number of characters is severely limited—usually no more than six or eight.	5. Has a profusion of characters, sometimes several dozen.
6. Plot is linear and moves in a single line with few subplots or counterplots.	6. Is frequently marked by several threads of action, such as two parallel plots, or scenes of comic relief in a serious play.
7. Line of action proceeds in a cause-and-effect chain. The characters and events are closely linked in a sequence of logical, almost inevitable development.	7. Scenes are juxtaposed to one another. An event may result from several causes; or it may have no apparent cause, but arises in a network or web of circumstances.

The table outlines the chief characteristics of climactic and episodic forms and illustrates the differences between them. It is clear that the climactic and episodic forms differ from each other in their fundamental approaches. One emphasizes constriction and compression on all fronts; the other takes a far broader view and aims at a cumulative effect, piling up people, places, and events.

is one of the most serious moments of the play, but the man who goes to open the door is a comical character, a drunken porter, whose speech is a humorous interlude in the grim business of the play.

The Overall Effect Is Cumulative   With regard to cause and effect in episodic drama, the impression created is of events piling up: a tsunami, a tidal wave of circumstances and emotions sweeping over the characters. Rarely does one letter, one telephone call, or one piece of information determine the fate of a character. Time and again, Hamlet has proof that Claudius has killed his father; however, what eventually leads him to kill Claudius is not a single piece of hard evidence but a rush of events.

In modern theatre both climactic form and episodic form have been adopted, sometimes by the same playwright. This is characteristic of the diversity of our age. Ibsen, for example, wrote a number of "well-made" or climactic plays—*Ghosts, A Doll's House,* and others—but also several episodic plays, such as *Brand* and *Peer Gynt.*

Combinations of Climactic and Episodic Form

There is no law requiring a play to be exclusively episodic or exclusively climactic. It is true that during certain periods one form or the other has been predominant. Also, it is

COMBINING CLIMACTIC AND EPISODIC STRUCTURES
Though we often separate the episodic and climactic structures, there have been a number of times when the two forms are combined, joining together characteristics from each. Good examples are plays from the English Restoration and, 200 years later, the plays of the Russian dramatist Anton Chekhov. Shown here is a scene from a Restoration comedy, William Congreve's *The Way of the World,* directed by Michael Kahn at the Shakespeare Theatre Company. The play has some of the economy of climactic drama but features a number of characters, as shown here, which are typical of the episodic form. (© Carol Rosegg)

not easy to mix the two forms, because—as we have seen—each has its own laws and its own inner logic. In several periods, however, they have been successfully integrated.

A group of plays that combine elements of the climactic and episodic forms are the comedies of the Restoration period in England (from 1660, when the English monarchy was restored, to 1700). These comedies usually had a large cast, a subplot as well as a main plot, and several changes of scene. They did not, however, cover extended periods of time or move rapidly from place to place as the plays of Shakespeare did.

The climactic and episodic forms have frequently been combined successfully in the modern period. Chekhov, who generally wrote about one principal action and set his plays in one household, usually has more characters than is customary in climactic drama. For instance, there are fifteen in *The Cherry Orchard.* Frequently, too, Chekhov's plays cover a period of several months or years.

Rituals as Dramatic Structure

Like acting, ritual is a part of everyday life of which we are generally unaware. Basically, **ritual** is a repetition or reenactment of a proceeding or transaction that has acquired special meaning. It may be a simple ritual like singing the national anthem before a sports contest, or a deeply religious ritual such as the Roman Catholic mass or the Jewish kaddish, a prayer for the dead.

All of us develop rituals in our personal or family life: a certain meal we eat with the family once a week, for example, or a routine we go through every time we take an examination in school. Occasions like Thanksgiving, Christmas, and Passover become family rituals, with the same order of events each year, the same menu, and perhaps even the same conversation. Rituals give us continuity, security, and comfort. Often, as in the case of primitive tribes, people assume that if they perform a ritual faithfully, they will be blessed or their wishes will be granted. Conversely, they assume that failure to follow a ritual to the letter will lead to punishment.

In theatre, ritual is an activity where the old and new come together. Traditional plays are full of rituals: coronations, weddings, funerals, and other ceremonies. And in modern theatre, ritual has been discovered and given new life. Certain avant-garde theatre groups, for example, have made a conscious attempt to develop new rituals or revive old ones. Ritual has structure. Actions are repeated in a set fashion; these actions have a beginning, a middle, and an end; and there is a natural progression of events.

RITUAL IN MODERN THEATRE

Many avant-garde playwrights and groups use ceremonies and rituals. *The Blacks,* a highly theatrical piece by the French playwright Jean Genet, is part ritual, part minstrel show, part court trial. It takes place in an imaginary Africa. As a part of the various ceremonies and other actions, Genet uses masks, such as the ones shown here. (© Dennis Stock/Magnum Photos)

Patterns as Dramatic Structure

Related to ritual is a pattern of events. In Samuel Beckett's *Waiting for Godot,* the characters have no personal history, and the play does not build to a climax in the ordinary way. But if Beckett has sacrificed traditional plot structure, he has replaced it with a repeated sequence of events containing its own order and logic. The play has two acts, and in each act a series of incidents is duplicated.

Each act opens with the two chief characters coming together on a lonely crossroads after having been separated. Then, in both acts, a similar sequence of events occurs: they greet each other; they despair of Godot's ever coming; they attempt to entertain themselves. Two other men, Pozzo and Lucky, appear and, following a long scene, disappear. The first two men are left alone once more. The two acts continue to follow the same sequence: a small Boy comes to tell the men that Godot will not come that day, the Boy leaves, and the men remain together for another night. There are important differences between the two acts, but the identical sequence of events in each act achieves a pattern, which takes on a ritualistic quality.

Serial Structure

Another kind of structure is a series of acts or episodes—individual theatre events—offered as a single presentation. In this case, individual segments are strung together like beads on a necklace. Sometimes a central theme or common thread holds the various parts together. Sometimes there is little or no connection between the parts.

The musical *revue* is a case in point. In a revue, short scenes, vignettes, skits, dance numbers, songs, and possibly even vaudeville routines are presented on a single program. There may be an overall theme, such as political satire or the celebration of a past event or period. Sometimes a master of ceremonies provides continuity between the various segments. Also, in today's theatre we frequently see a program of short plays. Sometimes there will be a bill of one-act plays by the same author; at other times there will be two or three plays by different authors. On some occasions an attempt is made to relate the separate plays to a central theme; but sometimes the plays are chosen simply to complete an evening's entertainment.

Structure in Experimental and Avant-Garde Theatre

Special Structures   In the second half of the twentieth century, a number of theatre groups in Europe and the United States experimented with forms such as ritual. These included the Polish Laboratory Theater, headed by Jerzy Grotowski; and the Living Theater, the Open Theater, the Performance Group, Mabou Mines, and the Wooster Group in the United States. These groups questioned long-held beliefs about theatre. They had two things in mind. On one hand, they felt that the traditional theatre of the past was no longer relevant to the problems of the present and that new forms had to be found to match the unique challenges and aspirations of the modern world. On the other hand, they wanted to look back beyond the traditions of the past 2,500 years to the beginning of theatre, to scrape off the many layers of formality and convention that had accumulated through the centuries, and to rediscover the roots of theatre.

In many cases these two impulses led to similar results. From the experiments of this radical theatre movement, several significant departures from traditional theatre practice were developed. Among them were the following: (1) emphasis on *nonverbal theatre,* that is, theatre in which gestures, body movements, and sounds without words are stressed rather than logical or intelligible language; (2) reliance on improvisation or a scenario developed by performers and a director to tell the story, rather than a written text; (3) interest in ritual and ceremony; and (4) stress on the importance of the physical environment of theatre, including the spatial relationship of the performers to the audience.

The theatre groups that developed these ideas were referred to as *avant-garde,* a French term that literally means "advance guard in a military formation." The term has come to mean an intellectual or artistic movement in any age that breaks with tradition and therefore seems ahead of its time.

Segments and Tableaux as Structure   The experimental pieces of the directors Robert Wilson (noted in Chapters 5 and 6) and Richard Foreman (b. 1937), like other types of avant-garde theatre, often stress nonverbal elements. At times they include *non sequitur* as well. In spite of this, their work does have structure. Often the various elements are united by a theme, or at least by a pronounced point of view on the part of the director. Also, the material is organized into units analogous to the

SEGMENTS AND TABLEAUX IN AVANT-GARDE THEATRE
The works of many modern experimental theatre directors consist of separate segments, almost like pictorial tableaux. The emphasis is on the visual aspect, and also on images, sounds, music, and dancelike movement. An example of segments and tableaux can be seen in this production by the avant-garde director-auteur Robert Wilson, an adaptation of classic French tales of animals, *The Fables of La Fontaine*, presented at the Lincoln Center Festival in New York City. (© Richard Termine)

frames of film and television, or to the still-life tableaux of painting or the moving tableaux of dance. (In theatre, a *tableau*—plural, *tableaux*—is a static scene onstage featuring performers in costume.)

Robert Wilson, in productions such as *A Letter to Queen Victoria, Einstein on the Beach,* and *CiVil WarS: A Tree Is Best Measured When It Is Down,* begins a segment with a visual picture—like a large painting, but three-dimensional. The performers move from this static image into the activities of the segment. When one segment has concluded, another picture or tableau will be formed to initiate the next segment.

Frequently directors like Foreman and Wilson will use rapid movements—as in silent films—or slow-motion movements. At times several activities will occur simultaneously. All of these, however, relate both to an image and to a tableau or frame.

Structure in Musical Theatre

In musical theatre, structure often involves alternation and juxtaposition. Musical numbers alternate with spoken scenes; solos and duets alternate with choral numbers; singing alternates with dance numbers; and sometimes comic songs and scenes alternate with serious ones.

An example of structural principles in musicals is found in *My Fair Lady,* with book and lyrics by Alan Jay Lerner and music by Frederick Loewe. The story is based on George Bernard Shaw's play *Pygmalion.*

My Fair Lady concerns a speech teacher, Henry Higgins, who claims that the English judge people by how they speak. He bets his friend Colonel Pickering that he can take an ordinary cockney flower girl, Eliza Doolittle, and by teaching her correct diction, pass her off as a duchess. The comic subplot of *My Fair Lady* deals with Eliza's father, Alfred P. Doolittle, a ne'er-do-well who doesn't want to achieve middle-class respectability, because if he does he will have to marry the woman he lives with.

The first song in the show is sung by Higgins—"Why Can't the English Learn to Speak?" The next song shifts to Eliza and her dreams of luxury as she sings "Wouldn't It Be Lovely?" She is joined in this number by a chorus. The action now shifts to the subplot, and Alfred Doolittle is joined by two buddies to sing of how he hopes to avoid working "With a Little Bit of Luck." We then move back to a scene with Higgins, who is pushing Eliza very hard to learn to speak properly. After a song by Higgins, "I'm an Ordinary Man," Eliza vows revenge on him in her next song: "Just You Wait."

The musical proceeds in this manner, moving from one character to another, from a solo to a trio to a dance routine to an ensemble. There is variety in these numbers—some are serious; some are comic; some explain the characters' feelings; some describe a situation. It is on such alternation that structure in musical theatre is based. Always, too, it must be remembered, spoken scenes are interspersed with musical numbers, and ballet or modern dance routines with other numbers.

DRAMATIC CHARACTERS

Along with structures, the playwright creates dramatic characters. These can range from fully rounded human beings to so-called *stock characters* who are two-dimensional.

Extraordinary Characters

In most important dramatic works of the past, the heroes and heroines are extraordinary in some way. They are larger than life. Historically, major characters have been

photo essay

Extraordinary Characters

In dramas of the past, the leading characters are often people who are exceptional in some way. Shown here is a gallery of exceptional characters from a range of dramas.

Dominic West as Segismundo, the lead character in Helen Edmundson's adaptation of Calderón de la Barca's *Life Is a Dream,* directed by Jonathan Munby at the Donmar Warehouse in London.

(© Johan Persson/ArenaPAL)

(© Geraint Lewis) Frances Barber as Cleopatra, the powerful, alluring queen of Egypt with whom Antony fell in love in Shakespeare's *Antony and Cleopatra,* in a production at Shakespeare's Globe in London.

Anne-Marie Duff as the exceptional historical figure
Saint Joan in the play of that name by George Bernard
Shaw at the National Theatre, London.

(© Kevin Cummins)

A quintessential extraordinary figure, King Oedipus, from
the play by Socrates, as portrayed by Peter Macon, in a new
version by Ellen McLaughlin, directed by Lisa Peterson at the
Guthrie Theater.

(© T Charles Erickson)

THE TRAGIC FIGURE: AN EXCEPTIONAL CHARACTER
A good example of an extraordinary figure in tragedy is Tamburlaine, a larger-than-life character who through terror and cunning conquered much of the known world in central Asia and was the hero of two plays by Christopher Marlowe in the late 1580s. Shown here are Avery Brooks and the cast of the Shakespeare Theatre Company's *Tamburlaine,* adapted and directed by Michael Kahn. (© Carol Rosegg)

kings, queens, bishops, members of the nobility, or other figures clearly marked as holding a special place in society. In drama, as in life, a queen is accorded respect because of her authority, power, and grandeur; a high military official is respected because of the position he holds.

Dramatists go one step farther, however, in depicting extraordinary characters. In addition to filling prestigious roles, dramatic characters generally represent men and women at their best or worst—at some extreme of human behavior. Lady Macbeth is not only a noblewoman; she is one of the most ambitious women ever depicted onstage. In virtually every instance, with extraordinary characters we see men and women at the outer limits of human capability and endurance.

Comic characters can also be extremes. The chief character in *Volpone* by Ben Jonson (1572–1637) is an avaricious miser who gets people to present him with expensive gifts because they think he will remember them in his will.

Characters may also be extraordinary because of their exceptional personalities or achievements. A good example is Joan of Arc, the heroine of George Bernard Shaw's *Saint Joan,* a simple peasant girl who rises to become commander of an army that triumphs in the name of the king of France.

Some characters are mixtures, combining extreme virtue and extreme vice. Faustus, treated by Christopher Marlowe in *Doctor Faustus* and by Johann Wolfgang von Goethe in *Faust,* is a great scholar but becomes so bored with his existence and so ambitious that he makes a compact with the devil, forfeiting his soul in return for unlimited power. Cleopatra, an exceedingly vain, selfish woman, also has "immortal longings." Queen Elizabeth I of England and Mary Queen of Scots, rivals in real life, have made admirable dramatic characters—women of strong virtues and telling weaknesses.

In sum, larger-than-life characters become the heroes and heroines of drama not only because of their station in life but also because they possess traits common to us all—ambition, generosity, malevolence, fear, and achievement—in such great abundance.

In the eighteenth century, ordinary people began taking over from royalty and the nobility as the heroes and heroines of drama—a reflection of what was occurring in the real world. But despite this move away from royalty and the nobility, the leading figures of drama continued in many cases to be exceptional men and women at their best and worst.

Representative or Quintessential Characters

When characters from everyday life replaced kings and queens as the leading figures in drama, a new type of character emerged alongside the extraordinary character. Characters of this new type are in many respects typical or ordinary, but they are significant because they embody an entire group. Rather than being notable as "worst," "best," or some other extreme, they are important as *representative* or *quintessential* characters.

A good example of such a character is Nora Helmer, the heroine of Henrik Ibsen's *A Doll's House*. A spoiled, flighty woman, she has secretly forged a signature to get money for her husband when he was very ill and needed medical attention. All her life, first by her father, then by her husband, she has been treated like a doll or a plaything, not as a mature, responsible woman. In the last act of the play, Nora rebels against this attitude; she makes a declaration of independence to her husband, slams the door on him, and walks out. It has been said that Nora's slamming of the door marks the beginning not only of modern drama but of the emancipation of modern women. Certainly Nora's defiance—her demand to be treated as an equal—has made her typical of all housewives who refuse to be regarded as pets. In one sense, Nora is an ordinary wife and mother—far from Antigone or Lady Macbeth—but she is unusual in the way she sums up an entire group of women. *A Doll's House* was written in 1879; but today, well over a century later, Nora is still a symbol of modern women, and the play is revived year after year.

In *Who's Afraid of Virginia Woolf?* by Edward

QUINTESSENTIAL CHARACTERS
Certain key characters in drama, especially in modern drama, are not extraordinary or exceptional in the same way as royalty or military leaders, but become important because they embody qualities of an entire group of people. Included in this description would be the lead characters in Edward Albee's *Who's Afraid of Virginia Woolf?*—Martha and George, named after Martha and George Washington. They are the epitome of a contemporary warring couple. Shown here in the original Broadway production are (left to right) Ben Piazza as the guest, Uta Hagen as Martha, and Arthur Hill as George. (Photofest)

Albee, the main characters are a husband and a wife who are in many ways quite commonplace. He is a somewhat ineffectual college professor; she is the daughter of the college president. They argue and attack each other almost to the point of exhaustion. Another unhappily married couple? Yes. But again, they are quintessential. To Albee, they represent an American type: a bitter, alienated couple, bored with themselves and each other. To underline this point, he names them Martha and George—the same first names as Martha and George Washington, America's "first couple."

Another example is Willy Loman, in Arthur Miller's *Death of a Salesman,* who sums up all salesmen, traveling in their territories on a "smile and a shoeshine." Willy has lived by a false dream: the idea that if he puts up a good front and is "well liked," he will be successful and rich. Still another example is Troy Maxon in *Fences* by August

THE AUDIENCE'S RESPONSE

- Look at the cast of characters in a Shakespearean play you have seen or read. Place each character in a category: major character; minor character; or a character in between—that is, a character with a clear personality but not a large role. Which characters are in opposition to one another? Which characters in the play dominate in the struggle? Is there a reversal of their fortunes?

- While you are watching a modern play or drama involving a small group of characters locked in a struggle for dominance or control, how does the action usually play out? Is first one person in the ascendency and then another? What do shifts of power and control have to do with revealing the personalities of the characters? What do these changes have to do with the meaning of the play?

- During the last performance you attended, did the action take place in one locale (one room, for instance) or, instead, in three or four locations? Did the action move frequently, returning at times to a former location? What effect did these elements of place or location have on your experience of the play?

Wilson. Maxon epitomizes the proud, headstrong man who in order to survive in a world of oppression and prejudice has developed firmness and resolution, which serve him well but take their toll on his wife and son.

Nora Helmer, Martha and George, Willy Loman, and Troy Maxon: all are examples of characters who stand apart from the crowd, not by standing above it but by summing up in their personalities the essence of a certain type of person.

Stock Characters

The characters we have been describing, whether extraordinary or representative, are generally fully rounded figures. Many characters in drama, however, are not complete or three-dimensional; rather, they exemplify one particular characteristic to the exclusion of virtually everything else. Frequently they are known by their station in life, their sex, and their occupation along with some tendency of personality: the clever servant, for instance, or the absentminded professor. They are referred to as *stock* characters, and they appear particularly in comedy and melodrama, though they can be found in almost all kinds of drama.

Some of the most famous examples of stock characters are found in ***commedia dell'arte,*** a form of popular comedy that flourished in Italy during the sixteenth and seventeenth centuries. In commedia dell'arte, there was no script but rather a scenario, which gave an outline of a story. The performers improvised or invented words and actions to fill out the play. The stock characters of commedia were either straightforward or exaggerated and were divided into servants and members of the ruling class. In every character, however, one particular feature or trait was stressed.

Whenever such a character appeared, he or she would have the same propensities and would wear the same costume. The bragging soldier, called *Capitano,* always boasted of his courage in a series of fictitious military victories. *Pantalone,* an elderly merchant, spoke in clichés and chased girls; and a pompous lawyer called *Dottore* spoke in Latin phrases and attempted to impress others with his learning. Among servants, *Harlequin* was the most popular; displaying both cunning and stupidity, he

STOCK CHARACTERS OF COMMEDIA DELL'ARTE
Italian Renaissance comedy developed stereotyped characters who were always the same: each of them was famous for a certain trait—greed, boastfulness, gullibility, or the like—and was always easily identifiable by his or her costume. Accompanying these characters were clever servants, such as Harlequin. Here is an eighteenth-century engraving of a commedia troupe onstage. By then the characters were no longer masked, as they had been in the sixteenth and seventeenth centuries. (© Bettmann/Corbis)

was at the heart of most plot complications. These are but a few of a full range of commedia characters, each with his or her own peculiarities.

As for examples of stock characters in melodrama, we are all familiar with such figures as the innocent young heroine, "pure as the driven snow"; and the villain, lurking in the shadows, twirling his moustache. In today's television, the familiar figures on weekly situation comedies are examples of stock or stereotypical characters.

Characters with a Dominant Trait

Closely related to stock characters are characters with a single trait or "humor." During the Renaissance, there was a widely held theory that the body was governed by four humors, which must be kept in balance for a person to be healthy. In the sixteenth century this theory was expanded to include psychological traits, and the dramatist Ben Jonson followed it extensively in his plays. In *Every Man in His Humour* and *Every Man Out of His Humour,* for instance, Jonson portrayed characters in whom one humor came to dominate all others, making for an unbalanced, often comic, personality. Jonson often named his characters for their single trait or humor. His play *The Alchemist* includes characters with names like Subtle, Face, Dapper, Surly, Wholesome, and Dame Pliant.

CHARACTERS WITH A DOMINANT TRAIT
Many comic plays feature characters with one predominant trait—greed, ambition, self-importance, and so forth. The extremes of the character are one of the elements that create the comic effect. The French playwright Molière often named his plays for such characters. Shown here are Nancy Robinette as Toinette and René Auberjonois as Argan in the Shakespeare Theatre Company's production of Molière's *The Imaginary Invalid,* directed by Keith Baxter. (© Carol Rosegg)

Minor Characters

Stock characters or characters with a dominant trait are not to be confused with *minor characters.* Minor characters are those—in all types of plays—who play a small part in the overall action. Generally they appear briefly and serve chiefly to further the story or to support more important characters. Typical examples of minor characters are servants, soldiers, and so forth; but even figures such as generals, bishops, judges, dukes, and duchesses are considered minor if they play only a small role in the action. Since we see so little of these characters, the dramatist can usually show only one facet of their personalities; but this is a different case from that of a main character who is deliberately portrayed as one-sided.

A Narrator or Chorus

A special type of character is a narrator or the members of a chorus. Generally, a *narrator* speaks directly to the audience. He or she may or may not assume a dramatic persona as the other characters do. In Tennessee Williams's *The Glass Menagerie* and Thornton Wilder's *Our Town,* for instance, a performer appears both as a narrator and as one or more characters in the play. Ancient Greek drama had a chorus (usually consisting of fifteen performers) who in song and dance commented on the action of the main plot and reacted to events in the story. Use of a chorus or narrator creates a *dialectic* or *counterpoint* between a party outside the play and characters in the central action. (*Counterpoint* is a term from music denoting a second melody that accompanies or moves in contrast to the main melody.)

Bertolt Brecht used a narrator, and sometimes singers, in a pointed way: to startle the audience by making a sudden shift from the main story to the presentation of a

THE NARRATOR OR CHORUS

A role in drama in which a performer or group steps out of character to address the audience directly is a narrator or a chorus. In Thornton Wilder's *Our Town,* the character of the Stage Manager is the narrator of the piece, and he also plays small roles such as the preacher who marries the young couple. Here, Frank Craven (center) plays the role in the original Broadway production, 1938. (Vandamm Collection/Theatre Collection, Museum of the City of New York)

moral or political argument. In *The Caucasian Chalk Circle,* for instance, Grusha—an innocent, peace-loving peasant woman—steps out of character at one point to sing a song extolling the virtues of a general who loves war. Grusha, in other words, momentarily becomes a sort of chorus when she is asked to sing a song with a point of view opposite to her own. This wrenching of characters and attitudes is deliberate on Brecht's part: it is meant to make us think seriously about some issue, such as war and the ravages of war.

THE CHORUS: A TIME-HONORED DEVICE

The Greeks were the first to use a chorus. It extended the range and sweep of their plays, which otherwise adhered closely to the climactic form. Here we see the chorus in the London production of *Bacchai* by Euripides, directed by Peter Hall at the National Theatre.

(© Donald Cooper/Photo*stage*)

NONHUMAN CHARACTERS

Sometimes characters are nonhuman, although they usually have human characteristics. This tradition goes back at least as far as the comedies of the Greek writer Aristophanes in the fifth century BCE in Greece. Frequently they are animals of some sort. A nonhuman character in Shakespeare is Bottom when he is turned into an ass in *A Midsummer Night's Dream,* shown here directed by Peter Hall, with Judi Dench as Titania and Oliver Chris as Bottom, the ass, at the Rose Theatre. (© Geraint Lewis)

Nonhuman Characters

In Greece in the fifth century BCE, and in many primitive cultures, performers portrayed birds and animals, and this practice has continued to the present. Aristophanes, the Greek comic dramatist, used a chorus of actors to play the title parts in his plays *The Birds* and *The Frogs.* In the modern period, Eugène Ionesco has men turn into animals in *Rhinoceros;* and the French playwright Edmond Rostand wrote a poetic fable called *Chantecler,* about a rooster.

Occasionally performers are called on to play other nonhuman roles. Karel Čapek (1890–1938) wrote a play, *R.U.R.,* in which people enact robots. (The initials in the title stand for "Rossum's Universal Robots," and it is from this play that the word *robot* derives.) In the medieval morality play *Everyman,* characters represent ideas or concepts, such as Fellowship, Good Deeds, Wordly Possessions, and Beauty.

Dramatic characters in the guise of animals or robots are the exception rather than the rule, however. When they do occur, it is the human quality of the animal or robot that is being emphasized.

The Audience and Character Types

Classifying characters in categories is neither artificial nor arbitrary. Different types of characters are part of the fabric of various dramatic forms, and being aware of them is a helpful tool in appreciating and understanding those forms. It should also be remembered that not every character fits neatly into a single category, and that various character types are not necessarily mutually exclusive. For example, an extraordinary or quintessential character might also be a character with a dominant trait. At the same time, knowledge of the character types we have been studying can greatly help audiences understand how characters function in a drama and enhance their experience when seeing a performance. This is a key phrase: *seeing a performance.*

When a playwright in ancient Greece or Elizabethan England wrote a tragedy, he did not think of the central figure in his drama as an extraordinary character. In nineteenth-century France, when a dramatist composed a bedroom farce, he was not consciously employing stock characters. And when a twentieth-century playwright wrote a serious drama, he or she did not focus on developing quintessential figures as the play's chief characters. Dramatists create characters, not labels. In the same way, an audience member attending a performance should not be preoccupied with assigning the characters onstage to a specific category. During a theatre event a spectator should let the action onstage unfold, taking it in as a whole, and observing particular elements only when they appear evident or are especially striking. Focusing on character types should be undertaken in studying a play before seeing it, or in analyzing it afterward.

Juxtaposition of Characters

We turn now from single characters to the way characters interact with and relate to one another. Often in the creation of a dramatic work, characters are combined in important, significant ways to bring out certain qualities.

Protagonist and Antagonist   From Greek theatre we have the terms ***protagonist*** and ***antagonist.*** The *protagonist* in a play is the main character—Othello, for instance—and the *antagonist* is the main character's chief opponent. In *Othello,* the antagonist is Iago. It is through the contest between these two characters that their individual qualities are developed.

Contrasting Characters   Another way characters are contrasted is by setting them side by side rather than in opposition. Sophocles created two exceptionally strong-willed, independent female characters—Antigone and Electra—each one the

CONTRASTING CHARACTERS
Playwrights often set two characters beside each other, or against each other, so that they stand in sharp contrast. In Henrik Ibsen's *Hedda Gabler,* the frustrated, volatile, reckless Hedda is juxtaposed with her friend Mrs. Elvsted, a calmer, wiser, quieter person. In this scene Polly Maberly as Mrs. Elvsted is on the left and Gillian Kearney as Hedda is on the right, under the direction of Matthew Lloyd in a production in the United Kingdom. (© Marilyn Kingwill/ArenaPAL)

title character in a play. Both are young women intent on defying an older person and willing to risk death to fight for a principle. But unlike other dramatists who had told the same story, Sophocles gave each of them a sister with a sharply contrasting personality. To Antigone he gave Ismene, a docile, compliant sister who argues that Antigone should obey the law and give in to authority. To Electra he gave Chrisothemis, a meek, frightened creature who protests that as women they are powerless to act. Sophocles strengthened and clarified Antigone and Electra by providing them with contrasting characters to set off their own determination and courage.

Orchestration of Characters

Anton Chekhov, the Russian dramatist, is said to have "orchestrated" his characters. The reference is to a musical composition in which the theme is played first by one section of the orchestra, such as the violins; and then by another, such as the brasses or woodwinds. Not only is the theme taken up by various sections, but it can be played in different ways as well—first in a major key, for instance, and then in a minor key. Beyond that, there is the way the various segments of the orchestra—strings, brass, woodwinds, percussion—are blended together, how they play with one another or in counterpoint to one another. In a similar fashion, Chekhov created his characters, giving each a distinctive voice. But his real genius was in the way he blended his characters, creating differences, similarities, subtle shadings, and contrasts.

In each of his plays, Chekhov drew a series of characters with a common problem, and each character represented some aspect of the central theme. In *Uncle Vanya,* for example, Chekhov's theme of disillusionment and frustration with life is reflected by virtually every character in the play, each of whom longs for a love that cannot be fulfilled. The title character, Vanya, has been working on an estate to help support a professor whom he discovers to be a fraud. In the midst of his disillusionment, Vanya falls in love with the professor's young wife, but she does not return his love. A neighbor, Dr. Astrov, has made sacrifices to be a doctor in a small rural community and then has grown dissatisfied with his life. He too loves the professor's wife, but nothing can come of it. Vanya's niece, a plain woman who works hard for little reward, is in love with Dr. Astrov, but he does not return her love. And so it goes; practically everyone embodies the theme of unrequited love. But all this is done subtly and carefully. The theme is brought out through gradations and shadings of meaning which are interwoven in the characters like threads in a tapestry.

Chekhov was a master at orchestrating his characters, but he was not the only dramatist to use the technique. In one way or another, most dramatists try to arrange their characters so as to produce a cumulative effect. It is not what one character does or says but what all the characters do together that creates the effect.

In this chapter we examined the creation of dramatic structure and dramatic characters. In Chapter 9 we turn to point of view, or genre—in other words, the type of drama, whether tragic, comic, or some combination of the two.

SUMMARY

1. There are several basic types of dramatic structure. *Climactic* form was adopted by the ancient Greeks and has been used frequently ever since. Its characteristics are a plot beginning quite late in the story, a limited number of characters, a limited number of locations and scenes, little or no extraneous material, and tight construction, including a cause-and-effect chain of events.

2. *Episodic* form involves a plot covering an extended span of time, numerous locations, a large cast of characters, diverse events (including mixtures of comic and serious episodes), and parallel plots or subplots. Shakespeare's plays are good examples of episodic form.

3. The climactic and episodic forms can be combined, as they have been in the Restoration period and in the modern period, in the works of Anton Chekhov and others.

4. Ritual or pattern is often used as the basis of dramatic structure. Words, gestures, and events are repeated; they have a symbolic meaning acquired both through repetition and through the significance invested in them from the past.

5. Theatre events are sometimes strung together to make a program. Examples are a group of unrelated one-act plays and a group of skits and songs in a revue. In this case, structure is within the individual units themselves; among the units the only structure might be the unfolding of the separate elements; or there can be a common theme uniting them.

6. Avant-garde theatre sometimes arranges events in a random way to suggest the random or haphazard manner in which life unfolds in everyday situations.

7. Experimental groups in the modern period have often used radical forms, including non-verbal and improvisational structures.

8. Segments and tableaux have also been used as structure.

9. Structurally, musical theatre consists of different elements put together in a sequence, in which solo musical numbers alternate with group numbers and dances and these musical elements alternate with dramatic scenes.

10. Dramatic characters symbolize people and fall into several categories. Frequently the chief characters of theatre are extraordinary characters: men and women at the outer limits of human behavior. Also, these characters often hold important positions: king, queen, general, admiral, duchess.

11. In modern serious theatre we frequently find typical or ordinary characters—complete, fully rounded portraits of people—who embody a whole group or type. An example is Willy Loman, the salesman in *Death of a Salesman*.

12. Some characters are stereotypes. Stock characters, for instance, are predictable, clearly defined types. Other characters have one dominant trait, which overshadows all other features.

13. A special type of character in drama of many periods is a narrator or the members of a chorus.

14. Occasionally performers are asked to play nonhuman parts—animals, birds, etc.—but these parts generally have a strong human flavor.

15. Characters are placed together by the playwright in certain combinations to obtain maximum effectiveness. A protagonist may be opposed by an antagonist; minor characters support major characters; and individual characters are orchestrated into a whole.

Tragedy, Comedy, and Tragicomedy

Tragedy, comedy, tragicomedy, farce, melodrama: these are various categories or types of drama. Such a category is often referred to by the French term *genre* (pronounced JAHN-ruh). People have found that speaking of plays in these terms can be helpful in studying and understanding theatre. An audience member who has knowledge of genres or types of plays will have a better grasp of a production he or she is attending.

In this chapter we will describe and explain the various types of drama. Before we begin, however, we should offer a word of caution about the notion of assigning plays to a particular category or genre. Although designations can serve a valuable purpose, attempting to separate and organize plays according to categories can also be a hindrance to developing a free and open understanding of theatre. Shakespeare makes fun of this problem in Hamlet when he has Polonius announce that the players who have come to court can perform anything: "tragedy, comedy, history, pastoral, pastoral-comedy, historical-pastoral, tragical-historical, tragical-comical-historical-pastoral." In spite of such absurdities, there are those who continue to try to pigeon-hole or label every play that comes along.

Having heard this warning, however, we will find that it is still helpful to understand the various genres into which stage works can fall. A play that aims at a purely melodramatic effect, for instance, should be looked at differently from one that aspires to tragedy. A lighthearted comedy should not be judged by the same standards as a philosophical play. It is to understand these differences that we study dramatic genres.

In this chapter we will look first at tragedy and other forms of serious drama, and then turn to comedy, tragicomedy and alternative forms that have developed through the years.

◀ **DRAMATIC GENRE: COMEDY**

Drama is often divided into categories or types, often referred to as genres. The Greeks separated tragedy from comedy. To those two genres have been added others such as farce and tragicomedy. Shown here is a comedy of wit by Oliver Goldsmith, She Stoops to Conquer, *which he called a "laughing comedy." The production was directed by Nicholas Martin at the McCarter Theatre; sets, David Korins; lighting, Ben Stanton; costumes, Gabriel Berry. (© T Charles Erickson)*

TRAGEDY

Serious drama takes a thoughtful, sober attitude toward its subject matter. It puts the spectators in a frame of mind to think about what they are seeing and to become involved with the characters onstage: to love what these characters love, fear what they fear, and suffer what they suffer. The best-known form of serious drama, to which we turn first, is *tragedy*. Other forms of serious theatre are *heroic drama, domestic drama,* and *melodrama.*

Tragedy asks very basic questions about human existence. Why are people sometimes cruel to one another? Why is the world unjust? Why are men and women called on to endure suffering? What are the limits of human suffering and endurance? In the midst of cruelty and despair, what are the possibilities of human achievement? To what heights of courage, strength, generosity, and integrity can human beings rise?

EXTRAORDINARY CHARACTERS CAUGHT IN A TRAGIC WEB
In traditional tragedy the fall of a hero or heroine has a special significance because of the combination of his or her personality and position. An example of an exceptional tragic heroine is Medea in Euripides's play of the same name. The heroine has been wronged by her husband, Jason, and for revenge she sends a poisoned robe to the woman he has turned to. In addition, to further punish him, Medea kills the sons she has had with Jason. Shown here is the British actress Fiona Shaw holding one of the sons she has murdered while Jason (Jonathan Cake) rages. The production was directed by Deborah Warner. (© Donald Cooper/Photo*stage*)

Tragedy assumes that the universe is indifferent to human concerns and often cruel and malevolent. Sometimes the innocent appear to suffer while the evil prosper. In the face of this, some humans are capable of despicable deeds, but others can confront and overcome adversity, attaining a nobility that places them "a little lower than the angels."

We can divide tragedy into two basic kinds: traditional and modern. *Traditional tragedy* includes works from several significant periods of the past. *Modern tragedy* generally includes plays from the late nineteenth century to the present day.

Traditional Tragedy

Three noteworthy periods of history in which tragic drama was produced are Greece in the fifth century BCE, England in the late sixteenth century and early seventeenth century, and France in the seventeenth century. Tragedies from these three ages have in common the following characteristics, which help define traditional tragedy.

Tragic Heroes and Heroines Generally, the hero or heroine of a tragedy is an extraordinary person: a king, a queen, a general, a nobleman or noblewoman—in other words, a person of stature. In Greek drama, Antigone, Electra, Oedipus, Agamemnon, Creon, and Orestes are members of royal families. In the plays of Shakespeare, Hamlet, Claudius, Gertrude, Lear, and Cordelia are also royal; Julius Caesar, Macbeth, and Othello are generals; and others—Ophelia, Romeo, and Juliet—are members of the nobility.

Tragic Circumstances   The central figures of the play are caught in a series of tragic circumstances: Oedipus, without realizing it, murders his father and marries his mother; Antigone must choose between death and dishonoring her dead brother; Phaedra falls hopelessly and fatally in love with her stepson, Hippolytus; Othello is completely duped by Iago; and Lear is cast out by the daughters to whom he has given his kingdom. In traditional tragedy, the universe seems determined to trap the hero or heroine in a fateful web.

Tragic Irretrievability   The situation becomes irretrievable: there is no turning back. The tragic figures are in a situation from which there is no honorable avenue of escape; they must go forward to meet their fate.

Acceptance of Responsibility   The hero or heroine accepts responsibility for his or her actions and also shows willingness to suffer and an immense capacity for suffering. Oedipus puts out his own eyes; Antigone faces death with equanimity; Othello kills himself. King Lear suffers immensely, living through personal humiliation, a raging storm on a heath, temporary insanity, and the death of his daughter, and finally confronts his own death. A statement by Edgar in *King Lear* applies to all tragic figures: "Men must endure their going hence even as their coming hither."

Tragic Verse   The language of traditional tragedy is verse. Because it deals with lofty and profound ideas—with men and women at the outer limits of their lives— tragedy soars to the heights and descends to the depths of human experience; and many feel that such thoughts and emotions can best be expressed in poetry. Look at Cleopatra's lament on the death of Mark Antony. Her sense of admiration for Antony, and her desolation, could never be conveyed so tellingly in less poetic terms:

> Oh, wither'd is the garland of war,
> The soldier's pole is fall'n! Young boys and girls
> Are level now with men. The odds is gone,
> And there is nothing left remarkable
> Beneath the visiting moon.

These words have even more effect when heard in the theatre spoken by an eloquent actress.

The Effect of Tragedy   When the elements of traditional tragedy are combined, they appear to produce two contradictory reactions simultaneously. One is pessimistic: the heroes or heroines are "damned if they do and damned if they don't," and the world is a cruel, uncompromising place, a world of despair. And yet, in even the bleakest tragedy—whether *Hamlet, Medea, Macbeth,* or *King Lear*—there is affirmation. One source of this positive feeling is found in the drama itself. Sophocles, Euripides, Shakespeare, and the French dramatist Jean Racine, although telling us that the world is in chaos and utterly lost, at the same time affirmed just the opposite by creating brilliant, carefully shaped works of art.

There is another positive element, which has to do with the tragic heroes and heroines themselves. They meet their fate with such dignity and such determination that they defy the gods. They say: "Come and get me; throw your worst at me. Whatever happens,

GLOBAL CROSSCURRENTS

THE ASIAN INFLUENCE ON THE PLAYWRIGHTS BRECHT AND WILDER

Two mid-twentieth-century dramatists from the west who were strongly influenced by Asian theatre were the German playwright Bertolt Brecht (1889–1956) and the American playwright Thornton Wilder (1897–1975).

Brecht, for example, drew from Asian legends, and used techniques borrowed from Chinese, Japanese, and Indian theatre. Chinese theatre and literature were to prove particularly important for his *Good Woman of Setzuan* (1938–1949) which was set in China; and *The Caucasian Chalk Circle* (1944–1945), based on a Chinese play, *The Story of the Chalk Circle*.

Both Brecht and Wilder had seen Beijing opera and adopted certain features of this dramatic style into their own work. Beijing opera (also called

Bertolt Brecht. (© Hulton-Deutsch Collection/Corbis)

Thornton Wilder. (© Bettmann/Corbis)

jingju and Peking opera) blends song, dance, martial arts, theatre, acrobatics, and dance and uses much symbolism. Beijing opera takes place on an almost bare stage (often with just a table and a few chairs onstage throughout) and uses simple props brought on by stage attendants, and symbolic movements by the actors. For example, an actor walking in a circle around the stage indicates a long journey; a banner with a fish design indicates water, although rolled up on a tray, the same banner would represent a fish.

Brecht used such symbolic props and actions to achieve his alienation or distancing effect, which prevented the audience from identifying emotionally with the drama. In 1935, Brecht saw a performance by the Beijing opera star Mei Lanfang (1894–1961) in Moscow, and the following year he wrote his essay "Alienation Effects in Chinese Acting," which noted aspects of Beijing opera conducive to the distancing effect he desired.

Similarly, Wilder had been exposed to Chinese theatre first at an early age, when his father's work took him to Hong Kong and Shanghai; and then as an adult, when he saw Mei Lanfang perform in New York in 1930. Aspects of Beijing opera that Wilder adopted can best be seen in his Pulitzer Prize–winning *Our Town* (1938). In this play, Wilder uses an almost bare stage with just two tables and six chairs positioned by the stage manager (who also acts as a narrator), and other locales are suggested by very simple alterations; in the third act, for example, the cemetery is suggested by just ten or twelve people sitting in chairs.

Both playwrights illustrate the increasing prevalence of Asian influences in twentieth-century playwriting.

Prepared by Naomi Stubbs, CUNY Graduate Center.

I will not surrender my individuality or my dignity." In Aeschylus's play *Prometheus,* the title character—who is one of the earliest tragic heroes—says: "On me the tempest falls. It does not make me tremble." In defeat, the men and women of tragedy triumph.

As for the deeper meanings of individual tragedies, there is a vast literature on the subject, and each play has to be looked at and experienced in detail to obtain the full measure of its meaning. Certain tragedies seem to hold so much meaning, to contain so much—in substance and in echoes and reverberations—that one can spend a lifetime studying them.

Modern Tragedy

Tragedies of the modern period—that is, beginning in the late nineteenth century—do not have queens or kings as central figures, and they are written in prose rather than poetry. For these as well as more philosophical reasons, purists argue that modern tragedies are not true tragedies.

In answer to this, it should be pointed out that today we have few kings or queens—either in a mythology or, except in certain places like Great Britain, in real life. At the same time, we may ask: do we not have characters today who can stand as symbolic figures for important segments of society? Many would answer that we still do.

In attempting to create modern tragedy, the question is not whether we view the human condition in the same way as the French in the seventeenth century or the Greeks did in the fifth century BCE—the truth is that those two societies did not view life in

A MODERN TRAGIC FAMILY

In Federico García Lorca's play *The House of Bernarda Alba,* a widow who has grown to hate and distrust men keeps her daughters confined as virtual prisoners in their own home, preventing them from going out. In this production, directed by Elizabeth Huddle at the Madison Repertory Theatre, we see four of the daughters, with the mother in the center. Left to right, the performers are Jamie England, Monica Lyons, Elisabeth Adwin, Margaret Ingraham, and Diane Robinson. (Zane Williams/Madison Repertory Theatre)

the same way either—but whether our age allows for a tragic view on its own terms. The answer seems to be yes. Compared with either the eighteenth or the nineteenth century—ages of enlightenment, progress, and unbounded optimism—our age has its own tragic vision. Modern tragic dramatists probe the same depths and ask the same questions as their predecessors: Why do men and women suffer? Why do violence and injustice exist? And perhaps most fundamental of all: What is the meaning of our lives?

On this basis, many commentators would argue that writers like Ibsen, Strindberg, García Lorca, O'Neill, Williams, and Miller can lay claim to writing legitimate modern tragedy. The ultimate test of a play is not whether it meets someone's definition of tragedy but what effect it produces in the theatre and how successful it is in standing up to continued scrutiny. Eugene O'Neill's *Long Day's Journey into Night* takes as bleak a look at the human condition, with, at the same time, as compassionate a view of human striving and dignity as it seems possible to take in our day.

HEROIC DRAMA

The term **heroic drama** is not used as commonly as *tragedy* or *comedy,* but there is a wide range of plays for which *heroic drama* seems an appropriate description. I use the term specifically to indicate serious drama of any period that incorporates heroic or noble figures and other features of traditional tragedy—dialogue in verse, extreme situations, and the like—but differs from tragedy in having a happy ending, or in assuming a basically optimistic worldview even when the ending is sad.

Several Greek plays ordinarily classified as tragedies are actually closer to heroic drama. In Sophocles's *Electra,* for instance, Electra suffers grievously, but at the end of the play she and her brother Orestes triumph. Another example is *The Cid,* written by Pierre Corneille (1606–1684) in France. It has a hero who leads his men to victory in battle but who is not killed; in the end, he wins a duel against his rival. In the late seventeenth century in England, a form of drama also called *heroic drama,* or sometimes *heroic tragedy,* was precisely the type about which I am speaking: a serious play with a happy ending for the hero or heroine.

Many Asian plays—from India, China, and Japan—though resisting the usual classifications and including a great deal of dance and music, bear a close resemblance to heroic drama. Frequently, for example, a hero goes through a series of dangerous adventures, emerging victorious at the end. The vast majority of Asian dramas end happily.

A second type of heroic drama involves the death of the hero or heroine, but neither the events along the way nor the conclusion can be thought of as tragic. Several of the plays of Johann Wolfgang von Goethe (1749–1832) follow this pattern. (Many of Goethe's plays, along with those of his contemporaries in the late eighteenth century and early nineteenth century, form a subdivision of heroic drama referred to as *romantic drama.* **Romanticism,** a literary movement that took hold in Germany at the time and spread to France and throughout much of Europe, celebrated the spirit of hope, personal freedom, and natural instincts.)

A number of plays in the modern period fall into the category of heroic drama. *Saint Joan,* by George Bernard Shaw, is a good example: although Joan is burned at the stake, her death is actually a form of triumph. As if that were not enough, Shaw provides an epilogue in which Joan appears alive again.

In the history of theatre, the plays I refer to as *heroic drama* occupy a large and important niche, cutting across Asia and western civilization and across periods from the Greek golden age to the present.

BOURGEOIS OR DOMESTIC DRAMA

With the changes in society that resulted from the rise of the middle class and the shift from kings and queens to more democratic governments, we move from classic tragedy to modern tragedy. In the same way, during the past 150 years heroic drama has largely been replaced by **bourgeois** or **domestic drama.** *Bourgeois* refers to people of the middle or lower middle class rather than the aristocracy, and *domestic* means that the plays often deal with problems of the family or the home rather than great affairs of state. In the Greek, Roman, and Renaissance periods, ordinary people served as main characters only in comedies; they rarely appeared as heroes or heroines of serious plays. Beginning in the eighteenth century, however, as society changed, there was a call for serious drama about men and women with whom members of the audience could identify and who were like themselves.

In England in 1731, George Lillo (1693–1739) wrote *The London Merchant,* a story of a merchant's apprentice who is led astray by a prostitute and betrays his good-hearted employer. This play, like others that came after it, dealt with recognizable people from the daily life of Britain, and audiences welcomed it.

From these beginnings, bourgeois or domestic drama developed through the balance of the eighteenth century and the whole of the nineteenth, until it achieved a place of prominence in the works of Ibsen, Strindberg, and more recent writers such as Arthur Miller, Tennessee Williams, Lorraine Hansberry, Edward Albee, August Wilson, and Paula Vogel. Problems with society, struggles within a family, dashed hopes, and renewed determination are typical characteristics of domestic drama. When sufficiently penetrating or profound, domestic drama achieves the level of modern tragedy.

In one form or another, bourgeois or domestic drama has become the predominant form of serious drama throughout Europe and the United States during the past hundred years.

DOMESTIC DRAMA OF EVERYDAY LIFE

Domestic drama concerns itself with family problems: parents and children, husbands and wives, growing up, growing old. The characters in it are recognizable people, and it has long been a mainstay of modern drama. Shown here is a scene from the Hartford Stage production of *A Raisin in the Sun* directed by Seret Scott. It is a sensitive drama about a family in Chicago trying to buy a home in a white neighborhood. The actors are, left to right, standing: April Yvette Thompson (Ruth), Lynda Gravátt (Lena, the mother), and Crystal Noelle (Beneatha). Billy Eugen Thomas (Walter Lee) is on the floor. (© T Charles Erickson)

photo essay

Modern Domestic Drama

Serious drama in America came of age in the mid-twentieth century, with plays by Eugene O'Neill, Tennessee Williams, Arthur Miller, and Lillian Hellman, among others. Though all four experimented with nonrealistic dramatic devices, much of their strongest work was realistic domestic drama. Included here are examples, in photographs from the original productions.

(Carl Mydans/Time Life Pictures/ Getty Images)

Long Day's Journey Into Night, 1956, with Fredric March, Florence Eldridge, Jason Robards Jr., and Bradford Dillman.

A Streetcar Named Desire, 1947, with Marlon Brando as Stanley Kowalski and Jessica Tandy as Blanche DuBois.

(Theatre Collection, Museum of the City of New York)

204

All My Sons, 1947, with Karl Malden and Lois Wheeler.

Tallulah Bankhead (right) as Regina Giddons and Eugenia Rawls as Alexandra in the 1939 production of Lillian Hellman's *The Little Foxes.*

205

MELODRAMA

During the eighteenth and nineteenth centuries, one of the most popular forms of theatre was **melodrama.** The word, which comes from Greek, means "music drama" or "song drama." Its modern form was introduced by the French in the late eighteenth century and applied to plays that had background music of the kind we hear in movies: ominous chords underscoring a scene of suspense and lyrical music underscoring a love scene.

Among the effects for which melodrama generally strives is fright or horror. It has been said that melodrama speaks to the paranoia in all of us: the fear that someone is pursuing us or that disaster is about to overtake us. How often do we have a sense that others are ganging up on us or a premonition that we have a deadly disease? Melodrama brings these fears to life; we see people stalked or terrorized, or innocent victims tortured. Murder mysteries and detective stories are almost invariably melodramas because they stress suspense, danger, and close brushes with disaster. This type of melodrama usually ends in one of two ways: either the victims are maimed or murdered (in which case our worst paranoid fears are confirmed); or, after a series of dangerous episodes, they are rescued (in which case the play is like a bad dream from which we awaken to realize that we are safe in bed and everything is all right).

Probably the easiest way to understand melodrama is to look at films and television. Among the kinds of melodrama we find in movies and on television is the *western,* with its heroes and villains and a shootout on Main Street for the finale, as in *High Noon.* We also find television *soap operas,* with their perpetual crises, complicated love interests, adulterous affairs, sudden turns of fortune, and wicked, insincere villains; *science fiction* epics like *Star Trek, Star Wars,* and *X-Men,* in which once again the good characters oppose the bad and which feature a series of spectacular narrow escapes; *horror films* like *Saw, The Haunting in Connecticut,* and *Friday the 13th,* which try to frighten the audience as much as possible; and *detective stories* or *spy mysteries* like the 1940s classic *The Maltese Falcon* or James Bond films and *The Bourne Identity* series, which feature a succession of sensational, dangerous adventures.

Still another form of melodrama argues a political or moral issue. Melodrama invariably shows us the good guys against the bad guys. Therefore, a playwright who wants to make a strong political case will often write a melodrama in which the good characters represent his or her point of view.

Lillian Hellman (1905–1984), in order to depict the predatory nature of greedy southern materialists, wrote a forceful melodrama called *The Little Foxes.* The play takes place around 1900. The leading character, Regina Giddens, wants to take control of the family cotton mills so that she will be rich and can move to Chicago. She will do anything to obtain her objectives: flirt with a prospective buyer, blackmail her own brothers, and even allow her husband to die. In one horrifying scene, her husband has a heart attack, while she stands by, refusing to get his medicine.

A list of significant melodramas would range over most of theatre history and would include writers from Euripides through Shakespeare and his contemporaries to dramatists throughout Europe and the Americas in the modern period. Other types of serious drama, tragic and nontragic, frequently have strong melodramatic elements as well.

Aside from a basically serious point of view, there are two other fundamental approaches to dramatic material. One is *comedy,* with its many forms and variations; the other is a mixture of the serious and the comic, called *tragicomedy.*

COMEDY

People who create **comedy** are not necessarily more frivolous or less concerned with important matters than people who create serious works; they may be extremely serious in their own way. Writers of comedy like Aristophanes, Molière, and George Bernard Shaw cared passionately about human affairs and the problems of men and women. But those with a comic view look at the world differently: with a smile or a deep laugh or an arched eyebrow. Writers like these perceive the follies and excesses of human behavior and develop a keen sense of the ridiculous, with the result that they show us things that make us laugh.

It should also be noted that there are many kinds of laughter. They range all the way from mild amusement at a witty saying or a humorous situation to a belly laugh at some wild physical comedy to cruel, derisive laughter. Theatre, which reflects life and society, encompasses comedies that display a similar range, from light comedies to outrageous farces.

Characteristics of Comedy

If we cannot fully explain comedy, we can at least understand some of the principles that make it possible.

Suspension of Natural Laws   One characteristic of most comedy is a temporary suspension of the natural laws of probability, cause and effect, and logic. Actions do not have the consequences they do in real life. In comedy, when a haughty man walking down the street steps on a child's skateboard and goes sprawling on the sidewalk, we do not fear for his safety or wonder if he has any bruises. The focus in comedy is on the man's being tripped up and getting his comeuppance.

In burlesque, a comic character can be hit on the backside with a fierce thwack, and we laugh, because we know that it does not hurt anything but his or her pride. At one point in stage history a special stick consisting of two thin slats of wood held closely together was developed to make the sound of hitting someone even more fearsome. The stick is known as a **slapstick,** a name that came to describe all kinds of raucous, knockabout comedy.

Prime examples of the suspension of natural laws in comedy are silent movies and film cartoons. In animated cartoons, characters are hurled through the air like missiles, are shot full of holes, and are flattened on the sidewalk when they fall from buildings. But they always get up, with little more than a shake of the head. In the audience, there are no thoughts of real injury, of cuts or bruises, because the cause-and-effect chain of everyday life is not operating.

Under these conditions, murder itself can be viewed as comic. In *Arsenic and Old Lace,* by Joseph Kesselring (1902–1967), two sweet elderly women—sisters—thinking they are being helpful, put lonely old men "out of their misery" by giving them arsenic

SUSPENSION OF NATURAL LAWS IN COMEDY
Frequently in various kinds of comedy, particularly in farce, our natural reaction to events is reordered to achieve the comic effect, and the audience goes along with this. An excellent example is the play *Arsenic and Old Lace* by Jospeh Kesselring, in which two elderly women, who appear to be helpless and harmless, actually murder a number of old men by giving them elderberry wine laced with poison. Because we have accepted the comic premise of the play, we do not condemn their acts, but rather become amused. Shown here in a London production of the play are Marcia Warren, Stephen Tompkinson, Thelma Barlow, and Brian Poyser. (© Geraint Lewis)

in elderberry wine. The two sisters let their brother, who thinks he is Teddy Roosevelt, bury the bodies in the cellar, where he is digging his own version of the Panama Canal. All together, these innocent-seeming sisters murder twelve men before their scheme is uncovered. But we do not really think of it as murder, and we have none of the feelings one usually has for victims. The idea of suffering and harm has been suspended, and we are free to enjoy the irony and incongruity of the situation.

The Comic Premise   The suspension of natural laws in comedy makes possible the development of a *comic premise.* The comic premise is an idea or concept that turns the accepted notion of things upside down and makes this upended notion the basis of a play. The premise can provide thematic and structural unity and can serve as a springboard for comic dialogue, comic characters, and comic situations.

Aristophanes, the Greek satiric dramatist, was a master at developing a comic premise. In *The Clouds,* Aristophanes pictures Socrates as a man who can think only when perched in a basket suspended in midair. In *The Birds,* two ordinary men persuade a chorus of birds to build a city between heaven and earth. The birds comply, calling the place Cloudcuckoo Land, and the two men sprout wings to join them. In another play, *Lysistrata,* Aristophanes has the women of Greece agree to go on a sex strike to end a war: they will not make love to their husbands until the husbands stop fighting and sign a peace treaty with their opponents.

Techniques of Comedy

The suspension of natural laws and the establishment of a comic premise in comedy involve exaggeration and incongruity, and the contradictions that result from these show up in three areas—verbal humor, characterization, and comic situations.

Verbal Humor   Verbal humor can be anything from a pun to the most sophisticated discourse. A *pun*—usually considered the simplest form of wit—is a humorous use of words with the same sound but different meanings. A man who says he is going to start a bakery if he can "raise the dough" is making a pun.

Close to the pun is the *malaprop*—a word that sounds like the right word but actually means something quite different. The term comes from Mrs. Malaprop, a character in *The Rivals* by the English playwright Richard Brinsley Sheridan (1751–1816). Mrs. Malaprop wants to impress everyone with her education and erudition

VERBAL HUMOR
Among the elements of comedy is verbal wit. No one was more the master of wit than the playwright Oscar Wilde, whose epigrams and clever wordplay are still quoted today. Shown here is a scene from his play *The Importance of Being Earnest* in a production at the Guthrie Theater, directed by Joe Dowling. It featured (left) Erin Krakow as Cecily Cardew and Linda Thorson as Lady Bracknell. (© Michal Daniel)

but ends up doing just the opposite because she constantly misuses long words. For example, she insists that her daughter is not "illegible" for marriage, meaning that her daughter is not "ineligible," and when asked to explain a situation she says that someone else will provide the "perpendiculars" when she means the "particulars."

A sophisticated form of verbal humor is the *epigram*. Oscar Wilde (1854–1900), a man devoted to verbal humor, often turned accepted values upside down in his epigrams. "I can resist anything except temptation," says one of his characters; and "A man cannot be too careful in the choice of his enemies," says another.

Comedy of Character

In comedy of character the discrepancy or incongruity lies in the way characters see themselves or pretend to be, as opposed to the way they actually are. A good example is a person who pretends to be a doctor—using obscure medicines, hypodermic needles, and Latin jargon—but who is actually a fake. Such a person is the chief character in Molière's *The Doctor in Spite of Himself.* Another example of incongruity of character is Molière's *The Would-Be Gentleman,* in which the title character, Monsieur Jourdain, a man of wealth, but without taste or refinement, is determined to learn courtly behavior. He hires a fencing master, a dancing master, and a teacher of literature (the last tells him, to his great delight, that he has been speaking prose all his life). In every case Jourdain is made a fool of: he dances and fences awkwardly and even gets involved in a ridiculous courtship with a noblewoman. All along he is blind to what a ridiculous figure he makes, until the end, when his follies and pretenses are exposed.

Comedy of character is a basic ingredient of Italian commedia dell'arte and all forms of comedy where stock characters, stereotypes, and characters with dominant traits are emphasized.

Plot Complications

Still another way the contradictory or the ludicrous manifests itself in comedy is in plot complications, including coincidences and mistaken identity. A time-honored comic plot is Shakespeare's *The Comedy of Errors,* based on *The Menaechmi,* a play of the late third century BCE by the Roman writer Titus Maccius Plautus (c. 254–184 BCE). *The Comedy of Errors* in turn was the basis of a successful American musical comedy, *The Boys from Syracuse,* with songs by Richard Rodgers (1902–1979) and Lorenz Hart (1895–1943).

In *The Comedy of Errors,* identical twins and their identical twin servants were separated when young, with one master and servant growing up in Syracuse and the other master and servant growing up in Ephesus. As the play opens, however, both masters and both servants—unknown to one another—are in Ephesus. The wife and the mistress of one master, as well as many other characters, mistake the second master and his servant for their counterparts in a series of comic encounters leading to ever-increasing confusion, until at the end, all four principals appear onstage at the same time to clear up the situation.

A classic scene of plot complication occurs in Sheridan's *The School for Scandal,* written in 1777. Joseph Surface, the main character in the play, is thought to be an upstanding man but is really a charlatan, whereas Charles, his brother, is mistakenly considered a reprobate. In a scene called the "screen scene," the truth comes out and the accepted images are reversed. As the scene opens, Lady Teazle, a married woman, is visiting Surface secretly. When her husband, Sir Peter Teazle, unexpectedly appears, she quickly hides behind a floor screen, but shortly after Sir Peter's arrival, Surface's brother Charles

PLOT COMPLICATIONS: A HALLMARK OF FARCE

Frequently used devices of comedy include twists and turns in the plot, mistaken identity, unexpected developments, and ridiculous situations. Michael Frayn's comedy *Noises Off* contains an abundance of these elements. The production shown here was at the Hartford Stage Company, directed by Malcolm Morrison. Scenic design, Tony Straiges; Costume design, Ilona Samogyi. (© T Charles Erickson)

turns up as well, and in order not to be seen by Charles, Sir Peter starts for the screen. Sir Peter notices a woman's skirts behind the screen, but before he can discover that it is his wife, Surface sends him into a closet. Once Charles enters the room, he learns that Sir Peter is in the closet and flings it open. As if this discovery were not enough, he also throws down the screen and in one climactic moment reveals both the infidelity of Lady Teazle and the treachery of Surface. The double, even triple, comic effect is due to the coincidence of the wrong people being in the wrong place at the wrong time.

Forms of Comedy

Comedy takes various forms, depending on the dramatist's intent and on the comic techniques emphasized.

Farce   Most plays discussed in the section on plot complications are *farces.* Farce thrives on exaggeration—not only plot complications but also broad physical humor and stereotyped characters. It has no intellectual pretensions but aims rather at entertainment and provoking laughter. In addition to excessive plot complications, its humor results from ridiculous situations as well as pratfalls and horseplay, not on the verbal wit found in more intellectual forms of comedy. Mock violence, rapid movement, and

photo essay

Forms of Comedy

(Sara Krulwich/The New York Times/Redux)

Comedy takes a number of forms, depending on whether the emphasis is on verbal wit, plot complications, or the characters' eccentricities. It can range all the way from intellectual comedy, to high comedy (dealing with the upper classes), to domestic comedy (similar to sit-coms on TV), to slapstick farce. Shown here is a variety of types of comedy.

A well-known British farceur is the playwright Alan Ayckbourn, who combines outrageous comic situations with serious personal problems and situations. The scene shown here is comic simply in the appearance of the costumes and the body language of the characters. The play is Ayckbourn's *Absurd Person Singular,* and the performers are Deborah Rush, Alan Ruck, and Clea Lewis.

Shown here is Mikelle Johnson as Dromio of Ephesus in Shakespeare's *The Comedy of Errors* in a Yale Repertory Theatre production. The humorous scene and costume designs are by two Yale graduate students: Evonne Esther Griffin and Alixandra Gage England, respectively.

(© Geraint Lewis)

Farce as satire is demonstrated by Steve Martin's *The Underpants,* an adaptation of a German farce from 1910 about a small-town mayor whose wife's underpants won't stay on. Shown here are Dolly Wells as Louise, the wife; and Graeme Eton as Klinglehoff, at the Red Lion Pub Theatre in England.

(© Joan Marcus)

Political satire is an age-old form of comedy. One of the best-known plays of this type is *The Government Inspector* by the Russian dramatis Nikolai Gogol. In the play, a number of politicians assume that an innocent man passing through their village is really a high-ranking figure from Moscow. Shown here are Lee Mark Nelson (Dobchinsky), Kris L. Nelson (Bobchinsky), and Sally Wingert (Anna Andreyevna). This production, adapted by Jeffrey Hatcher from the original, was directed by Joe Dowling at the Guthrie Theater.

(© Michal Daniel)

One of the finest comic playwrights of all time was the French dramatist Molière. One of his most famous creations was the title character in his play *Tartuffe,* a man who dressed in clerical clothing and pretended to be extremely pious. He completely fooled a man named Orgon, who considered him religious when in reality he was after Orgon's money and his wife. Shown here is a scene with the wife, the husband, and Tartuffe, played by Rachel Botchan, T. J. Edwards, and Bradford Cover at the Pearl Theatre.

(© Gregory Costanzo)

accelerating pace are hallmarks of farce. Marriage and sex are the objects of fun in *bedroom farce*, but farce can also poke fun at medicine, law, and business.

Burlesque *Burlesque* also relies on knockabout physical humor, as well as gross exaggerations and, occasionally, vulgarity. Historically, burlesque was a ludicrous imitation of other forms of drama or of an individual play. In the United States, the term *burlesque* came to describe a type of variety show featuring low comedy skits and attractive women.

Satire A form related to traditional burlesque, but with more intellectual and moral content, is *satire.* Satire uses wit, irony, and exaggeration to attack or expose evil and foolishness. Satire can attack specific figures; for example, the revue *Forbidden Broadway* makes fun of the more flamboyant or excessive stars in Broadway musicals. It can also be more inclusive, as in the case of Molière's *Tartuffe,* which ridicules religious hypocrisy generally.

Domestic Comedy The comic equivalent of domestic or bourgeois drama is *domestic comedy.* Usually dealing with family situations, it is found most frequently today in television situation comedies—often called *sitcoms*—which feature members of a family or residents of a neighborhood caught in a series of complicated but amusing situations. Television shows such as *Two and a Half Men, How I Met Your Mother,* and *My Name Is Earl* are examples. This type of comedy was once a staple of theatre and can still be found onstage in plays by writers like Neil Simon (b. 1927).

Comedy of Manners *Comedy of manners* is concerned with pointing up the foibles and peculiarities of the upper classes. Against a cultivated, sophisticated background, it uses verbal wit to depict the cleverness and expose the social pretensions of its characters. Rather than horseplay, it stresses witty phrases. Pointed barbs are always at a premium in comedy of manners. In England a line of comedies of manners runs from William Wycherley, William Congreve, and Oliver Goldsmith (1730–1774) in the seventeenth and eighteenth centuries to Oscar Wilde in the nineteenth century and Noël Coward (1899–1973) in the twentieth.

Comedy of Ideas Many of George Bernard Shaw's plays could be put under a special heading, *comedy of ideas,* because Shaw used comic techniques to debate intellectual propositions and to further his own moral and social point of view. Though witty and amusing, Shaw's plays frequently include provocative discussions of controversial social issues. *Mrs. Warren's Profession,* about a woman who runs a house of prostitution, deals with hypocrisy in society; *Arms and the Man* is not only an amusing story of a pompous soldier but also a treatise on war and heroism; *Major Barbara* poses difficult questions about philanthropy and the source of funds needed to carry out reforms.

In all its forms, comedy remains a way of looking at the world in which basic values are asserted but natural laws are suspended in order to underline human follies and foolishness—sometimes with a rueful look, sometimes with a wry smile, and sometimes with an uproarious laugh.

COMEDY OF MANNERS

Comedy of manners usually deals with the upper class in a given society. It stresses verbal humor, repartee, and irony. The precursors of modern comedy of manners were the Restoration comedies popular in London in the late seventeenth century. In the nineteenth century, Oscar Wilde was a master of comedy of manners, and in the twentieth century it was Noël Coward. One of Coward's best-known plays is *Private Lives,* about two upper-class couples whose marriages become comically entangled. Seen here in a production at the Guthrie Theater are Tracey Maloney (Sibyl), Kris L. Nelson (Victor), Stephen Pelinski (Elyot), and Veanne Cox (Amanda). (© Michal Daniel)

TRAGICOMEDY

In twentieth-century theatre a new genre came to the forefront—***tragicomedy.*** In this section, we will examine this form that has proved so important in the modern period.

What Is Tragicomedy?

In the past, comedy has usually been set in opposition to tragedy or serious drama: serious drama is sad, comedy is funny; serious drama makes people cry, comedy makes them laugh; serious drama arouses anger, comedy brings a smile. True, the comic view of life differs from the serious view, but the two are not always as clearly separated as this polarity suggests. Many comic dramatists are serious people; "I laugh to keep from crying" applies to many comic writers as well as to certain clowns and comedians.

A great deal of serious drama contains comic elements. Shakespeare, for instance, included comic characters in several of his serious plays. The drunken porter in *Macbeth,* the gravedigger in *Hamlet,* and Falstaff in *Henry IV, Part 1* are examples. In

TRAGICOMEDY: FUNNY AND SAD AT THE SAME TIME

In *The Visit,* by Friedrich Dürrenmatt, serious and comic elements are intertwined. The chief character, the richest woman in the world, demands the death of the leading citizen of a small town because he wronged her when she was young. At the same time there are also comic, ironic elements. This scene is from the original Broadway production, starring Alfred Lunt and Lynn Fontanne, directed by Peter Brook, 1956. (Photograph by Snowdon, Camera Press London/Billy Rose Theatre Division, The New York Public Library for the Performing Arts, Astor Lenox and Tilden Foundations)

medieval plays, comic scenes are interpolated in the basically religious subject matter. In a play about Noah and the ark, Noah and his wife argue, like a bickering couple on television, with Mrs. Noah refusing to go aboard the ark with all those animals. Finally, when the flood comes, she relents, but only after she has firmly established herself as a shrewish, independent wife.

One of the best-known of all medieval plays, *The Second Shepherds' Play,* concerns the visit of the shepherds to the manger of the newborn Christ child. While they stop in a field to spend the night, Mak, a comic character, steals a sheep and takes it to his house, where he and his wife put it in a crib, pretending that it is their baby (a parody of Christ lying in the manger). When the shepherds discover what Mak has done, they toss him in a blanket, and after this horseplay the serious part of the story resumes.

•The alternation of serious and comic elements is a practice of long standing, particularly in episodic plays; but *tragicomedy* does not refer to plays that shift from serious to comic and back again. It is a view in which one eye looks through a comic lens and the other through a serious lens; and the two points of view are so intermingled as to be one, like food that tastes sweet and sour at the same time. In addition to his

COMBINING TRAGEDY AND COMEDY
Tragicomedy has become more and more prominent in the modern period, and has taken its place alongside traditional tragedy, comedy, and other genres as a major form of our time. In several of Shakespeare's so-called problem plays, comic and serious elements are intermixed in the manner of tragicomedy. A good example is *All's Well That Ends Well*, which features a strange, almost bizarre, mixture of fairy-tale elements with cynical realism. Shown here is a scene from a production at London's National Theatre, directed by Marianne Elliott, with Conleth Hill as Parolles and Michelle Terry as Helena. (© Geraint Lewis)

basically serious plays and his basically comic plays, Shakespeare wrote others that seem to be a combination of tragedy and comedy, such as *Measure for Measure* and *All's Well That Ends Well*. Because they do not fit neatly into one category or the other, these plays have proved troublesome to critics—so troublesome that they have been officially dubbed *problem plays*. •

The "problem," however, arises largely because of difficulty in accepting the tragicomic point of view, for these plays have many of the attributes of the fusion of the tragic and the comic. A sense of comedy pervades these plays, the idea that all will end well and that much of what happens is ludicrous or ridiculous; at the same time, the serious effects of a character's actions are not dismissed. Unlike true comedy, in which a fall on the sidewalk or a temporary danger has no serious consequences, these plays contain actions that appear quite serious. And so we have tragicomedy.

In *Measure for Measure,* for instance, a man named Angelo—a puritanical, austere creature—condemns young Claudio to death for having made his fiancée pregnant. When Claudio's sister, Isabella, comes to plead for her brother, Angelo is overcome by passion and tries to make her his mistress. Angelo's sentencing of Claudio is deadly serious, but the bitter irony that arises when he proves to be guilty of "sins of the flesh"—even guiltier than Claudio—is comic. The result is that we have tragic and comic situations simultaneously.

THE AUDIENCE'S RESPONSE

- A play by Henrik Ibsen, Anton Chekhov, Tennessee Williams, Lorraine Hansberry, or August Wilson might be set in a time 50 years ago or 100 years ago. What do you think it is about these dramas that allows an audience member in the twenty-first century to identify strongly with the characters and the situations in the play?

- Which kind of play do you prefer: a classic tragedy, a serious contemporary drama, a knockabout farce, a comedy, a musical? Can you explain why you prefer one type over the others?

- Do you favor a play with a strong story line, a tight plot, and unexpected twists and turns? Or do you prefer a looser play that reflects the randomness of everyday life? What do you think attracts you to these characteristics?

Modern Tragicomedy

In the modern period—during the past hundred years or so—tragicomedy has become the primary approach of many of the best playwrights. As suggested in Chapter 3, these writers are not creating in a vacuum; they are part of the world in which they live, and ours is an age that has adopted a tragicomic viewpoint more extensively than most previous ages. As if to keynote this attitude and set the tone, the Danish philosopher Søren Kierkegaard (1813–1855) made the following statement in 1842: "Existence itself, the act of existence, is a striving and is both pathetic and comic in the same degree." The plays of Anton Chekhov, written at the turn of the twentieth century, reflect the spirit described by Kierkegaard. Chekhov called two of his major plays *comedies;* but Stanislavsky, who directed them, called them *tragedies*—an indication of the confusion arising from Chekhov's mixture of the serious and the comic.

An example of Chekhov's approach is a scene at the end of the third act of *Uncle Vanya,* first produced in 1899. Vanya and his niece, Sonya, have worked and sacrificed for years to keep an estate going in order to support her father, a professor. At the worst possible moment, just when Vanya and Sonya have both been rebuffed by people they love, the professor announces that he wants to sell the estate, leaving Vanya and Sonya with nothing. Sonya explains how cruel and thoughtless this is, and a few moments later Vanya comes in to shoot the professor. He waves his pistol in the air like a madman and shoots twice, but he misses both times and then collapses on the floor. In this scene, Vanya and Sonya are condemned to a lifetime of drudgery and despair—a serious fate—but Vanya's behavior with the gun (there is doubt that he honestly means to kill the professor) is wildly comic. Again, serious and comic elements are inextricably joined.

Theatre of the absurd (discussed below) is an example of modern tragicomedy. It probes deeply into human problems and casts a cold eye on the world, and yet it is also imbued with a comic spirit. The plays of Harold Pinter (b. 1930), a writer associated with theatre of the absurd, have been called *comedies of menace,* a phrase suggesting the idea of a theatre simultaneously terrifying and entertaining.

COMEDIES OF MENACE
Comedies range widely, from the pure entertainment of farce and light comedy to more substantive and probing comedies with a strong serious component. The playwright Harold Pinter calls many of his plays *comedies of menace,* meaning that they can provoke laughter but also have a deeper, more disturbing, sometimes frightening element. One of Pinter's best-known plays exemplifying this is *The Birthday Party.* A recent London production directed by Lindsay Posner starred Eileen Atkins and Paul Ritter, shown here. (© Geraint Lewis)

THEATRE OF THE ABSURD

After World War II, a new type of theatre emerged in Europe and the United States, which the critic Martin Esslin called ***theatre of the absurd.*** Although the dramatists whose work falls into this category do not write in identical styles and are not really a "school" of writers, they do have enough in common to be considered together. Esslin took the name for this form of theatre from a quotation in *The Myth of Sisyphus* by the French writer, dramatist, and philosopher Albert Camus (1913–1960). Camus maintained that in the modern age we have lost the comfort and security of being able to explain the world by reason and logic: one cannot explain the injustice, inconsistency, and malevolence of today's world in terms of the moral yardsticks of the past. In *The*

Myth of Sisyphus, Camus says that there is a separation between "man and his life, the actor and his setting," and that this separation "constitutes the feeling of Absurdity."[1]

Plays falling into the category of absurdism convey humanity's sense of alienation and its loss of bearings in an illogical, unjust, and ridiculous world. Although serious, this viewpoint is generally depicted in plays with considerable humor; an ironic note runs through much of theatre of the absurd.

A prime example of theatre of the absurd is Beckett's *Waiting for Godot.* In this play Beckett has given us one of the most telling expressions of loneliness and futility ever written. There is nothing bleaker or more desolate than two tramps on a barren plain waiting every day for a supreme being called "Godot," who they think will come but who never does. But they themselves are comic. They wear baggy pants like burlesque comedians, and they engage in any number of vaudeville routines, including one in which they grab each other's hats in an exchange where the confusion becomes increasingly comical. Also, the characters frequently say one thing and do just the opposite. One says to the other, "Well, shall we go?" and the other says, "Yes, let's go." But having said this, they don't move.

Absurdist plays suggest the idea of absurdity both in what they say—that is, their content—and in the way they say it, their form. Their structure, therefore, is a departure from dramatic structures of the past.

Absurdist Plots: Illogicality

Traditional plots in drama proceed in a logical way from a beginning through the development of the plot to a conclusion, an arrangement that suggests an ordered universe. In contrast, many absurdist plays not only proclaim absurdity but also embody it.

An example is *The Bald Soprano* by Eugène Ionesco. The very title of the play turns out to be nonsense; a bald soprano is mentioned once in the play, but with no explanation, and it is clear that the bald soprano has nothing whatever to do with the play as a whole. The absurdity of the piece is manifest the moment the curtain goes up. A typical English couple are sitting in a living room when the clock on the mantle strikes seventeen times; the wife's first words are, "There, it's nine o'clock."

Absurdist Language: Nonsense and Non Sequitur

Events and characters are frequently illogical in theatre of the absurd, and so too is language. *Non sequitur* is a Latin term meaning "it does not follow"; it implies that something does not follow from what has gone before, and it perfectly describes the method of theatre of the absurd. Sentences do not follow in sequence, and words do not mean what we expect them to mean.

An example of the irrationality or debasement of language is found in Beckett's *Waiting for Godot.* The character Lucky does not speak for most of his time onstage, but at the end of the first act he delivers a long speech consisting of incoherent religious and legalistic jargon. The opening lines offer a small sample.

> Given the existence as uttered forth in the public works of Puncher and Wattmann of a personal God quaquaquaqua with white beard quaquaquaqua outside time without extension who from the heights of divine apathia divine athambia divine aphasia loves us dearly with some exceptions for reasons unknown but time will tell. . . .[2]

THEATRE OF THE ABSURD

Non sequitur, nonsensical language, existential characters, ridiculous situations—these are hallmarks of theatre of the absurd, which can also be viewed as a type of tragicomedy. One example is Eugene Ionesco's *Exit the King.* Shown here, left to right, are Lauren Ambrose (as Queen Marie), Geoffrey Rush (King Berenger), William Sadler (the Doctor, in the background), and Susan Sarandon (Queen Marguerite, the King's wife) in a recent Broadway production adapted and directed by Neil Armfield. (© Joan Marcus)

Numerous examples of such language appear not only in the plays of Ionesco and Beckett but in those of many other absurdist writers.

Absurdist Characters: Existential Beings

A significant feature of absurdist plays is the handling of characters. Not only is there an element of the ridiculous in the characters' actions, but they frequently exemplify an ***existential*** point of view. According to this viewpoint, existence precedes essence; a person creates himself or herself in the process of living. Beginning with nothing, the person develops a self in taking action and making choices.

In theatre, existentialism suggests that characters have no personal history and therefore no specific causes for their actions. The two main characters in *Waiting for Godot,* for example, are devoid of biography and personal motivation; we know nothing of their family life or their occupations. They meet every day at a crossroads to wait for Godot, but how long they have been coming there, or what they do when they are not there, remains a mystery.

In addition to the plays of the absurdists, other modern plays also incorporate the tragicomic spirit. In *The Visit,* by Friedrich Dürrenmatt (1921–1990), a Swiss dramatist, a wealthy woman returns to her birthplace, a small, poverty-stricken village. She offers a huge sum of money to the village on the condition that the citizens murder a storekeeper who wronged her when she was young. The townspeople express horror at the idea, but at the same time they begin buying expensive items on credit—some from the man's own store. There is a comic quality to these scenes: the shopkeeper's wife, for instance, shows up in a flashy fur coat. The conclusion, however, is not funny, for the man is eventually murdered by his greedy neighbors.

In tragicomedy, a smile is frequently cynical, a chuckle may be tinged with a threat, and laughter is sometimes bitter. In the past, the attitude that produced these combinations was the exception rather than the rule. In our day, it seems far more prevalent, not to say relevant. As a result, tragicomedy has taken its place as a major form alongside the more traditional approaches.

In Part Three we have been examining the work of the playwright in creating a play, including the development of dramatic structure, dramatic characters, and genre (tragedy, comedy, tragicomedy, and so forth). In Part Four, we turn to those responsible for the visual and aural design of a production: scenery, costumes, light, and sound.

SUMMARY

1. Tragedy attempts to ask very basic questions about human existence: Why do men and women suffer? Is there justice in the world? What are the limits of human endurance and achievement? Tragedy presupposes an indifferent and sometimes malevolent universe in which the innocent suffer and there is inexplicable cruelty. It also assumes that certain men and women will confront and defy fate, even if they are overcome in the process.

2. Tragedy can be classified as traditional or modern. In traditional tragedy the chief characters are persons of stature—kings, queens, and the nobility. The central figure is caught in a series of tragic circumstances, which are irretrievable. The hero or heroine is willing to fight and die for a cause. The language of the play is verse.

3. Modern tragedy involves ordinary people rather than the nobility, and it is generally written in prose rather than verse. In this modern form, the deeper meanings of tragedy are explored by nonverbal elements and by the cumulative or overall effect of events as well as by verbal means.

4. There are several kinds of nontragic serious plays, the most notable being heroic drama, bourgeois or domestic drama, and melodrama.

5. Heroic drama has many of the same elements as traditional tragedy—it frequently deals with highborn characters and is often in verse. In contrast to tragedy, however, it has a happy ending or an ending in which the death of the main character is considered a triumph, not a defeat.

6. Bourgeois or domestic drama deals with ordinary people, always seriously but not always tragically. It stresses the problems of the middle and lower classes and became a particularly prominent form in the twentieth century.

7. Melodrama features exaggerated characters and events arranged to create horror or suspense or to present a didactic argument for some political, moral, or social point of view.

8. Comedy takes a different approach from serious forms of drama. It sees the humor and incongruity in people and situations. Comic dramatists accept a social and moral order and suspend natural laws (a man falls flat on his face but does not really hurt himself).

9. Comedy is developed by means of several techniques. *Verbal humor* turns words upside down and creates puns, malapropisms, and inversions of meaning. *Comedy of character* creates men and women who take extreme positions, make fools of themselves, or contradict themselves. *Plot complications* create mistaken identity, coincidences, and people who turn up unexpectedly in the wrong house or the wrong bedroom. There are also physical aspects to comedy: slapstick and horseplay.

10. From these techniques, the dramatist fashions various kinds of comedy. For instance, depending on the degree of exaggeration, a comedy can be *farce* or *comedy of manners;* farce features strong physical humor, whereas comedy of manners relies more on verbal wit.

11. Another type of comedy is *domestic comedy,* which deals with ordinary people in familiar situations. Depending on its intent, comedy can be designed to entertain, as with *farce* or *burlesque;* or to correct vices, in which case it becomes *satire.* Many of Shaw's plays represent *comedy of ideas.*

12. Serious and comic elements can be mixed in theatre. Many tragedies have comic relief—humorous scenes and characters interspersed in serious material.

13. Authentic tragicomedy fuses, or synthesizes, two elements—one serious, the other comic. We laugh and cry at the same time. Plays by Chekhov, Beckett, Dürrenmatt, and writers of theatre of the absurd use tragicomedy. Some commentators feel that this is the form most truly characteristic of our time.

4

The Designers

THE VISION OF THE DESIGNERS

The scenic, costume, lighting, and sound designers are essential members of any production. They give visual and aural life to the ideas of the playwright and director. They create an environment for the performers and a milieu in which the audience can place the play and enjoy the production. An example of an enchanting world onstage is this scene for a production of Shakespeare's *Love's Labour's Lost.* Note the beautiful costumes, the colorful "trees" at the top, and the eye-catching reflections of the actors and costumes on the floor below. The production at the Royal Shakespeare Company was directed by Gregory Doran, with set design by Francis O'Connor and costumes by Katrina Lindsay. (© Robbie Jack/Corbis)

Part Four

The Designers

The theatre experience does not occur in a visual vacuum. Spectators sit in the theatre watching what unfolds before them. Naturally, they focus most keenly on the performers who are speaking and moving about the stage. But the visual images of scenery, costumes, and lighting are always present. Spectators also become aware of the elements of sound that are part of the production. The creation of these effects is the responsibility of designers.

As in other areas, there is a parallel between design elements in theatre and our experiences in everyday life. Every building or room we enter can be regarded as a form of stage set. Interior decorating, along with architectural design—the creation of a special atmosphere in a home or a public building—constitutes scene design in real life. A church decorated for a wedding is a form of stage set; so too is the posh lobby of a hotel, or an apartment interior with flowers, candlelight, and soft music. In every case the "designer"—the person who created the setting—has selected elements that signal something to the viewers, thus making an impression.

Just as scenic design surrounds our daily lives, costumes are all around us. For instance, there are the outfits people wear in a holiday parade, at a masquerade ball, or in a pageant. Other obvious examples of the costumes we frequently see are in fashion magazines and runway shows. The dresses and other outfits created by top-name designers for haute couture shows are not what women would ordinarily wear; they are exotic, extreme, and offbeat.

In a less obvious way, costumes also play a significant role in daily life. People wear clothing not only for comfort, but also for the information they want to convey to others about themselves. If we look around us, we are surrounded by costumes every day: the formal, subdued uniform of a police officer; the sparkling outfits of a marching band at a football game; a judge's long black robe; the cap and gown for graduation; the dresses worn by bridesmaids at a formal wedding. In this sense, everything we wear is a form of costume.

Stage lighting, quite simply, includes all forms of illumination on the stage. The lighting designer makes decisions in every area of lighting: the color of the lights, the mixture of colors, the number of lights, the intensity and brightness of the lights, the angles at which lights strike performers, and the

The main reading room of the New York Public Library—a grand environment where researchers, scholars, and readers can do their work. (Mark Lennihan/AP/Wide World Photos)

length of time required for lights to come up or fade out. As with costumes and scenery, one encounters lighting design in daily life: a nightclub may use varying levels of light in addition to strobes or black lights to create a party atmosphere or to encourage people to dance.

A fourth type of designer in theatre is often referred to as the *aural* or *sound designer.* This is the person who arranges the sound components. Sound, of course, is all around us: the conversations in a meeting place; trains, trucks, and automobiles that pass by; music that blares from sound systems. In theatre, the sound designer is responsible for sound effects, recorded music, and the placement and synchronization of microphones for the performers.

Not only must he or she create all aural material not originating with the performers; the sound designer must also blend the sound from all sources.

In Part Four we examine the work of the scenery, costume, lighting, and sound designers, which includes the various skilled theatre technicians who assist designers in bringing their visions and sounds to life.

The austere plain black robes worn by judges indicate authority and formality. Seen here are the judges of the Texas Court of Criminal Appeals in Austin. (© Bob Daemmrich/ The Image Works)

High Fashion—a model walks the runway during a show at the Paris Womenswear Fashion Week for the Spring/Summer 2010 season. (Karl Prouse/Catwalking/ Getty Images)

Fireworks are part of colorful pyrotechnic displays on many occasions, such as these starbursts in Paris on Bastille Day, France's most important holiday, celebrated on July 14. (Brand X Pictures/ PunchStock)

10

Scenery

When audience members attend a theatre production, they first encounter the environment—the look and size of the space. Is it large or small, formal or informal? Then, as the presentation begins, the spectator becomes aware of the performers and the roles they are playing, as well as the story that begins to unfold. But along with these elements, which initially strike the audience, there are other factors: the scenery, the costumes, the lighting, and the sound. In their own way, these are as crucial to the theatre experience as any other aspects.

THE AUDIENCE'S VIEW

As the audience members begin to take in the visual and aural elements of a performance, they should look for specifics. Is the scenery realistic, resembling a recognizable kitchen, bedroom, or office? Or is the scenery abstract: shapes, steps, levels, platforms on a relatively bare stage? Is it futuristic or dreamlike? What about the costumes? Are they like everyday clothes, or do they suggest some period: ancient Rome, the American Revolution, the Civil War, the 1920s? Are the costumes fanciful, like Halloween outfits, or do they resemble clothes from daily life: judges' robes, police uniforms, cheerleaders' outfits? As for lighting, is it what one would expect in a normal setting, coming from sunlight outdoors, or lamps indoors? Or perhaps the lighting is abstract and arbitrary: beams of light cutting through the darkness, special lighting illuminating one part of the stage while the rest is dark. Sound, too, must be taken into account. Are there arbitrary sounds: a music track, specials effects such as sudden eruptions of synthetic noises? Or is the sound realistic: sirens for ambulances, thunder for a storm?

◀ **SCENE DESIGN PROVIDES THE VISUAL ENVIRONMENT**

The set designer Marjorie Bradley Kellogg has created a bilevel set for the Syracuse Stage production of The Diary of Anne Frank. *On the lower level are the people who are hiding Anne's family; on the upper level is the hiding space. In this production, directed by Timothy Bond, costumes were by Lydia Tanji and lighting by Les Dickert. (© T Charles Erickson)*

In all these areas, the audience should be conscious of the visual and aural signals that are being sent continuously. As for who prepares these signals, they are the designers and all the technicians and others who work with them.

THE SCENE DESIGNER

The scene designer creates the visual world in which a play unfolds. Together with the playwright and the director, the scene designer determines whether a scene is realistic or in the realm of fantasy. He or she decides on the colors, the shapes, the visual style that the spectators view and the actors inhabit. The set indicates the kind of world we are in—outdoors or indoors; an affluent environment or a humble one; a time period long ago, today, or in the future. When different locales are called for—in a play with an episodic structure, for instance—the scene designer must ensure that we move smoothly and quickly from one locale to another.

Designers and lead technicians in their respective areas must deal with practical as well as aesthetic considerations. A scene designer must know in which direction a door should open onstage and how high each tread should be on a flight of stairs. A lighting designer must know exactly how many feet above a performer's head a particular light should be placed and whether it requires a 500- or 750-watt lamp. A costume designer must know how much material it takes to make a certain kind of dress and how to "build" clothes so that performers can wear them with confidence and have freedom of movement. A sound designer must know about acoustics, be familiar with echoes, and understand electronic sound systems.

As in other elements of theatre, symbols play a large role in design. A single item onstage can suggest an entire room: a bookcase, for instance, suggests a professor's office or a library; a stained-glass window suspended in midair suggests a church or synagogue. A stage filled with a bright yellow-orange glow suggests a cheerful sunny day, whereas a single shaft of pale blue light suggests moonlight or an eerie graveyard at night. How designers deal with the aesthetic and practical requirements of the stage will be clearer when we examine the subject in detail: scene design in this chapter, costumes in Chapter 11, and lighting and sound in Chapter 12.

A BRIEF HISTORY OF STAGE DESIGN

At the beginning of both western and Asian theatre there was little of what we now call scene design. The stage itself was the background for the action. In Greek theatre, for instance, the facade of the stage house usually represented a palace or some other imposing edifice. In medieval theatre, "mansions" were set up in town squares. These were small set pieces representing such things as Noah's ark, the whale that swallowed Jonah, and the manger in which Christ was born. The Elizabethan and Spanish theatres of the Renaissance had bare stages in which the facade of the stage house functioned as the background for the action, just as it had in Greece. In Elizabethan England and Spain, set pieces as well as furniture such as thrones were used, but there was still no scenery as we know it. Actual scenery began to appear along with the proscenium theatres in Italy and later in France and England. These were the theatres (described in Chapter 4) where designers such as the Bibiena family came to the forefront.

Since then, theatre has experienced a combination of improved stage machinery—the means by which scenery is shifted—and increasing realism in depicting scenes. This growing realism has been the basis of much modern stage scenery.

SCENIC DESIGN TODAY

We are accustomed to "stage settings" in everyday life; but, as with other elements in theatre, there is an important difference between interior decoration in real life and set designs for the stage. For example, the stage designer must deal with scale: the relationship of the performer in the set to his or her surroundings. This must in turn correspond to the scale of settings we experience in the world outside the theatre. The scale in a stage set may be different from that of a living room or a courtroom in real life. Robert Edmond Jones, who is often considered the most outstanding American scene designer of the first half of the twentieth century, put it in these terms:

> A good scene should be, not a picture, but an image. Scene-designing is not what most people imagine it is—a branch of interior decorating. There is no more reason for a room

THE SIGNIFICANCE OF SCENE DESIGN

Scene design creates the visual environment in which the action occurs. It signals the tone, the style, and the degree of reality or fantasy in the presentation. Shown here is a production by the innovative French auteur-director Ariane Mnouchkine of a piece entitled *Le Dernier Caravansérail*. It has all scenery on dollies wheeled swiftly on and off the stage to reinforce the continued movement of the refugees who are the subject of this epic drama. The cast members in this scene are bringing a movable piece of scenery downstage; note also the potted plant at the left, on a movable platform that can take various positions onstage in different scenes. (© Martine Franck/Magnum Photos)

on a stage to be a reproduction of an actual room than for an actor who plays the part of Napoleon to be Napoleon or for an actor who plays Death in the old morality play to be dead. Everything that is actual must undergo a strange metamorphosis, a kind of sea-change, before it can become truth in the theater.[1]

A stage set does signal an atmosphere to the viewer in the same way as a room in real life, but the scene designer must go a step farther. As has been pointed out many times, theatre is not life: it resembles life. It has, as Jones suggests, both an opportunity and an obligation to be more than mere reproduction.

The special nature of scenery and other elements of scene design will be clearer when we examine the objectives and functions of scene design.

OBJECTIVES OF SCENE DESIGN

The scene designer has the following objectives:

1. Creating an environment for the performers and for the performance.
2. Helping to set the mood and style of the production.
3. Helping to distinguish realistic from nonrealistic theatre.
4. Establishing the locale and period in which the play takes place.
5. Evolving a design concept in concert with the director and other designers.
6. Where appropriate, providing a central image or visual metaphor for the production.
7. Ensuring that the scenery is coordinated with other production elements.
8. Solving practical design problems.

Objectives 1 through 7 encompass the aesthetic aspects of stage design. Objective 8 encompasses several practical aspects.

AESTHETIC ASPECTS OF STAGE DESIGN

The Scenic Environment

There have been times in the history of theatre when scene design was looked on as painting a large picture. In Chapter 4, in discussing the proscenium stage, I noted the temptation to use the proscenium arch as a frame and put a large picture behind it. The tradition of fine scene painting, begun in Italy in the late seventeenth century, continued throughout Europe in the eighteenth and nineteenth centuries, and into the twentieth.

Scene painting as an end in itself has not been the only case where the visual side of stage spectacle took precedence over other elements and was featured for its own sake. In the seventeenth century, the elaborate stage effects at the "Hall of Machines" in Paris—clouds descending, rocks opening, turntables rotating—were the main attraction. Throughout the nineteenth century, spectacular effects, such as chariot races and houses burning down onstage, were extremely popular. Many modern musicals, such as *The Phantom of the Opera, The Lion King,* and *Wicked* have tended to rely on the visual side of the production fully as much as on other elements such as the book or score.

The person responsible for these visual extravaganzas is the scene designer. He or she is always an important member of the creative team in a theatre production, and for an elaborate musical such as *The Lion King* or an avant-garde visual piece, the

SCENERY: AN ENVIRONMENT FOR A PLAY

Scenery provides the visual world in which a performance takes place. It indicates whether a play is realistic, expressionistic, or fantastic; where the action takes place (inside a home, at various locations, in some exterior setting); and whether the story occurs in a past era or at the present time. For a production of Horton Foote's *Dividing the Estate* at the Hartford Stage, the scenic designer Jeff Cowie created the living and dining room area of a three-generation family in a small Texas town. It is a rather well-to-do family, quareling angrily over the estate of the dying mother; and the setting against which these family squabbles take place is handsome. The production seen here was directed by Michael Wilson, with lighting design by Rui Rita. (© T Charles Erickson)

work of the scene designer becomes a major ingredient. A stage picture that constantly engages the attention of the audience and makes a comment all by itself requires inventiveness and imagination of a high order, not to mention a firm grasp of stage effects.

To arrive at a design for a production, the scenic designer looks first at the script and analyzes the world the characters inhabit. How do they speak? How do they move? In what kind of home or office or outdoor setting do they function? What are their goals and objectives? What do they wear? Does their life seem cramped, or does it appear free and open? From the answers to these questions, the designer begins to form visual impressions, sometimes jotting down pencil sketches, sometimes making notes. The object is to absorb the play and the characters and to begin to move toward a concrete manifestation of the visual world of the drama—an environment in which the characters can interact.

Mood and Style

A stage setting can help establish the mood, style, and meaning of a play. Is the play happy or sad, frightening or uplifting? A Roman farce, for example, might call for comic, exaggerated scenery—in the manner of a cartoon, perhaps, with outrageous colors. A satire might call for a comment in the design, like the twist in the lines of

MOOD AND STYLE
The designers should establish the mood, tone, and style of a production; this is accomplished with architectural shapes, colors, fabrics, furniture, and other elements. Shown here is a cool, modern, bilevel design by Todd Rosenthal for a production at the Goodman Theatre of Sarah Ruhl's *The Clean House.* The drama, which won a Susan Smith Blackburn Award, concerns a young woman (Guenia Lemos), a maid who wants to be a comic, and her employer (Mary Beth Fusger) on the lower level, and the husband and his lover (Patrick Clear and Marilyn Dodds Frank), on the upper level. The design—clean and contemporary—is the backdrop for family turmoil. (Liz Lauren, courtesy of the Goodman Theatre)

a caricature in a political cartoon. A serious play calls for sober, straightforward scenery, even in a nonrealistic piece.

As examples of what is called for in scene design, let us consider two works by the Spanish playwright Federico García Lorca. His *Blood Wedding* is the story of a young bride-to-be who runs away with a former lover on the day she is to be married. The two flee to a forest, and in the forest the play becomes expressionistic: allegorical figures of the Moon and a Beggar Woman, representing Death, appear and seem to echo the fierce emotional struggle taking place within the characters. It would be quite inappropriate to design a realistic, earthbound set for *Blood Wedding,* particularly for the forest scenes. The setting must have the same sense of mystery, of the unreal, that rules the passions of the characters. We must see this visually in the images of the forest as well as in the figures of the Moon and the Beggar Woman.

Another play of García Lorca's, *The House of Bernarda Alba,* is about a woman and her five daughters. The woman has grown to hate and distrust men, and so she locks up her house, like a convent, preventing her daughters from going out. The action takes place in various rooms of the house and an enclosed patio. From the designer's point of view it is important to convey the closed-in, cloistered feeling of the house in which the women are held as virtual prisoners. The sense of entrapment must be omnipresent. In other words, the setting here stands in sharp contrast to that of *Blood Wedding.*

Realistic and Nonrealistic Scenery

The stage designer's role is of special importance in distinguishing between realism and nonrealism. *Realistic theatre* calls for settings that look very much like their counterparts in real life. A kitchen resembles a kitchen, a bedroom resembles a bedroom, and so on.

A complete reproduction, however, is an extreme. Even in realistic theatre the stage designer selects items to go onstage, and his or her talent and imagination play an important role. The point is to make the room resemble, but not duplicate, its

REALISTIC AND NONREALISTIC SCENERY

Generally, realism and nonrealism call for different design elements, underscoring the difference in style between these two types of theatre. Here (top), we see an extremely realistic set, designed by Andrea Bechert for a production of *To Kill a Mockingbird*, adapted by Christopher Sergel from the novel by Harper Lee, and directed by Jane Page at the Colorado Shakespeare Festival. The bottom scene is a surrealistic landscape designed by the avant-garde director Robert Wilson for his rock opera *POEtry*, about Edgar Allan Poe. There is no attempt to portray reality; rather, there is a surrealistic presentation of images and ideas. (*Top:* © University of Colorado; *Bottom:* © Hermann and Clärchen Baus)

real-life counterpart. It must also support the visual and thematic "world" of the play. A playwright does not simply take a tape recorder into the streets and record conversations; nor does a scene designer reproduce each detail of a room. A set calls for selectivity and editing. In a realistic setting, it is up to the designer to choose those items, or symbols, that will give the appropriate feeling and impression. At times the designer may provide only partial settings for realistic plays. We will see a portion of a room—a cutout with only door frames and windows, but no walls, or walls suggested by an outline. Whether a set is complete or partial, though, the result should convey to us not only the lifestyle but the individual traits of the characters in the play.

In *nonrealistic theatre,* the designer can give free rein to imagination, and the use of symbol is of special importance. Chinese theatre affords a graphic example of the possibilities of symbol in stage design. During its long history, it has developed an elaborate set of conventions in which a single prop or item represents a complete locale or action. An embroidered curtain on a pole stands for a general's tent, an official seal signifies an office, and an incense tripod stands for a palace. A plain table may represent a judge's bench; but when two chairs are placed at each end of the table, it can become a bridge. When performers climb onto the table, it can be a mountain; when

SCENE DESIGN SETS THE TONE
Good scene design sets the tone and style of a production, letting the audience know where and when the action takes place and whether the play is a tragedy, a comedy, or some other type of drama. Also, it harmonizes with other elements of the production—script, acting, and direction—to create a unified whole. The scene designer Patrick Carl created this rural Russian setting for Chekhov's *The Three Sisters,* directed by Joe Dowling at the Guthrie Theater. The costumes are by Paul Tazewell. (© T Charles Erickson)

they jump over it, a wall. A banner with fish on it represents the sea, a man with a riding crop is riding a horse, and two banners with wheels are a chariot. Interestingly enough, such symbols are thoroughly convincing, even to westerners.

Productions in the United States also provide examples of imaginative nonrealistic scenery. For a revival of Sophocles's *Electra,* Ming Cho Lee (b. 1930) suspended large stone formations on three sides of the stage, suggesting the three doors of ancient Greek theatre and conveying the solidity, dignity, and rough-hewn quality of the play. In contrast, for the musical *Company,* Boris Aronson (1900–1980) designed a sharp, sleek set constructed partly of chrome and Lucite with straight lines, which symbolized the chic, antiseptic world of sophisticated urban living.

Locale and Period

Whether realistic or nonrealistic, a stage set should tell the audience where and when the play takes place. Is the locale a saloon? A bedroom? A courtroom? A palace? A forest? The set should also indicate the time period. A kitchen with old-fashioned utensils and no electric appliances sets the play in the past. An old radio and an icebox might tell us that the time is the 1920s. A spaceship or the landscape of a faraway planet would suggest the future.

In addition to indicating time and place, the setting can tell us what kinds of characters the play is about. For example, the characters may be neat and formal or lazy and sloppy. They may be kings and queens or an ordinary suburban family. The scene design should tell us these things immediately.

The Design Concept

In order to convey information, the scene designer frequently develops a *design concept* similar to the directorial concept discussed in Chapter 6. The design concept is a unifying idea carried out visually. Examples of design concepts would be the claustrophobic setting for *The House of Bernarda Alba* and Ming Cho Lee's Greek-influenced setting for *Electra,* described above.

A strong design concept is particularly important when the time and place of a play are shifted. Modern stage designs for Shakespeare's *A Midsummer Night's Dream* illustrate the point. In most productions it is performed in palace rooms and a forest, as suggested by the script. But for a production by Peter Brook (b. 1925) in the early 1970s, the designer Sally Jacobs (b. 1932) fashioned three bare white walls—like the walls of a gymnasium. Trapezes were lowered onto the stage at various times, and in some scenes the performers actually played their parts suspended in midair.

The concept developed by a scene designer for a stage setting is closely related to the central image or metaphor, discussed next.

The Central Image or Metaphor

Stage design not only must be consistent with the play but also should have its own integrity. The elements of a design—lines, shapes, and colors—should add up to a whole. In many cases, a designer tries to develop a central image or metaphor.

In *Mother Courage* by Bertolt Brecht, the playwright has provided a central image for the designer to work with. This is the wagon which Mother Courage pulls throughout the play and from which she sells wares to support her family. The play takes place

A CENTRAL DESIGN IMAGE

For a production of John Steinbeck's *The Grapes of Wrath,* the scene designer, Marion Williams, selected an old jalopy as a central design image. The design conveys the futility of a deserted land, the Dust Bowl in the 1930s. In later scenes, trapdoors open to reveal a stream, and then a horrendous rainfall showers down, showing the extremes of weather faced by these wanderers. Through it all, however, an overstuffed jalopy is pushed around the stage by some of the actors, remaining a constant visual image and giving a sense of the characters' movements from place to place. The play was adapted by Frank Galati and directed by Joe Discher at the Shakespeare Theatre of New Jersey, with costumes by Maggie Dick. (© Gerry Goodstein)

in the seventeenth century, during the Thirty Years' War in Europe, and Mother Courage is a survivor. She sells goods to all sides in order to keep herself going. The wagon, which she has with her at all times, is a symbol of her transitory life—she is always on the move—and of her need to peddle merchandise. The wagon signifies the whole notion of commerce and its relationship to war. A designer, therefore, must create a wagon that will work onstage and that will embody all the characteristics called for in the script and the character of Mother Courage. It becomes a sort of mobile central image or metaphor around which the scene designer develops an entire visual concept.

Coordination of the Whole

Because scenic elements have such strong symbolic value and are so important to the overall effect of a production, the designer has an obligation to provide scenery consistent with the intent of the play and the director's concept. If the script and acting are highly stylized, the setting should not be mundane or drab. If the script and acting are realistic, the setting should not overpower the other elements in the production. Regardless of how the visual world of the play is defined, it is essential for the technical director to engineer the construction in such a way that the visual elements are not compromised but can still safely and effectively support the stage action. It is a question, once again, of how the various parts of a production should contribute to an overall effect.

PRACTICAL ASPECTS OF SCENE DESIGN

We now move from aesthetic considerations to the practical side of creating a visual environment.

The Physical Layout

The playing area must fit into a certain stage space, and, more important, it must accommodate the performers. In terms of space, a designer cannot plan a gigantic stage setting for a theatre where the proscenium opening is only 20 feet wide and the stage is no more than 15 feet deep. By the same token, to design a small room on a 40-foot stage would no doubt be ludicrous.

GLOBAL CROSSCURRENTS

THE MAGIC OF THE DESIGNER JOSEF SVOBODA

The Czech scene designer Josef Svoboda (1920–2002) developed a number of significant techniques in stage design, which have since been adopted and utilized by designers in many countries around the world. Svoboda's work centered on his understanding of the *kinetic stage* and *scenography.* The term *kinetic stage* refers to his belief that the set should not function independently of the actors, but rather should develop and adapt as a performance progresses. *Scenography* was what he called his art, conveying the sense that he created a whole physical space, not just designs on paper intended for the back of the stage. His experiments with these ideas led to many significant concepts in modern stage design, most notably the *laterna magika, polyekran,* and *diapolyekran.*

Polekran literally means multiscreen and was the practice, devised by Svoboda, of using multiple screens

at multiple angles and heights. Although real people and objects were projected, the aim was to convince the spectators not that they were looking at the real object, but rather that they were looking at a projection, or a collage of projections. A later development of this technique was *diapolyekran,* which employed whole walls of small, square screens making up a composite image. The wall of screens could be used to present one unified image, cubist images, or collage.

Laterna magika, the best-known of his innovations, used screens in conjunction with actors; the actors were part of the film, and the film was part of the action. The projections used in this form were not simply for decoration, or for communicating images independent of the action; rather, the projections and action functioned together, creating a new manner of performance.

These developments were introduced to the global community in 1958 at the Brussels World Fair, where they instantly commanded attention from the wider theatrical community. Svoboda had been the chief designer at the National Theatre in Prague at the time of the World Fair, and a showcase of the work of the theatre was displayed to the global audience, winning him three medals. What was seen as ingenious in 1958 was quickly adopted and adapted by numerous practitioners in many countries, and the effect of these means of design can still be witnessed in contemporary theatre, in performance art, and on Broadway, as well as at rock concerts and sporting events. This incorporation of screens and projections into onstage action has infiltrated the world of the theatre to the extent that it has become one of the conventional tools of theatre worldwide.

Josef Svoboda. (© Franco Origlia/Sygma/Corbis)

Prepared by Naomi Stubbs, CUNY Graduate Center.

The designer must also take into account the physical layout of the stage space. If a performer must leave by a door on the right side of the stage and a few moments later return by a door on the left, the designer must obviously make allowance for crossing behind the scenery. If performers need to change costumes quickly offstage, the scene designer must make certain that there is room offstage for changing. If there is to be a sword fight, the performers must have space onstage in which to make their turns, to advance and retreat.

GROUND PLAN

To aid the director, performers, and stage technicians, the designer draws a ground plan, or blueprint, of the stage, showing the exact locations of furniture, walls, windows, doors, and other scenic elements.

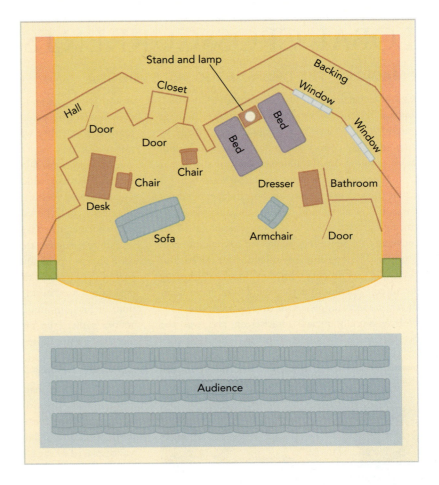

Any physical movement requires a certain amount of space, and the scene designer must allow for this in the ground plan. A *ground plan* is a floor plan, drawn to scale, outlining the various levels on the stage and indicating the placement of scenery, furniture, doors, windows, and so on. It is similar to a map in that the viewer is looking down on the plan from above. Working in conjunction with the director, the designer is chiefly responsible for developing a practical ground plan.

The way doors open and close, the way a sofa is set, the angle at which steps lead to a second floor—all these are the responsibility of the designer and are important to both the cast and the play. If a performer opens a door onstage and is immediately blocked from the view of the audience, this is obviously an error on the part of the scene designer. Also, actresses and actors must have enough space to interact with other performers naturally and convincingly.

To designate areas of the stage, the scene designer uses terminology peculiar to the theatre. *Stage right* and *stage left* mean the right and left sides of the stage, respectively, as seen from the performer's position facing the audience. In other words, when we look at a stage, the side to the audience's left is stage right, and the side to the audience's right is stage left. The area of the stage nearest the audience is known as *downstage,* and the area farthest away from the audience is *upstage.*

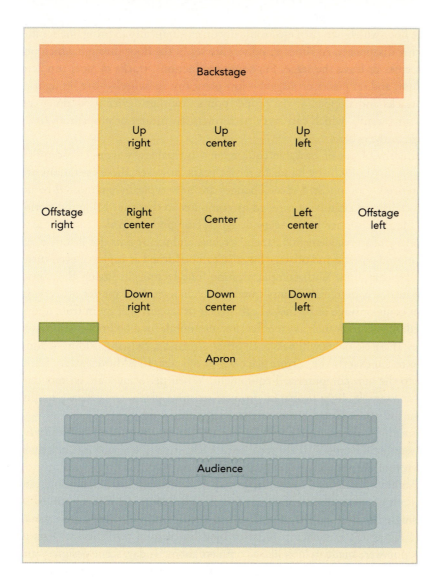

	Backstage	
Up right	Up center	Up left
Right center	Center	Left center
Down right	Down center	Down left

Offstage right

Offstage left

Apron

Audience

STAGE AREAS

Various parts of the stage are given specific designations. Near the audience is *downstage;* away from the audience is *upstage. Right* and *left* are from the performers' point of view, not the audience's. Everything out of sight of the audience is *offstage.* Using this scheme, everyone working in the theatre can carefully pinpoint stage areas.

The designations *downstage* and *upstage* come from the eighteenth and nineteenth centuries, when the stage was raked—that is, it sloped downward from back to front. As a result of this downward slope, a performer farther away from the audience was higher, or "up," and could be seen better. This is the origin of the expression to *upstage someone.* The term has come to mean that one performer grabs the spotlight from everyone else and calls attention to himself or herself by any means whatever. Originally, however, it meant that one performer was in a better position than the others because he or she was standing farther back on the raked stage and hence was higher.

Materials of Scene Design

In creating a stage set, the designer must be aware of several elements. For example, there is the stage floor itself. Sometimes the stage floor is a *turntable,* that is, a circle set into the floor which can turn electronically or mechanically to bring one set into view as another disappears. At times trapdoors are set in the floor through which performers can enter or leave the stage. For some productions, tracks or slots run across the stage floor, and set pieces or *wagons*—low platforms on wheels—are brought onstage in the tracks and stopped at the proper point. Another device used along the stage floor is a treadmill, which can carry performers, furniture, or props from one side of the stage to the other.

Formerly, pieces of movable equipment—turntables, wagons, treadmills—were moved mechanically or by hand. In recent years, however, these operations are often computerized. Complicated scene changes are now typically engineered by automation specialists and can be controlled by computer so that they bring the world of the play to life as envisioned by the scene designer. Computers can also control the turning and shifting of scenic elements. Panels, screens, and scenic flats, for instance, not only can be moved onstage and offstage but also can be turned at angles or even turned 180 degrees by computer. With computerization, one technician sitting at a console can control intricate, extremely complicated scene changes. In a matter of seconds, wagons will come onstage or be moved off; panels or screens will fly in from above or be removed; scenic units such as an office, an automobile, or a bedroom will move on- or offstage. These elements will pass each other—turning, twisting, sliding—and finally come to rest at exactly the correct place on- or offstage. In addition, safety features are built into the new computerized equipment. When performers are on moving treadmills, for example, light beams or pressure-sensitive plates can detect a malfunction and shut the system down before anyone is injured.

Instead of coming from the sides, scenery can be dropped from the **fly loft**—to *fly,* as noted in Chapter 4, is the term used when scenery is raised into the fly loft out of the view of the audience.

From floor level, ramps and platforms can be built to any height. To create walls or divisions of other kinds, the most common element is the **flat,** so named because it is a single flat unit. In the past, flats consisted of canvas stretched on wood, with the side facing the audience painted to look like a solid wall. Several flats used in conjunction were made to look like a complete room. Today, scene designers and shop technicians usually employ the *hard flat,* sometimes called a *movie* or *Hollywood* flat; it consists of a plywood material called lauan placed on a wooden or hollow metal frame. A hard flat can be painted; in addition, three-dimensional plastic moldings can be attached to it, creating cornices, chair rails, and other interesting features. The hard flat also has the advantage of not flapping when it is touched. Other vertical units are *cutouts*—small pieces made like flats or cut out of plywood. These too can be painted to look like a solid architectural element.

The scene designer's art comes into play in creating an illusion—with flats and other units—of virtually any type of room or architecture required. To accomplish this, designers not only use traditional materials but also take advantage of a wide range of nonscenic materials. Examples are scaffolding, inflatable scenery, reflective Mylar (which can be used for mirror effects), and erosion cloth—the crosshatch material used in highway construction.

A special type of scenery is the **scrim**—a gauze or cloth screen which (like a regular flat) can be painted with thin paint or dye. The wide mesh of the cloth allows light

SPECIAL SCENIC EFFECTS: THE SCRIM

Scene designers use various materials and devices to achieve their effects. One popular scenic element is the scrim, which can be transparent when light comes from behind it and opaque when light comes from the front. It is especially effective for scenes of memory and fantasy. Shown here, in front of a scrim, is a character from a production at the Huntington Theatre entitled *36 Views*. The scenery was designed by Adam Stockhausen, the costumes by Teresea Snider-Stein, and the lighting by Chris Parry. (© T Charles Erickson)

to pass through. When light shines on a scrim from in front—that is, from the audience's point of view—it is reflected off the painted surface, and the scrim appears to be a solid wall. When light comes from behind, the scrim becomes transparent and the spectators can see performers and scenery behind it. The scrim is particularly effective in scenes where ghosts are called for or an eerie effect is desired. Scrims are likewise useful in memory plays or plays with flashbacks: the spectators see the scene in the present in front of the scrim, and then, as lights in the front fade and those behind come up, they see through the gauzelike scrim a scene with a cloudy, translucent quality, indicating a memory, a dream, or a scene in the past.

Another scenic device is *screen projection*. A picture or drawing is projected on a screen either from in front—as in an ordinary movie theatre—or from behind. The advantage of projection from behind is that, because the performers will not be in the beam of the light, there will be no shadows or silhouettes. Obviously, projections offer many advantages: pictures can change with the rapidity of cinema, and there is an opportunity to present vast scenes onstage in a way that would hardly be possible otherwise.

SCENIC PROJECTIONS
An increasingly popular scenic resource is projections: rear-screen and front-screen projections, produced on an opaque surface or on a scrim. Projections allow rapid changes of locale, panoramic views, and abstract designs. Shown here are the projections of film footage of a plane flying low over the house in Arthur Miller's *All My Sons,* directed by David Esbjornson at the Huntington Theatre. The set design was by Scott Bradley and the lighting by Christopher Akerlind. (© T Charles Erickson)

In looking at the materials used in scene design, it is important to remember that the designer must have the experience and the know-how to design, paint, build, create drawings and models, engineer, and assemble in a manner that creates an appropriate and exciting "world" for the players and the play to inhabit.

Special Effects

Scrims and projections bring us to the subject of *special effects.* These are effects of scenery, lighting, sound, and props that seem unusual or even miraculous. (The term **prop** comes from the word *property.* It refers to any object onstage that is not a permanent part of the scenery or costumes. Props include such things as lamps, ashtrays, water glasses, computers, walking sticks, and umbrellas.)

Special effects include fog, ghosts, knives or swords that appear to stab victims, walls that fall apart, and so on. In the modern era, films and television—because of their technical capabilities—have brought extreme realism to special effects; examples include burning buildings, exploding cars, and scenes in outer space. Special effects onstage, however, are almost as old as theatre itself. From the Greeks on, theatre has tried to suspend natural laws and create an illusion of miraculous or extraordinary effects. The see-through scrim and projections (described above) are used to create a number of special effects, such as dream sequences. Fog machines create a cloudy

SPECIAL EFFECTS

An important element in many productions comes under the heading of special effects. These can run the gamut from swords that pierce bodies and the blood that flows from the wound to walls that collapse to smoke and fog, even fires onstage. Here we see such a fire in a production of *Everyman*. From left to right, Clemens Schick in the role of Death, Peter Simonischek as Everyman, and Sven-Eric Bechtolf as the Devil. This revival of a version by Hugo von Hoffmannsthal was directed by Christian Stueckl and presented as part of the Salzburg Festival in Austria. (Kerstin Joensson/AP Images)

vapor that can be blown across the stage, giving an impression of clouds or fog. In *The Phantom of the Opera,* a huge chandelier falls from the top of the auditorium onto the stage.

Several special lighting effects can be used to create interesting visual pictures. A simple technique is positioning the light source near the stage floor and shining the light on the performers from below. This creates shadows under the eyes and chin and gives the performers a ghostly or horrifying quality. Another special effect is created with ultraviolet light—a dark blue light that causes phosphorus to glow. When the stage is very dark, even black, costumes or scenery that have been painted with a special phosphorus paint will "light up." An effect of slow motion or silent movies, where performers seem to be moving in jerks, can be created by using a *strobe light,* a very powerful, bright gas-discharge light which flashes at rapid intervals.

There are also a number of special sound effects. Sometimes speakers are placed completely around the audience so that the sound can move from side to side. Computerized noises and electronic music can be used to create special sounds for various situations, and tape loops can repeat the same sound over and over for a long time. Echoes can be created by a machine that causes reverberations in sound waves. Applications of light and sound are discussed more fully in Chapter 12.

THE PROCESS OF SCENE DESIGN

Elements of Design

In bringing her or his ideas to fulfillment, the designer makes use of the following elements:

1. *Line,* the outline or silhouette of elements onstage—for example, predominantly curved lines versus sharply angular lines.
2. *Mass and composition,* the balance and arrangement of elements: for example, a series of high, heavy platforms or fortress walls versus a bare stage or a stage with one tree on it.
3. *Texture,* the "feel" projected by surfaces and fabrics: for example, the slickness of chrome or glass versus the roughness of brick or burlap.
4. *Color,* the shadings and contrasts of color combinations.
5. *Rhythm,* that is, "visual rhythm"—the repetition of shape, color, and texture in a regular or irregular pattern in a design.
6. *Movement* between scenes and within scenes—the way the action unfolds and the way it progresses from one scene to the next. This may involve rapid scene changes, turntables, and other devices for smooth transitions.

The designer will use these six elements to produce effects in conjunction with the action and other aspects of the production. Sometimes the designer will bring the director rough sketches showing several possible ideas, each emphasizing different elements to achieve different results.

Steps in the Design Process

In meeting the objectives described earlier in this chapter, how does the scene designer proceed? Although every designer has his or her own method, usually a general pattern is followed.

The designer reads the script carefully and begins to form ideas about how the play should come to life visually. Meanwhile, the director reads the script and develops ideas about the scenery. Following that, the director and the designer meet at a preliminary conference. Both have read the script, and they exchange ideas about the design. During these discussions the director and designer will develop and discuss questions of style, a visual concept for the production, the needs of the performers, and so on.

Next, the designer develops rough sketches, sometimes called *thumbnail sketches,* and rough plans to provide the basis for further discussions about the scenic elements. As the designer proceeds, he or she attempts to fill out the visual concept with sketches,

STEPS IN THE SCENE DESIGN PROCESS

In designing a production, the scenic, costume, lighting, and sound designers look closely at the script and work cooperatively with the director and with one another. Scene designers often make sketches, computer-generated designs, and models in preparing for the scenic aspect of a production. Here we see three stages in the scene design for the musical *In the Heights,* which originated off-Broadway at the 37 Arts Theatre in New York and later moved to Broadway. The scene designer Anna Louizos carefully scouted out the Washington Heights neighborhood in Manhattan where the play takes place and made many rough pencil sketches, one of which is shown here at the top (© Anna Louizos). The second photo shows one of various set models she built (© Anna Louizos), and the bottom photo shows the completed set with actors onstage. (Sara Krulwich/The New York Times/Redux)

- What production that you have attended had the most elaborate scenery, lighting, costumes, and special effects? What effect did these visual elements have on you? Were you captivated by the visual elements, or did you think that they were overdone?

- What production that you have seen had the least amount of scenery and visual effects? Did you miss seeing extensive design elements, or did you enjoy using your imagination to create the visual environment inside your head?

- In a production that you have seen that had many changes of scene, how efficiently and effectively were scene changes carried out? Were transitions smooth and seamless, or were they awkward and did they appear to interrupt the action?

drawings, models, and the like. Throughout this period there is a good deal of give-and-take, of tossing ideas back and forth, between the director and the designer. Gradually the director and the designer move toward a mutually agreeable design.

When the designer and the director have decided on an idea and a rough design they like, the designer will make a more complete sketch, often in color, called a *rendering*. If the director approves of this, the designer will make a small-scale three-dimensional *model,* which the director can use to help stage the show. There are two types of models. One shows only the location of the platform and walls, with perhaps some light detail drawn in; it is usually all white. The other is a complete finished model: everything is duplicated as fully as possible, including color and perhaps moldings and texture.

Today more and more designers are using computers and computer graphics to develop not only ground plans but also three-dimensional models of what a set will look like. Computerized design, known technically as *computer-assisted design* (CAD), is very flexible: the designer can make instantaneous changes in what appears on the screen and can easily indicate to the director and others alternative plans and features of a stage set. Not only ground plans but also the three-dimensional look of a set can be instantaneously rearranged to let both director and designer see what various configurations would look like. Not only can the scene be shown in three dimensions; it can also be looked at from various perspectives: from the right or left, from above, from the front.

It is important to note that this design process does not necessarily unfold from one step to the next in a predictable fashion. Discussions will be followed by further sketches, which in turn will be subject to consultation with the director and other designers. More than once in creating a production, the designer will feel it necessary to "go back to the drawing board."

The Scene Designer's Collaborators and the Production Process

As with every element of theatre, there is a collaborative aspect to scene design: in addition to the director there are a number of other important people with whom the scene designer works. In fact, any scene design would be little more than a creative idea without the input of the following collaborators: technical directors, property designers, scenic charge artists, stage managers, design assistants, and skilled technicians working in every one of these areas, often with expanded new technologies. These scenic collaborators are essential at every level of production, from university to regional professional theatre to Broadway.

A few definitions: the *technical director* is responsible for solving overall technical problems; he or she is in charge of scheduling, constructing and painting scenery, and in general, making certain that all designs are executed as conceived by the scene designer. The *property designer* creates and executes all props; this work may include building special pieces of furniture, finding or devising magical equipment, and selecting items such as lamps and other accessories. *Scenic charge artists* are responsible for seeing that sets are built and painted according to the specifications and requirements of the scene designer. In the case of painting the set, the person in charge is referred to as the *paint charge artist*. As noted earlier in this chapter, projection design is becoming a more common feature of the scenic environment, also requiring additional skilled technicians to bring the world of the play to life.

Realizing the design typically begins with drafting (predominantly with CAD these days) all production ground plans, also known as floor plans, which are detailed layouts of each scenic location drafted within the context of a specific theatre space. Drawings that show all exacting scenic details from the point of view of the audience are known as *designer/front elevations*. The drafting of the designer/front elevations is completed either by the scene designer or by various design assistants. These drawings are then used to construct accurate scenic models or perspective renderings that are useful visual tools for anyone involved in the production. Once they have been given final approval by the director, the floor plans are delivered to the stage manager, who will tape on the floor of the rehearsal spaces an accurate, full-scale version of all platforms, ramps, staircases, and entrances and exits to be used by the director and the actors in rehearsal. The technical director uses the floor plans to determine where all the construction elements will go, as well as to determine backstage escapes for actors. The technical director then completes construction drawings for all those floor plan elements. The technical director also converts the complete set of designer/front elevations into a complete set of rear elevations or working drawings for construction purposes. Without this critical engineering and drafting step, the scenery could never be built accurately or safely. The technical director and scenic designer work together in much the same way an engineer will work with an architect in completing the blueprints to plan construction of a building.

It is interesting to note that the realm of scene design on Broadway is one of the last areas to begin the switch over to CAD drafting and design. Many of the designers who have been working for years on Broadway were already well along in their professional careers when CAD became common. Therefore they required their own assistants to "draft by hand" as they had done in the past. The use of CAD is now happening gradually as younger trained associate and assistant designers are bringing advanced CAD skills with them to Broadway design studios and demonstrating the flexibility of CAD and the opportunity to make changes very quickly.

The visual world of many production designs is so complex that a property designer typically works as an essential collaborator with the scenic designer. The property area is also broken down into two areas: (1) functional props used by actors, and (2) set dressing, which fills out the visual stage reality. Once the scene designer has approved all of the property designer's research, solutions, and drawings, those are also forwarded to the technical director to be worked into the construction schedule. It is also frequently the property designer who completes the mechanical special effects used in theatrical production. Owing to developments in computer and electronic technology, special effect solutions are frequently crafted by projection designers or electricians as well. Projection technology solutions are finding their way into many production designs for special visual effects requiring the presence of yet another essential scenic collaborator.

The scene designer and her or his assistants also complete a full series of paint elevations that are delivered to the scenic charge artist, who works with a group of scenic artists in completing the painting of the actual scenery. Paint charge and scenic artists require both talent and technique: to create, for instance, the feeling of rare old wood in a library, or of bricks, or of a glossy, elegant surface in an expensive living room. In commercial theatre, construction drawings and paint elevations are sent to scenic houses separate from the theatre that specialize in both construction and painting. In regional theatres and university settings there are typically support spaces and support staff for scenic, property, painting, and costume construction on-site. In these settings the entire production team is typically present at all times, allowing for convenient tracking of the construction and painting process. In Broadway and other professional producing theatres without technical support spaces and staff, it is necessary for the designer or the assistant designers (or both) to visit the scenic houses and paint studios to check on progress and to ensure consistency with the original design intent.

When the time comes for technical rehearsals, dress rehearsals, and the actual performances after the official opening, a production requires backstage leadership by the stage management team. The members of this team call all the cues for lights, sound, projections, scenic shifts, and actors' entrances. An entire crew of stagehands will work together to coordinate every change, no matter how small, in the visual world of the play. These changes may involve a fly crew for flown scenery, a shift crew for either automated or manual shifting of entire settings, and a property crew for any preparation or movement of furniture and properties onstage or off. Meanwhile a crew of dressers, whose work will be covered in more detail in Chapter 11, will work backstage with the actors, helping prepare them for the next scene. Once a production moves beyond opening night, it is controlled by the stage manager, who is also responsible for maintaining the director's artistic intent as well as maintaining consistency in cue placement and the visual world of the play.

Designing a Total Environment

Sometimes a designer goes beyond scenery and special effects to design an entire theatre space, rearranging the seating for spectators and determining the relationship of the stage area to the audience. For instance, in an open space such as a gymnasium or warehouse, a designer might build an entire theatre, including the seats or stands for the audience and the designated acting areas. In this case, the designer considers the size and shape of the space, the texture and nature of the building materials, the atmosphere of the space, and the needs of the play itself. This is also true of multifocus theatre. Even in Broadway theatres some designers change the architecture of the theatre space in creating the world of the play. The Broadway scene designer Eugene Lee, designer of the musical *Wicked,* won two of his three Tony Awards doing just that for the original productions of *Candide* and *Sweeney Todd: The Demon Barber of Fleet Street.*

In this chapter we have examined the work of the scene designer. In Chapter 11, we turn to someone whose work is closely related: the costume designer.

SUMMARY

1. We encounter forms of scene design in everyday life: in the carefully planned decor of a restaurant, in a hotel lobby, or in a decorated apartment.

2. Scene design for the stage differs from interior decorating in that it creates an environment and an atmosphere that are not filled until occupied by performers.

3. In addition to creating an environment, the scene designer has the following objectives: to set tone and style, distinguish realism from nonrealism, establish time and place, develop a design concept, provide a central design metaphor, coordinate scenery with other elements, and deal with practical considerations.

4 As in other aspects of theatre, in scene design there has been more and more crossover, and interaction, between theatre design and design for many types of popular entertainment.

5. In practical terms the scene designer must deal with the limits of the stage space and the offstage area. For example, ramps must not be inclined too steeply, and platforms must provide an adequate playing area for the performers. In short, the stage designer must know the practical considerations of stage usage and stage carpentry, as well as the materials available, in order to achieve desired effects. Close work with the technical director allows the scene designer to push the limits of construction in creating a unique visual world while maintaining a safe environment for performers.

6. In theatrical productions that stress visual elements over the play or the acting, the scene design must constantly engage and entrance the spectator.

7. Special effects are elements of scenery, lighting, costumes, props, or sound that appear highly unusual or miraculous. Technical expertise is required to develop them properly.

8. Elements of design include line, mass, composition, texture, color, rhythm, and movement.

9. The scene designer works closely with the director and other designers and creates a series of drawings (sketches and renderings) and models of what the final stage picture will look like.

10. In dealing with created or found space, the designer must plan the entire environment: the audience area as well as the stage area.

11. The technical director, with his or her staff, supervises the construction of scenery, special effects, and the like, in order to meet the designer's specifications.

12. A scenic charge artist and additional scenic artists must translate the look shown in models, renderings, and paint elevations into the full-scale version of the design.

13. Working with the technical director and the scenic charge artist are the property designer and the paint charge artist.

11

Stage Costumes

Costumes are the most personal aspect of the visual elements in theatre. To members of the audience, a performer and his or her costume are perceived as one; they merge into a single image onstage. At the same time, costumes have a value of their own, adding color, shape, texture, and symbolism to the overall effect. Other elements or accessories, such as makeup, hairstyles, masks, and personal items like bracelets and necklaces, are an important component of costumes.

Clothes have always indicated or signaled a number of things regarding the wearer, including the following:

- Position and status
- Sex
- Occupation
- Relative flamboyance or modesty
- Degree of independence or regimentation
- Whether one is dressed for work or leisure, for a routine event or a special occasion

As soon as we see what clothing people are wearing, we receive messages about them and form impressions of them. We instantaneously relate those messages and impressions to our past experience and our preconceptions, and we make judgments, including value judgments. Even if we have never before laid eyes on someone, we feel we know a great deal when we first see what he or she is wearing.

◀ **STAGE COSTUMES: AESTHETIC, SYMBOLIC, AND SUITED TO THE CHARACTER**

In addition to being stylish and beautiful, costumes can convey a wealth of information to the audience. Here we see Shannon Antalan as Yolanda, in the front, and behind her, left to right: Valerie Payton as Mable, and Chandra Currelley as Mother Shaw in Crowns, *by Regina Taylor, directed and choreographed by Patdro Harris, Syracuse Stage, 2009, with costumes designed by Reggie Ray and lighting by Jennifer Setlow. (© T Charles Erickson)*

chapter eleven

COSTUMES FOR THE STAGE

In theatre, clothes send us signals similar to those in everyday life, but, as with other elements of theatre, there are significant differences between the costumes of everyday life and theatrical costumes. Stage costumes communicate the same information as ordinary clothes with regard to sex, position, and occupation; but onstage this information is magnified because every element in theatre is a focus of attention. Also, costumes on a stage must meet other requirements not normally imposed in everyday life. These requirements will be clearer after we look at the objectives of costume design.

Objectives of Costume Design

Stage costumes should meet the following seven requirements:

1. Help establish the style of a production.
2. Indicate the historical period of a play and the locale in which it occurs.
3. Indicate the nature of individual characters or groups in a play—their stations in life, their occupations, their personalities.
4. Show relationships among characters—separating major characters from minor ones, contrasting one group with another.
5. Where appropriate, symbolically convey the significance of individual characters or the theme of the play.
6. Meet the needs of individual performers, making it possible for an actor or actress to move freely in a costume, perhaps to dance or engage in a sword fight, and (when required) to change quickly from one costume to another.
7. Be consistent with the production as a whole, especially other visual elements.

The Process of Costume Design

In order to achieve these objectives, the costume designer goes through a process similar to that of the scene designer. He or she reads the script, taking particular note of the characters: their age, gender, physical qualities, and special traits, as well as their roles in the play.

Early in the process, the costume designer also meets with the director and other designers to discuss the "look" that the show will have and how the various elements will be coordinated. The costume designer may make preliminary sketches to show the director and other designers. These may include not only suggestions about style (for example, historical, modern, futuristic) but also ideas for colors and fabrics. Once agreed upon, these designs will move from sketches to renderings of what the costumes will look like in their final form. Swatches of material may be attached to these designs, indicating the texture and color of the fabrics to be used.

As part of this process, the costume designer will meet with the members of the cast, measuring each performer and making certain that the costumes will be workable and appropriate for the individual actresses and actors.

The following sections discuss how the various objectives of costume design are realized by the designer in this process.

Indicating Style Along with scenery and lighting, costumes should inform the audience about the style of a play. For a production set in outer space, for instance, the costumes would be futuristic. For a Restoration comedy, the costumes would be quite elegant, with elaborate gowns for the women and lace at the men's collars and cuffs. For a tragedy, the clothes would be formal and dignified—seeing them, the audience would know immediately that the play itself was serious.

For the musical *The Phantom of the Opera,* which is set in Paris in 1911, the designer Maria Bjornson fashioned romantic period outfits: the men in top hats with canes and capes, the women in long dresses with full skirts and elaborate hats and coats. For *Brooklyn Boy,* a play by Donald Margulies, the costume designer Jess Goldstein created contemporary costumes suitable for men and women today: informal, casual, with the women in slacks, and the men in sports shirts with jackets. The ill father wore a hospital gown. Angela Wendt, costume designer for the musical *Rent,* clothed the characters in all manner of informal pickup attire appropriate to free-spirited young people living on the Lower East Side in New York City, struggling to make their way.

A Girl

Dumas

Benoit

Cyrano de Bergerac costume for Coquelin

Eleonora Duse

Sarah Bernhardt

COSTUME DESIGN: THE PROCESS
Costume designers often make preliminary sketches of costumes as they begin to design a production. Shown here are sketches for *The Ladies of the Camellias* by the costume designer Jess Goldstein for a production at the Yale Repertory Theatre. (© Jess Goldstein)

Indicating Period and Locale Costumes indicate the period and location of a play: whether it is historical or modern, whether it is set in a foreign country or the United States, and so on. A play might take place in ancient Egypt, in seventeenth-century Spain, or in modern Africa. Costumes should tell us when and where the action occurs.

For most historical plays, the director and the costume designer have a range of choices, depending on the directorial concept. For a production of Shakespeare's *Julius Caesar,* for instance, the costumes could indicate the ancient Roman period when Caesar actually lived; in this case, the costumes would include Roman togas and soldiers' helmets. Or the costumes could be Elizabethan. We know that in Shakespeare's day costumes were heightened versions of the English clothes of the time, regardless of the period in which a play was set. As a third option, the designer could create costumes for an entirely different period, including our own day—with the men in business suits, modern military uniforms, and perhaps even tuxedos. Whatever the choice, the historical period should be clearly indicated by the costumes.

Identifying Status and Personality Like clothing in everyday life, costumes can tell us whether people are from the aristocracy or the working class, whether they are blue-collar workers or professionals. But in theatre, these signals must be clear

photo essay

Stage Costumes Make a Strong Visual Statement

(© T Charles Erickson)

Shown on these pages are five examples of striking costumes. Costume designers, using colors, fabric, intricate cuts and shapes of cloth, accessories, and other elements, create a special look for each production. The costumes must fit the actor and allow for easy movement, as well as be visually appealing. They must also be appropriate for the play, and communicate to the audience the period and the social status and the financial level of the characters wearing the costumes.

Seen here is a magical image for a production of a Shakespearean play: Ellen McLaughlin as Titania and Jay Goede as Oberon in *A Midsummer Night's Dream* at the McCarter Theatre, Princeton, directed by Tina Landau, with costumes designed by Michael Krass.

Brandon Hearnsberger as Marquis 1 with Jeffrey Bean as Cyrano de Bergerac in the Alley Theatre production of *Cyrano de Bergerac*; the director Gregory Boyd stages Brian Hooker's adaptation; costume design by Alejo Vietti.

(© Michal Daniel)

Julius Caesar by William Shakespeare, Royal Shakespeare Company production directed by Lucy Bailey. Greg Hicks as Julius Caesar, Noma Dumezweni as Calpurnia. Stratford Upon Avon 2009, costumes by Fotini Dimou.

Don Burroughs as Elyot Chase and Carol Linnea Johnson as Amanda Prynne in the Utah Shakespearean Festival's 2009 production of Noël Coward's *Private Lives*. Director, Joseph Hanreddy; costume designer, David Kay Mickelsen; scenic designer, Bill Forrester.

(© Geraint Lewis)

(© Utah Shakespearean Festival. Photo by Karl Hugh)

Linda Thorson as Lady Bracknell in Oscar Wilde's *The Importance of Being Earnest,* directed by Joe Dowling at the Guthrie Theater; costumes by Mathew J. LeFebvre.

(© Michal Daniel)

and unmistakable. For example, in real life a woman in a long white coat could be a doctor, a laboratory technician, or a hairdresser. A costume onstage must indicate the occupation exactly—by giving the doctor a stethoscope, for instance.

Costumes also tell us about the personalities of characters: a flamboyant person will be dressed in flashy colors; a shy, retiring person will wear subdued clothing.

Costumes also indicate age. This is particularly helpful when an older performer is playing a young person, or vice versa. A young person playing an older character, for instance, can wear padding or a beard.

Showing Relationships among Characters   Characters in a play can be set apart by the way they are costumed. Major characters, for example, will be dressed differently from minor characters. Frequently, the costume designer will distinguish the major characters by dressing them in distinctive colors, in sharp contrast to the other characters. Consider Shaw's *Saint Joan,* a play about Joan of Arc. Obviously, Joan should stand out from the soldiers surrounding her. Therefore, her costume

COSTUMES INDICATE SOCIAL RELATIONSHIPS
Along with their many other properties, costumes can signal the relationships and contrasts among characters in a production. Not only can costumes indicate the time period when a drama takes place, and the locale where it occurs, but they can and should indicate occupations and relative social positions. Who, for example, is a laborer or tradesman and who is a professional businessperson? In this scene from August Wilson's *Radio Golf* at the Goodman Theatre, we see John Earl Jelks as Sterling Johnson and Hassan El-Amin as Harmond Wilks in costumes designed by Susan Hilferty. The man on the right is a succcessful businessman; the man on the left is a laborer. (Peter Wynn Thompson)

might be bright blue while their costumes are steel gray. In another play of Shaw's, *Caesar and Cleopatra,* Cleopatra should stand out from her servants and soldiers. If she is dressed like them in an Egyptian costume, she should wear an outfit that has brighter colors and is more elegant.

Costumes underline important divisions between groups. In *Romeo and Juliet,* the Montagues wear one color and the Capulets another. In a modern counterpart of *Romeo and Juliet,* the musical *West Side Story,* the two gangs of young men are dressed in contrasting colors: the Jets might be in various shades of pink, purple, and lavender; the Sharks in shades of green, yellow, and lemon.

Creating Symbolic and Nonhuman Characters

In many plays, special costumes are called for to denote abstract ideas or give shape to fantastic creatures. Here the costume designer must develop an outfit that conveys the appropriate imaginative and symbolic qualities. In *Macbeth,* for instance, how does one clothe the witches or the ghost of Banquo? Some way must be found to symbolize the qualities they represent.

To illustrate how costumes can suggest ideas or characteristics, a costume of animal skins can symbolize bestiality; a costume of feathers can indicate a birdlike quality; a costume of a metallic material can suggest a hard, mechanical quality.

The Balcony by the French playwright Jean Genet calls for exaggerated as well as symbolic costumes. The play is set in a house of prostitution where ordinary men act out their fantasies: one man pretends to be a general, another a bishop, and a third a judge. They dress in exaggerated costumes, looking almost like caricatures, with platform shoes, shoulder pads wider than their own shoulders, and high headpieces. The women who serve them also dress fantastically. The woman serving the general is dressed as a horse, and the costume designer has the task of making a costume for her which will bring out her attractiveness as a person but still give her a horse's tail and mane.

For *The Lion King,* the director Julie Taymor, who was also the costume designer, used puppets, masks, and other devices to create outfits for numerous animal characters, such as lions, tigers, giraffes, and elephants. The musical *Avenue Q* has large puppets as characters, manipulated by actors visible onstage and interacting with them.

Meeting Performers' Needs

Virtually every aspect of theatre has practical as well as aesthetic requirements, and costume design is no exception. No matter how attractive or how symbolic, stage costumes must work for the performers. A long, flowing gown may look beautiful, but if it is too long and the actress wearing it trips every time she walks down a flight of steps, the designer has overlooked an important practical consideration. If actors are required to duel or engage in hand-to-hand combat, their costumes must stand up to this wear and tear, and their arms and legs must have freedom of movement. If performers are to dance, they must be able to turn, leap, and move freely. Each of these examples points to the absolute importance of skilled *stitchers* (technicians who sew all the costumes) and *drapers* (technicians who pattern, pin, and drape the fabric to fit individual actors perfectly) in a costume shop.

Quick costume changes are frequently called for in theatre. At the end of the musical *Gypsy,* when an emerging young star sings "Let Me Entertain You," she goes offstage between choruses and reappears a few seconds later in a different costume. The actress goes through three or four dazzling costume changes in seconds, to the astonishment of the audience. The costumes must be made so that the actress, with the

Many productions—especially musicals—call for rapid costume changes by performers. A good example is the musical *La Cage aux Folles,* in which some male performers dress as women (known as Les Cagelles). Here, Will Taylor is helped with a rapid costume change by the dresser Lizz Hirons (holding a flashlight in her mouth). (Sara Krulwich/The New York Times)

help of dressers offstage, can rapidly shed one outfit and get into another. Tear-away seams and special fasteners are used so that one costume can be ripped off quickly and another put on. Broadway audiences have loved watching Bernadette Peters's Witch change to a beauty before their very eyes during *Into the Woods.* Some fast costume changes may require Velcro or snaps like Whopper Poppers. Still others require a magician's special effects touch.

Unlike scenery, which stays in place until it is moved, a costume is always in motion, moving as the performer moves. This provides an opportunity for the designer to develop grace and rhythm in the way a costume looks as it moves across the stage, but with that goes the great responsibility of making the costume workable for the performer. This movement also requires special stitching techniques not typically used in basic contemporary clothing, since costumes must often withstand eight active performances per week. On Broadway and in national touring productions it is also necessary to make costumes for more than one actor for the same role, although this is not typically the case in shorter runs in regional or university theatre productions. (An interesting note about *The Phantom of the Opera:* this musical, which has now been touring for more than twenty years, has two chorus costumes that are so expensive to make that a small cadre of actresses who fit those gowns have been kept under contract over the years to fill in during vacations and to take over the role for a brief time. Also, new performers are regularly auditioned who not only are able to play the parts but also can fit into those costumes.)

At times it is important for the costume designer to work closely with individual performers. Actresses and actors must know how to use the accessories and costumes provided for them. For example, the character Sparkish in the Restoration comedy *The Country Wife* by Wycherley is an outrageous fop. Sparkish wears a fancy wig, a hat, and flamboyant breeches. He uses a handkerchief, a snuffbox, and other hand accessories. In creating a costume for Sparkish, the designer must provide an outfit that not only is correct for the style of the production but also suits the physique and appearance of the individual actor. If the actor has never worn a wig or breeches of this kind and has never worked with a handkerchief—which he keeps in the cuff of his jacket—or with a snuffbox, he must learn to use these items, working closely with both the director and the costume designer and frequently with a movement specialist.

Maintaining Consistency   Finally, costumes must be consistent with the entire production—especially with the various other visual elements. A realistic production set in the home of everyday people calls for down-to-earth costumes. A highly stylized production requires costumes designed with flair and imagination.

The Costume Designer at Work

The Costume Designer's Responsibilities   As noted earlier, the person who puts all these ideas into effect is the costume designer. Every production requires someone who takes responsibility for the costumes. This is true whether the costumes are *pulled* or *built*.

Pulling is a term used when costumes are rented and the designer goes to a costume house or storeroom and selects outfits that are appropriate for the production. The designer must already know about period, style, and the other matters discussed above. He or she must also have the measurements of all the performers for whom costumes are to be pulled. Seldom will pulled or rented costumes fit the actor perfectly, and it is the responsibility of stitchers, often with tailoring experience, to complete the necessary alterations.

When costumes are *built,* they are created in a costume shop under the direction of the shop supervisor, who works closely with a costume designer in much the same way the technical director and scene designer work together. Before making a costume out of expensive fabrics, well-staffed costume shops will make *muslin mock-ups* of the costumes first, and those are then fitted to the actor. Next, the mock-ups are taken apart and used as patterns for the actual costume fabric. In these shops, costumes are built in two different ways. Some are drafted as flat patterns based on the performer's measurements, and some are draped. Draping involves pinning and tucking the fabric directly to a dress form of the proper size and marking the fabric while it is on the dress form, in preparation for stitching and detailed finish work and closures.

The Costume Designer's Resources   Among the elements a costume designer works with are (as discussed below) (1) line, shape, and silhouette; (2) color; (3) fabric; and (as discussed later) (4) accessories.

Line   Of prime importance is the cut or line of the clothing. Do the lines of an outfit flow, or are they sharp and jagged? Does the clothing follow the lines of the body,

photo essay

The Costume Designer at Work

(© Carol Rosegg)

Costume designer Jane Greenwood, who has designed costumes for well over 100 Broadway shows, several dozen regional theatre productions and numerous films, is seen here in her studio. Shown also are her sketch for Hermione's red costume in a production of Shaw's *Heartbreak House* and Swoosie Kurtz wearing the red costume on stage. Greenwood makes sketches of what the costumes will look like, chooses the colors and fabrics, fits the costumes to the performer, and oversees the construction of the costume.

(Courtesy of Jane Greenwood)

(© Joan Marcus)

or is there some element of exaggeration, such as shoulder pads for a man or a bustle at the back of a woman's dress? The outline or silhouette of a costume has always been significant. There is a strong visual contrast, for instance, between the line of an Egyptian woman's garment, flowing smoothly from shoulder to floor, and that of an empire gown of the early nineteenth century in France, which featured a horizontal line high above the waist, just below the breasts, with a line flowing from below the bosom to the feet. The silhouettes of these two styles would stand in marked contrast to a woman's outfit in the United States during the early 1930s: a short outfit with a prominent belt or sash cutting horizontally across the hips.

Undergarments are an aspect of costume design often overlooked by audiences. For women's costumes, one example is the hoopskirt. In *The King and I,* a musical of 1951 that was revived on Broadway in 1996, Anna, an English schoolteacher in Siam, wears dresses with hoopskirts several feet in diameter, which were in fashion in England in the mid-nineteenth century, the time of the play.

Other undergarments include bustles, which exaggerate the lines in the rear; and corsets, which can greatly alter a woman's posture and appearance. For example, some corsets pull in the waist and cause the wearer to stand very straight. But in the first decade of the twentieth century, women in society often bent forward because they wore a curved corset that forced them to thrust their shoulders and upper body forward. A costume designer will be aware of the importance of undergarments and will use them to create the appropriate silhouette. During the nineteenth century there were times when men would also wear corsets to achieve the fashionable posture of the day. It is often necessary to make actual boned corsets in a costume shop for period theatre productions, since the dominant period silhouettes (especially female silhouettes) were so often based on the line created by tight-fitting corsets and undergarments, and boning is the only way to achieve the appropriate look.

Color   A second important resource for costume designers is color. Earlier, we saw that leading characters can be dressed in a color that contrasts with the colors worn by other characters, and that characters from one family can be dressed in colors different from those of a rival family. Color also suggests mood: bright, warm colors for a happy mood; dark, somber colors for a more serious mood.

Beyond these applications, however, color can indicate changes in character and changes in mood. Near the beginning of Eugene O'Neill's *Mourning Becomes Electra,* General Manon, who has recently returned from the Civil War, dies, and his wife and daughter wear dark mourning clothes. Lavinia, the daughter, knows that her mother had something to do with her father's death, and she and her brother conspire to murder the mother. Once they have done so, Lavinia feels a great sense of release. She adopts characteristics of her mother, and as an important symbol of this transformation, she puts on brightly colored clothes of the same shades her mother had worn as a young woman.

Fabric   Fabric is a third tool of the costume designer. In one sense, this is the costume designer's medium, for it is in fabric that silhouette and color are displayed. Just as important as those qualities are the texture and bulk of the fabric. What is its reflective quality? Does it have a sheen that reflects light? Or is it rough, so that it absorbs light? How does it drape on the wearer? Does it fall lightly to the floor and outline

physical features, or does it hide them? Does it wrinkle naturally, or is it smooth? Ornamentation and trim can also be used. Fringe, lace, ruffles, feathers, beads—all these add to the attractiveness and individuality of a costume.

Beyond its inherent qualities, fabric has symbolic values. For example, burlap and other roughly textured cloths suggest people of the earth or of modest means. Silks and satins, on the other hand, suggest elegance and refinement—perhaps even royalty.

The connotations of fabrics may change with passing years. Two or three generations ago, blue denim was used only for work clothes, worn by laborers, or by cowboys who actually rode horseback on a ranch. Today, denim is the fabric of choice in informal clothes for people of all incomes and all ages.

Using the combined resources of line, color, fabric, and trims, the costume designer arrives at individual outfits, which tell us a great deal about the characters who wear them and convey important visual signals about the style and meaning of the play as a whole.

The Costume Designer's Collaborators   Once again, it is important to recognize that a number of collaborators aid in the process of costume design. As noted previously, the costume shop supervisor is the lead costume technician, and there are many other very specific job responsibilities in a typical costume shop. Often young professionals beginning a career will start as buyers for professional shops that have copies of the designers' renderings. In New York City, for example, they will scour the garment district to find actual fabrics that best match the designer's renderings and notes. That fabric comes back to the shop, and after the muslin mock-ups are made, it will go to a cutter-draper. A costume designer's first hand (see below) will often build the initial costume and complete the fitting with the designer and the actor.

THE AUDIENCE'S RESPONSE

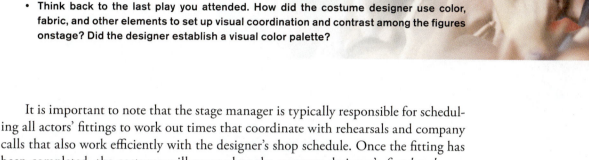

- What kinds of "costumes" do you encounter in everyday life? What characteristics do they convey?

- Onstage, costumes look just as one imagines they do in life, but on closer examination they may be exaggerated or heightened. How might the designer achieve this effect?

- Think back to the last play you attended. How did the costume designer use color, fabric, and other elements to set up visual coordination and contrast among the figures onstage? Did the designer establish a visual color palette?

It is important to note that the stage manager is typically responsible for scheduling all actors' fittings to work out times that coordinate with rehearsals and company calls that also work efficiently with the designer's shop schedule. Once the fitting has been completed, the costume will proceed to the costume designer's *first hand,* or a lead stitcher, who completes the detailed sewing and adds all costume closures. It is not always desirable that costumes look like crisp, new, clean clothes. Once construction is completed the costumes are frequently turned over to design assistants or costume crafts specialists for purposes of *distressing.* Try to imagine a *Pirates of the Caribbean* movie with all the pirates wearing clothes that look brand-new.

Once costumes are completed and ready for dress rehearsals and performances, they become the responsibility of the wardrobe supervisor, who coordinates the wardrobe crew for a production. All decisions related to costume organization and preparation in the theatre are made by the wardrobe supervisor. The wardrobe crew's responsibilities begin with backstage preparation before every performance until the laundry is completed following every performance. During rehearsal and performance, depending on the complexity of the production, there are numerous dressers from the wardrobe crew assigned to various actors. Some dressers will work solely with a single lead actor in the show, whereas others will work with various members of the production ensemble. There are other areas of specialty, and artisans integral to the realm of costume design, to be discussed with other elements in the next section.

OTHER ELEMENTS

Makeup

A part of costume is makeup—the application of cosmetics (paints, powders, and rouges) to the face and body. With regard to age and the special facial features associated with ethnic origins, an important function of makeup is to help the performer personify and embody a character.

Theatrical makeup used to be more popular than it is today. In a modern small theatre, performers playing realistic parts will often go without makeup of any consequence; in that case, the actors handle their own makeup. Anything beyond the most simple makeup, however, demands an accomplished makeup designer to plan specifically what changes will take place. This design process will typically start with photographs or drawings of the actors with design overlay drawings indicating details

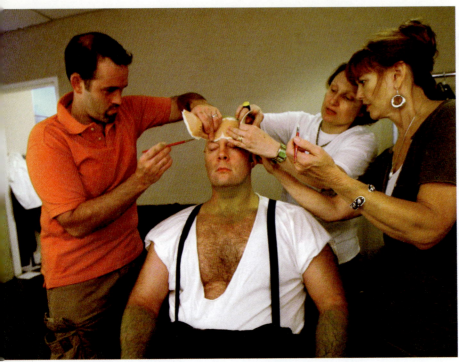

MAKEUP: CHANGING A FACE OR CREATING A NEW ONE

Makeup is an ancient theatre tradition. Makeup can highlight features of the face or parts of the body that might be washed out under the glare of stage lights. Makeup can also be used to alter the appearance of the face altogether. In these two photographs we see Shuler Hensley being made up for his role as the "Dreadful Monster" in Mel Brooks's musical *Young Frankenstein*. From the left: Vincent T. Schicchi, makeup prosthetics supervisor; Angelina Avallone, makeup designer; and Pam Farrow, hair and makeup supervisor. (Greg Gilbert/Seattle Times)

of makeup. Historical figures are frequently incorporated into realistic plays and may demand extensive use of extremely realistic prosthetic makeup. A recent example on Broadway was William Gibson's one-woman play *Golda's Balcony,* with Tovah Feldshuh as the former Israeli prime minister Golda Meir. One makeup artist from Long Island, New York, made nine prosthetic noses, cast in foam latex, each week for more than a year that the show ran on Broadway. The same show then toured nationally for eight more months, with Valerie Harper requiring a different set of noses each week to fit her face perfectly.

Makeup has a long and important history in theatre, and sometimes it is a necessity—one good example being makeup to highlight facial features that would not otherwise be visible in a large theatre. Even in a smaller theatre, bright lights tend to wash out cheekbones, eyebrows, and other facial features.

Makeup is often essential because the age of a character differs from that of the performer. Suppose that a nineteen-year-old performer is playing a sixty-year-old character. Through the use of makeup—a little gray in the hair or simulated wrinkles on the face—the appropriate age can be suggested. Another situation calling for makeup to indicate age is a play in which the characters grow older during the course of the

action. The musical *I Do! I Do!* with book and lyrics by Tom Jones and music by Harvey Schmidt, is based on the play *The Fourposter* by Jan de Hartog. In the musical, a husband and wife are shown in scenes covering many years in their married life, from the time when they are first married until they are quite old. In order to convey the passing years and their advancing age, the actress and actor must use makeup extensively.

Makeup is also a necessity for fantastic or other nonrealistic creatures. Douglas Turner Ward (b. 1930), a black playwright, wrote *Day of Absence* to be performed by black actors in whiteface. The implications of this effect are many, not the least being

HISTORICAL PERSPECTIVES

CLASSIC JAPANESE THEATRE: REMARKABLE COSTUMES, MAKEUP, & MASKS

Japanese classic theatre is unique in the history of world theatre. Between the early fifteenth century and the early seventeenth century, not one but three theatre traditions emerged: nō, bunraku, and kabuki. The remarkable fact is that all three have been performed continuously since they first developed and are still on view today.

Under Zeami, the actor discussed in the opening section of Chapter 1, **nō** became a fully developed theatrical form; it remained the dominant type of production in Japan for the next 200 years. The stories on which nō plays were based often came from literary or historical sources. The nō stage has remained roughly the same since the time of Zeami and his successors. The stage has a bridge, called a *hashigakari,* which leads from the actors' dressing room offstage to the stage proper. The main playing space is about 18 feet square, is roofed, and has a ceremonial pine tree painted on the rear wall. At the back of the playing space is a narrow section for four or five musicians, who accompany the play. Nō theatres were originally outdoors, but a modern nō theatre is placed inside a larger shell as though it were a giant stage set.

Nō actors move in a highly stylized way that has important elements of both dance and pantomime. During the performance of a nō text, the actors alternate sections of chanting with a heightened speech that might best be compared to recitative in western opera. Costumes made for nō are usually of great elegance, and the masks worn by the chief character are among the most beautiful, subtle, and effective ever created for any theatre. The elegance, mystery, and beauty of nō have continued to fascinate the Japanese, and the tradition has been passed on from teacher to disciple through succeeding generations.

Nō remained the most popular theatrical form during Japan's long medieval period. Civil wars and other disturbances, however, caused increasing political disarray until in 1600 a general, Tokugawa Ieyasu, unified the country. All through the long Tokugawa period (1600–1868), Japan was unified and at peace, and these conditions led to a rapid development of commerce and trade and a growing merchant class, which demanded its own entertainment.

The first of the new popular forms of theatre to flourish was a puppet theatre known as **bunraku.** Bunraku is a highly unusual type of theatre featuring musicians and a chanter who tells the story and creates the voices of all the characters. The puppets that enact the drama were smaller in the beginning but are today approximately two-thirds human size and are operated by three men dressed in black. One man moves the legs of the puppet, one moves the left arm, and the chief handler moves the head and the right arm. At times the chief handler is dressed in an ornate costume. The puppeteer's black outfits are a convention: they signify that the audience should consider these men invisible.

Bunraku first became popular in the early seventeenth century and is still performed in Japan today. The first and undoubtedly the best of the writers for bunraku, Chikamatsu Monzaemon (1653–1725), contributed enormously to the transformation of this popular theatre into a true art form. Chikamatsu wrote both historical plays and domestic dramas dealing with life in his own day; his domestic dramas have remained popular to the present time. His emphasis on ordinary people was new to the Japanese stage and foreshadowed later developments in European theatre. Because of his great talent and

(continued)

the wide-ranging subject matter of his many dramas, he is sometimes spoken of as the "Shakespeare of Japan."

Shortly after bunraku had become established, another form of popular theatre—*kabuki*—developed, in the early and middle seventeenth century. Kabuki drew its material from plays written for nō and bunraku; the exaggerated gestures of kabuki are often attributed to the fact that in its early phases a conscious attempt was made to imitate puppets. Despite these exaggerated and stylized gestures, kabuki was less formal and distant than nō, which remained largely the theatre of the court and nobility. Kabuki quickly became a tremendously popular form of theatre, and it remains a favorite of Japanese audiences today. Kabuki was performed first by all-female troupes, then by boys, and finally—beginning in 1652—by all-male companies. Kabuki actors are trained from childhood in singing, dancing, acting, and physical dexterity. The actors who play women's parts are particularly skillful at suggesting the essence of a feminine personality through stylized gestures and attitudes. The costumes and makeup are elegant as well as colorful. Musicians—sometimes onstage, sometimes offstage—generally accompany the stage action.

The stage used for kabuki performances underwent various changes during the history of the art, but the same principles were observed after the middle of the nineteenth century. The stage is long and has a relatively low proscenium. Kabuki features elaborate and beautiful scenic effects, including the revolving stage, which was developed in Japan before it was used in the west. Another device used in kabuki is the *hanamichi*, or "flower way," a raised narrow platform connecting the rear of the auditorium with the stage. Actors often make their entrances on the hanamichi and occasionally perform short scenes there as well.

the reversal of the old minstrel performances in which white actors wore blackface. Ward was not the first to put black actors in whiteface; Genet had part of the cast of his play *The Blacks* wear white masks. A popular recent musical on Broadway, Steven Schwartz's *Wicked,* portrays a green witch named Elphaba, from birth until she becomes better known as the Wicked Witch of the West. Perhaps even more amazing in *Wicked* is the makeup used on the numerous flying monkeys in the production.

Asian theatre frequently relies on heavy makeup. For instance, Japanese kabuki, a highly stylized theatre, uses completely nonrealistic makeup. The main characters must apply a base of white covering the entire face, over which bold patterns of red, blue, black, and brown are painted. The colors and patterns are symbolic of the character. In Chinese theatre, too, the colors of makeup are symbolic: all white suggests treachery, black means fierce integrity, red means loyalty, green indicates demons, yellow stands for hidden cunning, and so forth.

When makeup is used, the human face becomes almost like a canvas for a painting. The features of the face may be heightened or exaggerated; or symbolic aspects of the face may be emphasized. In either case, makeup serves as an additional tool for the performer in creating an image of the character.

Hairstyles and Wigs

Another important component of costume design includes hairstyles and wigs. When costume designers create their renderings, they include characters' hairstyles as a part

WIGS AND HAIRSTYLES
Hairstyle indicates social status and other facts about a character; it provides information about when and where a play is taking place. Beyond that, hairstyles and wigs can make a comment. Shown here, in period costumes, are two characters wearing elaborate wigs in a hairstyle that exaggerates the normal and has an immediate comic effect all on its own: Mara Davi (Mrs. Whitehead) and Joey Slotnick (Captain Jeffrey T. Spaulding/Groucho) in *Animal Crackers,* written by George S. Kaufman and Morrie Ryskind, directed by Henry Wishcamper at the Goodman Theatre; costumes designed by Jenny Mannis. (Photo by Eric Y. Exit)

of the design, which will later require a hair and wig specialist as a part of the crew. In certain periods men have worn wigs: the time of the American Revolution is one example. In England, judges wear wigs to this day.

For women, hairstyles can denote period and social class. In the middle of the nineteenth century, for example, women often wore ringlets like Scarlett O'Hara's in the film *Gone with the Wind.* A few decades later, in the 1890s, women wore their hair piled on top of the head in a pompadour referred to as the Gibson girl look. In the 1920s, women wore their hair marcelled in waves, sometimes slicked down close to the head. In the modern period, women wear their hair in more natural styles. But again there is tremendous variety—some women have short, curly hair; others have long hair, perhaps even down to the waist. The musical *Hairspray* featured young women in the bouffant hairdos of the 1960s.

For men, too, hairstyles are significant and sometimes symbolic. A military brush cut, an Elvis Presley–style pompadour, and a ponytail each point to a certain lifestyle, but each may be interpreted in several ways.

Audiences would actually be surprised to know how often wigs are used in theatrical productions. They may not even recognize an actor or actress outside the theatre, because such a complete visual transformation can be accomplished with the use of wigs made from real hair. Hair and wig specialists are typically assigned to every production. The hair designers will fashion the wigs in the shop before dress rehearsals. A hair and wig specialist is also required backstage to care for the wigs throughout the performance process to keep the hair looking exactly as the designer envisioned it and to maintain the actors' comfort. One of the most amazing uses of a wig in recent memory on Broadway was the extraordinary design by Paul Huntley for *Jekyll and Hyde the Musical*: the actor could manipulate the character's wig instantaneously, allowing him to shift back and forth between Jekyll and Hyde within the same song.

Masks

Masks seem to be as old as theatre, having been used in ancient Greek theatre and in the drama developed by primitive tribes. In one sense, the mask is an extension of the performer—a face on top of a face. There are several ways to look at masks. They remind us, first of all, that we are in a theatre, that the action going on before our eyes is not real in a literal sense but is a symbolic or an artistic presentation. For another thing, masks allow a face to be frozen in one expression: a look of horror, perhaps, which we see throughout a production. Masks can also make a face larger than life, and they can create stereotypes, similar to stock characters (see Chapter 8) in which one particular feature—for example, cunning or haughtiness—is emphasized to the exclusion of everything else. More often today, audiences will see half masks, like those used in commedia dell'arte, as these allow for stylized character expressions but also give the actor more freedom to speak clearly and effectively. Characters' mask designs are also incorporated into the costume renderings and are typically built by a makeup or crafts specialist in the costume shop. Neutral masks are also frequently used in actors' training, to prompt them to use more dynamic physical movement without the benefit of facial expression to express character.

Millenary, Accessories, and Crafts

A number of the seven objectives of costume design noted at the beginning of this chapter are actually achieved through the design and use of accessories to the base costume pieces. Accessories include items like hats, walking sticks, jewelry, purses, parasols, and royal staffs. All these items instantly refer to various historical periods and also make visual statements about character and locale. Virtually every major costume shop will have a technician who specializes in millenary and crafts. Each of these pieces must be carefully designed and constructed to connect visually to the costumes and to other areas of design. It is hard to imagine a production of Shakespeare's

photo essay

Masks

Masks are as old as theatre—they were part of ancient Greek theatre and early Asian theatre, and of ceremonial costumes in Africa and elsewhere. Masks can have a variety of uses: they can be highly decorative, but they can also convey the character and temperament of the actor wearing them. Here we see a variety of masks in old and new plays.

(© Geraint Lewis)

Atandwa Kani as Ariel in *The Tempest* by William Shakespeare, set in Africa in a production by the Baxter Theatre Centre of Capetown, in association with the Royal Shakespeare Company, directed by Janice Honeyman; Nicky Gillibrand, costume designer; Giles Cradle, set designer.

Masks are prominent in *The Royal Hunt of the Sun,* a historical play about the conquistadors in South America by Peter Shaffer, directed by Trevor Nunn in London. Paterson Joseph is Atahuallpa; the designer was Anthony Ward.

(© Geraint Lewis)

Commedia dell'arte masks: Tommaso Minniti as Dr. Lombardi, Stefano Guizzi as Brighella, and Giorgio Bongiovanni as Pantalone in *Arlecchino: Servant of Two Masters,* by Carlo Goldoni in a production by the Piccolo Teatro di Milano; costumes, Ezio Frigerio.

Greg Hicks is Dionysus in a production of *Bacchai* by Euripedes, directed by Peter Hall at the National Theatre, London, with designs by Alison Chitty.

273

A Midsummer Night's Dream without some kind of delightful donkey's headpiece or mask made specifically for the character Bottom. It just wouldn't be the same. Theatre design and execution in all areas rely heavily on extensive details to make the visual world of the play compelling for audiences.

Masks offer other symbolic possibilities. In his play *The Great God Brown,* Eugene O'Neill calls for the performers at certain times to hold masks in front of their faces. When the masks are in place, the characters present a facade to the public, withholding their true selves. When the masks are down, the characters reveal their inner feelings.

COORDINATION OF THE WHOLE

Actors and actresses would have great difficulty creating a part without costumes and accessories, and in some cases without makeup or a mask. These elements help the performer define his or her role and are so closely related to the performer that we sometimes lose sight of them as separate entities. At the same time, costumes, makeup, hairstyles, and masks must be integrated with other aspects of a production, and each demands special technical skills in order to complete the visual design.

For example, these elements are essential in carrying out a point of view in a production. Masks, for instance, are clearly nonrealistic and signal to the audience that the character wearing the mask and the play itself are also likely to be nonrealistic. Costumes suggest whether a play is comic or serious, a wild farce or a stark tragedy.

Costumes, makeup, hairstyles, and masks must also be coordinated with scenery and lighting. The wrong kind of lighting can wash out or discolor costumes and makeup. It would be self-defeating, too, if scenery were in one mood or style and the costumes in another. Ideally, these elements should support and reinforce one another, and spectators should be aware of how essential it is for them to work together.

In this chapter we have looked at costume design, and in Chapter 10 at scene design. At this point, it is appropriate to stress again that the designers do not work in isolation. We have seen that the director confers with designers, and it is important to note that the designers themselves also consult frequently with one another. In the production process there are regular meetings between two or more designers to coordinate their efforts—not only on such matters as colors and style but also regarding cues and the way various design elements work together. In Chapter 12 we turn to a third visual element, lighting, and to the use of sound in theatre.

SUMMARY

1. The clothes we wear in daily life are a form of costume. They indicate station in life, occupation, and a sense of formality or informality.

2. Onstage, costumes—like clothes in real life—convey information about the people wearing them; more than that, these costumes are chosen consciously and are designed to give the audience important information.

3. The objectives of costume design are to set tone and style, indicate time and place, characterize individuals and groups, underline personal relationships, create symbolic outfits

when appropriate, meet the practical needs of performers, and coordinate with the total production.

4. The designer works with the following elements: line and shape, color, fabric, and accessories.

5. Costumes can be pulled or built. When they are pulled, they are drawn from a preexisting costume collection. Building costumes means creating the complete costume: sewing and constructing the outfit in a costume shop.

6. Those working with a costume designer include a first hand (or lead sticher) and other assistants.

7. Makeup and hairstyles are also important to the appearance of the performers and are part of the designer's concern.

8. Where called for, masks, too, are under the direction of the costume designer.

9. Often, costume, makeup, and wig assistants work with actors during a performance.

12

Lighting and Sound

Like scenery, costumes, and other elements of theatre, stage lighting and sound have counterparts in everyday life. For example, in real life the basic function of lighting is, of course, illumination—to allow people to see at night and indoors. But there are also many theatrical uses of light in daily life. Advertising signs often have neon lights or brightly colored bulbs. Restaurants feature soft lights, candles, and background music to help establish mood and atmosphere.

With the explosion of such hand-held devices as iPhones, several millions of people live each day with their own sound track. In homes, people put spotlights on special parts of a room, such as a dining-room table. Also, in homes people frequently use a rheostat so that they can dim lights to create a mood. What home does not have projected images available through a television screen or now even the ability to change digital images in picture frames?

STAGE LIGHTING

Lighting was historically the last element of visual design to be incorporated in theatre production—and it is perhaps the most advanced in terms of equipment and techniques. Most of the advances have occurred in the past 100 years; and before we look at theatre lighting today, it will be helpful to have a short historical view of its development.

◀ **LIGHTING AND SOUND IN ACTION**

Lighting is one of the most versatile and potent visual resources in theatre. It can be used to establish focus, to indicate mood, and to create special effects. Here we see two dancing figures in a bright light, while behind them we have a silhouetted projection of the same two figures, providing an interesting visual effect. The show is The Play What I Wrote, *by Sean Foley and Hamish McColl (pictured) and Eddie Braben in a London production directed by Kenneth Branagh, with choreography by Irving Davies and Heather Cornell, set and costume designs by Alice Power, lighting design by Tim Mitchell, and sound design by Simon Baker for Autograph. (© Geraint Lewis)*

277

A Brief History of Stage Lighting

For the first 2,000 years of its recorded history, theatre was held mostly outdoors during the day—a primary reason being the need for illumination. The sun, after all, is an excellent source of light.

Since sophisticated lighting was unavailable, playwrights used imagination—the handiest tool available—to suggest nighttime or shifts in lighting. Performers brought on torches, or a candle, as Lady Macbeth does, to indicate night. Playwrights also used language to indicate lighting. In *The Merchant of Venice,* Shakespeare has Lorenzo say, "How sweet the moonlight sleeps upon this bank"; this is not just a pretty line of poetry but also serves to remind us that it is nighttime. The same is true of the eloquent passage when Romeo tells Juliet that he must leave because dawn is breaking.

> Look, love, what envious streaks
> Do lace the severing clouds in yonder East:
> Night's candles are burnt out, and jocund day
> Stands tiptoe on the misty mountain tops.

Around 1600 CE, theatre began to move indoors. Candles and oil lamps were used for illumination, and the chief refinements were more sophisticated uses of these basic elements, such as those achieved in the 1770s by David Garrick, the actor-manager of the Drury Lane Theatre in London; and Philippe Jacques DeLoutherbourg (1740–1812), a French designer whom Garrick brought to the Drury Lane. DeLoutherbourg, for example, installed lighting above the stage and used gauze curtains and silk screens to achieve subtle effects with color. In 1785 an instrument known as the Argand lamp (after its inventor, Aimé Argand of Geneva) was introduced. It made use of a glass chimney and a cylindrical wick to create a steadier, brighter light.

Not until 1803, however, when a theatre in London installed gaslights, was there a genuine advance in stage lighting. With gas, which was the principal source of illumination during the nineteenth century, lighting was more easily controlled and managed. Lighting intensity, for example, could be raised or lowered. Its effectiveness, however, remained limited. In addition, the open flames of gas and other earlier lighting systems posed a constant threat of fire. Through the years there were several tragic and costly fires in theatres, both in Europe and in the United States.

In 1879 Thomas Edison invented the incandescent lamp (the electric lightbulb), and the era of imaginative lighting for the theatre began. Not only are incandescent lamps safe, but they can also be controlled. Brightness or intensity can be increased or decreased: the same lighting instrument will produce the bright light of noonday or the dim light of dusk. Also, by putting a colored film over the light or by other means, color can be controlled.

Beyond the power and versatility of electric light, there have been numerous other advances in controls and equipment over the past fifty years. Lighting instruments have been continually refined to become more powerful, as well as more subtle, and to throw a more concentrated, more sharply defined beam. Also, lighting has lent itself more successfully than other theatre elements to miniaturization and computerization. After all, costumes must still be sewn individually, and scenes on flats or backdrops are still painted by hand. Lighting intensity, however, is controlled by electricity and therefore offers a perfect opportunity to take advantage of advances in electronics.

First came resistance dimming systems, then thyratron vacuum tubes, and after that a series of technical innovations with names such as *magnetic amplifiers* and *silicon-controlled rectifiers.*

When applied to lighting, these developments in dimming systems allowed for increasingly complex and sophisticated controls. For a large college theatre production, 200 to 300 lighting instruments may be hung around and above the stage. For a large Broadway musical there may be 800 or more. Each of these instruments can be hooked up to a central computer board, and light settings can be stored in the computer. By pushing a single button, an operator can, in a split second, bring about a shift in literally dozens of instruments. The resulting flexibility and control are remarkable tools for achieving stage effects.

Objectives and Functions of Lighting Design

Adolphe Appia (1862–1928), a Swiss scene designer, was one of the first to see the vast aesthetic, artistic possibilities of light in the theatre. He wrote: "Light is to the production what music is to the score: the expressive element in opposition to the literal signs; and, like music, light can express only what belongs to the inner essence of all vision's vision." Norman Bel Geddes (1893–1958), an imaginative American designer who was a follower of Appia, put it in these words: "Good lighting adds space, depth, mood, mystery, parody, contrast, change of emotion, intimacy, fear." Edward Gordon Craig (1872–1966), an innovative British designer, spoke of "painting with light." The lighting designer can indeed paint with light, but far more can be done. On the deepest sensual and symbolic level, the lighting designer can convey something of the feeling, and even the substance, of a play.

It is intriguing that today's leading lighting designers still speak of the artistic potential and aesthetics of light in precisely the same way as these innovators did. In a sense the art of lighting has not changed, but the technology has exploded in the last twenty years of innovation, and that innovation continues. In fact the most serious problem in lighting for the theatre today is to prevent the technology from taking over the aesthetics of the design, which is where the greatest distinction exists between contemporary lighting technicians and lighting designers.

The following are the primary functions and objectives of stage lighting:

1. Provide visibility.
2. Reveal shapes and forms.
3. Provide a focus onstage and create visual compositions.
4. Assist in creating mood and reinforcing style.
5. Help establish time and place.
6. Establish a rhythm of visual movement.
7. Reinforce a central visual image, establish visual information, or both.

An experienced lighting designer will be capable of accomplishing all these functions simultaneously and will emphasize various objectives at various times during a production to help maintain the *kinesthetic* connection between the audience and the world of the play.

Visibility   On the practical side, the chief function of lighting is illumination or visibility. We must be able, first and foremost, to see the performers' faces and their actions onstage. Occasionally, lighting designers, carried away with atmospheric possibilities, will make a scene so dark that we can hardly see what is happening. Mood is important, of course, but seeing the performers is obviously even more important. It is true that unless you can see the actors and actresses, the lighting designer has not carried out his or her assignment; however, the accomplished designer will establish a balance that allows for visibility while meeting other design objectives effectively.

Shape and Form   The lighting designer must enhance the visual world of the play by revealing the objects in that world as interestingly as possible. Lighting objects from the front, with lights above the audience illuminating the stage, visually washes out all three-dimensional objects onstage, making them look flat and uninteresting. The designer must therefore enhance the actors and other visual elements of the *world of the play* with lighting and color from the side, top, and behind them.

Focus and Composition   In photography, the term *focus* means adjustment of the lens of a camera so that the picture recorded on the film is sharp and clear. In theatre lighting, *focus* refers to the fact that beams of light are aimed at—focused on—a particular area. In stage action the director and lighting designer collaborate in creating a continually moving visual composition that always keeps the audience focused on the central action of the play. This kind of collaboration and compositional focus also allows a character—Count Dracula, for example—to slip into position without the audience ever realizing how he got there until it is time to reveal him. Careful focus of light is integral to successful visuals onstage. Adjacent lighting and acting areas must be overlapped in focus to allow actors to move across the stage without going into and out of the edges of light beams. At the same time, the designer must control the *spill* of the light in front of and behind the actor so that it will not distract the audience from the action.

By means of focus and changes in light cues the lighting designer and director keep the audience focused on the essential action. These compositions or *looks* can vary from turning the stage into one large area to creating small, isolated areas all intended to take the audience on an interesting visual journey through the world of the play.

Mood and Style   Theatre, as a collaborative art form by definition, combines all areas of a production to establish the mood and world of the play. Once that predominant mood is established for an audience, the individual production areas can manipulate mood throughout the play, especially through lighting and sound. A production can also effectively manipulate the audience's reaction. For example, early in a play the audience may see two or three romantic moments when the stage is filled with blue moonlight; then, in a later scene the look may seem the same until the action starts and the audience realizes that the mood has changed to a cold, dark, evil situation. Action, scenery, and words, in conjunction with light, tell us exactly what the mood is. Experienced playwrights and designers know how an audience can be manipulated and will often take advantage of its expectations to make its journey more interesting.

LIGHTING CREATES MOOD AND STYLE
Along with scenery and costumes, lighting is a key element in creating the mood and style of a production. Shown here is a magical, imaginative lighting design for a production of Shakespeare's *Much Ado about Nothing*. Note the dappled light on the stage floor, which could suggest moonlight on a lake, or a meadow; and the blue night sky and the background, outlining the single red balloon. The lighting design was by Michael Gilliam. The production, at the Alley Theatre, was directed by Scott Schwartz, with set design by Walt Spangler and costume design by Fabio Toblini. (© T Charles Erickson)

In terms of style, lighting can indicate whether a play is realistic or nonrealistic. In a realistic play, the lighting will simulate the effect of ordinary sources—table lamps, say, and outside sunlight. In a nonrealistic production or a highly theatrical musical, the designer can be more imaginative: shafts of light can cut through the dark, sculpting performers onstage; a glowing red light can convey a scene of damnation; a ghostly green light can cast a spell over a nightmare scene; a hard-edged spotlight can let the audience members know that what they are now seeing is not a realistic moment in a character's life.

Time and Place   By its color, shade, and intensity, lighting can suggest the time of day, giving us the pale light of dawn, the bright light of midday, the vivid colors of

photo essay

The Many Uses of Stage Lighting

Stage lighting can be used for many purposes: to illuminate, to highlight characters or stage areas, to create mood.

Here we see lighting creating the background behind and above the character of Hilda Wangel in a production of Ibsen's *The Master Builder.* Meanwhile, the character, played by Susan Heyward, is highlighted by spotlights from in front and above, so that she stands out, as the center of attention. The production was directed by Evan Yionoulis at the Yale Repertory. Set design, Timothy Brown; costumes, Katherine Akiko Day; lighting, Paul Whitaker.

This photograph from a production of *The Glass Menagerie* by Tennessee Williams, directed by Scott Schwartz at the Alley Theatre in Houston, shows a skillful use of local front lighting: the candles illuminate the two characters, Judith Ivey as Amanda Wingfield and Patch Darragh as Tom. Lighting by Michael Gilliam; costumes by Fabio Toblini; sets by Walt Spangler.

282

A fascinating example of the powerful effects of lighting onstage is demonstrated in this scene with Hannah Barrie as Queen Isabel and Jonathan Slinger as King Richard in a production of Shakespeare's play *Richard II* at the RSC, Stratford-upon-Avon. Note the marvelously eerie effect of the downlighting on Richard, and the side- and backlighting on both characters, creating an intriguing atmosphere and visual stage picture. Design by Tom Piper.

This scene illustrates the powerful visual effect of silhouette, created by lighting in which dancing figures are outlined against a striking background. The scene is from the musical *Fela!*—about an iconic African musical figure. The production was choreographed and directed by Bill T. Jones, with lighting by Robert Wierzel.

sunset, or the muted light of evening. Lighting can also indicate the season of the year, because the sun strikes objects at very different angles in winter and summer. Lighting can also suggest place, by showing indoor or outdoor light.

Rhythm   Since changes in light occur on a time continuum, they establish a rhythm running through a production. It is absolutely imperative that the seemingly simple lighting changes from scene to scene help establish the kind of rhythm and timing that the director needs for the audience to be drawn into the action. Abrupt, staccato changes with stark blackouts might unsettle an audience if that is called for, and languid, slow fades and gradual cross-fades can allow the audience a more thoughtful transition between scenes. However, do we fade out the previous scene slowly while the next scene is beginning, thus prompting the audience to think about the connection? Or do we make the lights fade in very slowly, prompting the audience to ask what is to come and pulling their attention in? Either way these changes in rhythm have an effect on the audience's interaction and understanding of the world of the play.

Since many lighting changes are coordinated with scene changes and changes in other production elements, it is a challenge for the lighting designer to make artistic choices that will support the director's vision, whether a change is pragmatic or solely aesthetic. Either way the importance of this synchronization is recognized by directors and designers, who take great care to ensure the proper changes—"choreographing" shifts in light and scenery like dancers' movements.

Reinforcement of the Central Image   Lighting—like scenery, costumes, and all other elements—must be consistent with the overall style and mood of a production. Over the past thirty years there has been a dramatic change in the style of writing in plays. Long, extended scenes taking place in a single location are less and less common. Today's audiences are most accustomed to film and television editing, and to shorter scenes with multiple locations. Most of our contemporary plays tend to be written in a style that also cuts frequently from location to location; the actors may be on a bare stage with only the most essential props or suggested props to support the action. These kinds of changes in writing style prompt the lighting designer to provide more visual information than ever before about place and locale to allow for such simple staging. The wrong lighting can distort or even destroy the effect of a play. At the same time, because lighting is the most flexible and the most atmospheric visual element of theatre, it can aid enormously in creating the theatre experience.

The Lighting Designer

The person responsible for creating, installing, and setting controls for stage lighting is the lighting designer. It is important for the lighting designer to have a background in the technical and mechanical aspects of lighting as well as a broad, creative visual imagination. The ability to translate words and actions and feelings into color, direction, and intensity comes only after much training and experience.

The Process of Lighting Design   In creating the lighting design for a production, the lighting designer first reads the script and begins to form some rough ideas and develop some feelings about the play. He or she meets with the director and other designers to discuss visual concepts. The lighting designer receives from the set designer copies of all the scenery plans and usually consults with the costume designer to learn the shape and color of the costumes.

The lighting designer will do a great deal of visual research and will also see one or perhaps several rehearsals to get the feel of the production, to see the exact location of various pieces of furniture and stage business, and to consult with the director about possible effects. Following this, the lighting designer draws a plan called a *light plot*. This includes the location and color of each lighting instrument. Also indicated is the kind of instrument called for and the area of the stage on which it is focused. When lighting instruments are moved into the theatre and hung (that is, placed on pipes and other supports), the designer supervises the focusing.

During technical rehearsals, the lighting designer works with the director to establish light cues: that is, instructions about when the lights go on and off. The designer also sets the length of time for light changes and the levels of intensity on the computer-controlled light board, which sends a digital signal to the actual dimmers to adjust the lighting instrument levels. (The actual dimmers, which allow lighting intensities to be changed smoothly and at varying rates, are located in a remote offstage location.)

Properties of Stage Lighting When working on the design for a production, the lighting designer knows what controllable properties of light will achieve the objectives discussed above. The lighting designer can manipulate four different properties of light for any visual change onstage: intensity, color, distribution, and movement.

Intensity The first property of light is brightness, or intensity. Intensity can be controlled (as noted above) by devices called dimmers, which make the lights brighter or darker. A dimmer is an electric or electronic device that can vary the amount of power going to the lights. This makes it possible for a scene at night to take place in very little light and a daylight scene to take place in bright light. Since the advent of computer-control systems, lighting intensities can be set at any level between 1 percent and 100 percent of full, as opposed to levels 1 through 10 on older manual controls.

Color The second property of light is color. Color is a very powerful part of lighting, and theatre lights can very easily be changed to one of several hundred colors simply by placing colored material in slots at the front of the lighting instruments. This material is usually called a gel—short for gelatin, of which it was originally made. Today, however, these color filters are generally made of plastic, Mylar, or acetate. Also in recent years, color *scrollers* have been introduced. These devices typically make it possible to change up to fifteen colors for each lighting, and the scrollers are also programmed into each light cue along with intensity and timing. Color is often mixed so that the strong tones of one shade will not dominate, since such dominance would give an unnatural appearance. Colors are most often selected to support choices made by the scenic and costume designers while still including sufficient dramatic color to support the varied action of the play. Quite often scenes will call for special effects; we expect stark shadows and strange colors, for example, when Hamlet confronts the ghost of his father.

THE USE OF COLOR IN LIGHTING

One of the prime elements in stage lighting is color: it can alter and transform a stage set, changing and establishing different moods. Here we see the same set from *The Underpants* by Carl Sternheim, adapted by Steve Martin, presented at the Alley Theatre, Houston. Note the stark white of the first photograph and the pink and purple hue of the second, contrasting the mood and the tone from one visual picture to another. All this is done with light. The director was Scott Schwartz, with lighting design by Pat Collins, costume design by David C. Woolard, and set design by Anna Louizos. (© T Charles Erickson)

Distribution   The third property of light that the lighting designer can use is distribution: the position and type of lighting instrument being used and the angle at which the light strikes the performers onstage. (Another term for this property could be *direction,* that is, the source from which the light comes, the type of instrument used, and the points on the stage at which a light beam is aimed.) In earlier days, footlights—a row of lights across the front of the stage floor—were used, primarily because this was almost the only location from which to light the front of the performers. However, footlights, which were below the performers, had the disadvantage of casting ghostly shadows on their faces. Footlights also created a kind of barrier between performers and audience. With the development of more powerful, versatile lights, footlights have been eliminated and they are now used only when a production is trying to re-create the look and style of a classic play of the eighteenth or nineteenth century.

Today, most lighting hits the stage from above, coming from instruments in front of the stage and at the sides. The vertical angle of light beams from the *front of the house* is typically close to 45 degrees; this is an excellent angle for lighting the actor's face without creating harmful shadows, and it also gives a sense of sunlight or an overhead light source found in most locations.

There are a wide variety of lighting instruments available today, both conventional instruments and automated moving light fixtures. They all have distinctive features, and each instrument is selected for the quality of light and the design options it allows. What visual qualities or "texture" does the light produce? Is it a single shaft of light, like a single beam of moonlight through the trees or a spotlight in a nightclub? Or is the light in a pattern, such as dappled sunlight through the leaves of trees in a forest? Are the edges of the light sharp, or soft and diffused? In conventional ellipsoidal lighting instruments light can be shaped by special shutters that close in at the edges (very few moving lights even have that capability). All these are additional tools for the designer.

Movement The last property of light the designer can work with is movement, and in fact this is where the lighting design comes to life. On one level, the eye is carried from place to place by the shifting focus of lights: follow spots moving from one person or one area to another, automated lights changing directions, a performer carrying a candle or flashlight across the stage. The subtlest and often the most effective kind of movement of light comes with shifting the audience's focus when lights go down in one area and come up in another. Lighting cross-fades like this can shift the focus from location to location and from color to color, but even within single scenes a good lighting design will force the audience members to change their focus without even realizing it. Also, time of day, sunsets, and so on can help provide visual information for the audience.

For an example of how these properties function, consider the lighting for a production of *Hamlet*. To emphasize the eerie, tragic quality of this play, with its murders and graveyard scene, the lighting would generally be cool rather than warm, but it could also have a slash of red cutting through the otherwise cool light. As for angles, if the production took place on a proscenium stage, there would be more dramatic downlighting and backlighting to give the characters a sculptured, occasionally unreal quality. In terms of movement, the lights would change each time there was a shift in locale, or a low-angle special could come on diagonally from behind the ghost of Hamlet's father. This would give a rhythm of movement throughout the play and would also focus the audience's attention on particular areas of the stage as well as supporting the thematic elements of the play.

The Lighting Designer's Resources Among the resources of the lighting designer are various kinds of lighting instruments and other kinds of technical and electronic equipment.

Types of Stage Lights Most stage lights have three main elements: a lamp that is the source of the light, a reflector, and a lens through which the beams pass. The two basic categories of lighting fixtures are conventional lighting instruments and automated or moving light fixtures. Conventional lights are fixed instruments with a single focus and design purpose. Intelligent moving light fixtures are able to alter focus, change color, project multiple patterns, rotate the patterns at varying speeds, change the size of the beam, and give a sharp or diffused focus.

Examples of common conventional lights are the ellipsoidal reflector spotlights, Fresnel spotlights, strip/cyc/flood/border lights, PARs, and follow spots:

1. *Ellipsoidal reflector spotlight.* This is the most widely used conventional fixture. It creates a bright, hard-edged spot. However, the edges can be softened with focus adjustment or with a diffusion filter. Lenses of different focal lengths allow for eight different standard-size beams depending on the distance from a theatre's hanging positions to the stage; this instrument is therefore useful from almost any position in the theatre. Clearly, it is the "workhorse" of contemporary lighting practice. It also has a special *gobo* slot for pattern projection. A *follow spot* is another typically hard-edged spotlight controlled by an operator that is designed to follow the leading performer across the stage. This type of follow spot has been in use since about 1856. Originally, the light was created by igniting the mineral lime in front of a reflector in the back end of a long metal tube. The chemical reaction created a bright but slightly green light, which led to a common expression for someone who likes attention as "being in the limelight."

Variable beam profile spot. (Courtesy of Selecon)

Selecon 1200 Fresnel. (Courtesy of Selecon)

2. *Soft-edged spotlights.* The most popular soft-edged spotlight is the Fresnel (pronounced "fruh-NEL"). It is a high-wattage spot, and the Fresnel lens helps dissipate the heat, but it can create only a soft-edged beam of light that can be focused down to a small spot or flooded to cover a larger stage area. The lens is named for Auguste Fresnel, who designed, for lighthouses, the first lenses that would not crack with intense heating and cooling. The concentric rings he cut into the lens allowed the lens to function properly while preventing the buildup of heat from cracking the lens after the light was turned off. Many lighting designers use this instrument for toplighting and backlighting and to cover a large stage area with a wash of color. The Fresnel is generally used in positions near the stage—behind the proscenium opening, or mounted close to the action on an arena or thrust stage. Another common soft-edged lighting instrument is the parabolic aluminized reflector (PAR), which emits an oval beam. *Barn doors,* with flaps that can cut off an edge of the beam, and *color changers/scrollers,* which increase the options from one color to fifteen colors on a single instrument, are common accessories used on both PARs and Fresnels.

3. *Floodlights, strip lights, and border lights.* These lights bathe a section of the stage or scenery in a smooth, diffused wash of light. Floodlights are used, singly or in groups, to provide general illumination for the stage or scenery. The light from floods can be blended in acting areas, or used to "tone" settings and

Selecon Acclaim flood. (Courtesy of Selecon)   Vari*Lite VL6 spot luminaire. (Courtesy of Vari*Lite)

costumes. They are most often used to illuminate cycloramas at the rear of the stage, or ground rows along the floor of the stage.

4. *Automated or moving light.* The moving light is the newest and most versatile instrument of the group, although there are still only a few moving lights with an independent shutter function that can be focused in a theatre like an ellipsoidal spotlight. Automated light fixtures are able to alter focus, change color using dichroic color mixing, project multiple patterns, rotate the patterns at varying speeds, change the size of the beam, and give a sharp or diffused focus. One mover used as a special can replace numerous conventional fixtures. Most contemporary lighting designers use a combination of both types of instruments. Automated fixtures are particularly useful in elaborate musical productions and are widely used in rock concerts.

Lighting Controls   Technologically, lighting is easily the most highly developed aspect of theatre. We have already considered some of the advances in this area. Lighting instruments can be hung all over the theatre and aimed at every part of the stage; and these many instruments can be controlled by one person sitting at a console. The development of intelligent lighting fixtures and other digital accessories has also prompted a great deal of change in the design of lighting control systems. Ideally, in a theatre it is best to have a newly designed console that combines the typical theatrical programming for conventional light cues with full moving light capability and ease of operation. In recent years such lighting boards have been developed. Currently there are ideal control systems for movers with the ability to control more traditional lighting cues, though not in the traditional fashion; and there are traditional theatrical lighting boards that can control movers, though the programming for those moving lights is cumbersome and time-consuming. Lighting control systems are extremely expensive, so the eventual change to another system for most theatre operations will happen only gradually.

Lighting changes—or ***cues,*** as they are called—are usually arranged ahead of time. Sometimes, in a complicated production (a musical, say, or a Shakespearean play), there will be from 75 to 150 or more light cues. A cue can range from a ***blackout*** (in which all the lights are shut off at once), to a *fade* (the lights dim slowly,

- During the last play you attended, what did you notice about the lighting? Were the light instruments throughout the theater aimed at the stage? When the performance began, where did the beams of light appear to come from?

- What colors were created onstage by lighting? Did you think the colors were appropriate for the production? How did the color of the lights affect your overall experience?

- Were you able to spot the sound speakers? During the performance, did you notice if microphones were attached to the actors? Do you think there were microphones elsewhere onstage?

changing the scene from brighter to darker), to a *cross-fade* (one set of lights comes down while another comes up) or a split cross-fade (the lights that are coming up are on a different fade count from the lights that are coming down). Thanks to computerized control, the split cross-fade is the most common. Although light board programming is complicated and somewhat time-consuming the actual running of a show has become a fairly simple task because of well-designed computer control systems. The most critical aspect of the lighting design is the ability of the stage manager to fully understand the pacing and design aesthetic in calling the lighting and sound cues. Even the process of calling cues has been simplified in some ways by technology. In lighting for dance or for large-scale musicals it is critical to merge the lighting and sound cues. Through the use of new digital sound technology a computer-controlled sound program can interface with a computer light board and both light and sound cues can be run simultaneously with one tap of the keyboard space bar.

For instance, Strindberg's *A Dream Play* has innumerable scene changes—like a dream, as the title implies—in which one scene fades into another before our eyes. At one point in the play, a young woman, called the Daughter, sits at an organ in a church. In Strindberg's words, "The stage darkens as the Daughter rises and approaches the Lawyer. By means of lighting the organ is transformed into a wall of a grotto. The sea seeps in between basal pillars with a harmony of waves and wind." At the light cue for this change, a button is pushed, and all the lights creating the majesty of the church fade as the lights creating the grotto come up. In many ways stage lighting technology has finally started to catch up with, and serve, the creative ideas that artists like Strindberg and Appia had at the start of the twentieth century.

The Lighting Designer's Collaborators   As in every aspect of theatre, in lighting too there is collaboration. A number of people work with the lighting designer. These include assistant designers and people who help create the light plot, as well as a master electrician responsible for the preparation, hanging, and focusing of the lights and all accessories (often, if not always, electricians must climb on catwalks and ladders to remote areas above, behind, and in front of the stage). One of the newer jobs is that of the moving light programmer. Until the advent of moving lights, programming light cues had always fallen to either the lighting designer or the lead associate designer. More recently, however, the complexity of programming has grown exponentially with automated fixtures and other digital accessories, thus requiring another technical specialty. Large-scale musical productions, for example, are often so complex that even calling all the cues is impossible for one person to do. For that reason, all follow-spot cues (usually three or four follow spots in a design) are typically called by the lead spot operator. In the concert industry, this gets even more complex, as there are usually a minimum of eight follow spots and often as many as sixteen or more on a major tour in addition to almost unimaginably complex moving light packages.

SOUND IN THE THEATRE

Scenery, costumes, and lighting can all be described as visual elements of theatre. Another design element, sound, is aural. In recent years, it has become an increasingly important aspect of theatre, with its own artistry, technology, and designers. In fact, in 2007 the Tony Awards Committee voted to include sound design as a category beginning with the 2008 awards.

Sound Reproduction: Advantages and Disadvantages

Amplification In the past few decades, sound reproduction has become increasingly prominent in theater. For some audience members, it has sometimes proved to be controversial as well. At popular music concerts, intense amplification has come to be expected, and personal stereo systems have made listeners expect widespread sound reproduction in the theater. As a result, large musicals, whether presented in Broadways houses or in spacious performing arts centers across the country, are now extensively amplified. Most audiences, accustomed to amplified sound in many other settings, take such amplification for granted.

Some critics charge, however, that amplification in theatre is sometimes overdone, with the sound too loud, as well as too mechanical and artificial. In opera the objections are even stronger. In today's theatre, those continuing to oppose amplification appear to be the "purists." Their objections stem, no doubt, from the experience of theatergoing half a century ago. It may be difficult for young people in the early twenty-first century to imagine, but the great American musicals of the 1940s and the 1950s—by composers like Rodgers and Hammerstein, Cole Porter, and Irving Berlin—were all produced without any sound amplification whatsoever. Today, however, electronic amplification is a way of life in theatre, and sound design has become an indispensable part of any production.

It should be noted at the same time that the issue is less pressing in smaller venues: in "black boxes," for example, or fringe theaters in lofts or warehouses that seat perhaps 100 spectators. In such spaces, the sound component, both because of economics and because of size, is likely to be less elaborate and less noticeable. We are speaking here, therefore, of larger spaces: college or university theatres of 400 or 500 seats, and professional theatres that might range from 800 to 2,000 seats.

Sound Effects Aside from the argument about the volume or pervasiveness of voice amplification, it should be noted that sound has always been an important, and necessary, component of theater production. One aspect of this is sound effects. In earlier years—for several centuries, in fact—various devices were developed to create such sounds.

Historically, for example, the sound of wind was produced by a wooden drum made from slats. The drum was usually 2 or 3 feet in diameter, and covered with a muslin cloth. When the drum was turned, by means of a handle, it made a noise like howling wind. Thunder was suggested by hanging a large, thick metal sheet backstage and gently shaking it. For the sound of a door slamming, a miniature door or even a

There are times when sound takes over in a production. Of course, in most musical productions, all the voices, as well as the instruments of the orchestra, are enhanced by sound equipment. But in many productions there are certain moments when sound is crucial. An example is the scene shown here from a production of *Summer and Smoke* by Tennessee Williams, directed by Michael Wilson at the Hartford Stage Company. One of the characters fires a gun at another character. All action stops; the shot becomes the defining event. Sound design was by John Gromada. (© T Charles Erickson)

full-size door in a frame was placed just offstage and opened and shut. Two hinged pieces of wood slammed shut simulated the sound of a closing door. A gunshot sound could also be created with these hinged pieces of wood, as well as by firing a gun loaded with blank cartridges. (It should be noted that in some states, blank guns are illegal. But live ammunition should never be used onstage.)

Today, of course, sound effects are far more sophisticated. The developments in computer programs to support sound design and playback are extensive. There are many programs available on the Internet for free download as well, so it is not difficult to get started using simple sound programs. Most often these same programs have more advanced and complex capabilities that are available for purchase. You can record and play back a myriad of sound cues, but if you want to interface those sound cues through a lighting control board or projection system, for creation and alteration, then you may use Pro Tools, Final Cut Pro, or Garage Band. Also available are SFX and CueLab computer playback systems.

The Sound Designer

The person responsible for arranging and orchestrating all the aural aspects of a production is the sound designer. Like his or her counterparts in visual design, the sound designer begins by reading the script, noting all the places where sound might be needed. For a large-scale musical, the designer also decides on the number and type of microphones to be used, the placement of speakers throughout the theatre, and all other aspects of sound reproduction.

After reading the script, the sound designer consults with the director to determine the exact nature of the sound requirements, including sound effects and amplification. The designer then sets about preparing the full range of components that constitute sound for a production. Encompassing anything from preshow and intermission music to any and all microphones to special prerecorded sound effects to preshow announcements about cell phones to live voice-overs, sound is an essential component of every theatre production.

Understanding Sound Reproduction and Sound Reinforcement

One way to classify sound design is as *sound reproduction* and *sound reinforcement.* Reproduction is the use of motivated or environmental sounds. *Motivated sounds* would be, for instance, the noise of a car crunching on gravel, a car motor turning off, and a door slamming—a sequence that would announce the arrival of a character at a house where a scene is taking place. Motivated sounds, then, are those called for by the script. *Environmental sounds* are noises of everyday life that help create verisimilitude in a production: street traffic in a city, crickets in the country, loud rock music coming from a stereo in a college dormitory. Such sounds are usually heard as background.

Sound effects, as noted above, are one form of sound reproduction. A sound effect can be defined as any sound produced by mechanical or human means to create for the audience a noise or sound associated with the play. In recent years, most sound effects have been recorded on compact discs. Virtually every sound imaginable—from birds singing to dogs barking to jet planes flying—is available on CDs or can be downloaded from the Internet, not only for expensive professional productions but also for college, university, and community theatres.

Reinforcement is the amplification of sounds produced by a performer or a musical instrument. With the growth of electronics in music, more and more instruments have been amplified. At any rock concert, you can see wires coming out of the basses and guitars. In an orchestra pit in a theatre, the quieter acoustic instruments such as the guitar are miked to achieve a balance of sound with the louder instruments. In today's Broadway theatres it is not unusual to have some members of the orchestra in a separate room in another part of the building with a television monitor showing the conductor. In most cases, the audience would never know about this seating arrangement. The total sound can overwhelm a singer, especially one who has not been trained—as opera singers are—to project the voice into the farther reaches of a theatre. As a result, we have body mikes on the performers.

At first, a body mike was a small microphone attached in some way to the performer's clothing. A wire ran from the mike to a small radio transmitter concealed on the performer; from the transmitter, the sound was sent to an offstage listening device that fed it into a central sound-control system. In today's large musical productions, the microphone worn by a performer is frequently a small instrument, hardly larger than a piece of wire, worn over one ear alongside the temple or placed elsewhere near the performer's head, that carries the sound to the body transmitters. In some musicals, the performers wear a small microphone attached to a headpiece coming around one side of the head, similar to that worn by telephone switchboard operators. Head microphones are used so that they will be as close as possible to the performer's mouth and at a constant distance away from it. (How many people realize while watching a musical that tap dancers are frequently wearing wireless microphones near their feet?)

Still another kind of sound that must be added to the final mix is musical or other *underscoring,* which one hears between scenes or acts, and sometimes during spoken sections of a performance to add emphasis or create mood.

Sound Technology

Microphones and Loudspeakers

In preparing the sound for a production, the designers and engineers not only must assemble all the necessary sounds but also must be certain that the appropriate microphones are used correctly and must place the speakers effectively onstage and in the auditorium.

Several types of microphones are used. A *shotgun mike* is highly directional and is aimed from a distance at a specific area. A *general mike* picks up sounds in the general area toward which it is aimed. A *body mike,* as described above, is a wireless microphone attached to a performer's body or clothing. Microphones not worn by performers are placed in various locations. One position is alongside the downstage edge of the stage. Another position is hanging in the air above the stage. Any type of microphone must be hooked up to an amplifier that increases the electronic energy of the sound and sends it through the speakers.

The placement of loudspeakers is both an art and a science. It is necessary to determine the correct speakers for the size and shape of the theatre, and to position them so that they carry sound clearly and evenly into the auditorium—to the upper reaches of the balcony, to the side seats, and to areas underneath the balcony as well as the first few rows in the orchestra. Also, live sound from the performers must reach the sides and back of the theatre at the same time that it reaches the spectators in front. One problem in this regard is that sound travels much more slowly than light. The speed of sound is only 1,100 feet per second—which means that for a spectator seated at the back of a large theatre, sound from a speaker at the rear of the auditorium will be heard before the human voice from the stage. Developments in digital electronics have led to devices that process, sample, and synthesize sound for various effects; and one useful device addresses this problem, delaying the electronic sound so that it arrives through a loudspeaker at the same time as the much slower live sound.

Sound Recordings

The process of assembling sound recordings is similar for professional and nonprofessional productions. First, a list is made of all sound required. This list is usually developed by the sound designer in consultation with the director, and possibly with a composer: for a show with a great deal of sound or music, there may be both a sound designer and a music composer. Once the list is drawn up, a master recording is made and the sounds are arranged in their order of appearance in the script. This process is called *editing.* When the production moves into the theatre, there is a technical rehearsal without performers, during which each sound cue is listened to and the volume is set. When rehearsals with the performers start in the theatre, more changes will be made. Depending on the action and the timing of scenes, some cues will be too loud and others too soft; some will have to be made shorter and others made longer.

During an actual performance of a production using sound reinforcement, an operator must sit at a complex sound console *mixing* sound or use a computerized playback system such as SFX or CueLab. In this way the operator blends all elements from the many microphones and from the master sound recording—so that there is a smooth, seamless blend of sound. Also, the operator must make certain not only that all sound is in balance but also that sound does not intrude on the performance or call attention to itself, away from the stage and the performers.

New Technologies in Sound   As with lighting, in recent years we have seen frequent advances and breakthroughs in sound equipment and technology. The new body microphones and a device that delays the delivery of electronic sound have already been mentioned. There are other developments as well.

Analog reel-to-reel tape decks, which were standard only a few years ago, are now giving way to digital technology such as recordable compact discs and direct playback from a computer's hard drive. Sound is now recorded and edited at digital audio workstations, based on personal computers. Such stations allow easier editing of sound, more complex effects, and higher-quality sound. Digital playback systems allow very easy and precise cueing of shows, as well as greatly improved sound quality.

Lighting and sound, like scenery and costumes, are means to an end: they implement the artistic and aesthetic aspects of a production. The colors, shapes, and lines of lighting effects and the qualities of sound interact with other elements of theatre and contribute to the overall experience.

In Part Four we have looked at the design component of the theatre experience—at both the aesthetic and the technical sides of various aspects of design: scenic, costume, lighting, and sound. In Part Five we move to a discussion of three important types of theatre we experience when we attend performances: musical theatre, today's global theatre, and contemporary American theatre.

SUMMARY

1. Stage lighting, like other elements of theatre, has a counterpart in the lighting of homes, restaurants, advertisements, etc.

2. Lighting was historically the last visual element to be fully developed for the stage but is today the most technically sophisticated. Once the incandescent electric lamp was introduced, it was possible to achieve almost total control of the color, intensity, and timing of lights. Lighting controls have also benefited from computerization, with extensive light shifts being controlled by an operator at a computerized console.

3. Lighting design is intended to provide illumination onstage, to establish time and place, to help set the mood and style of a production, to focus the action, and to establish a rhythm of visual movement.

4. Lighting should be consistent with all other elements.

5. The lighting designer uses a variety of instruments, colored gels, special accessories, and advanced dimmer controls as well as computerized control consoles to achieve effects. Electronic developments and computers have greatly increased the flexibility and control of lighting instruments and equipment.

6. Sound is taking its place alongside scenery, costumes, and lighting as a key design element. Rapid advances in technology allow for sophisticated delivery in a theatre of both sound reproduction—sound effects and such—and sound reinforcement, of both musical instruments and the human voice. The sound designer and engineer must (a) prepare the sound track, (b) place microphones and speakers appropriately, and (c) mix recorded and live sounds during the performance to achieve the desired effect.

5

The Theatre
Landscape Today

TODAY'S THEATRE: INCLUSIVE AND DIVERSE

Global theatre today reaches across all continents and encompasses the tragic and comic, the traditional and experimental, and straight plays and musicals. Many contemporary productions are multicultural; a good example is *Fela!* This Afrobeat dance musical about Fela Kuti, a Nigerian singer and revolutionary, was choreographed and directed by Bill T. Jones. Shown here is Sahr Ngaujah in the title role. (Sara Krulwich/The New York Times/Redux)

Part Five

The Theatre Landscape Today

During the past 100 years, the world has seen unprecedented, earth-shattering changes. Discoveries and inventions have abounded, and, at the same time, war, civil unrest, unimaginable horrors, and natural disasters have marked our world.

On the positive side, we have experienced an astounding series of achievements in science, medicine, technology, communications, travel, and commerce. In medicine, for example, great strides have been made: diseases have been cured and people enabled to live much longer.

Also, in information technology worldwide communication has become instantaneous, as e-mail and mobile phones allow us to reach the other side of the world in a matter of seconds. Television has brought into our homes the triumphs and disasters of this fast-paced world, shown up-close and graphically, as they occur.

On the other side of the ledger, in the past 75 years we have experienced World War II—in which, among other things, the Nazi regime carried out the systematic and ruthless extermination of 6 million people, most of them

Jews. In the 1960s and 1970s, the Vietnam War brought a frightening number of casualties and images of horror to the American consciousness. Civil wars and genocide took place in several African countries. There has also been the continuing, bloody conflict between Israel and the Palestinians in the Middle East. Terrorist attacks took place inside the United States on September 11, 2001. The costly and deadly wars in Iraq and Afghanistan have continued this pattern of despair and destruction.

In the midst of all this, the one thing missing from our amazing

Cell phones (some with built-in digital cameras and Internet access), laptop computers, hand-held electronic devices, and digital music players have become ubiquitous. (Russel A. Daniels/AP Images)

Today's world has seen unbelievable progress and heartbreaking tragedies. This impromptu memorial for U.S. military personnel killed in the Iraq War was set up near a village 150 miles from Baghdad. (Pier Paolo Cito/AP/Wide World Photos)

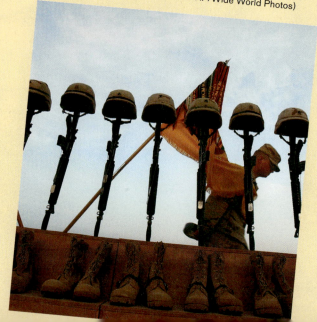

medical advances, from our instantaneous communication, from the powerful images we see on television and film, is human contact—two groups of people in the presence of one another at the same time: the performers and the audience. As the world seems to grow more impersonal and frightening, the need for human interaction becomes more important than ever. And at the forefront of contact between people is the theatre experience.

This is a primary reason why, in spite of the multitude of challenges theatre has faced—radio, film, television, computers—it remains alive and well. In fact, in some ways it is more vital than ever. Theatre, like the best of human institutions, is all-embracing. It's safe to say that at no time in the past have audiences in the United States, in Canada, and in many other places had as wide or varied a choice of theatrical offerings as they have today. To begin with, there is an amazing multiplicity of theatrical venues: large theatres, midsize resident professional theatres, small intimate theatres, college and university theatres, community theatres, theatres with all types of audience and stage configurations. The various theatres house large spectacular productions, classics, new plays, performance art, ensemble creations, and avant-garde presentations.

The season of a resident professional theatre or a college and university theatre might include a classic from the past (the most widely produced playwright in America is William Shakespeare), an important work from the early modern period (Ibsen, Chekhov, Strindberg), a play from the mid-twentieth century (García Lorca, O'Neill, Miller, Williams, Hansberry, Albee), contemporary plays from around the world, and premieres of works by young playwrights.

A further development in contemporary theatre has been the incredibly wide range of the types of offerings: global theatre, multinational theatre (African American, Asian American, Hispanic, Native American); gender-specific drama (gay theatre, lesbian theatre, transsexual theatre), and political theatre, which would include feminist theatre and theatre of social commentary.

In Part Five, we look closely at the landscape of contemporary theatre: in Chapter 13, we focus on musical theatre; in Chapter 14, we examine global theatre; and in Chapter 15, we look at American theatre.

Controversial subjects that have been addressed in contemporary theatre include same-sex unions and other gay and lesbian issues. (© Alex Wong/Getty Images)

Jada Pinkett Smith playing the video game "Enter the Matrix," at a party to celebrate the game's release. (Chris Pizzello/AP Images)

13

Musical Theatre

Today's theatre is global, diverse, and eclectic. Contemporary theatre includes the widest possible types of stage offerings, from the most traditional to the most extreme experimental and avant-garde, and it is truly international. In the next three chapters, we will examine the depth, scope, and range of theatre today, beginning with an important, invaluable part of this rich mix: musical theatre. The following pages offer a brief history of musical theatre, its characteristics today, and a discussion of its special qualities.

BACKGROUND

Drama and Music

Throughout theatre history, drama has been closely associated with music and dance. In ancient Greek tragedy, choral sections were performed to the accompaniment of music and dance. Opera, which began in Italy around 1600, was originated by men who thought that they were imitating Greek drama. Shakespeare, who wrote at about the same time opera began, included songs as an important part of his comedies. The nineteenth-century term *melodrama* came from "song dramas" in which music accompanied the action onstage. In other forms of nineteenth-century theatrical entertainment, such as vaudeville and *burlesque,* singing and dancing were an important element.

It was in the twentieth century, however, that the form of musical theatre with which we are most familiar reached its highest development—for example, in *Oklahoma!, West Side Story, My Fair Lady, Fiddler on the Roof, A Chorus Line,* and Stephen

◀ **MUSICAL THEATRE**

During the twentieth century, American artists were important in developing musical theatre as a distinct art form, in terms of both music itself and its integration with dramatic structure. The beginnings occurred in the first three decades of the twentieth century; then there was a "golden age" of book musicals from the mid-1940s to the mid-1960s. Here is Christina Applegate as Charity Hope Valentine in the musical Sweet Charity. *(© Paul Kolnik)*

Sondheim's musicals. Moreover, these musicals represent a form that came to full flower in the United States. Every other type of drama at which American playwrights and performers have excelled—such as modern tragedy, domestic drama, and farce—traces its origins to another time and another country. Though modern musical theatre has antecedents in forms such as European operetta, it is largely a product of American talent and creativity. Proof of its significance and universal appeal is the fact that it is imitated and performed throughout the western world and in numerous other countries.

The Appeal of Music and Dance

Before we look more closely at musical theatre, it will be helpful to consider the special appeal that music and dance have as part of theatre.

It is not difficult to understand why singing and dancing have frequently been combined with dramatic productions. To begin with, all three are performing arts, and so there is a natural affinity among them. Second, singing and dancing have wide popular appeal. People enjoy listening to music at home as well as in the theatre. Also, in today's world through the earphones they carry with them people hear music everywhere—while they are walking, or riding in cars, planes, or buses. In terms of music, listeners respond to rhythms and to the emotional pull of a memorable melody, especially when it is performed by a singer with a captivating voice and personality. Dancing can also be immensely appealing. The grace and agility of a talented, expertly trained solo dancer or ensemble and the precision of a group of dancers moving in unison provide entertainment of a high order.

Beyond their value as entertainment, singing and dancing possess an unmatched ability to capture the beauty of sound and movement and to communicate a wide range of emotions. In language there are thoughts and feelings that cannot be adequately expressed in everyday prose, and for these we turn to poetry. In the same way, there are expressions of beauty, anguish, and spirituality that can best be conveyed in vocal and instrumental music and in dance.

Opera

Before discussing musical theatre we should take a brief look at a close relative and predecessor, opera. Opera can be defined as a drama set entirely to music. Every part of the performance is sung, including not only the arias but also the transitional sections between them, known as *recitatives*. Having begun in Florence, Italy, around 1600 as drama set to music, opera spread to other parts of Italy during the seventeenth century. For three centuries, from 1600 to 1900, it spread and developed throughout not only Italy, but France, Germany, and much of the European continent, as well as England.

During this time, it took on the characteristics that we have come to know as defining opera. Arias (strong, melodic solos), stirring duets, trios, quartets, and choruses all found their place as components of opera. The stories of opera used myth, history, and contemporary fictional and real events as source material. Also, comic opera *(opera buffa)* joined more serious opera as an option for composers. Important figures in the history of opera include the Italian Alessandro Scarlatti (1659–1725), who established the supremacy of the aria. Wolfgang Amadeus Mozart (1756–1791) brought comic opera to a peak of perfection. Richard Wagner (1813–1883), a German composer, imposed on opera his ideas of monumental works based on legends and myths, with sweeping scores, all joined together in a unified theatre piece. And the Italian composer Giuseppe Verdi (1813–1901) was a superb musician with a mastery of orchestral techniques and an impressive instinct for dramatic effect.

In the late nineteenth century and the early twentieth century, Giacomo Puccini (1858–1924) composed operas that were extremely popular, thanks to their romantic stories and appealing melodies. After that, during the course of the twentieth century, the great days of opera seem to have passed. This was a century in which revivals of operas from earlier years became the standard repertoire. Operas continued to be composed—in the latter part of the century, many of them were commissioned by opera companies—and some found favor with audiences. Others, however, because they incorporated the dissonances and atonality of modern music, were not embraced by a wide public. In addition to the standard repertoire, it is not unusual for works from musical theatre to be presented by opera companies. Two examples are Gershwin's *Porgy and Bess* and Sondheim's *Sweeney Todd.* Thanks to its rich heritage, opera continues to have a significant place in the performing arts.

Opera has many of the qualities of drama: vivid characters and stories with plot twists and unexpected reversals. But it has long been considered within the realm of music rather than drama. This is largely because the composer and the score predominate. For example, *Don Giovanni* has a libretto by Lorenzo Da Ponte, but it is never said to be "by Da Ponte." It is always "Mozart's *Don Giovanni.*" Similarly, *Falstaff* is based on Shakespeare's play *The Merry Wives of Windsor,* but it is known only as Verdi's *Falstaff.* In opera, the composer reigns supreme. By contrast, musical theatre is considered primarily in the realm of theatre.

OPERA

An important musical form related to musical theatre is opera, which originated in Italy at the beginning of the seventeenth century and for three centuries spread through the European continent and England. Opera stresses music: solos, duets, choruses, and other combinations of singers. Also, there is a premium on great singing rather than acting. Shown here are Ramon Vargas as Alfredo and Renée Fleming as Violetta in *La Traviata* at New York's Metropolitan Opera. (Ken Howard/Metropolitan Opera)

Types of Musical Theatre

To understand modern **musical theatre,** it is necessary to define certain terms. Aside from *opera,* they include *operetta, musical comedy, musical theatre,* and *revue.*

Unlike opera, an *operetta* is not entirely set to music; certain portions are spoken by the performers, as in a regular drama. Operetta generally features a romantic story set in a far-off locale. An air of unreality and make-believe makes most operettas remote from everyday life. But the best ones have beautiful, soaring melodies and a plot that tells a complete story, however fanciful. Operetta features solos, duets, and trios as well as stirring choral numbers.

Musical comedy is a form of musical entertainment which emerged in the United States in the 1920s and which features a light, comic story interspersed with popular music. Originally, the story was often far-fetched or even silly, but it did relate to contemporary people and events, and thus musical comedy was closer to everyday life than operetta was. The *musical,* also called *musical theatre,* evolved out of operetta and musical comedy. Examples of this form—*Show Boat, Porgy and Bess, Oklahoma!,* and *My Fair Lady*—will be discussed in the pages that follow.

To round out the range of musical entertainment, we should note the *revue* (discussed in Chapter 8), in which sketches and vignettes alternate with musical numbers. The important thing to remember about the revue is that there is no single story carrying through from beginning to end; the scenes and songs stand alone and may have very little relationship to each other, although they often have a common theme.

A BRIEF HISTORY OF THE AMERICAN MUSICAL

Antecedents

The modern American musical had a number of antecedents in the theatre of the nineteenth century and early twentieth century. One of these was operetta; two others were vaudeville and burlesque. Though burlesque eventually became synonymous with vulgar sketches and "girlie shows," for most of the nineteenth century it featured dramatic sketches and songs that satirized or made fun of other theatrical forms. Vaudeville was a series of variety acts—music, sketches, juggling, animal acts—that

THE MUSICAL REVUE

One variation of the musical is the revue: a series of songs, sketches, and other acts strung together. In the early part of the twentieth century, the revue was a staple of American musical theatre. Singers, dancers, actors, specialty acts, and comic stars were all featured in revues. In addition, the scenic and costume effects were often extremely lavish. One well-known aspect of a revue such as the Ziegfeld Follies was the chorus of beautiful young women, wearing elaborate costumes or barely any costumes at all. The scene here is from the Ziegfeld Follies of 1919. (Bettmann/Corbis)

made up an evening's entertainment. Another form of musical production that flourished in the nineteenth century was the minstrel show, a variety show that featured white performers wearing blackface.

In short, there was a movement toward the development of the *book musical,* which refers to a show with a story that traces the fortunes of the main characters through a series of adventures with a beginning, middle, and end. (The book of a musical is sometimes referred to as the *libretto,* and the person who writes it as the *librettist;* the person who writes the lyrics to a musical score is called a *lyricist.*)

By the early twentieth century, with burlesque, vaudeville, and American imitations of European operettas, the seeds of American musical comedy had been sown.

The 1920s and 1930s: Musical Comedies

Around the time of World War I (1914–1918), a truly native American musical began to emerge. The story was often frivolous, but at least it was a story rather than a series of patched-together blackout sketches, as in earlier attempts at musical shows. More important than the story—or book—was the music. A group of exceptional composers and lyricists wrote the songs for these shows. These songs from the musical comedies of the 1920s and 1930s became known as *standards.* That is, they were so popular that they were played over and over again, and many of them are still played on radio and television and are available to the public through recordings.

Among the composers were Irving Berlin (1888–1989), Jerome Kern (1885–1945), George Gershwin (1898–1937), Cole Porter (1893–1964), and Richard Rodgers. The work of these men was fresh and innovative. Their melodies ranged from the sprightly to the haunting and featured surprising modulations and developments in the melodic line. Matching the inventiveness of the composers were the words of the lyricists. Ira Gershwin (1896–1983) wrote lyrics for many of his brother George's tunes, and Lorenz Hart teamed up with Richard Rodgers. Irving Berlin and Cole Porter wrote their own lyrics.

The lyrics were generally witty and clever, and they reflected a high order of intelligence; the rhymes were resourceful and often unexpected. For example, in "You're the Top" Cole Porter compares the singer's beloved to a wide range of superlative objects, stating that the person is the Colosseum and the Louvre Museum, comparing the loved one to a Bendel bonnet and a Shakespeare sonnet, then rhyming the tower of Pisa with the smile on the Mona Lisa.

The 1920s and 1930s: Advances in Musicals

While composers and lyricists were perfecting their art, a few shows were steps forward for the form of the musical itself. A landmark musical of this era was *Show Boat,* which opened in 1927. The music was by Jerome Kern and the book and lyrics were by Oscar Hammerstein II (1895–1960). It represented an advance over previous musicals in several respects.

Show Boat was based on a novel by Edna Ferber about life on a Mississippi riverboat. Thus the story itself was thoroughly American, not an exotic romantic fable of the kind that was generally found in operetta. But it was a serious story, and this set *Show Boat* apart from lighthearted musical comedies. The story concerns Magnolia Hawks and Gaylord Ravenal, who meet, fall in love, perform on the showboat, later lose their money because of Gaylord's gambling, and eventually separate. Meanwhile, a subplot—a second romance, between the characters Julie and Steve—represented a first for the American musical: it was the love story of an African American woman and a white man. At the time, nothing like this had been shown onstage. There was further daring, and realism, in the depiction of the lives of black workers on the levees of the Mississippi, as exemplified in the song "Ol' Man River."

The score of *Show Boat* included songs that would achieve lasting fame, such as "Why Do I Love You?," "Make Believe," and "Bill." Moreover, these songs were more carefully integrated into the plot than had previously been the case. Another innovation in *Show Boat* was the elimination of a line of chorus girls, which had always been considered indispensable.

Another milestone for the American musical was passed in 1931, when *Of Thee I Sing* was awarded the Pulitzer Prize. This was the first time that a musical had been so honored and a sign that the form was beginning to be taken more seriously. With music and lyrics by George and Ira Gershwin, *Of Thee I Sing* was a satire on political and cultural institutions such as presidential elections and Miss America contests.

In 1935, eight years after *Show Boat,* another important musical opened. This was *Porgy and Bess,* with music by George Gershwin, book by DuBose Heyward (1885–

SHOW BOAT: A LANDMARK MUSICAL
When *Show Boat* opened in 1927, it began a new chapter in the history of the American musical. The chorus line was eliminated, miscegenation (a romance between a white man and a black woman) was treated for the first time, and other problems facing African Americans were touched on. Also, it had a glorious score by Jerome Kern and Oscar Hammerstein. Shown here is a revival staged by Harold Prince. (© Catherine Ashmore)

1940), and lyrics by Heyward and Ira Gershwin. Once again, the story was powerful and realistic—even more so than in *Show Boat*. And the score by George Gershwin, which included "Summertime," "It Ain't Necessarily So," and "Bess, You Is My Woman Now," represented some of the finest compositions written for musical theatre.

Porgy and Bess is set in a black community in Charleston, South Carolina, known as "Catfish Row," and deals with Porgy, a crippled man who falls in love with Bess, who has been the woman of a man named Crown. So forceful and complete is the musicalization of the story that there is some debate over whether *Porgy and Bess* should be considered musical theatre or opera. It has been performed in both theatres and opera houses, including the Metropolitan Opera in New York.

Meanwhile, other steps were being taken that advanced the musical. A musical of 1936 called *On Your Toes* was about a Russian ballet company being persuaded to present a modern ballet. The musical score was by Rodgers and Hart, and the co-author of the book was George Abbott (1887–1995). In addition to writing a number of the musicals of this period, Abbott was the best-known director of musicals, and he was recognized for the energy, ebullience, and fast pace of his productions. The innovative aspect of *On Your Toes* was its introduction of a serious dance into musical comedy—in this case, a ballet called "Slaughter on Tenth Avenue."

THE AUDIENCE'S RESPONSE

- Musical theatre can be of several types: classic Broadway musicals, such as *My Fair Lady*; musicals that address serious issues, such as *Next to Normal*; musicals based on films, such as *Hairspray*; musicals resembling operettas, such as *Phantom of the Opera*; and musicals emphasizing dance, such as *A Chorus Line*. Which of these do you enjoy the most?

- Musicals contain many different elements, including story, songs, dance, and spectacular visual effects. Is one of these more important, or should one be more prominent, than the others?

- What is your favorite stage musical? Which element or elements make it stand out in your mind?

In another Rodgers and Hart musical, *Pal Joey* (1940), the hero is a heel: a nightclub singer who takes advantage of women to get ahead. The presentation of an antihero as a leading character was a further step in the development of American musical theatre, which emerged full-blown in the 1940s and 1950s.

Musical Theatre of the 1940s and 1950s

In 1943 a musical opened that was to herald the golden era of American book musicals. This was *Oklahoma!*—which brought together for the first time the team of Richard Rodgers and Oscar Hammerstein II. Both had been involved in musical theatre since the 1920s, but they had never collaborated before.

Oklahoma! is sometimes hailed as more revolutionary than it really was. Many of the innovations it is credited with had actually appeared in earlier musicals. Set against the background of the founding of the state of Oklahoma, it tells the love story of Curly and Laurey, who are thwarted by a character named Jud. During the course of the action, Curly kills Jud onstage. This was considered extremely daring, but several years earlier, Porgy had killed Crown onstage in *Porgy and Bess. Oklahoma!* was also praised for integrating the songs with the story, but this too had happened previously.

Even so, *Oklahoma!* in many respects offers a prime example of how complete and effective a musical can be. An important achievement was its inclusion, for the first time, of ballet as a crucial element throughout the piece. Agnes de Mille (1905–1995), a choreographer with classical training, created several dances that carried the story forward and became a part of the fabric of the musical. What's more, the entire piece—story, music, lyrics, dances—fitted together in tone, mood, and intention to present a seamless whole. From *Oklahoma!* on, American musicals could tackle any subject, serious as well as frivolous, and present it as an integrated art form with acting, dancing, and singing masterfully intertwined. For Rodgers and Hammerstein, *Oklahoma!* was the first in a long line of successful musicals that included *Carousel* (1945), *South Pacific* (1949), *The King and I* (1951), and *The Sound of Music* (1959).

Choreography, which became such an integral part of musical theatre in the decades to follow, encompassed a number of dance forms, from the classical lifts and

THE GOLDEN AGE OF AMERICAN MUSICALS
Emblematic of the exciting era of American musicals in the twenty years from the mid-1940s to the mid-1960s were the productions created by Richard Rodgers and Oscar Hammerstein II. The example shown here is a recent revival of *South Pacific.* The outpouring of musicals, with works by Irving Berlin, Cole Porter, Lerner and Loewe, Frank Loesser, Leonard Bernstein, and numerous others, was unprecedented. Shown here are Paulo Szot and Kelli O'Hare in the Lincoln Center production directed by Bartlett Sher. (© Joan Marcus)

turns of Agnes de Mille's work to the energetic athleticism favored by Jerome Robbins (1918–1999) to the sharp, angular, eccentric moves created by Bob Fosse (1927–1987). In order to execute the many kinds of steps required, dancers became highly trained and enormously versatile, and they were able to perform everything from classical pirouettes to muscular leaps and rapid-fire tap dancing.

The outpouring of first-rate musicals in the 1940s and 1950s remains unparalleled today. Several writers who had been involved in musicals in previous decades did their best work during this period. These include Irving Berlin, with *Annie Get Your Gun* (1946), a musical version of the life of Annie Oakley; and Cole Porter, with *Kiss Me, Kate* (1948), the story of a theatre company putting on a version of Shakespeare's *Taming of the Shrew.*

In addition, a number of new composers, lyricists, and writers appeared on the scene and produced memorable musicals: Frank Loesser (1910–1969), who wrote the words and music for *Guys and Dolls* (1950); Alan Jay Lerner (1918–1986) and Frederick Loewe (1904–1988), who wrote *My Fair Lady* (1956), a musical version of George

Bernard Shaw's *Pygmalion;* and the composer Leonard Bernstein (1918–1990) and the lyricist Stephen Sondheim (b. 1930), who created *West Side Story* (1957), a modern version of *Romeo and Juliet.*

The 1940s and 1950s were remarkable not only for the number of outstanding musicals produced but for the range and depth of those musicals. They covered a wide variety of subjects, and the quality was impressive not only in the better-known shows but in many shows in the second rank as well. Along with composers and writers, performers, directors, designers, and choreographers were all working at the top of their form.

Musicals from the 1960s through the 1980s

Fiddler on the Roof, which opened in 1964, is believed by many to mark the end of the golden era of book musicals. *Fiddler on the Roof,* with music by Jerry Bock (b. 1928), lyrics by Sheldon Harnick (b. 1924), and book by Joseph Stein (b. 1912), tells of a Jewish family whose father tries to uphold the traditions of the past in a small village in Russia, where the Jewish community faces persecution and a pogrom. It was directed and choreographed by Jerome Robbins, who gave it an overall style and point of view that represented the best of the American musical.

One indication of changes in the musical was the opening in 1967 of *Hair,* a celebration of the informal, antiestablishment lifestyle of young people in the 1960s. *Hair,* with music by Galt MacDermot (b. 1928) and lyrics by Gerome Ragni (1942–1991) and Joseph Rado (b. 1932), had no real story line and represented a radical departure from the book musicals that had dominated the scene for the past 25 years.

After *Hair,* musical theatre became increasingly fragmented. In the 1970s and 1980s, fewer and fewer book musicals were written, though some successful ones continued to appear. In place of book musicals there were other approaches, one being the *concept musical,* in which a production is built around an idea or a theme rather than a story. A pioneer in developing the concept musical was the composer-lyricist Stephen Sondheim (b. 1930). A frequent collaborator with Sondheim was the director Harold Prince (b. 1928). Two examples of Sondheim's concept musicals are *Follies* (1971) and *Assassins* (1990). The first paid tribute of the stars and music of a bygone era, but also underscored a theme of the negative effects of the passing years in terms of nostalgia and self-delusion. *Assassins* was an examination in songs and scenes of the motives and delusions of people who murdered American presidents. In addition to his concept musicals, Sondheim has also written more traditional musicals, such as *A Little Night Music* (1973) and *Sweeney Todd, the Demon Barber of Fleet Street* (1979).

Occasionally a musical came up with a variation on old formulas and appeared to break fresh ground. Such a musical was *A Chorus Line,* which presents a group of aspiring dancers auditioning for a Broadway show. *A Chorus Line,* which was directed by Michael Bennett (1943–1987), opened in 1975 and ran until 1990. It was successfully revived on Broadway in 2006.

A Chorus Line symbolized the ascendancy of dancers and choreographers in the musical. Beginning with Jerome Robbins, the "vision" of musicals was furnished more and more by choreographers who had become directors. In addition to Robbins and Bennett, these included Bob Fosse, who directed *Sweet Charity* (1966) and *Pippin*

MUSICALS: 1940s THROUGH THE 1960s
From the 1940s through the mid-1960s, there was an outpouring of memorable American musicals. In the period after that, the composer Stephen Sondheim was one of those who dominated the scene. Seen here is the original production of Sondheim's *Sunday in the Park with George,* about the painter Seurat. (© Martha Swope)

(1972); and Tommy Tune (b. 1939), who was a performer and choreographer and has won nine Tony Awards. Among the well-known musicals for which Tune provided choreography were *My One and Only* (1983), *Grand Hotel* (1990), and *Will Rogers' Follies* (1991). For the last two he was also the director. A more recent example of an outstanding director-choreographer is Susan Stroman (b. 1954), who was responsible for such musicals as *The Producers* (2001) and *Contact* (2003). Stroman continues to be active not only with new musicals but with revivals, as well as opera and television.

In recent years, choreographer-directors have often not worked with a solid book or with inspired scores, and as a result, they have emphasized the outward aspects of their productions, stressing the look and style. The result in many cases has been a substitution of style for substance.

Still another trend of the 1970s and 1980s was the emergence of British composers and lyricists in the creation of musicals. The composer Andrew Lloyd Webber (b. 1948) and the lyricist Tim Rice (b. 1944) wrote *Jesus Christ Superstar* (1971) and *Evita* (1979), the story of Eva Perón of Argentina. Webber also wrote the music for *Cats* (1982), *The Phantom of the Opera* (1987), and *Sunset Boulevard* (1993). Two other large-scale British musicals of the period were *Les Misérables* (1986) and *Miss Saigon* (1989). In 2008 *Billy Elliot* arrived from Britain.

GLOBAL CROSSCURRENTS

THE THEATRE OF JULIE TAYMOR

The American director and designer Julie Taymor (b. 1952) is known predominately for her vibrant productions, which draw on theatrical traditions from across the globe. Her use of puppetry (adopted predominantly from Indonesia) and her costume designs mark her as a designer who uses eastern traditions.

Taymor has traveled to Sri Lanka, Indonesia, Japan, and India, and her travels have allowed her to encounter the very different theatrical forms of those countries. Her experiences of Japanese nō, bunraku, and avant-garde theatre, and Indonesian rod puppets (*wayag golek*) and shadow puppets (*wayang kulit*), were particularly influential in her later productions. In her early experiments with blending theatrical forms, she founded the theatrical company Teatr Loh, which included performers from Java, Bali, Sudan, and the west. This blending of eastern theatrical traditions has been continued through her many productions in the east and west.

Among Taymor's productions are an adaptation of a German novella set in India called *The Transposed Heads* (1984); a production of *Juan Darien* (1988, 1990), which drew on the puppet traditions of Indonesia and Japan and the music of Australia, South America, and Africa; and an opera adaptation of *Oedipus Rex* (1992), which drew on Greek sculpture and Japanese nō costumes. However, she is best known for her productions of *The King Stag* and *The Lion King*.

The King Stag was written in eighteenth-century Italy by Carlo Gozzi and tells of King Derramo and his evil prime minister, Tartaglia. In order to ensure that his daughter will marry the king, Tartaglia tricks the king into transferring his soul into the body of a stag, with the prime minister then taking control of the king's body. By her own count, Taymor identifies nine different countries whose theatrical traditions she drew from in creating *The King Stag*. She used masks from eighteenth-century Italian commedia dell'arte troupes, white ruffs from Elizabethan England, Japanese prints and colors, Taiwanese paper bird kites, Indonesian puppetry, Japanese bunraku, and ancient Chinese mirror stone techniques (through her use of Plexiglas puppets). The end result was an imaginative, colorful production that could not be defined by any one theatrical tradition. Similarly, her Broadway production of *The Lion King* used elements of numerous theatrical cultures from across Asia, especially from Indonesia and Japan; also prominent was music from South Africa. Many of the scenes combine actors, masks, and puppets, illustrating once again her distinctive fusion of numerous theatrical forms. Owing to the wide range of sources, her productions are not re-creations of any one theatrical source, but rather compositions drawn from theatrical traditions across the globe.

Prepared by Naomi Stubbs, CUNY Graduate Center.

Julie Taymor (AP Images)

BRITISH MUSICALS

Musicals created in Great Britain took center stage on both sides of the Atlantic in the era beginning in the early 1970s and continuing through the next two decades. The best-known composer of these was Andrew Lloyd Webber, who wrote the music for *Cats* and for *Phantom of the Opera*. Both were presented by the British producer Cameron Macintosh. The era of the British musicals also included such productions as *Les Misérables* and *Miss Saigon*. The scene here shows Michael Crawford and Sarah Brightman in *Phantom of the Opera*, directed by Harold Prince and designed by Maria Bjornson. (© Clive Barda/ArenaPAL)

Musicals from 1990 to the Present

In musical theatre from 1990 to the present, four trends are discernible. One is the unprecedented number of major revivals of past musical successes. This time frame saw revivals of such shows as *Annie Get Your Gun; Chicago; Wonderful Town; Carousel; Oklahoma!; Kiss Me, Kate; Fiddler on the Roof; La Cage aux Folles; Sweet Charity;* and many more. One reason for the increase in revivals was the increasing cost of producing musicals on Broadway and for road tours. Advertising, rental, wages, and other costs rose year after year, and producers decided that presenting a revival of a tried and true musical classic was safer economically. At the same time, this was a clear indication that there is not the same output of new work today as in earlier years. On the positive side, the trend confirmed that these shows form part of an important heritage and that they have lasting value.

photo essay

The Diverse American Musical

(© Geraint Lewis)

The modern American musical has covered a wide range of subjects, some lighthearted but others quite serious. Also, American musicals have embraced different styles—some reminiscent of operetta, some comic, some avant-garde. Shown here are examples of the diversity of musicals through the years.

A Funny Thing Happened on the Way to the Forum, by Stephen Sondheim, is based on Roman farce and so it is a musical with a classic source in the tradition of pure entertainment.

A serious musical, *Fiddler on the Roof* by Jerry Bock and Sheldon Harnick, is based on the Jewish experience in czarist Russia in 1905, when Jewish tradition and even survival are put to a severe test. Here, Alfred Molina plays the lead role of Tevye.

(© Carol Rosegg)

A landmark musical was *West Side Story,* based on Shakespeare's *Romeo and Juliet,* with direction and choreography by Jerome Robbins, music by Leonard Bernstein, and lyrics and music by Stephen Sondheim and Arthur Laurents. Shown here in a revival marking the show's fiftieth anniversary is Karen Olivo, center, in the role of Anita.

(Sara Krulwich/The New York Times/Redux)

A theatre piece in the long-standing tradition of American musical comedy, intended primarily for entertainment, is *Guys and Dolls,* with words and music by Frank Loesser. The story of a gambler who bets he can woo a Salvation Army worker, features memorable melodies that run the gamut from ballads to comic numbers. An example of the latter is a song called "Sit Down, You're Rocking the Boat," shown in this scene from a production at the Paper Mill Playhouse in New Jersey.

(© Gerry Goodstein)

MUSICALS IN THE NEW CENTURY
In the early twenty-first century, the American musical scene was a cross section of different types of musicals: old and new, traditional and experimental, serious and comic. An example of the contemporary serious musical is *Next to Normal,* about a woman suffering from bipolar disorder, and the effect that this condition has on her as well as the members of her family. Shown here are Aaron Tveit, Alice Ripley, and J. Robert Spencer as the son, mother, and father. Directed by Michael Greif, with lyrics by Brian Yorkey and score by Tom Kitt. (Sarah Krulwich/The New York Times/Redux)

A second trend—a refreshing counterpoint to the rush of revivals—was the periodic appearance of fresh, offbeat musicals, indicating that the genre remains full of vitality. For example, *Rent* (1996), about a group of nonestablishment young people, won numerous awards, including the Pulitzer Prize and the Tony Award for best musical of the year. Another example is *Avenue Q,* a lively, iconoclastic musical featuring puppets operated by onstage characters. Two other examples are *In the Heights* and *Next to Normal.* Winner of the 2008 Tony Award, *In the Heights* covers three days in the lives of characters in the Dominican-American section of Washington Heights in Manhattan, and features hip-hop, meringue, salsa, and soul music. *Next to Normal,* which was awarded the 2009 Tony Award, concerns a mother who is struggling with bipolar disorder and the effects her disease has on her family. As her condition worsens, other concerns surface—suicide, drug abuse, psychiatric ethics—none of which are typical subjects for a musical.

A third trend was musicals based on films. This list would include *The Producers, Monty Python's Spamalot, Hairspray, Young Frankenstein,* and musicals presented by the Disney organization, such as *The Lion King* and *Mary Poppins.*

The fourth trend is the creation of productions out of the music of former popular stars and groups, sometimes referred to as "jukebox" musicals. The most successful of these has been *Mamma Mia!*—a story taking place in the Greek islands and based on the music of the group ABBA. The music of Billy Joel formed the basis of Twyla Tharp's dance musical *Moving Out.* In the years that followed, show after show was created by stringing together hits from one music group or another, a good example being *Jersey Boys* (2005).

It is clear that the musical theatre scene at the present time is a patchwork quilt, featuring old and new, revues and book musicals, imports and original material. All in all, the musical remains a mainstay of Broadway, and of those large theatres across the United States that feature shows with music, spectacular scenery, and well-known performers. In Chapters 14 and 15 we turn to an examination of global and American theatre today.

SUMMARY

1. At many points in theatre history, music and dance have been combined with drama. An important art form, related to theatre, is opera, which is a drama set entirely to music.

2. In addition to opera, types of musical theatre include *operetta,* scenes of spoken dialogue alternating with songs; *musical comedy,* a light, comic story interspersed with popular music; the *musical,* also known as *musical theatre,* which evolved from musical comedy; and the *revue,* a series of individual, independent songs and comic sketches.

3. The modern musical is largely an American creation—the only theatrical form developed primarily in the United States.

4. There were many forerunners of the modern musical in the nineteenth century and early twentieth century, including operetta, vaudeville, burlesque, and the minstrel show.

5. During the 1920s and 1930s, musical comedy emerged: comic, sometimes silly stories that had glorious music with intelligent, witty lyrics, written by people like Irving Berlin, Jerome Kern, Cole Porter, Richard Rodgers, and Lorenz Hart.

6. The period from the early 1940s to the late 1960s was the golden age of the American musical, with a profusion of successful shows, many of them modern classics. These musicals integrated dancing and singing to form an overall structure that had great variety as well as unity.

7. In the past three decades, musical theatre has become fragmented: fewer book musicals are being produced; choreographer-directors rather than writers or directors have been responsible for the total vision of the show; experiments are being made with other forms, such as the concept musical; and more musicals are being imported from Great Britain.

8. Current trends in musical theatre include (a) revivals, (b) offbeat or experimental musicals, (c) musicals made from films, and (d) musicals made from the songs of a popular composer or group.

Global Theatre Today

In approaching global theatre, three points should be kept in mind. The first is that in many cultures, theatre has a long, illustrious history. Unlike American theatre, which has a relatively short history, world theatre goes back more than 2,000 years in both Europe and Asia. In Europe, preceding contemporary theatre, the theatre tradition of the past begins with Greek theatre and moves through Roman, medieval, Renaissance, eighteenth-century, and nineteenth-century theatre into modern theatre. In Asia, theatre in India began earlier than 2,000 years ago and Chinese theatre a few centuries after that; Japanese theater was established by 800 CE.

In other parts of the world—for instance, in Africa, in pre-Columbian Latin America, and in the Native American culture of North America—there are rich traditions of rituals and ceremonies imbued with theatrical elements: costumes, song and dance, and impersonation of people, animals, and divinities.

When we look at European, Asian, and other theatres, therefore, we are looking at a tradition preceding the theater that exists in those parts of the world today. At various points in *The Theatre Experience*, we have referred to some of these theatres and to their playwrights, stage spaces, production practices, and acting companies. In this chapter, we will concentrate on contemporary theatre throughout the world outside the United States, not just in Europe and Asia, but in Africa and other parts of the Americas as well.

A second point to be borne in mind is that beginning around 1900, Asian and other non-European theatres were influenced by developments of modern theatre in the west: the realism introduced by Ibsen, Strindberg, and Chekhov; and a number of

◄ **JAPANESE SHAKESPEARE**

A Japanese director well known for presenting western classics in a distinctly Japanese style is Yukio Ninagawa. He has directed Shakespeare, the classic Greek playwrights, and Tennessee Williams. In every case he creates his own vision, a Japanese vision, of the play in question. Shown here is his adaptation of Shakespeare's Twelfth Night *presented in kabuki style in London. The actors are Nakamura Tokizo V as Olivia (*onnagata*) and Onoe Kikugoro VII as Malvolio. Onnagata are male actors who play women's roles in kabuki. (© Geraint Lewis)*

INTERNATIONAL FESTIVALS: THEATRE FROM CHILE

A representative piece from the Chilean troupe Compañia Teatro Cinema blends theatrical and cinematic techniques. The play shown here, *Gemelos,* featured Diego Fontecilla, Juan Carlos Zagal, and Laura Pizarro. It was presented at the Lincoln Center Festival in New York City, only one of a number of international festivals that have become more and more an integral part of today's theatre scene. (Kitra Cahana/The New York Times/Redux)

departures from realism, such as expressionism. Thus in a country like Japan you had the traditional theatre of nō and Kabuki alongside modern theatre.

The third point, and in many ways, the most significant point for modern audiences, is the development of global exchanges—in communication, in ideas, in commerce, and in the arts. Thomas Friedman, in his book *The World Is Flat,* analyzes how globalization has affected business and industry in contemporary society. One can no longer tell whether a product is made by a company of a specific country, since most major corporations are multinational. The automobile industry clearly reflects the trend toward industrial globalization, as does the personal computer industry. A car created today by a Japanese, Korean, or German manufacturer may be assembled in the United States. A PC may be assembled in the United States, but the 24-hour help desk may be located in India.

The same is true in today's theatre. Many diverse groups influence one another to create the contemporary theatrical landscape. Theatre artists cross national boundaries to stage their works with artists of other countries. Popular works tour the world and cross-pollinate other theatrical ventures. International theatre festivals bring artists of various nationalities to interact with those in the host community.

The global nature of today's theatre can be seen in the offerings each summer at the International Theatre Festival at Lincoln Center in New York City. Productions from all parts of the world are presented side by side. In recent years the countries represented have included Japan, Indonesia, China, Singapore, Switzerland,

Germany, Ireland, Argentina, Chile, Spain, Mexico, Italy, and France. Experimental artists appropriate the styles and techniques of traditional theatres from around the world. Artists mix and match all sorts of styles, historical antecedents, materials, and techniques.

What this suggests is that we can no longer easily classify theatre productions and artists by specific national designations. Ease of travel, electronic communication, and the commerce of theatre have all led to a blurring of national theatres. Like the global economy, theatre today is a global activity. In order to bring some structure to our discussion, we will organize this chapter along traditional national boundaries. However, we will frequently point to the global interplay and impact of the various theatre artists and companies.

THEATRES IN INDIA, CHINA, AND JAPAN IN THE MODERN PERIOD

The Asian continent is immense and includes roughly 40 countries and hundreds of ethnicities, languages, and theatre traditions. In the limited space of this book, it would be impossible to do justice to such diversity and multiplicity. Therefore, we will confine our discussion to three Asian countries: India, China, and Japan. In all three countries, traditional theatre continues today: kathakali in India, Beijing (Peking) opera in China, and nō and kabuki in Japan. But the influences of western theatre are undeniable. As in Latin America, Asian countries were influenced in the early twentieth century by western dramatic forms, particularly the modernist traditions of realism and departures from realism. The colonial influence also led to a weakening of the traditional forms of theatrical practice, both popular and classical.

Following World War I, there was a politicization of Asian theatres. Some theatre artists opposed western influences and the colonial mentality. As a result, in the past five decades, there has been a unique return of traditional forms blended into the sociopolitical sensibilities of Asian theatre artists. This return to traditional forms, in itself, is a rejection of colonial and postcolonial western intrusions into the continent.

In India several changes occurred a few decades into the twentieth century. For one thing, World War I was disruptive. Perhaps more pervasive, though, was the advent of cinema. In India, film became extremely popular, from the standpoint of both producers and consumers. Films began to be produced in great numbers, and audiences flocked to them. These productions feature theatrical staging, lighting, costumes, and choreography and are often referred to as "Bollywood" films. The term combines Hollywood, the center of American cinema, with the Indian city Bombay (now Mumbai). At mid-century, this trend, and the effects of World War II, led to a decrease in professional theatre in many parts of India.

The theatre that emerged in the latter half of the twentieth century was primarily an amateur theatre. It is estimated that Calcutta has as many as 3,000 registered amateur theatre groups, Mumbai perhaps has as many as 500, and Madras at least 50. Many of these theatres do not have a permanent home, but some do. Also, some of them present professional-quality theatre. Moreover, these theatres keep alive plays written by Indian playwrights, past and present, as well as plays from other nations. There was also a strain of experimental theatre in India, led by such figures as Badal Sircar (b. 1925), whose plays reflect the experience of urban life in India.

In China after the civil war and Mao Zedong's rise to power following World War II in 1949, spoken drama continued to be written, but additional emphasis was given to traditional forms of popular theatre. These traditional forms were familiar in the countryside and became a medium for carrying messages from the government to remote corners of the nation. During the cultural revolution, which began in 1966, theatrical activity—particularly spoken drama—was more restricted; increasing emphasis was placed on a few dance-dramas, elaborately staged and performed, that had very heavy ideological or propagandistic content. For the most part, theatre artists, along with intellectuals, were seen as subversive and suffered greatly during this era in Chinese history.

Since the death of Mao, and the opening up of China to the west in the late 1970s, there has been cross-fertilization between Chinese traditions and western drama. Theatre artists from the United States and Europe have visited and performed in China. Arthur Miller, for example, directed a production of *Death of a Salesman* in Beijing in 1983. These western influences can be seen in plays like *The Peach Blossom Fan,* by Ouyang Yuqian (1889–1962), which tells the story of the romance between a high-class courtesan and an army general in the late Ming dynasty; and *Jesus, Confucius, and John Lennon* by Sha Yexin (b. 1939), a play about the absurdities Christ, Confucius, and Lennon encounter during their travels on the moon and around the world as representatives of God.

In addition to new drama, traditional forms, such as Beijing (Peking) opera and other forms of classic music-drama, which were repressed during Mao's rule, are becoming popular again. While much of the drama still remains socialist in point of view and realistic in style, there have been a number of artists who push the boundaries of subject matter and style, fusing classical traditions with contemporary forms and issues. Ping Chong's puppet theatre production with the Shaanxi Folk Art Theatre of Xian, China, *Cathay: Three Tales of China* (2005), is just one example of the merging of avant-garde and traditional forms in contemporary China.

Since the end of World War II, contemporary theatre in Japan has thrived. A number of truly gifted playwrights have emerged, chief among them Kinoshita Junji (1914–2006), whose work combines social concerns with humor and, when appropriate, with elements from Japanese folk tradition. In his play *Twilight Crane,* for example, he weaves a story of greed and loss using the central image of a crane, which in Japanese culture is a symbol of long life.

In the second half of the twentieth century there were three main branches of theatre in Japan. One was traditional theatre—nō, bunraku, and kabuki, of which the most active was kabuki. Despite western influences, these three ancient theatre traditions in Japan have remained vital and active today.

A second branch consisted of various manifestations of *shingeki,* a word that means "new theatre." *Shingeki* began in the late nineteenth century and in one form or another continued throughout the twentieth century. Broadly speaking, it was a modern theatre, in contrast to the traditional classic theatres. For one thing, it was more realistic than the traditional theatres. In addition, at the beginning it was influenced by such western playwrights as Ibsen and Chekhov. In the early twentieth century, shingeki banished the gods and the fantastic from theatre, partly because they had played such a large role in classic theatre. Later, after World War II, nonrealistic elements were admitted to shingeki dramas. Despite its changes and western influences,

A CHINESE AMERICAN PRODUCTION
A prime example of international cooperation in theatre was *Cathay: Three Tales of China,* a production created jointly by the American avant-garde director Ping Chong and the Shaanxi Folk Art Theatre of Xian, China. An innovative, experimental theatre director and producer, Ping Chong has developed more than fifty productions with his company in the past three decades. *Cathay,* which featured puppet figures, was a satisfying collaboration, taking the best from two theatrical cultures. (© Richard Termine)

shingeki remains a theatre in which the playwright is a central figure. In recent years it has included female playwrights, who were almost nonexistent in earlier times.

The third strain of modern Japanese theatre has been avant-garde or experimental theatre. A good example of this movement is the work of Tadashi Suzuki, who began his work at Waseda University in Tokyo and then developed a theatre community in the mountains at Toga. (A profile of Suzuki appears in "Global Crosscurrents" in this chapter.) Other theatre figures created their own brand of avant-garde work, some of it paralleling that being done in the west, but some distinctly Japanese. One example is the performance artist Issei Ogata (b. 1952), whose one-man shows underscore the humor in everyday situations: for example, an inebriated businessman attempting to catch a taxi, or a father overwhelmed by the responsibility of looking after his children.

From Zeami's performances at the Kitano temple in Japan (discussed in Chapter 1) to the elaborate Bollywood producions in India, Asian theatre continues to evolve to reflect political and social changes. Theatre in these countries has triumphed and continues to acknowledge and celebrate the traditions that established roots for the work of contemporary artists like Tadashi Suzuki and Issei Ogata, whose productions reveal and document life in Asia today.

GLOBAL CROSSCURRENTS

TADASHI SUZUKI: JAPANESE INTERNATIONALIST

Among important international theatre artists, a key figure is Tadashi Suzuki (b. 1939), a director, writer, and teacher who calls Japan his home but has worked with and influenced artists around the world. Suzuki first attracted attention as a part of Japan's *Shōgekijō undō,* or "little theatre movement," in the 1960s and 1970s. *Shōgekijō* was a resonse to what was seen as the restrictive realism and limited viewpoint of *shingeki,* the Japanese retelling of western theatre. Like proponents of "little theatre" and avant-garde movements in the west, *shōgekijō* artists largely rejected the mainstream, preferring smaller, more adventurous audiences who were willing to engage with provocative, experimental material. The directors Shūji Terayama (1935–1983), Shogo Ohta (1939–2007), and Yukio Ninagawa (b. 1935) were also part of this movement. Today, Tadashi Suzuki is among the world's most famous theatre directors. His Suzuki Company of Toga, in the mountains of Japan, is well-known for combining stories and traditions from various cultures; this includes creating theatre pieces that remain distinctively Japanese while also entering into conversation with theatres across the globe. His work also frequently comments on international political situations. In addition to his own company in Japan, Suzuki cofounded the SITI company in 1992, with the prominent American director Anne Bogart (b. 1951).

Two examples of Suzuki's international work are his productions of Euripides's *The Bacchae.* In 1981, Suzuki worked with students at the University of Wisconsin to develop a dual-language version of the play, which he had been working on in Japan for a number of years. In this production, the American actors spoke English and the Japanese actors spoke Japanese, the characters responding as if they understood each other. The production also emphasized the cyclical nature of violence and power, suggesting that one tyrant dies only to be replaced by another.

Beginning in 1991, Suzuki introduced *Dionysus,* a new adaptation of the play which focused on the clash between religion and government. This production was widely interpreted as a comment on the escalating violence in the Middle East in general and on the wars between the United States and Iraq more specifically.

Suzuki's actors are praised for their onstage presence and incredible athleticism. His actor-training system, the Suzuki method, combines elements of traditional Japanese theatre techniques with the experimental work that emerged from international theatre in the 1960s and 1970s. Actors spend a great deal of time focusing on their feet and the ground beneath them, building strength, flexibility, and balance through a physical connection to the earth. Many observers feel that Suzuki's most lasting impact on world theatre will be his work on actor training.

Prepared by Frank Episale, CUNY Graduate Theatre Program.

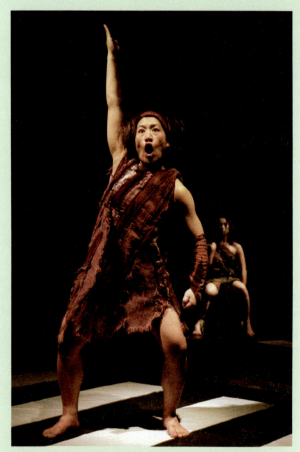

Tadashi Suzuki's *Electra,* after the Greek playwright Euripides, with Yukiko Saito in the title role. (© Jack Vartoogian/www.frontrowphotos)

THEATRES IN THE MIDDLE EAST

Although the Islamic religion has strong prohibitions against theatre, there have always been traditions of storytelling, folklore, and popular comedy throughout the middle east, before Islamic times and since. In Turkey and Egypt, for example, religious stories were often brought to life with the use of shadow puppets. Professional storytellers would also bring to audiences tales of religious or historic events, often accompanied by musical instruments. It wasn't until the nineteenth century, however, that stage theatre was embraced as a popular means for conveying life in the middle east. Today theatre in the Arab world is greatly affected by the politics of the region.

As in Asia and Latin America, the close of the nineteenth century and the beginning of the twentieth century saw a rise in western colonial influence on the theatres of the Arab middle east. The adaptation of historic events into plays became very popular. Three early playwrights are widely credited with the introduction of western dramatic techniques into the Arab world: the Lebanese author Marun al-Naqqash (1817–1855), who combined drama with opera in his work, such as his interpretation of Molière's *L'Avare*; Abu Khalil al-Qabbani (1851–), a Syrian who came to Egypt after his theatre was closed in Damascus; and Ya'qub Sannu (1839–1912), a Jewish-Egyptian dramatist. Western influence was particularly prevalent in the years following World War I.

After World War II and through the 1970s, there was significant development of professional theatrical activity throughout the middle eastern region, including Egypt, Iran, Syria, Lebanon, and Iraq. The theatres of these countries continued to be influenced by western practices and artists, but there also developed a good deal of theatrical cross-fertilization. Iran, for example, hosted the Shiraz Arts Festival through the 1970s until the Islamic revolution in 1979. The festival featured works by such notable western artists as Peter Brook, Jerzy Grotowski, and Robert Wilson, and many of these works clearly reflected the influence of middle eastern theatre and literature. However, the works of many Arab theatre artists were highly nationalistic during this era and returned to traditional folk materials; examples are the works of the Iraqi playwright-director Qassim Mohammed (b. 1935).

With the rise of Islamic fundamentalism and totalitarianism in many of these countries, theatrical activities have been halted, significantly curtailed, or rigidly controlled by the state. For example, the theatrical infrastructure in Iraq was severely damaged by Iraq's war with Iran in the 1980s and by economic hardships after the Persian Gulf war in the early 1990s, and then again with the invasion and occupation of Iraq by the United States and Britain beginning in 2003. In Saudi Arabia, the state-sponsored Saudi Society for Culture and Arts, established in 1972, oversees much theatrical activity; however, there is great controversy over the support of theatrical art.

There are currently a number of significant theatre artists who deal with the contemporary political turmoil of the middle east, including the ongoing battles with Israel, particularly in Egypt and in the Palestinian territories. In Jordan, the ministry of culture has sponsored annual theatre festivals, and there have also been independent festivals that bring together theatre artists from many parts of the Arab world.

There has been Palestinian theatre since the 1850s, but historians have focused most on theatrical activities since the Israeli occupation in 1967. Many companies

THEATRE IN THE MIDDLE EAST

When the current turmoil in the middle east became increasingly intense, Al-Kasaba Theatre in Ramallah had difficulty mounting its regular schedule. One way to keep its theatre alive was to present plays like *Alive from Palestine: Stories under Occupation,* a series of monologues developed by actors and writers responding to the situation in Ramallah. Shown here is a scene from the play, featuring Hussam Abu Eisheh, Mahmoud Awad, and Georgina Asfour. (© Geraint Lewis)

and playwrights have created theatrical works that express the Palestinian point of view toward Israel's control of the West Bank and, until recently, Gaza. A Palestinian company that is gaining international recognition from its visits to the Royal Court Theatre in London is Al-Kasaba Theatre, originally founded in Jerusalem in 1970 but now located in Ramallah in the occupied West Bank. In 2001, Al-Kasaba staged *Alive from Palestine: Stories behind the Headlines,* which consists of a series of monologues dealing with the intifada, the Palestinian uprising against Israel. The company's artistic director is George Ibrahim.

Two other productions that reflect the Palestinians' existence under Israeli occupation are *The Alley* (1992), a one-woman production written and performed by Samia Qazmouz al-Bakri, which focuses on the lives of Palestinian women since 1948; and *We Are the Children of the Camp* (2000) by al-Rowwad Theatre for Children in the Aida refugee camp near Bethlehem. This production, performed primarily by children, toured the United States in 2005.

Israeli theatre has also developed since the founding of the state of Israel in 1948. Israeli drama has been influenced by the eastern European origins of many of its founders as well as the middle eastern traditions of those Jews who left Arab nations to settle in the Jewish state.

One national theatre of Israel is the Habimah, which was established in Russia in the early twentieth century and settled in what was then British-controlled Palestine in 1931. The other large national theatre in Israel is the Tel Aviv Municipal Theatre, referred to as the Cameri, founded in 1944 by the director Yossef Milo (b. 1916). There are many other active Israeli theatres throughout the country—in Tel Aviv, Jerusalem, Haifa, and elsewhere. As in Europe and the United States, there are also smaller fringe theatrical groups, which experiment with avant-garde techniques, and performance artists. Most of the theatres in Israel receive some governmental subsidy. Israeli drama also reflects the tumultuous history of the nation. Early drama dealt with the establishment of the state and nationalism. More recent dramatic works explore the complexities of middle eastern politics, including Israel's relationship with the Palestinians.

In the 1950s, Israel's best-known playwrights were Aharon Megged (b. 1920) and the poet Leah Goldberg (1915–1970). Nissim Aloni (1926–1998), in the 1950s and 1960s, was Israel's first author to focus exclusively on theatre. In the 1970s and 1980s, Hanoch Levin (1943–1999) was the prominent playwright and director. The most internationally recognized Israeli dramatist is Joshua Sobol (b. 1939), whose play *Ghetto* (1984) was produced throughout the world. In the 1980s, Sobol served as an artistic director with the Municipal Theatre in Haifa, frequently combining Israeli and Palestinian actors in controversial productions.

AFRICAN THEATRES AND DRAMA

Early African societies had many traditional performances that were connected to ceremonies and rituals and used music, song, and dance. Colorful, exotic, symbolic costumes were also a key element of many rituals and ceremonies. African theatre artists in the twentieth century used these traditional forms and subverted forms of popular western theatre in order to create work that reflects anticolonial struggles as well as attacks against totalitarian regimes in the newly independent African nations.

Contemporary African theatre and society are divided into English-speaking Africa; French-speaking Africa; Portuguese-speaking Africa; and Arabic-speaking Africa, which includes the northern African countries Egypt, Tunisia, Algeria, and Morocco. In the nations that were originally defined by nineteenth-century colonial powers, there are also attempts to experiment with the indigenous languages of the peoples of this region of Africa.

In Portuguese-speaking Africa, which includes Angola, Cape Verde, Guinea-Bissau, Mozambique, and São Tomé and Principe, missionaries introduced religious drama in order to spread Catholicism. Before independence in 1975, much of the theatre of this part of Africa was like vaudeville, although some anticolonial dramas were written. After independence, there was a greater focus on theatre that would arouse social consciousness, and plays followed the model of agitprop dramas; theatrical companies created collaborative works that focused on political and social issues. In Angola, for example, the National School of Theatre was founded in 1976 and staged works that focused on African liberation.

Among the best-known works from Portuguese-speaking Africa are *The Devil's Skin* (Angola, 1977) by Manuel Santos Lima; *Bombo's Chalk Circle* (Angola, 1979) by Henrique Guerra; *The Old Man Is Untouchable* (Angola, 1980) by Costa Andrade; *Shameless* (Cape Verde, 1979) by Donald Pereira de Macedo; and the plays by the Mozambican author Orlando Mendes.

French-speaking (francophone) Africa includes areas south of the Sahara as well as some nations in northern Africa. There is a vital theatre in the sub-Saharan nations, influenced by traditional forms of storytelling and music as well as by French theatre traditions. Many of the plays written in this part of French-speaking Africa have been produced in festivals organized in Paris. In addition, some of these African plays were also read and performed in New York during the 1990s by the off-off-Broadway Ubu Repertory Theatre. The plays of this region usually focus on historical chronicles, social concerns, and political circumstances. Among the most significant playwrights of this region are Senegal's Cheik Ndao (b. 1933), the Ivory Coast's Bernard Dadié (b. 1916), the Congo's Sony Labou Tansi (b. 1947) and Felix Tchicaya U'Tamsi (1931–1988), Cameroon's Guillaume Oyono-Mbia (b. 1939), and Togo's Senouvo Zin sou (b. 1946). Theatre in French-speaking Africa also received international attention when such well-known contemporary directors as Roger Blin and Peter Brook employed actors from this region in some of their productions.

English-speaking (anglophone) Africa, which includes Nigeria, South Africa, Uganda, and Zambia, has had a significant international impact. Anglophone theatre became more highly developed in the 1950s because of the influence of universities in this region. Universities encouraged the work of dramatists and also organized traveling theatre troupes.

Among the influences on the theatre of English-speaking Africa are traditional forms, popular theatre, and the indigenous languages of the peoples; in fact, there has been considerable debate over whether theatre should be created in the language of the African peoples or in English. Among the leading theatre artists from anglophone Africa are the Nigerians Hubert Ogunde (1916–1990), the playwright who is often cited as the founder of modern Nigerian theatre; Moses Olaiya Adejumo (b. 1936), an actor-manager; and Olu Obafemi (b. 1951), a playwright, director, and actor. Among the leading playwrights in Zimbabwe are S. J. Chifunyise (b. 1948), Ben Shibenke (b. 1945), and Thompson Tsodzo (b. 1947). In Kenya, the playwright Ngugi wa Thiong'o (b. 1938), who has created individual and collaborative works in Kenyan languages, was arrested by the oppressive government between 1977 and 1978 and then forced to live in exile. South Africa produced many significant playwrights and theatre companies in the 1970s, including the Market Theatre, People's Space Theatre, and Junction Avenue Theatre Company; these companies frequently produced works that questioned South Africa's apartheid.

Concern for political and social equality is at the heart of the works of the South African playwright Athol Fugard (b. 1932) and the Nigerian playwright Wole Soyinka (b. 1934), and these two authors have become the most internationally renowned of all contemporary African playwrights.

Fugard, who is white, attacked apartheid in such plays as *The Blood Knot* (1964), *Sizwe Banzi Is Dead* (1973), *Master Harold . . . and the Boys* (1982), *A Lesson from Aloes* (1987), and *Playland* (1992). Some of Fugard's early works, such as *Sizwe Banzi* and *Statements after an Arrest under the Immorality Act* (1972), were written in collaboration with black actors. His works are in the tradition of the plays of Henrik Ibsen and Arthur Miller, so he has sometimes been criticized for taking a simplistic liberal point of view. Nonetheless, his dramas clearly represent the racial turmoil of South Africa during apartheid and postapartheid.

Another significant African playwright is the Nigerian Wole Soyinka, who is also a poet, essayist, and novelist. Soyinka began his career with the Royal Court Theatre in London in the late 1950s. His politically charged works led to his arrest in Nigeria in 1967, and to 2 years' imprisonment. In 1973, he adapted Euripides's *The Bacchae* for the National Theatre in England. Soyinka gained international recognition in 1986,

AFRICAN THEATRE: WOLE SOYINKA

A major African playwright of the past half century is the Nigerian Wole Soyinka, who is also a poet and author. Soyinka won the Nobel Prize for Literature in 1986. Before that he had been imprisoned in Nigeria for his political views. Mixing traditional African ceremonial elements with modern themes and characters is the play shown here, *Death and the King's Horseman.* It featured Nonso Anozie (as Elesin, Horseman of the King, center) and was recently presented in London. (© Elliott Franks/ArenaPAL/The Image Works)

when he received the Nobel Prize in literature. Among his best-known dramas are *The Swamp Dwellers* (1957), *The Road* (1965), *Death and the King's Horsemen* (1975), and *Play of Giants* (1985).

In recent years an important group of dramatists, writing in Arabic, emerged in the countries of northern Africa. This group includes two Egyptian playwrights, Alfred Farag (1929–2005) and Lenin El-Ramli (b. 1945); the Tunisian dramatist Jalila Baccar (b. 1952); the Algerian playwright Abdelkader Alloula (1929–1994); and Tayed Saddiki (b. 1937) of Morocco. Farag was the leading Egyptian playwright of the post-1952 revolution period; El-Ramli is considered Egypt's leading comic dramatist. Baccar is an author, director, and actress in films and television as well as onstage. Her Tunisian company has been featured in festivals in Europe and the United States. Alloula, Algeria's leading dramatist after its independence, was assassinated by extremists in 1994. Saddiki is considered the outstanding playwright in contemporary Morocco.

RUSSIA AND EASTERN EUROPE

A pivotal event for theatre in eastern Europe, as for so much else, was the fall of the Soviet Union in 1989–1991. From World War II until that time, theatre in Russia and the territories under its domination was a double-edged sword. On the one hand, there was state-supported theatre through much of the Soviet Union, which meant theatre was available as well as affordable. On the other hand, all theatrical activity was heavily censored and required to hew to the party line, with the result that experimentation, creativity and protest were stifled if not eliminated altogether.

In the last two decades new theatrical energy has emerged throughout the region, but at the same time, there has been a struggle for financial support. The two theatrical centers in Russia itself remain Moscow and Saint Petersburg. Three important traditional theatres are still very much a presence in Moscow: the Moscow Art Theatre, the Maly, and the theatre of Vakhtangov. Among newer well-known theatres are the Taganka, the theatre of Oleg Tabakov, and the first gay theatre in Russia: the Roman Viktiuk Theatre.

Among the leading contemporary playwrights in Russia, Lyudmila Petrushevskaya (b. 1938) specializes in three types of drama: plays that expose the shadowy part of life, including extreme loneliness; joke plays, often based on famous literary figures; and plays exploring relationship problems. Alexander Galin (b. 1947) wrote *Retro,* the most frequently performed drama in Russia in the 1980s. The Presnyakov brothers, Oleg (b. 1969) and Vladimir (b. 1974), write plays that are extremely controversial, featuring the brutal alienation of today's world depicted in strong language. And Yevgeni Grishkovetz (b. 1967) writes, stages, and performs alone theatre pieces that are extremely personal and refreshingly humorous.

Among other countries formerly under Soviet domination, several have long, vibrant traditions of theatrical activity that have been rekindled. Three examples are Poland, the Czech Republic (formerly a part of Czechoslovakia), and Romania. Poland, for instance, in the twentieth century had an extremely influential pre-absurdist, experimental playwright, Ignacy Witkiewicz (1855–1939), as well as an internationally celebrated director, Tadeusz Kantor (1915–1990). During the Nazi occupation Kantor founded the underground Independent Theatre. After the war, he formed his own theatre, Cricot 2, and in the 1960s he became widely known for staging happenings. In the 1970s, Kantor began creating his own theatre pieces; the most famous of these was *Dead Class* (1970). During the next two decades, Kantor toured the world with his company and his productions, which included *Where Are the Snows of Yesteryear* (1982), *Let the Artists Die* (1985), and *Today Is My Birthday* (1990).

In the Czech Republic, Josef Svoboda revolutionized scene design in the mid-twentieth century. (See the profile of Svoboda in "Global Crosscurrents" in Chapter 10.) The playwright Václav Havel (b. 1936) challenged communist and Soviet authorities in his plays; as a result he was attacked and imprisoned, and his works were banned. In 1989, when the Czech Republic emerged as an independent nation, Havel was elected president.

In Romania, an auteur director, Radu Afrim, reinterprets and transforms classic texts to create extremely provocative theatre pieces. His version of Chekhov's *The Three Sisters,* for example, featured the sisters as scantily clad flash dancers, and his reworking of Lorca's *The House of Bernarda Alba* took place in a timeless location totally removed from Spain. It also transformed the matronly Bernarda of that play into a glamorous figure who engages in Olympic-style gymnastics.

WESTERN EUROPE, BRITAIN, AND IRELAND

The nations of western Europe, countries such as France, Germany, Italy, and Spain, as well as Britain and Ireland, have their own lengthy traditions of theatre. The traditions in this part of the world begin in ancient Greece and Rome and go through the Middle Ages, the Renaissance, and later centuries to the present.

KANTOR: INNOVATIVE POLISH DIRECTOR

Tadeusz Kantor was a Polish director who also worked as a scene designer and visual artist. He began as a proponent of the avant-garde but then decided to form his own theatre company to develop his personal vision. His later works—one of which, *Today Is My Birthday,* is shown here—have been described as personal reflections in which he reveals his deepest, inmost thoughts through stunning theatrical imagery. (© Geraint Lewis)

Contemporary theatre in these countries exists in three categories, or realms. One realm is classic theatre. Each nation has one or more theatres that continue to produce classics from the past. France, for example, has the Comédie Française in Paris, which was founded in 1680, more than 300 years ago. Britain has not one but two national theatres: the Royal Shakespeare Company and the National Theatre.

A second category of ongoing theatre in western Europe and Britain is modern theatre. It began in Europe in the late nineteenth century with the plays of Ibsen, Strindberg, and Chekhov and includes both the realistic drama of those playwrights and the many who followed them, as well as the nonrealistic drama that began at the same time and the playwrights who followed this path into such departures from realism as expressionism, surrealism, and absurdism.

A third category includes the many avant-garde and experimental works, sometimes produced by directors and sometimes by acting ensembles. It should be pointed out that in western Europe as well as Britain and Ireland, all three strands are very much alive today. What follows is a brief look at playwrights, directors, and theatre companies in this part of the world.

In Germany, for example, an important director has been Peter Stein (b. 1937), who became known in the 1970s for postmodernist productions in which he reworked classical texts to heighten ideological statements he felt were inherent in them and to express his own political viewpoints. He often used techniques of Brecht, Artaud, and naturalism. From 1970 to 1985, Stein was the artistic director of Berlin's Schaubühne

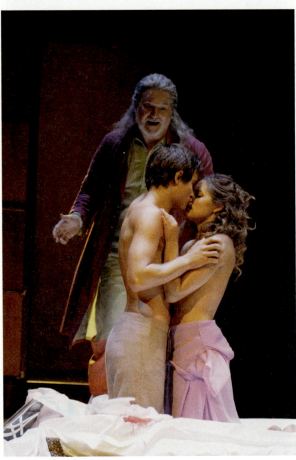

STEIN: POSTMODERN DIRECTOR
An important modern German director is Peter Stein, who became known for postmodernist productions in which he reworked classical texts to heighten ideological statements he felt were inherent in them and to express his own political viewpoint. Shown here is his version of Shakespeare's *Troilus and Cressida,* with Henry Pettigrew as Troilus, Arthur Cox as Calchus, and Annabel Scholey as Cressida. (© Geraint Lewis)

Theatre. In the mid-1980s Stein departed from his earlier experimentation and began to stage more traditional productions. Among his most recent productions are Sophocles's *Medea* at the 2005 Epidaurus Festival in Greece, *Blackbird* in 2005 at the Edinburgh Festival in Scotland, and *The Demons* in 2010.

Among German playwrights two important figures are Heiner Müller (1929–1995) and Peter Handke (b. 1942). Müller, who began his career in communist East Germany in the 1950s, became known for the short plays he wrote in the late 1970s and 1980s—explosions of images ridiculing traditional values and institutions. His most famous play is an Artaud-like scenario, *Hamletmachine* (1977). Handke's plays—including *Offending the Audience* (1966), *Ride across Lake Constance* (1970), *They Are Dying Out* (1973), and *Slow Homecoming* (1982)—focus on the shortcomings of language as a tool for communication and are surreal and symbolic in style.

In France there were a host of important playwrights throughout the twentieth century. One of the best-known of the newer playwrights is Yasmina Reza (b. 1959), whose plays include *Art* (1995) and *God of Carnage* (2007). Among French directors a signal figure is Ariane Mnouchkine, a profile of whom appears in this chapter. Another director who works in France, Peter Brook, is emblematic of the international, global nature of today's theatre. Brook is British and began his work in Britain, but he founded a theatre in Paris some years ago and has worked there ever since. Known as the International Theatre Research Center theatre, it incorporates not only European actors but a number of performers from Africa and Asia as well.

A key Italian theatre figure is the Italian playwright Dario Fo (b. 1926), known for his satirical political comedies, which attack capitalist institutions and are reminiscent of the Greek playwright Aristophanes. Fo, with his wife, the actress Franca Rame (b. 1929), has run his own theater companies, directing and acting in his plays. Among his best-known works are *The Accidental Death of an Anarchist* (1970); *We Won't Pay, We Won't Pay* (1974); and, with Franca Rame, *Female Parts* (1981). Fo won the Nobel Prize for literature in 1997.

Among the significant playwrights in England is Tom Stoppard (b. 1937), who continues to write dramas emphasizing wordplay and intellectual concerns. One of Stoppard's recent dramas in his long list of intellectually challenging and stimulating plays is *The Coast of Utopia,* three plays constituting a trilogy that lasts nearly nine hours and was presented in 2007 by the Lincoln Center Theatre.

A significant number of "angry" playwrights in Britain continue to attack traditional political, social, and economic institutions; among the best-known are David

BROOK'S *MARAT/SADE*

In the last half of the twentieth century, a number of creative, innovative directors emerged on the European continent and in Britain. In England, Peter Brook distinguished himself, first with Shakespeare, but then with far more experimental work. One of his bold productions, influenced by the theories of Antonin Artaud, was *Marat/Sade,* shown here; it was set in an insane asylum at the time of the French revolution. (© Dennis Stock/Magnum Photos)

Hare (b. 1947) and Howard Brenton (b. 1942). More contemporary sociopolitically oriented British playwrights include Patrick Marber (b. 1964), author of *Dealer's Choice* (1995) and *Closer* (1997); and Jez Butterworth (b. 1969), author of *Mojo* (1995).

A number of female English playwrights have achieved considerable recognition, including Timberlake Wertenbaker (b. 1946) and Pamela Gems (b. 1925). Sarah Kane (1971–1999) received considerable attention after she committed suicide. Her works include *Blasted* (1995), *Cleansed* (1998), and *Crave* (1998). A British playwright who has achieved immense worldwide recognition for politically charged feminist plays is Caryl Churchill (b. 1938). Churchill, whose plays include *Cloud Nine* (1979), *Serious Money* (1987), *Mad Forest* (1990), and *A Number* (2004), has received numerous awards, including the Susan Smith Blackburn Prize, which she won twice.

An English director who has developed a more experimental style of production, and has reinterpreted texts so as to focus on feminist, gender, and other sociopolitical issues, is Deborah Warner (b. 1959). Warner began her career with an alternative London troupe, the Kick Theatre Company, which she founded in 1980, when she

CONTEMPORARY WOMEN PLAYWRIGHTS

In the past quarter century, women playwrights have emerged throughout the English-speaking world. An award for the best new play in the English language, the Susan Smith Blackburn Prize, has coincided with this development. A play that was shocking to many people—though others applauded its honesty—was *Blasted* by Sarah Kane: it includes frank depictions of rape, torture, and cannibalism. Shown here, in a scene from a production at the Avignon theatre festival, are Katharina Schuettler and Ulrich Muehe. (The playwright hanged herself in 1999, at the age of twenty-eight.) (© Anne-Christine Poujoulat/Agence France-Presse/Getty Images)

was 21. She has since directed unique interpretations of the classics for the Royal Shakespeare Company and the National Theatre in London. She is best-known for the many productions she has directed that star the actress Fiona Shaw (b. 1959), including Shakespeare's *Richard II,* with Shaw in the title role; Beckett's *Footfalls;* and site-specific stagings of T. S. Eliot's *The Waste Land.* In the summer of 2000 and again in the winter of 2001, Warner directed Shaw in an adaptation of *Medea.*

There is also a new generation of young Irish playwrights who dramatize social, political, and historical issues. One of the best-known is Martin McDonagh (b. 1970), whose works include *The Beauty Queen of Leenane* (1996), *The Cripple of Inishmaan* (1996), *The Lonesome West* (1997), and *The Pillowman* (2005). Conor McPherson (b. 1971) has gained international attention for *St. Nicholas* (1996), *The Weir* (1997), and *Dublin Carol* (2000).

It should be pointed out that in all the areas of western Europe, Britain, and Ireland that we have discussed, there are numerous alternative theaters, which also exist in most major cities worldwide. In London, for example, there is an alternative

GLOBAL CROSSCURRENTS

ARIANE MNOUCHKINE: THÉÂTRE DU SOLEIL

Since her founding of the avant-garde Théâtre du Soleil in Paris in 1964, the French director Ariane Mnouchkine (b. 1939) has become one of the most widely admired directors in Europe and, in fact, around the world. Although strongly influenced by Copeau, Brecht, Artaud, and Meyerhold, she is also known for her effective use of nonwestern dramatic techniques, especially those of Japan and India. She was born in a small town near Paris, France, and attended Oxford University in England, majoring in psychology. There, she became involved with the Oxford University Drama Society and from that point on, her interest was theatre. In the early 1960s, Mnouchkine scraped together enough money to realize a lifelong dream of traveling to the far east. In Japan, Cambodia, and other parts of Asia, she found a beauty of form and a sense of ritual that she considered indispensable to theatre. When she returned to Paris in 1963, Mnouchkine and several of her friends established a "theatrical community," which was to become the Théâtre du Soleil (Theatre of the Sun).

The company has produced everything from loose collections of improvised materials to acclaimed versions of Shakespeare's works to a powerful 10-hour staging of the *Oresteia,* the cycle of Greek tragedies about the house of Atreus. Mnouchkine is strongly in favor of the collaborative process in creating theatrical pieces. The director, she has stated, has become all powerful. Her goal, she says, "is to move beyond that situation by creating a form of theatre where it will be possible for everyone to collaborate without there being directors, technicians, and so on." She and her company use many techniques in developing their productions. These include improvisational exercises

as well as styles such as commedia dell'arte and various Asian rituals.

Among the best-known collectively created productions of Théâtre du Soleil are *1789* (1970), which environmentally dramatized the historical background of the French Revolution; *The Age of Gold* (1975); and *Les Atrides* (1991), the adaptation of the *Oresteia.* Among her most recent productions are *And Suddenly Sleepless Nights* (1997), which deals with the plight of illegal immigrants; the two-part, 6-hour *Le Dernier Caravansérail (Odysées) (The Last Caravan Stop,* 2003), which deals with the hardships of refugees. For this last piece, she and members of her troupe spent three years collecting poignant and tragic stories from refugees from all parts of the world and then wove these stories into the drama. *Les Éphémères* (2009) consists of series of interwoven vignettes, chiefly about middle-class life in France.

A scene from *Les Éphémères,* with Camille Grandville, left, and Juliana Carneiro da Cunha. (Ruth Fremson/The New York Times/Redux)

to commercial theater known as *fringe theater,* and it is in fringe theater that many contemporary political playwrights began their careers. Among the well-known fringe theatres in London are the Donmar Warehouse, the Almeida, and the Menier Chocolate Factory. The British playwrights whose work appears in fringe theatre are often in the postmodernist tradition, mixing reality with theatrical techniques and fusing concerns of high art with techniques of popular art.

THE IRISH PLAYWRIGHT MARTIN McDONAGH
British and Irish playwrights come from a long line of well-known predecessors. In the case of the Irish, there is a strong tradition going back over a century. Among the prominent younger Irish dramatists is Martin McDonagh. Often mixing comedy and cruelty and continuing the strong oral tradition of Irish writing, McDonagh includes gruesome details and creates vivid scenes and characters. The scene here shows three characters from his play *A Behanding in Spokane,* his first play set in the United States, with the actors Christopher Walken, left, Zoe Kazan, and Anthony Mackie. (Sara Krulwich/The New York Times/Redux)

LATIN AMERICAN THEATRES

In twentieth century Latin America, there was a development of realistic drama, experimental theatre, radical sociopolitical drama, and popular forms, all existing side by side. While there have been economic, political, and social problems, including periods of censorship and governmental repression (for example, in Chile during the dictatorship of Pinochet from 1973 to 1989), all the countries in Latin America have significant theatres and playwrights. Frequently these artists have responded to the political and social turmoil in their societies.

At the beginning of the twentieth century, for instance, many comedies were written throughout Latin America—and especially in Argentina—that dealt with the unique local customs of each of the Latin American nations. In the period between the world wars, the dramatists of Latin America were clearly influenced by such European styles as surrealism and expressionism but often touched on nationalistic issues.

THE AUDIENCE'S RESPONSE

- In what ways does the enactment of a ritual or ceremony resemble a theatrical presentation? What elements do the two events have in common? What are the differences? What do we learn about both ceremonies and theatre by observing the differences?

- Have you ever seen a theatre presentation of a play or production from another part of the world—from Asia, eastern Europe, the middle east, Latin America, Canada, or Australia? What struck you about the performance: the similarities to your world, or the differences?

- What can we learn about other countries and other cultures by seeing their theatrical presentations? How does theatre compare with news accounts for providing insight into cultures and countries other than our own?

Following World War II, many Latin American dramatists began to focus on the unique national issues and concerns that confronted their individual countries. Some of Latin America's most developed and politically active playwrights and theatre companies can be found today in Argentina, Brazil, Chile, Mexico, and Peru. The theatre artists of these countries have fused the popular styles of their peoples with the modernist styles of modern western theatre, including realism, expressionism, absurdism, and performance art.

Among the most significant of the postwar Latin American dramatists are the Mexican Elena Garro (b. 1920), the Chilean Alejandro Sieveking (b. 1935), the Colombian Guillermo Maldonado (b. 1945), the Peruvian Mario Vargas Llosa (b. 1936), and the Brazilian Plinio Marcos (b. 1935).

One of the most renowned theatre artists of the era was the Brazilian playwright, director, and theorist Augusto Boal. In the 1960s, Boal created works about historical figures, theatrical and revolutionary. Because of his Marxist point of view, Boal was forced into exile. In exile, he traveled throughout South America and other parts of the world, experimenting with different types of theater. He became internationally known for his theoretical work *Theatre of the Oppressed* (1975), which became a manifesto for revolutionary and socially conscious theater. (A profile of Boal can be found in "Global Crosscurrents" in Chapter 2.)

Four contemporary playwrights from Argentina are Daniel Veronese (b. 1955), Lola Arias (b. 1976), Rafael Spregelburd (b. 1970), and Federica León (b. 1970). Veronese's *Women Dreamt Horses* features a sister and three brothers at a family dinner that goes terribly wrong for all concerned; Arias's *La Esquálida Familia* is set in an arctic frontier and tells the story of a developmentally disabled orphan boy whose discovery tears apart an incestuous family; in Spregelburd's *Panic* a woman facing a financial crisis searches frantically for the key to her husband's safe deposit box; León's *Ex-Antwone* is a dreamlike fantasy in which a young man attempts to connect with a girl who has Down syndrome and has had her face replaced with a normal one.

In addition to his writing, Varonese formed an important theatre company, El Periférico de Objetos, in 1989. Another important Argentine-based company, De

LATIN AMERICAN THEATRE: ARGENTINA

The Argentinian theatre group De La Guarda, in the piece *Fuerza Bruta* (*Brute Force*), has created a modern work that is part theatre, part rock concert, and part circus act. It typifies the mixing of styles and the eclecticism of much of contemporary theatre. There is no traditional stage. Performers soar through the air and, in the scene shown here, float in a transparent plastic water tank, which spectators view from below through a glass ceiling. (© Ronaldo Schemidt/AFP/Getty Images)

La Guarda, has brought several productions to New York and elsewhere, including *VillaVilla* and *Fuerze Bruta*.

Contemporary Mexican theatre, according to a young playwright, Richard Viqueira, "wants to unburden itself from the influence of European theatrical models, and is seeking to forge its own voice. The move in new writing," he says, "more and more is away from the folkloric toward the more recognizably idiomatic." Along with Viqueira (b. 1976), other recognized young Mexican playwrights include Javier Malpica (b. 1965); Sabima Berman (b. 1955), a political activist as well as playwright; Sylvia Peláez (b. 1965); and Alberto Villarreal (b. 1977).

CANADA AND AUSTRALIA SINCE WORLD WAR II

Canadian and Australian theatres before World War II developed commercially, presenting popular forms of entertainments that also reflected national identity. Two Australian examples are *The Squatter's Daughter, or, The Land of the Wattle* (1907), which focused on the Australian outlaw known as the bushranger; and the pantomime *The Bunyip, or The Enchantment of Fairy Princess Wattle Blossom* (1916), which included a mythological Aboriginal character.

During the period between the two world wars, Australia and Canada developed "little theatres"—some professional and some amateur—that presented noncommercial, and often politically charged, works. In Australia, three such companies were Sydney's New Theatre League, established in 1936; Melbourne's New Theatre Club, founded in 1937; and Brisbane's Unity Theatre, which also opened in 1937. Hart House Theatre, founded on the campus of the University of Toronto in 1919, was one example of the Canadian "little theatre" movement. It presented many of Canada's most important theatre artists in the two decades before World War II. After World War II, the Hart House became a venue for university productions, reflecting the vitality of university theatre across Canada.

Since World War II, the theatres of Canada and Australia have seen developments that parallel the complexity of the international theatre scene. For example, in Canada in the 1950s and 1960s, many regional theatres were established. One of the most famous is the Stratford Shakespeare Festival in Stratford, Ontario. This festival, established in 1952 under the artistic direction of Tyrone Guthrie, continues to produce classics, musicals, and contemporary works, in multiple venues. Australia also saw the development of theatres across the nation from the 1950s through the 1970s.

Both Australia and Canada also developed avant-garde companies and theatres from the late 1960s through the present. In 1967, Betty Burstall (b. 1926) established Melbourne's La Mama theatre, based on New York's famous experimental theatre. La Mama continues to function. Company B, which was established in Sydney in 1985 and is still producing, is known for presenting contemporary works and unique readings of classics. Among the stars who have recently appeared with the company are the film actors Geoffrey Rush (b. 1951) and Cate Blanchett (b. 1969).

Playwrights and theatre artists have dealt with issues related to these countries' diverse populations. Possibly the best-known of the Canadian playwrights is Michel Tremblay (b. 1942), who was born in Montreal. His French-language plays focus on working-class Canadians and gay issues. The theatre company Buddies in Bad Times, established in 1979 and still producing in Toronto, is committed to gay and lesbian

A DIRECTOR ON THE CUTTING EDGE
The Canadian director Robert Lepage is known for his inventive, striking visual imagery. Although *Lipsynch,* the work shown here, focuses on voices and speech, there is no shortage of his trademark visual fireworks. Writing in the *New York Times,* Charles Isherwood described this 9-hour work as "a feast of fluid, almost cinematic stage pictures created by blending sound, video, and live performance." Shown in this scene, at the left, are Lise Castonguay (Michelle) and Rick Miller (Jeremy).
(© Francis Loney/Arena PAL)

theatre. In the 1980s, feminist theatres in Australia included Home Cooking Theatre (1981) and Vital Statistix (1984). The Australian musical *Bran Nue Dae* (1990) dealt with Aboriginal life.

There are also Canadian and Australian artists who present performance art and multimedia works. The French-Canadian Robert Lepage (b. 1957) is a well-known director, creator of theatrical productions, and actor. In 1993, he founded Ex Machina, a multimedia performance center in Quebec City. Among Lepage's other well-known productions are a postmodernist version of Shakespeare's *A Midsummer Night's Dream* at the Naion Theatre in London in 1993 and his own *Far Side of the Moon* (2000), in which he played both of the work's two characters. Lepage is probably best-known for *KÁ,* the Cirque du Soleil production he staged in Las Vegas in 2005.

SUMMARY

1. A number of countries in Asia and the west have theatre traditions that stretch back hundreds, and in some cases thousands, of years.

2. The modern era is marked by increasing globalization in theatre, with more and more communication and cross-pollination—a feature of much of modern society, including the arts.

3. Asian theatre has both traditional and modern branches. In places like Japan, both types of theatre remain particularly active.

4. Theatre in India today is largely produced by numerous amateur groups.

5. Despite prohibition in Muslim countries, theatre has developed in certain middle eastern countries. In Israel, theatre is quite active.

6. The two best-known writers of African drama are Athol Fugard and Wole Soyinka.

7. Theatres in Russia and the countries of eastern Europe have long traditions, but many of these theatres were curtailed or interrupted during the years of the Soviet Union: the 1940s until 1989–1991.

8. European and British theatre has two active components: (a) traditional and establishment, and (b) alternative. Europe and Britain are known for national theatres; strong, innovative directors; and invigorating playwrights.

9. Latin American theatre has roots in Spanish and Portuguese drama. A well known Brazilian playwright is Augusto Boal.

10. Theatres in Canada and Australia remain active and vibrant.

Contemporary American Theatre

As we move into the twenty-first century, American theatre remains amazingly resilient, but at the same time it continues to face serious challenges. One constant challenge comes from various electronic media, which continue to proliferate. Not only film and television, but other new developments such as DVDs, iPods, and computer games are rivals to live theatre, particularly among young people.

Other challenges are more personal and political. Recurring threats to the arts in America are attacks by conservative movements against any advances made by gays, lesbians, feminists, and ethnic minorities. Conservative politicians, for example, have succeeded in sharply reducing the appropriations given annually to the National Endowment for the Arts (NEA). From the 1960s through the 1980s, grants from the NEA to theatres, coupled with earlier gifts from large foundations, made possible the creation of the network of resident professional theatres across the country. Appropriations from Congress to the NEA, however, were drastically reduced. In 1992, the amount was $175 million; in 1997, it had dropped sharply to $99 million; in 2007, it was roughly $120 million, which, when adjusted for inflation, is not much more than the amount for 1997. In other words, after 1992 there was a precipitous drop in the NEA budget, and this was at a time when the arts most needed support. When the Obama administration came in, a portion of the budget was restored. The 2009 budget was $155 million, still not at the level of 1992.

In America, there has never been a tradition of government support for the arts. By contrast, in Britain and many countries in continental Europe, national, state, and municipal governments each year make generous grants to arts organizations. To take

◀ **THEATRICAL DIVERSITY**

The work of the playwright Lynn Nottage is an excellent example of theatrical diversity, as well as global theatre. Her play Ruined, *directed by Kate Whoriskey, was jointly produced by the Goodman Theatre in Chicago and the Manhattan Theatre Club in New York. It is set in the Democratic Republic of the Congo in the year 2000 and tells the story of Sophie (Condola Phyleia Rashad) and her horrific experiences at the hands of men. She crosses paths with Mama Nadi, a sharp businesswoman who helps such women but also profits by them. (Liz Lauren/Courtesy of the Goodman Theatre)*

REGIONAL THEATRES

In the United States, regional, not-for-profit theatres are indispensable. These theatres, which emerged in the last half of the twentieth century, are spread all across America, in large cities and small ones. They present the classics and plays recently produced elsewhere, but they are also often the only theatres that give encouragement and crucial exposure to new works. Shown here is a scene from Arthur Miller's *All My Sons* directed by David Esbjornson at the Huntington Theatre in Boston. The play concerns a man whose pilot son died in World War II, at the same time that the man was selling defective airplane parts to the military. Shown here are Lee Aaron Rosen as Chris Keller, Will Lyman as Joe Keller (the father), and Diane Davis as the surviving son's fiance. (© T Charles Erickson)

only one example, the National Theatre in London receives the equivalent of more than $30 million per year from the British Arts Council. This grant to one theatre alone in Britain is roughly 20 percent of the entire appropriation for the NEA in the United States.

As a result of cuts in funding by the government and foundations, not-for-profit theatres have had to struggle in recent years. Among other things, there has been a shift from annual subscription sales to single ticket sales, and this together with the loss of funding has meant tighter budgets for many theatres. This, in turn, has led to fewer new plays, fewer large-cast shows, fewer musicals, and fewer plays with full-scale scenery.

Despite these very real difficulties, theatre has continued to play a vital role in the nation's art scene. In Chapter 3, I noted the impressive variety in contemporary American theatre. Audiences today can see revivals of the best theatre from the past: Greek, Elizabethan, French, and Spanish. They can see theatre from Asia, Africa, and Latin America; new plays; and avant-garde and experimental works. There are productions in translation of the best new plays from other countries. Audiences can see multi-cultural theatre—African American, Asian American, Hispanic, Native American—and they can see political theatre, and theatre reflecting the viewpoint of a number of minorities and special groups such as feminists and gays and lesbians. What's more, these productions can be seen in a wide variety of theatre environments.

One hallmark of contemporary theatre is that all these strands exist simultaneously. As this suggests, our contemporary theatre is complex. If theatre mirrors the society in which it is produced, it is not surprising that ours is fragmented, reflecting the complexity of today's life.

One way to understand the rich assortment of theatrical organizations and theatrical venues that make up the mosaic of contemporary theatre is to look at one locality as a microcosm of theatre across the United States. Take, for example, the city of Chicago. In many ways what is happening in Chicago mirrors what is happening elsewhere, in the diverse types of theatre on display, as well as in the variety of theatre spaces.

To begin with, there are traditional Broadway-style theatres, including the Ford Center, the Oriental, the Cadillac Palace, and the LaSalle Bank (formerly the Shubert). Not only do they offer touring Broadway shows, but the LaSalle Bank Theatre in recent years has been a tryout house for such musicals as *The Producers* and *Spamalot*.

As for not-for-profit theatre, Chicago has a number of resident professional theatres. The largest, the Goodman, is a flagship regional theatre; it has launched several plays by August Wilson as well as other important new works. Following closely behind the Goodman is Steppenwolf, founded in 1976. The original Steppenwolf company included many actors who became stars, such as John Malkovich (b. 1953), Gary Sinise (b. 1955), and Laurie Metcalf (b. 1955), and Steppenwolf itself evolved into a leading established regional theatre. In 2007 it launched the play *August: Osage County*, which went on to win a Pulitzer Prize; and in 2009 it launched *Superior Donuts*—both by Tracy Letts (b. 1965).

Steppenwolf is known as an *off-Loop* theatre, meaning that it is outside the downtown commercial section of Chicago (the equivalent in New York is off-Broadway and off-off-Broadway). Other major off-Loop Chicago theatres include Wisdom Bridge (where Robert Falls, currently artistic director of the Goodman, began his directing career), the Organic, the Body Politic, St. Nicholas, and Victory Gardens. These theatres have also introduced successful actors, including Joe Mantegna (b. 1947), and many significant playwrights. Lookingglass Theatre, founded in Chicago in 1988, has received praise for its productions of literary adaptations that use intriguing staging devices. In 2002, Lookingglass's artistic director, Mary Zimmerman, won the Tony Award for best direction, after her production of *Metamorphoses* (1998) moved to New York City.

Chicago also has the Chicago Shakespeare Theater, which is just one of a number of exceptional Shakespeare theatres and festivals around the country. All in all, there are more than 150 Shakespeare festivals in the United States, with over 30 located in California alone. Year after year, Shakespeare remains the playwright most frequently produced in America.

Along with the many professional theatres in Chicago, there are excellent college and university theatres, such as De Paul, and Northwestern in Evanston, Illinois, which produce high-quality work. The multiplicity of theatre activity in Chicago, at so many levels, can also be found in cities large and small in almost all 50 states as well as in Canada.

NONTRADITIONAL, ALTERNATIVE THEATRE

In the twenty-first century, traditional theatre remains vital and vigorous in America, as well as throughout the world. We will examine that theatre in considerable detail later in the chapter. But here, we should take note of a development that took root in the second half of the twentieth century and has become a full-blown movement in this century. It could be called nontraditional theatre, but it also goes variously by other names such as avant-garde, experimental, and postmodernist. It offers an alternative to traditional theatre, and it affords a different type of experience for theatre audiences.

A good way to begin examining nontraditional theatre is to look at what happened in the visual arts, particularly painting, in the last century. For hundreds of years painting in the western world was representational: that is, the subject on the canvas represented something recognizable, such as a landscape or a portrait. Then, in the early years of the twentieth century other approaches to painting began to appear: abstract expressionism, collage, montage, and all manner of nonrepresentational art.

No longer were observers looking at a mountain, a seascape, or a portrait of a family or an individual. They were looking at shapes, colors, designs that did not represent anything recognizable from daily life. Geometric shapes were arranged so that, say, blue squares, yellow triangles, and red circles appeared in a pattern that was either carefully delineated or seemingly thrown together at random. The flat surface of the canvas was even broken so that sections of the painting went beyond the frame or three-dimensional outgrowths appeared on the surface.

A number of people, content with centuries of representational art, resisted this approach to painting. Those who were attracted to it, however, or curious about it, had to come to terms with a new way of communicating. This different approach to art was challenging, provocative, sometimes disorienting. A spectator had to ask: "What is the artist trying to say?" The viewer, in other words, had to make sense of this new experience and embrace it at some level other than the familiar level of recognizable places or people.

Something similar occurred in theatre in the second half of the twentieth century. There were antecedents—the auteur director Vselovod Meyerhold in the early 1900s, as well as movements such as futurism, expressionism, and surrealism. The author Antonin Artaud, in the 1930s, proclaimed that there should be "no more masterpieces," meaning that texts like the plays of Shakespeare should no longer be revered but rather treated with no more respect than a run-of-the-mill drama by a second-rate dramatist. Following World War II this movement became more widespread. In the spirit of Artaud, a central element shared by all the new experimental and avant-garde approaches to theatre was a rejection of what was called "text-based" theatre, meaning theatre based on a script written by a playwright.

Instead of beginning with dialogue and a plot created by a dramatist, the new approach originated in a number of other ways: an ensemble of actors improvised material; a group of actors joined with dancers, or perhaps incorporated film or video into their presentations; a performance artist developed a one-person show; an auteur director created a piece according to his or her personal vision. In the process, entirely new material might be utilized; or, perhaps, a classical play would be turned upside down or inside out. Frequently, too, performances took place not in a conventional theatre setting, but in an unusual or site-specific locale. One rationale for this approach is that it reflected the confused, chaotic, often irrational world in which we live. Among the developments that took hold in the post–World War II era were happenings, multimedia, and environmental theatre.

Happenings were what the name suggests: unstructured events that occurred with a minimum of planning and organization. The idea was that art should not be restricted to museums, galleries, or concert halls but can and should happen any-where: on a street corner, in a grocery store, at a bus stop.

Multimedia is a joining of theatre with other arts—particularly dance, film, and television. In work of this sort, which is still being produced, live performers interact with sequences on film or television. The idea here is to fuse the art forms or to incor-porate new technology into a theatrical event. A current form that combines theatre, dance, and media is called *performance art* and will be discussed later in the chapter.

The term *environmental theatre* was coined in the 1960s by the American direc-tor and teacher Richard Schechner (b. 1934); many characteristics of environmental theatre, however, had developed out of the work and theories of earlier avant-garde art-ists such as Meyerhold and Artaud. Proponents of environmental theatre treat the entire theatre space as a performance area, suggesting that any division between performers and viewers is artificial. For every production, spatial arrangements are transformed.

The major influence on Schechner's theories was the Polish director Jerzy Grotowski (1933–1999). Works staged by Grotowski with the Polish Laboratory Theatre from its founding in 1959 until 1970 had many characteristics of environ-mental theatre. For each production, the theatre space and the performer-audience relationship were arranged to conform to the play being presented. Grotowski called his theatre *poor theatre,* meaning poor in scenery and special effects. It relied on the performers for its impact.

Two experimental directors are Robert Wilson (b. 1944) and Richard Foreman (b. 1937). Their work is typically unified by a theme or point of view determined by the director, and their material is often organized into units analogous to frames in television or film. Stunning theatrical images containing the essence of the ideas that interest these directors are often the key to their work.

Important off-off-Broadway theatres in which avant-garde works found a home included Café LaMama, the Living Theater, the Open Theater, the Performance Group, Mabou Mines, and the Wooster Group. These theatres were in New York City but had counterparts all across the United States. All have experimented with physi-cal performance techniques, improvisation, texts created by performers and directors, and environmental presentations.

Whatever the process, the result was not traditional theatre. Like their coun-terparts in painting, nonrepresentational theatre artists deal in images, impressions, fragments, and segments. There may be strong elements of improvisation, free associa-tion, and audience participation. Each presentation is an event, a time-based event, and it is up to the spectator to integrate its elements in some way, to determine its meaning and its impact. Another way of saying this is that viewing such theatre becomes a different kind of *experience* from the experience audiences are accustomed to in traditional theatre.

POSTMODERNISM

One term used to describe the nontraditional theatre we have been discussing is *postmodernism.* According to the film critic A. O. Scott, postmodernism has several attributes: "a cool, ironic effect; the overt pastiche of work from the past; the insouci-ant mixture of high and low styles." Although postmodernism is difficult to define specifically, it has certain distinctive facets.

CONTEMPORARY THEATRE: ECLECTICISM AND DIVERSITY
Theatre today is eclectic and widely diversified. Periods, styles, and theatrical purposes and approaches are often mixed. One such mixture of styles and material was a revival of *The Emperor Jones,* by the Wooster Group, known for its experimental work. The play was written in the early twentieth century by the American dramatist Eugene O'Neill, but in this production it was deconstructed and commented on at the same time that the original script was incorporated into the whole. Shown here are Scott Shepherd, Kate Valk (in the title role), and Ari Fliakos. (© Paula Court)

For one thing, postmodernism reflects issues of power in art. Postmodernists question the idea of an accepted "canon" of classics; they also ask why certain artists (such as playwrights) and certain groups (such as white males) should have held positions of power or "privilege" throughout theatre history.

Accordingly, postmodernists rebel against traditional readings of texts, arguing that theatre productions may have a variety of "authors," including directors and even individual audience members: they argue that each audience member creates his or her own unique reading. Postmodernist directors are noted for deconstructing classic dramas and trying to represent onstage the issues of power embedded in the text. When a classic is deconstructed in this way, it may serve simply as the scenario for a production.

One of the most famous groups known for deconstuction of texts is the Wooster Group, under the artistic direction of Elizabeth LeCompte (b. 1944). Its best-known productions are *Routes I & 9* (1981), which used sections of Thornton Wilder's classic *Our Town; L.S.D.* (1983); and *Brace Up* (1991), a performance adaptation of Chekhov's *The Three Sisters*. In 1997, the Wooster Group presented a highly theatricalized and physical version of Eugene O'Neill's *The Emperor Jones* in a run-down theatre in the Times Square area in New York City. In 2007, it presented a version of *Hamlet* that featured various filmed scenes of *Hamlet* interspersed with live action.

Postmodernists mix abstraction and realism, so that their works cannot be easily classified. Furthermore, the distinction between "high" art and popular art can no longer be clearly defined: postmodernists mix popular concerns and techniques with those of high art.

An intriguing example is the musical *The Lion King* (1997). This musical is based on a popular Disney animated film and has music by the rock composer Elton John. The director of *The Lion King*, as well as the designer of the masks and puppets, is Julie Taymor, who was profiled in Chapter 13. Taymor, who is a designer, director, and adapter of literature for the stage, is known for her avant-garde use of puppet techniques borrowed from Asian theatres. For example, she used puppets in staging Shakespeare's *The Tempest* (1986) at New York's Theatre for a New Audience; in her frequently revived adaptation of a short story, *Juan Darien* (1988); in a production of

Igor Stravinsky's opera *Oedipus Rex* in Tokyo (1992); and in a production of *The Green Bird* (1996), an eighteenth-century comedy by Carlo Gozzi.

AMERICAN THEATRE TODAY: TRADITIONAL AND NONTRADITIONAL

It is clear from the discussion above that today there are two broad kinds of theatre experience. One is the experience to which people have been accustomed throughout theatre history; the other is this new experience, which has been embraced by a number of today's imaginative, adventuresome theatre artists. It is important to understand that both are valid. It is also important to understand that exposure to traditional theatre remains the predominant experience most of us will encounter. One reason is that it includes not only a vibrant, vital traditional theatre alive today, but also the productions of the finest theatre from the past. As we examine the spectrum of theatre found in America today, and indeed in many parts of the world, we will discover that traditional theatre thrives alongside its more experimental counterpart.

In terms of traditional theatre, we begin with a look at a number of playwrights who have appeared on the scene in recent decades in the United States. The period just after World War II saw the emergence of Tennessee Williams, Arthur Miller, Lorraine Hansberry, and Edward Albee; then there were other playwrights who followed the traditional style, displaying an awareness of the craft of dramaturgy and also great originality. Included in this group were Sam Shepard (b. 1943) and David Mamet (b. 1947).

Like many of our contemporary playwrights, Shepard and Mamet mix concerns of high art—such as the plight of the American family and the demise of the American dream—with techniques borrowed from mass entertainments such as film, popular music, and melodrama. Also, they often blur the distinction between realism and abstraction.

Sam Shepard first developed his playwriting skills off-off-Broadway with works that fused surreal and absurdist styles and abandoned traditional plot structure and development. His later dramas include *Buried Child* (for which he won a Pulitzer Prize in 1979), *True West* (1980), *Fool for Love* (1982), and *A Lie of the Mind* (1985). Shepard's new plays deal with American mythology, the violence of American society, and the degeneration of the American family.

David Mamet's plays have naturalistic language and settings and some down-and-out characters whose struggles are clearly recognizable; but, unlike traditional realism, they do not provide clear-cut exposition or dramatic resolutions. His plays, like Shepard's, attack many accepted ideals of American life. Among his best-known works are *American Buffalo* (1977), *Glengarry Glen Ross* (1983), *Oleanna* (1992), *The Cryptogram* (1994), *Boston Marriage* (1999), and *Romance* (2005). Mamet has also written and directed a number of films.

A significant playwright bridging the twentieth and twenty-first centuries was Horton Foote (1916–2009), who wrote evocative dramas, mostly set in the south, for more than half a century. Other dramatists who made their mark in the closing decades of the twentieth century included John Guare (b. 1938), Lanford Wilson (b. 1937), Marsha Norman (b. 1947), Wendy Wasserstein (1950–2005), Donald

Margulies (b. 1954), Jon Robin Baitz (b. 1961), David Auburn (b. 1969), and David Lindsay-Abaire (b. 1971). A number of other contemporary figures will be discussed later in this chapter in the sections on minority, multiethnic, and women playwrights.

THEATRE OF DIVERSITY

Before we discuss specific multiethnic and minority points of view in theatre, it should be noted that while many theatre artists wish to write from a specific ethnic or gender viewpoint, there are others who happen to be members of a minority group or a specific gender group, or who espouse feminism or a political outlook, but who do not want to be identified solely, or even primarily, on that basis. For instance, there are playwrights who happen to be Hispanic or African American, but they want to be known as playwrights, without any ethnic identification. Also, there are people who are gay or lesbian, or who are strong feminists, but they want to be regarded chiefly, or even exclusively, as dramatists, not gay dramatists, lesbian dramatists, or feminist dramatists. It is also true that theatre companies, producers, or playwrights who are identified with an ethnic or gender group may well include in their work characters and a point of view belonging to those groups, but include them as part of a larger picture.

Having noted some of the variations within ethnic and minority playwriting and production, let us turn now to theatre identified with specific groups.

African American Theatre

African American theatre—also referred to as *black theatre*—is a prime example of theatre reflecting the diversity of American culture and the contributions of a particular group to that culture. African American theatre is theatre written by and for black Americans or performed by black Americans. It partakes of two important traditions. One is the western theatre tradition, in which actors like Paul Robeson (1898–1976) and writers like Lorraine Hansberry (1930–1965) have been significant. The other is a tradition that traces its origin to theatre in Africa and the Caribbean.

African American theatre has a long history, and therefore tracing its development from its beginnings will help us understand its significance and impact on our contemporary theatre. In American drama of the eighteenth and nineteenth centuries, comic black servants—who spoke a thick dialect, shuffled slowly, and wore ill-fitting costumes—were popular characters. These roles, however, were usually enacted by white performers; it was rare to see black performers on the American stage in the nineteenth century.

An exception was the African Grove Theater—a black company founded in New York during the 1820–1821 season by William Brown (an African American) and the West Indian actor James Hewlett. The company was particularly noted for Shakespearean plays. Hewlett was the first black to play Othello, and the renowned actor Ira Aldridge (c. 1806–1867) made his stage debut with the company. Here, too, the drama *King Shotaway* (1823)—believed to be the first play written and performed by African Americans—was presented. The African Grove closed in 1827, however, after attacks by white audience members.

The *minstrel show* was a popular nineteenth-century form, which caricatured blacks with comic and sentimental songs, skits, jigs, and shuffle dances. The performers were usually white entertainers dressed in colorful costumes, with their faces blackened and eyes and mouth enlarged by white and red lines.

At the turn of the twentieth century, the popular syncopated rhythms of ragtime had a strong influence on the emerging musical theatre and served as a bridge for a number of talented African Americans. Bob Cole (1864–1912) and William Johnson (1873–1954) conceived, wrote, produced, and directed the first black musical comedy, *A Trip to Coontown* (1898). The comedians Bert Williams (c. 1876–1922) and George Walker (1873–1911) and their wives joined composers and writers to produce musicals and operettas such as *In Dahomey* (1902) and *Abyssinia* (1906), in which Americans for the first time saw blacks on the Broadway stage without burnt-cork makeup, speaking without dialect, and costumed in high fashion.

The early twentieth century also saw the formation of African American stock companies. The most significant was the Lafayette Players, founded in 1914 by Anita Bush (1883–1974) as the Anita Bush Players. By the time it closed in 1932, this company had presented more than 250 productions and employed a number of black stars.

Black performers and writers were also making inroads into commercial theatre in the 1920s. Twenty plays and musicals with black themes were presented on Broadway in this decade, five of them written by African Americans, including *Shuffle Along* (1921), with lyrics and music by Noble Sissle (1889–1975) and Eubie Blake (1883–1983). The decade also saw some black performers achieve recognition in serious drama, among them Charles Gilpin (1878–1930), Paul Robeson, and Ethel Waters (1896–1977).

The Depression forced black performers to find other ways of earning a living or to invent ingenious ways of creating their own theatre. There were a few Broadway productions of plays by blacks, such as the folk musical *Run Little Chillun* (1933) and *Mulatto* (1935) by Langston Hughes (1902–1967).

Possibly the most significant development for black theatre during the 1930s was the Federal Theatre Project, which was meant to help theatre artists through the Depression. This project formed separate black units in twenty-two cities which mounted plays by black and white authors and employed thousands of African American writers, performers, and technicians. The Federal Theatre Project created a new generation of African American artists who would develop the theatre of the 1940s and 1950s. In 1941, Orson Welles directed, for his Mercury Theater, a dramatization of the controversial novel *Native Son* by Richard Wright (1908–1960). Other important Broadway ventures included Paul Robeson's record run of 296 performances in *Othello* in 1943, and *Anna Lucasta* (1944), adapted by Abram Hill (1911–1986).

The 1950s saw an explosion of black theatre that would continue over the next five decades. *Take a Giant Step* by Louis Patterson (b. 1922), a play about growing up in an integrated neighborhood, premiered in 1953. In 1954, the playwright-director Owen Dodson (1914–1983)—a significant figure in black theatre since the 1930s—staged *Amen Corner* by James Baldwin (1924–1987) at Howard University.

In 1932, *The Great Day* by Zora Neale Hurston (1891–1960) was produced on Broadway. Off-Broadway, the Greenwich Mews Theater began casting plays without regard to race and also produced *Trouble in Mind* (1956) by Alice Childress (1920–1994). Possibly the most important production of the postwar era was *A Raisin in the Sun* (1959) by Lorraine Hansberry. It is about a black family in Chicago, held

AFRICAN AMERICAN THEATRE

An important, irreplaceable component of American theatre for the past half century has been African American theatre. The dean of this group, the towering figure, was August Wilson, who wrote ten major plays, one for each decade of the twentieth century. The scene here is from his play *Gem of the Ocean,* in a production at the Huntington Theatre, directed by Kenny Leon. John Earl Jelks plays Citizen Barlow, Ruben Santiago-Hudson plays Caesar, and Phylicia Rashad plays Aunt Ester. (© T Charles Erickson)

together by a God-fearing mother, who is planning to move into a predominantly white neighborhood where the family will be unwelcome. The son loses money in a get-rich-quick scheme but later assumes responsibility for the family. Hansberry's play was directed by Lloyd Richards (1922–2006), the first black director on Broadway. Richards later became head of the Yale School of Drama, where in the 1980s he nurtured the talents of the black playwright August Wilson (1945–2005), author of *Jitney* (1982), *Ma Rainey's Black Bottom* (1984), *Fences* (1985), *Joe Turner's Come and Gone* (1986), *The Piano Lesson* (1990), *Seven Guitars* (1995), *King Hedley II* (2000), *Gem of the Ocean* (2003), and *Radio Golf* (2005). These plays are part of an impressive ten-part series in which each individual play focuses on one decade of the twentieth century. The magnitude of Wilson's achievement has led a number of commentators to call him the most important American playwright of the late twentieth century.

From 1960 to the 1990s, there was an outpouring of African American theatre, much of it reflecting the struggle for civil rights. Amiri Baraka (b. 1934) came to theatregoers' attention in 1964 with *Dutchman,* a verbal and sexual showdown between an assimilated black male and a seductive white woman, set in a New York subway. His plays *The Slave* (1965), *The Toilet* (1965), and *Slave Ship* (1970) also deal with the political, sociological, and psychological issues confronting blacks. Among other significant plays of these two decades were Adrienne Kennedy's *Funnyhouse of a Negro* (1964) and *The Owl Answers* (1969); Lonne Elder's *Ceremonies in Dark Old Men* (1969); Charles Gordone's *No Place to Be Somebody* (1969); Douglas Turner Ward's *Day of Absence* (1970); and Charles Fuller's *A Soldier's Play* (1981), which won a Pulitzer Prize for drama.

In 1970 the Black Theater Alliance listed more than 125 producing groups in the United States. Although only a few of these survived the decade, many had a significant impact. The Negro Ensemble Company, founded in 1967, holds the contemporary record for continuous production by a professional black theatre company. The New Lafayette Theatre, which operated from 1966 until 1972, introduced the playwright Ed Bullins (b. 1935), experimented with black ritual, and published the journal *Black Theater.* Other theatres of this period were the New Federal Theater (founded by Woodie King) and the National Black Theater (founded by Barbara Ann Teer).

In addition to the emergence of these producing organizations, another major change in the 1970s was the presence of a larger black audience at Broadway theatres, which accounted for a significant number of commercial African American productions, such as *Don't Bother Me, I Can't Cope* (1972); and *Bubbling Brown Sugar* (1976). This trend continued in the 1980s and 1990s with such hits as *Black and Blue* (1989), *Jelly's Last Jam* (1992), and *Bring in 'da Noise, Bring in 'da Funk* (1996). A later musical offering was *Fela!*—about a legendary African entertainer.

African American artists continued to make an impact on commercial and noncommercial theatre. For example, George C. Wolfe (b. 1955), author-director of *The Colored Museum* (1986), *Spunk* (1990), *Jelly's Last Jam,* and *Bring in 'da Noise, Bring in 'da Funk,* also directed both parts of the award-winning *Angels in America.* From 1993 to 2004, Wolfe was artistic director of the Public Theater, a renowned off-Broadway facility founded by the New York producer Joseph Papp (1921–1991).

Suzan-Lori Parks (b. 1964), Pearl Cleage (b. 1948), and Cheryl West (b. 1956) are three contemporary African American female playwrights whose works deal with issues of racism and feminism and have been produced in regional and alternative theatres. Parks's *Venus* (1996), for example, depicts the life of a nineteenth-century black woman who was exhibited in England as the Hottentot Venus, a sideshow freak. Parks's other critically acclaimed plays include *The America Play* (1993), *The Death of the Last Black Man in the Whole Entire World* (1990), and *Topdog/Underdog,* which won a Pulitzer Prize in 2002 and was directed by George C. Wolfe. In 2006 Parks wrote *365 Days/365 Plays,* a cycle that consisted of one short play each day for a year. In 2007 the cycle was produced by theatres all across the United States. Pearl Cleage's best-known plays are the one-act *Chain* (1992) and *Flyin' West* (1992), which was produced by Atlanta's Alliance Theatre Company. Cheryl West, trained as a social worker, deals with domestic crises in such works as *Before It Hits Home* (1989) and *Holiday Heart* (1994).

Another female African American dramatist whose work is politically charged is Kia Corthron (b. 1961). Corthron's works, which include *Seeking the Genesis* (1996), *Force Continuum* (2000), and *Breath, Boom* (2001), have been commissioned by leading regional and off-Broadway companies. An African American director, Kenny Leon (b. 1955), founded the True Colors Theatre in Atlanta in 2002 and directed a production of *A Raisin in the Sun* on Broadway in 2004.

Asian American Theatre

Asian American theatre should be seen against its background: the long, important heritage of the theatres of Asia. The three great Asian theatre traditions—Indian, Chinese, and Japanese—all reached a high point of artistic excellence many centuries ago at a time when religion and philosophy were central in each culture; and this has kept the focus of traditional theatre allied to these realms, even though the societies themselves have modernized and changed. In addition, these three cultures created and sustained a form of theatre in which many facets of theatrical art—acting, mime, dancing, music, and text—were combined.

It is against the backdrop of these ancient traditions that contemporary Asian American theatre developed. As early as the 1850s, puppet shows, acrobatic acts, and traditional operas were imported from China to California. For most of the nineteenth century and the first half of the twentieth century, however, Asians appeared in dramatic offerings strictly as stereotypes. In films, for instance, Asian Americans played such menial parts as cooks, spies, and vamps. Leading parts—even Asian characters—were played by whites in makeup.

ASIAN AMERICAN THEATRE

One of the best-known Asian American playwrights is David Henry Hwang, who won numerous awards for his Broadway show *M. Butterfly.* A recent play by Hwang is *Yellow Face,* shown here. It is an autobiographical play, in many ways like a revue, tracing Hwang's personal journey and development as an artist. Hoon Lee plays the part of Hwang, and Julienne Hanzelka Kim is the woman in this scene. (Sara Krulwich/The New York Times/Redux)

With the coming of cultural and ethnic awareness in the 1960s and 1970s, this situation began to change. In 1965 several Asian American performers and directors founded the East West Players in Los Angeles. In 1973, two more groups were formed—the Asian Exclusion Act in Seattle and the Asian-American Theatre Workshop in San Francisco—and in 1977 the director-actor Tisa Chang (b. 1945) founded the Pan Asian Repertory Theatre in New York. These groups employed Asian American performers, produced dramas from the Asian cultural heritage, and emphasized new plays written by and for Asian Americans.

A number of plays by Asian American writers were produced in the 1970s and 1980s, including a memory play by Philip Kan Gotanda (b. 1950) called *Song for a Nisei Fisherman* (1982). Gotanda has continued to be an active, prolific playwright. In 2003 the American Conservatory Theatre (ACT) premiered his *Yoheen,* about the difficult relationship between an African American man and his much younger Japanese American wife. In 2007 ACT presented Gotanda's *After the War,* an epic drama about a group of people living in a boardinghouse run by a former jazzman; the characters range from an unemployed African American to a Japanese accountant to a Russian-Jewish immigrant who once lived in Yokohama.

A playwright who came to prominence in the 1980s was David Henry Hwang (b. 1957), son of first-generation Americans who immigrated from China to California. Hwang wrote several plays that won wide recognition, beginning with *FOB,* produced in 1980; and *The Dance and the Railroad,* produced in 1981. Later in the decade, in 1988, Hwang's *M. Butterfly* opened successfully on Broadway. Based on a true story, the play deals with a French diplomat who meets and falls in love with a Chinese opera singer who he thinks is a woman but turns out to be a man and a spy. In 2003, Hwang collaborated with the composer Philip Glass on *The Sound of a Voice.* A younger Asian American playwright is Diana Son (b. 1965), whose play *The Moon Please* (2002) was produced at the New York Public Theatre.

Another Asian American writer is Young Jean Lee (b. 1974), who has gained wide recognition and is a director as well as a writer. One of her recent plays, *Songs of the Dragons Flying to Heaven* (2006), includes video, picturing the writer being slapped repeatedly on the cheek; monologues; and a scene with Korean Americans. Later, a white couple intrudes on the action.

Hispanic Theatre

Contemporary Hispanic theatre in the United States can be divided into at least three groups: Chicano theatre, Cuban American theatre, and Puerto Rican or Nuyorican

HISPANIC THEATRE

Theatres of all kinds have sprung up in recent decades, representing many cultures, ethnic groups, gender orientations, and the like. Hispanic plays, representing several branches of Hispanic theatre, have been particularly vibrant. Shown here is a scene from *Anna in the Tropics,* by Nilo Cruz, winner of a Pulitzer Prize, about a group of Cuban Americans who work in a cigar factory in Florida in the late 1940s. The performers are David Zayas, Jimmy Smits, John Ortiz, Vanessa Aspillaga, and Daphne Rubin-Vega. (© T Charles Erickson)

theatre. All three address the experiences of Hispanics living in the United States, and the plays are sometimes written in Spanish but are usually performed in English.

Chicano theatre, which originated primarily in the west and southwest, came to prominence during the civil rights movements of the 1960s. The theatre troupe known as El Teatro Campesino ("farmworkers' theatre") grew out of the work of Luis Valdéz (b. 1940), who joined César Chavez in organizing farmworkers in California. Valdéz wrote *actos,* short agitprop pieces dramatizing the lives of workers. (The term *agitprop* means "agitation propaganda"; it was applied in the 1930s to plays with a strong political or social agenda.)

El Teatro Campesino became the prototype for other groups such as Teatro de la Gente ("people's theatre"), founded in 1967; and Teatro de la Esperanza ("theatre of hope"), begun in 1971 in Santa Barbara, California. Also in 1971, a network of these theatres across the country was established. In the 1990s a well-known theatre, Teatro Vista, performed for Mexican and Hispanic communities in Chicago.

Valdéz's play *Zoot Suit* (1978), about racial violence in Los Angeles in 1943, opened in Los Angeles to considerable acclaim; it later moved to Broadway. Other plays about the Chicano experience followed, one of the most notable being *Roosters* (1987) by Milcha Sanchez-Scott (b. 1955), in which cockfighting is a metaphor used to explore Chicano concerns and family conflicts. Among other writers who have dealt with Chicano themes as well as wider themes is Arthur Giron (b. 1937), an American writer from Guatemala.

Cuban American theatre developed chiefly in Florida. The Federal Theatre Project of the 1930s resulted in fourteen Cuban American productions in 1936 and 1937. A highly regarded Cuban American dramatist who began to be produced in the 1970s was Maria Irene Fornés (b. 1930). Among the current generation of Cuban American writers who have emerged in the past quarter century are Manuel Martin, Mario Peña, Dolores Prida, Iván Acosta, and Omar Torres. (Torres's work is centered in Miami and New York.) Other Cuban American playwrights include Eduardo Machado (b. 1953) and Nilo Cruz (b. 1960), who won a Pulitzer Prize in 2003 for *Anna in the Tropics.*

Nuyorican is a term that refers to Puerto Rican culture, mostly in New York but elsewhere as well. Works by playwrights with a Puerto Rican orientation began to be produced in the 1960s and 1970s by groups such as the Teatro Repertorio Español; the Puerto Rican Traveling Theatre, founded by Miriam Colon; and the New York Public Theater, founded by Joseph Papp. The Nuyorican Poets' Café presented plays by a number of Hispanic writers, including an ex-convict, Miguel Piñero (1947–1988), whose *Short Eyes,* a harshly realistic portrait of prison life, proved to be very successful and won a number of awards in the 1973–1974 season. New Nuyorican playwrights have also come to prominence, including Yvette Ramírez, Cándido Tirado, Carmen Rivera, Edward Gallardo, and Juan Shamsul Alam.

Native American Theatre

Strictly speaking, there was no Native American theatre tradition; rather, there were spiritual and social traditions that had theatrical elements. These were found primarily in ancient rituals and communal celebrations, which were often infused with cosmic significance. Also, unlike traditional western theatre, these events had no audience as such: those observing were considered participants just as much as the principal performers. Many of these ceremonies and the like were outlawed by the American government in the nineteenth century. Thus the legacy of rituals and ceremonies, which had strong theatrical components—not to mention significant spiritual and cultural value—was lost or forced to go "underground."

The American Indian Religious Freedom Act of 1972 made it legal once again for certain ceremonies, such as the sun dance, to resume. The increased awareness of these rituals and celebrations contributed to the emergence of a Native American theatre. Two groups that led the way in the past three decades were the Native American Theatre Ensemble and Spiderwoman.

The Native American Theatre Ensemble, which was originally called the American Indian Theatre Ensemble, was founded by Hanay Geiogamah. (It is important to note that those familiar with Native American theatre invariably identify theatre companies and theatre artists not with the generic term *Native American theatre,* but in terms of their tribes. Thus, Geiogamah is identified as Kiowa-Delaware.) Geiogamah's organization gave its premiere performance at La Mama in New York City in 1972, and later toured widely, not only in North America but also in Europe and elsewhere.

Spiderwoman Theatre comes under the headings of both Native American theatre and feminist theatre. Founded in 1975, it is the longest continually running women's theatre in North America, as well as the longest-running Native American theatre. Three of its founding members—Lisa Mayo, Gloria Miguel, and Muriel Miguel—draw on storytelling and other theatrical traditions to celebrate their identity as American Indian women and to comment on stereotypes of women in general.

Another important Native American producing organization is Native Voices at the Autry. Randy Reinholz, a Native American; and his wife, Jean Bruce Scott, had developed a program presenting Native American drama at Illinois State University where they were on the faculty. In 2000, they were invited by the Autry Museum in Los Angeles to bring their project, Native Voices, to the Autry to become a full-time, professional producing organization. Since that beginning they have presented a series of readings, workshops, and full productions of a wide range of Native American dramatic writing.

One full production was *Kino and Teresa* (2005), a retelling by the dramatist James Lujan of the story of Romeo and Juliet. The play pits people from the Taos Pueblo against their Spanish conquerors. Another production was *Super Indian* (2007), based on a radio play by Arigon Starr. This play is in comic book style and includes, among other fantastic characters, a cross-gender Medicine Woman who spins around on the ceiling.[1]

What is important to note about Native American theatre today is that it is not primarily historical or ceremonial. Though elements of tribal traditions may be incorporated, the emphasis among playwrights and producers is really on contemporary work, fusing the problems and aspirations of today's Native Americans with their heritage. The challenges and preoccupations of young Native American playwrights are similar to those addressed by their Euro-American counterparts.

Several Native American playwrights have published single-author anthologies of their works. These include William F. Yellow Robe, Jr. (Assiniboine); Diane Glancy (Cherokee); and E. Donald Two-Rivers (Anishinabe). Another important contemporary playwright is Bruce King (Turtle Clan, Haudenosaunee-Oneida). King and Yellow Robe are also directors who have founded their own companies in the recent past and have taught playwriting and performance at the Institute of American Indian Arts in Santa Fe, New Mexico, an organization that nurtures the next generation of Native American theatre artists.

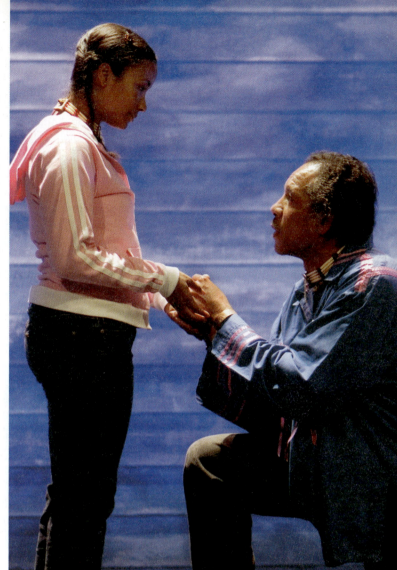

NATIVE AMERICAN THEATRE

Native American theatre, also known as indigenous theatre, is written by and for Native Americans. The participants frequently attempt to recapture not only themes and subjects appropriate to Native American culture, but also production styles and approaches of original theatrical presentations. The scene here is from a play written by William S. Yellow Robe, Jr., *Grandchildren of the Buffalo Soldiers*. It dramatizes the visit of a man, Craig Robe (James Craven), who returns to his tribe after having lived elsewhere. In this scene he is with August Jackson (Maya Washington) as part of his confrontation with his past and with the present circumstances of his people. The drama was coproduced by Penumbra Theatre Company and Trinity Repertory Company and directed by Lou Bellamy. (Ann Marsden, Penumbra Theatre Company)

Feminist Theatre

Feminist theatre is another significant movement that began in the socially active atmosphere of the late 1960s and early 1970s. It developed alongside the more general feminist movement, which stressed consciousness-raising to make people aware of the secondary position women had often been forced to occupy in social and political structures. Activists in this period attempted to revise cultural value systems and interpersonal relations in terms of an egalitarian ideology. In theatre this took the form of groups like the It's Alright to Be a Woman Theatre in New York, one of the first groups to translate consciousness-raising into stage performances.

Feminist theatre developed in several directions. For one thing, there was an attempt to make women writers, past and present, more widely acknowledged and recognized. Thus historical figures like Hrosvitha, a nun who wrote plays in her convent at Gandersheim in Germany in the tenth century, and the English playwrights Aphra Behn (1640–1689) and Susanna Centlivre (c. 1670–1723) have been brought to the forefront. In addition, attention was paid to several women playwrights who had made their mark in the early and middle twentieth century. One significant forerunner, for example, was the American playwright Rachel Crothers (1878–1958). Crothers wrote and directed many successful plays from 1906 to 1937; all of them dealt with women's moral and social concerns, and most of them were set in urban high society. Crothers's plays are skillful, entertaining comedies, but she always focused on the issue of sexual equality. Other notable women playwrights earlier in the twentieth century were Susan Glaspell (1876–1948), Sophie Treadwell (1890–1970), and Lillian Hellman (1905–1984).

The other direction for feminist theatre was the very active writing and production that emerged in the late 1960s, when many female playwrights questioned traditional gender roles and the place of women in American society. In the 1970s and 1980s, in response to the women's movement, which spurred women's playwriting and women's theatre companies, there were a number of critically and commercially successful female American playwrights. Representative works include *Fefu and Her Friends* (1977) by Maria Irene Fornés, which offered insight into female friendship and the struggles women experience in a patriarchal culture; *Still Life* (1981) by Emily Mann (b. 1952); *Painting Churches* (1983) by Tina Howe (b. 1937); and three plays that won the Susan Smith Blackburn Award, and later the Pulitzer Prize for Drama: *'Night, Mother* (1983) by Marsha Norman, *Crimes of the Heart* (1977) by Beth Henley (b. 1952), and *The Heidi Chronicles* (1988) by Wendy Wasserstein.

Although the women's movement weakened during the 1980s, women continued to write plays in increasing numbers. The playwrights who had broken new ground in the 1970s still wrote dramas, and now they were joined by other women's voices. *How I Learned to Drive* (1998) by Paula Vogel (b. 1951), about a girl's coming-of-age; and *Wit* (1998) by Margaret Edson (b. 1962), about a college professor who wrestles with a fatal illness, are examples of women's ongoing exploration of new subjects and new forms. Both plays won the Pulitzer Prize. Earlier in this chapter I noted four significant African American female playwrights: Suzan-Lori Parks (winner of a Pulitzer Prize in 2002), Pearl Cleage, Cheryl West, and Kia Corthron. In the past quarter century, women playwrights have been encouraged by receiving commissions from not-for-profit theatres and being recognized with special awards such as the Susan Smith Blackburn Prize, given annually to a woman who writes for the English-language theatre.

POLITICAL THEATRE: A FEMINIST PERSPECTIVE
A well-known contemporary woman playwright is Sarah Ruhl. In her play *In the Next Room (or The Vibrator Play),* she presents a feminist point of view about the circumstances of women in the late nineteenth century when society was dominated by men, and women's feelings of sexuality were often suppressed. In such a society, sexual fulfillment for some women could be found only indirectly and infrequently. Shown here are Mariza Dizzia and Michael Cerveris as patient and doctor in a scene from the play. (Sara Krulwich/The New York Times/Redux)

Some scholars estimate that more than 100 feminist companies have been founded in the United States; these companies include At the Foot of the Mountain, Women's Experimental Theatre, and Omaha Magic Theatre, founded by the playwright Megan Terry. One company, Split Britches, was started in 1981 by Lois Weaver, Peggy Shaw, and Deborah Margolin as an offshoot of Spiderwoman Theatre. Split Britches became well-known for its production of *Belle Reprieve* (1991), which made satiric references to Tennessee Williams's *A Streetcar Named Desire* and was created collaboratively with an English gay company, Bloolips. Many of the feminist companies that were started in the 1970s and 1980s, at the height of the women's movement, have closed. But several still remain, including Women's Project and Productions, which was founded in 1978 by Julia Miles. Feminist theatre companies have urged audiences to reexamine their own gender biases and those of their society.

A number of women dramatists, who may or may not express a feminist point of view, want to be known not as feminist or female playwrights but simply as playwrights, in the same way that male playwrights are identified. Many could be listed, but we will mention four: Sarah Ruhl, Theresa Rebeck, Carson Kreitzer, and Lynn Nottage. Sarah Ruhl (b. 1974) was awarded the Susan Smith Blackburn Prize in 2004, and was the recipient of a MacArthur "genius" grant. Ruhl's play *The Clean House,* a Pulitzer Prize finalist, concerns a Brazilian maid, who turns out to be a comedian and who refuses to clean the messy house of her disorganized employers. Ruhl's *Eurydice* tells the story of the Orpheus myth, from the point of view not of the hero but of his wife, whom he went to the underworld to rescue. A recent play by Ruhl, on Broadway in 2009, was *The Next Room,* about women's initiation into sexual satisfaction. A successful writer for television, Theresa Rebeck in her play *The Scene* wrote a sharp, pointed satire about today's television industry. Her play *The Water's Edge* transplanted the Greek story of Agamemnon, the returning warrior, to modern times and developed a seriocomic drama that mixes a tragic situation with amusing observations. Carson Kreitzer has written several plays about women who are driven to kill. One of these plays—*Self-Defense, or Death of Some Salesman*—was the story of Aileen Wuornos, a prostitute in Florida who became a serial killer. Kreitzer's *The Love Song of J. Robert Oppenheimer* concerns the soft-spoken man responsible for developing the atomic bomb. Nottage (b. 1964) has had plays about the African American experience produced throughout the United States. She is the winner of a Guggenheim Fellowship and a MacArthur "genius" grant, and her play *Ruined* won a Pulitzer Prize in 2009. The play, set in the Republic of Congo, tells of a young woman, who has experienced terrible hardships, and is taken in by a keen businesswoman who assists young women at the same time that she profits from them.

Gay and Lesbian Theatre

Lesbian theatre groups can be part of feminist theatre, but gay and lesbian theatre is also a distinct movement. A number of plays and performers introduced gay and lesbian themes into theatre before the 1960s. For example, in the nineteenth century and the early twentieth century there was a considerable amount of cross-dressing in performances: men often appeared in "drag" and women in men's clothing, raising questions about sexual and gender roles. Also, some plays included material on this subject; one example is Lillian Hellman's *The Children's Hour* (1934), in which a presumed lesbian relationship between two schoolteachers was presented.

Though considered too stereotypical by some, the play that first brought gay life to the attention of mainstream audiences was *The Boys in the Band* (1968), by Mart Crowley (b. 1935). Crowley depicted a group of men living an openly gay life. In the years that followed, complex gay characters were presented unapologetically. Plays in the 1970s and 1980s included *The Ritz* (1975) by Terrence McNally (b. 1939), Jane Chambers's *Last Summer at Bluefish Cove* (1980), and *Torch Song Trilogy* (1983) by Harvey Fierstein (b. 1954). Since then, more and more plays have dealt expressly with gay issues. In these dramas, not only is the lifestyle of gays and lesbians presented forthrightly, but frequently a gay or lesbian agenda is also put forward.

In addition to a general concern for gay and lesbian issues, there was a sense of urgency engendered by the AIDS crisis and gay rights issues. This led to a number of significant dramas, including *The Normal Heart* (1985) by Larry Kramer (1935–1999), *As Is* (1985) by William M. Hoffman (b. 1939), *The Baltimore Waltz* (1992) by Paula Vogel (b. 1951), Tony Kushner's two-part play *Angels in America* (1993–1994), Terrence McNally's *Love! Valour! Compassion!* (1995), and Richard Greenberg's *Take Me Out,* which won a Tony Award in 2003.

"Gender-bender" groups such as the Cockettes and the Angels of Light in San Francisco and Centola and Hot Peaches in New York are an offshoot of gay and lesbian theatre. An important company in New York was the Theater of the Ridiculous, founded by John Vaccaro, which developed an extraordinary writer and performer—Charles Ludlam (1943–1987). Ludlam rewrote the classics to include a good deal of wild parody and frequent cross-dressing; he also created the long-lived Ridiculous Theatrical Company. Another important group was the Five Lesbian Brothers, a col-

GAY AND LESBIAN THEATRE
Among the many alternative theatres that emerged in the last part of the twentieth century was theatre centering on the gay and lesbian experience. One important group calls itself the Five Lesbian Brothers. Shown here is its play *Oedipus at Palm Springs,* with Peg Healey, left, as Terri, and Dominique Dibbel as Prin. The play, written by four members of the troupe, is a modern, transgender view of the Greek myth of Oedipus. (© Joan Marcus)

lective of five women, including the solo performance artist Lisa Kron, who were based in New York City and staged plays parodying mainstream attitudes toward gender and sexuality.

Though a number of groups have not survived, individual performers and playwrights in gay and lesbian theatre remain very much a focus of attention.

POLITICAL THEATRE

Political theatre concerns itself with political ideas, causes, and individuals. It can run the gamut from dramas that take a strongly partisan point of view to those with a more evenhanded probing of ideas and causes. It can attack a target, espouse a cause, or engage in satire to expose what the dramatist considers a wrongheaded regime or a wrongheaded approach to a problem. Many dramatists of the past, such as George Bernard Shaw and Bertolt Brecht, have incorporated a clear political agenda into their work.

In the United States, there was a marked increase in political drama during the period of the Vietnam War, with such plays as Megan Terry's *Viet Rock,* Barbara Garson's *MacBird,* and the musical *Hair.* In the 1970s, the militant black power movement also created a number of plays that had a strong political purpose.

A number of the plays we have discussed in the previous sections of this chapter qualify as political plays, in addition to their other concerns or focus. Many of the plays in the multiethnic group—African American, Hispanic, Asian American, and others—have a political as well as an aesthetic purpose. These plays serve to speak up for the rights and for the recognition of a particular ethnic group. The same could be said of feminist theatre and of gay and lesbian theatre: the playwrights who focus on these concerns are often passionate about a particular political position that is clearly reflected in their work. Examples include the plays dealing with AIDS by Kramer, Vogel, and Kushner mentioned above. Another play with strong political implications

THE AUDIENCE'S RESPONSE

- Have you attended any performances, such as those described in this chapter, where the piece had no story or "through line" but rather there were segments—maybe a short dramatic scene, followed by a movement or dance section, interspersed with music or video? What is this performance supposed to "mean"? What did you take away from the experience?

- What themes might performances like those described above reflect on? How might themes such as betrayal, renewal, or hope be portrayed?

- What theatre environments are most conducive to productions that incorporate these types of characteristics?

was *The Vagina Monologues* (1996) by Eve Ensler (b. 1953), a dramatic presentation of actual women's stories of intimacy, vulnerability, and sexual affirmation.

In a reaction against the administration of George W. Bush and many of its policies, there was an outpouring of essentially political plays. To indicate the type and range of political plays presented during the Bush years, we will mention three pieces. The first is *Baghdad Burning: Girl Blog from Iraq* (2005), about everyday life in Iraq during the war; it was based on the blog of a girl living there, and actors read entries telling of both routine and horrific incidents leading to the girl's disappointment. Another is *The Treatment* (2006), Eve Ensler's dramatization of post-traumatic stress disorder as revealed in scenes between a male American war veteran and a female military psychologist; coming under particular scrutiny are the highly controversial, extreme interrogation practices carried out by the American military in Iraq. A third play was *My Trip to Al Qaeda* (2007), written by Lawrence Wright (b. 1947) and directed by Gregory Mosher; it was based on a book by Wright, *The Looming Tower: Al Qaeda and the Road to 9/11.*

Other political plays do not deal directly with a particular party or administration, but nevertheless have a strong political component. *Nine Parts of Desire* by Heather Raffo is a powerful portrait of a cross section of Iraqi women: their problems, their plight, and their distant hopes. Another political play is *Exonerated* by Jessica Blank and Erik Jensen, which includes actual transcripts of trials and other testimony of people who had been sentenced to death but were later proved to be innocent.

PERFORMANCE ART

In the past three decades, a number of artists have experimented with forms that force audiences to confront certain issues: What is performance? What is theatre? What is the subject of theatrical representation? Some of these artists are also political-minded; some are not. *Performance art* is one recent form that poses these questions and then some.

Performance art has two important antecedents: first, earlier avant-garde experiments of the twentieth century—such as dada, surrealism, and happenings, which stressed the irrational and attacked traditional artistic values and forms—and second, the theories of Antonin Artaud and Jerzy Grotowski.

During the past three decades, the term *performance art* has undergone several shifts of emphasis. In its earliest manifestations, performance art was related to painting and dance. In the 1970s, one branch of performance art emphasized the body as an art object: some artists suffered self-inflicted pain, and some went through daily routines (such as preparing a meal) in a museum or in a theatre setting. Another branch focused on site-specific or environmental pieces in which the setting or context was crucial: performances were created for a specific location such as a subway station, a city park, or a waterfront pier.

In some of the earliest forms of performance art, story, character, and text were minimized or even eliminated. The emphasis was not on narrating a story or exploring recognizable characters but rather on the visual and ritualistic aspects of performing. This type of theatre was often the work of an individual artist who incorporated highly personal messages, and sometimes political and social messages, into the event. The overall effect was often like a continually transforming collage. As might be expected, there was an affinity between this kind of theatre—with its emphasis of the visual picture formed onstage—and painting. Often, stage movement in performance art was also closely related to dance.

In an article in *Artsweek* in 1990, Jacki Apple explained how the emphasis in performance art shifted in the 1970s and 1980s:

> In the 1970s performance art was primarily a time-based visual art form in which text was at the service of image; by the early '80s performance art had shifted to movement-based work, with the performance artist as choreographer. Interdisciplinary collaboration and "spectacle," influenced by TV and other popular modes . . . set the tone for the new decade.[2]

In recent years the connotation of the term *performance art* has changed yet again. It is now often associated with individual artists who present autobiographical material onstage. Several such artists—Karen Finley (b. 1956) is one of the most visible—became a center of controversy when their work was seized on by ultraconservative religious groups and members of Congress as a reason to oppose funding the National Endowment for the Arts. These artists often espouse such causes as feminism and civil liberties for lesbians and gay men. Often nudity and other controversial representations of sexuality or sexual orientation are used to confront audiences. Such was the case in *Alice's Rape* (1989), in which Robbie McCauley performed nude as her great-great-grandmother, a slave on the auction block. These performance artists are continuing a trend begun by early realistic and antirealistic dramatists, whose works challenged the social status quo and were often banned.

Off-off-Broadway has been the initial home of many performance artists. Two artists who began performing solo pieces in alternative spaces but later received commercial productions are Spalding Gray (1941–2004) and Bill Irwin (b. 1950). Gray, a monologuist who discussed issues that ranged from his own personal concerns to politics, was reminiscent of ancient storytellers who created a theatrical environment single-handedly. Irwin's performances are mime-like, and he uses popular slapstick techniques to reflect on the contemporary human condition.

Anna Deavere Smith (b. 1952), an African American performance artist, won considerable acclaim in the early 1990s for pieces dealing with racial unrest. In her works, she portrays numerous real people whom she has met and interviewed. Her

PERFORMANCE ART
The category of performance art encompasses everything from storytelling to dramatic monologues to performances resembling cabaret turns. Usually the content is highly personal and strongly related to the individual artist. A particularly successful performance artist is Margaret Cho, seen here in her one-woman show *The Sensuous Woman*. Cho, who is a Korean American, deals with controversial social and personal problems, including a frank presentation of sexual issues, in a performance that in part resembles a nightclub act. (© Carol Rosegg)

Twilight: Los Angeles 1992 presented people affected by the uprising that followed the acquittals in the first trial of police officers charged with brutalizing Rodney King. A recent piece by Smith is *Let Me Down Easy* (2009). Other well-known performance artists are Ping Chong (b. 1946), an Asian American who mixed multimedia into his works; Eric Bogosian (b. 1953); John Leguizamo (b. 1965); Margaret Cho (b. 1968); Sarah Jones (b. 1974); and Holly Hughes (b. 1955).

A number of spaces have become recognized for their presentation of performance artists. These include two in New York City: PS 122, a converted public school in the East Village in downtown Manhattan; and the Kitchen, also located in downtown Manhattan. In addition, many museums throughout the United States are known for presenting series of performance artists, including the Walker Museum in Minneapolis and the Museum of Contemporary Art in Chicago. The fact that performance art is most often presented in converted, found spaces or museums again reflects the diversity of the form and its relationship to earlier avant-garde movements and the visual arts.

TODAY'S THEATRE: GLOBAL, ECLECTIC, DIVERSE

As we have pointed out, perhaps at no time in theatre history has there been such a wide-ranging group of live theatre events available to audiences. Despite the ever-present competition from electronic media—films, television, computers, and numerous handheld devices—live theatre remains very much a presence in our lives. It is truly global and international, with influences and exchanges from every corner of the world. Productions can regularly be seen not only in larger Broadway-style emporiums, but in excellent regional theatre and first-rate university and college productions. The kinds of theatre available range from the finest classics—Shakespeare is the most widely produced playwright in America—to the most cutting-edge, postmodern presentations. In short, the opportunities today for rewarding experiences in the theatre are truly global and diverse on all sides.

When we turn from the theatre of today to the theatre of the future, a question arises: Where will theatre go from here? It is impossible, of course, to answer with any certainty. We can assume, though, that the trends described in this chapter and Chapter 14 will continue. Theatre of the future will no doubt continue to present new works alongside a rich mixture of plays from the past. In both writing and production, theatre will draw on many sources. We cannot know whether or not new plays will attain the greatness of the past, but playwrights show no sign of abandoning theater, despite the larger financial rewards offered by film and television.

We can be sure that theatre will survive in a vigorous form, no matter what challenges it faces from electronic media. At the same time, modern technology will play an important role in theatre: in lighting effects with the use of computerized lighting boards, in the shifting of scenery, and in other ways. There will also, no doubt, continue to be multimedia experiments, fusing theatre with film, digital media, dance, and computer-generated media.

With all its innovations, however, theatre of the future will no doubt be an extension of theatre of the past. Theatre will continue to be enacted by women and men in person before an audience, and the plays they perform will deal primarily with the hopes, fears, agonies, and joys of the human race.

It is clear that the complexity of the modern world will result in a heterogeneous theatre. Ongoing exploration of the diversity of contemporary society means that diverse theatres will continue to spring up. There is no question that in the twenty-first century theatre will be as complex and fragmented as the world in which it exists. Yet from the start theatre has always focused on human concerns, and they will remain the source of its appeal as far ahead as we can see.

SUMMARY

1. Contemporary American theatre is a reflection of and a reaction to the complexity of modern times.

2. The city of Chicago, with its many types, levels, and sizes of theatres, offers a microcosm of American theatres across the country.

3. An important development of the past half century has been the emergence of non-text-based theatre, sometimes referred to as postmodernist. Rather than being initiated by a dramatist, a theatre event is created by an auteur director, an acting ensemble, a performance artist, or some combination of these.

4. Avant-garde and experimental theatre, which grew out of earlier approaches, is alive and well in the United States.

5. Multiethnic theatre in America is vibrant, with a number of facets: (a) African American theatre, (b) Asian American theatre, (c) Hispanic theatre, and (d) Native American theatre.

6. There are many active minority theatres and theatres with special points of view, including (a) feminist theatre, (b) gay and lesbian theatre, and (c) political theatre.

7. An important form of theatre today is performance art.

8. Much of the new theatre activity today is a reflection of the theories of postmodernism.

Glossary

Above Upstage or away from the audience.

Acting area One of several areas into which a stage space is divided in order to facilitate blocking and the planning of stage movement.

Ad lib To improvise lines of a speech.

Aesthetic distance Physical or psychological separation or detachment of audience from dramatic action, usually considered necessary for artistic illusion.

Allegory Symbolic representation of abstract themes through characters, action, and other concrete elements of a play.

Amphitheatre Large oval, circular, or semicircular outdoor theatre with rising tiers of seats around an open playing area; *also,* an exceptionally large indoor auditorium.

Antagonist Opponent of the protagonist in a drama.

Apprentice Young performer training in an Elizabethan acting company.

Apron Stage space in front of the curtain line or proscenium; also called the *forestage.*

Arena Stage entirely surrounded by the audience; also known as *circle theatre* or *theatre-in-the-round.*

Aside In a play, thoughts spoken aloud by one character (often, to the audience) without being heard or noticed by others onstage.

At rise Expression used to describe what is happening onstage at the moment when the curtain first rises or the lights come up.

Audition A tryout by performers before a director for a role in a play or musical.

Automated light Piece of lighting equipment that can change the direction, focus, color, and shape of the lighting beam by remote control. Made possible by advances in electronics and computerization.

Backdrop Large drapery or painted canvas that provides the rear or upstage masking of a set.

Backstage Stage area behind the front curtain; *also,* the areas beyond the setting, including wings and dressing rooms.

Ballad opera Eighteenth-century English form that burlesqued opera.

Basic situation Specific problem or maladjustment from which a play arises.

Batten Pipe or long pole suspended horizontally above the stage, on which scenery, drapery, or lights may be hung.

Beam projector Lighting instrument without a lens, which uses a parabolic reflector to project a narrow, nonadjustable beam of light.

Below Opposite of *above;* toward the front of the stage.

Biomechanics Vsevolod Meyerhold's theory that a performer's body should be machinelike and that emotion could be represented externally.

Black box A theatre space that is open, flexible, and adaptable, usually without fixed seating. The stage-audience configuration can be rearranged to suit the individual requirements of a given production, making it both economical and particularly well suited to experimental work.

Blackout Total darkening of the stage.

Blocking Pattern and arrangement of performers' movements onstage with respect to each other and to the stage space, usually set by the director.

Book (1) Spoken (as opposed to sung) portion of the text of a musical play. (2) To schedule engagements for artists or productions.

Bookholder Prompter who gave actors their lines in Elizabethan theatres.

Border Strip of drapery or painted canvas hung from a batten or pipe to mask the area above the stage; *also,* a row of lights hung from a batten.

Box Small private compartment for a group of spectators built into the walls of a traditional proscenium-arch theatre.

Box set Interior setting using flats to form the back and side walls and often the ceiling of a room.

Business Obvious, detailed physical movement of performers to reveal character, aid action, or establish mood.

Capa y espada ("CAH-pah ee ehs-PAH-dah") Literally, "cape and sword"; Spanish play about intrigue and duels of honor.

Casting Choosing performers to play specific roles in a play or musical. Usually performers are chosen who suit the part in age, gender, and other features, but at times there is "casting against type."

Catharsis ("kuh-THAR-sis") Greek word, usually translated as "purgation," which Aristotle used in his definition of tragedy, referring to the vicarious cleansing of emotions in the audience through their representation onstage.

Catwalk Narrow metal platform suspended above the stage to permit ready access to lights and scenery hung from the grid.

Cazuela ("cah-zoo-AY-lah") Gallery above the tavern in the back wall of the theatres of the Spanish golden age; the area where unescorted women sat.

Center stage Stage position in the middle acting area of the stage, or the middle section extended upstage and downstage.

Choregus ("koh-REE-guhs") Wealthy person who financed a playwright's works at an ancient Greek dramatic festival.

Chorus (1) In ancient Greek drama, a group of performers who sang and danced, sometimes participating in the action but usually simply commenting on it. (2) In modern times, performers in a musical play who sing and dance as a group.

City Dionysia ("SIT-ee digh-eh-NIGH-see-uh") The most important Greek festival in honor of the god Dionysus, and the first to include drama. Held in the spring.

Climax The high point in the development of a dramatic plot. The scene toward the end of a drama in which all the forces reach their highest pitch and the fate of all the characters is determined.

Comedia ("koh-MAY-dee-ah") Three-act full-length nonreligious play of the Spanish golden age.

Comedy of ideas A comedy in which the humor is based on intellectual and verbal aspects of comedy rather than physical comedy or comedy of character. A drama whose emphasis is on the clash of ideas, as exemplified in the plays of George Bernard Shaw.

Comedy of manners Form of comic drama that became popular in seventeenth-century France and the English Restoration, emphasizing a cultivated or sophisticated atmosphere and witty dialogue.

Compañias de parte ("cōhm-pa-NYEE-ahs day PAHR-teh") Acting troupes in the Spanish golden age, organized according to a sharing system.

Complication Introduction, in a play, of a new force, which creates a new balance of power and entails a delay in reaching the climax.

Computer-assisted design (CAD) Designs created by computer. All features of a set design, including ground plans, elevations, and walls, can be indicated by computer, and variations and alternations can be easily created and displayed.

Conflict Tension between two or more characters that leads to a crisis or climax; a fundamental struggle or imbalance—involving ideologies, actions, personalities, etc.—underlying the plot of a play.

Constructivism Post–World War I movement in scene design, in which sets—frequently composed of ramps, platforms, and levels—were nonrealistic and intended to provide greater opportunities for physical action.

Corral Theatre building of the Spanish golden age, usually located in the courtyard of a series of adjoining buildings.

Counterweight Device for balancing the weight of scenery in a system that allows scenery to be raised above the stage by ropes and pulleys.

Crew Backstage team assisting in mounting a production.

Crisis A point in a play when events and opposing forces are at a crucial moment, and when the course of further action will be determined. There may be a series of crises leading to the definitive climax.

Cross Movement by a performer across the stage in a given direction.

Cue Any prearranged signal—such as the last words in a speech, a piece of business, or any action or lighting change—that indicates to a performer or stage manager that it is time to proceed to the next line or action.

Cue sheet Prompt book marked with cues, or a list of cues for the use of technicians, especially the stage manager.

Curtain (1) Rise or fall of the actual curtain, which separates a play into structural parts. (2) Last bit of action preceding the fall of the curtain.

Curtain-raiser In nineteenth-century theatre, a short play presented before a full-length drama.

Cyclorama Permanent fixture or curved drop used to mask the rear and sides of a stage, usually representing sky or open space.

Dada Movement in art between the world wars, based on presenting the irrational and attacking traditional artistic values.

Denouement ("deh-noo-MAHN") Point near the end of a play when suspense is satisfied and "the knot is untied."

Designer (front) elevations Drawings that indicate the total, exact details of a set as seen from the point of view of the audience.

Deus ex machina ("DEH-oos eks MAH-kih-nah") Literally, "god from a machine," a resolution device in classic Greek drama; hence, intervention of supernatural forces—usually at the last moment—to save the action from its logical conclusion. In modern drama, an arbitrary and coincidental solution.

Dimmer Device for changing lighting intensity smoothly and at varying rates.

Dim out To turn out lights with a dimmer.

Director In American usage, the person responsible for the overall unity of a production and for coordinating the work of contributing artists. The American director is the equivalent of the British producer and the French *metteur-en-scène* ("meh-TURR ahn SENN").

Dithyramb ("DITH-ih-ramb") Ancient Greek choral song describing the adventures of a god or hero.

Double entendre ("DOO-bluh ahn-TAHN-druh") Word or phrase in comedy that has a double meaning, the second often sexual.

Doubling Term used when a performer plays more than one role in a play.

Downstage Front of the stage, toward the audience.

Dramaturg *Also,* literary manager. Position that originated in Europe and is now found in many theatres in the United States, particularly not-for-profit theatres. The dramaturg analyzes scripts, advises directors, and works with playwrights on new pieces.

Dress rehearsal The first full performances of a production before performances for the public.

Drop Large piece of fabric—generally painted canvas—hung from a batten to the stage floor, usually to serve as backing.

Ellipsoidal reflector spotlight Sharp, powerful light used at some distance from the stage.

Emotional recall Stanislavsky's exercise, which helps the performer to present realistic emotions. The performer feels a character's emotion by thinking of the conditions surrounding an event in his or her own life that led to a similar emotion.

Ensemble playing Acting that stresses the total artistic unity of a group performance rather than individual performances.

Entrance Manner and effectiveness with which a performer comes into a scene, as well as the actual coming onstage; *also,* the way this is prepared for by the playwright.

Epilogue Speech by one of the performers to the audience after the conclusion of a play.

Exit A performer's leaving the stage, as well as the preparation for his or her leaving.

Exposition Imparting of information necessary for an understanding of the story but not covered by the action onstage; events or knowledge from the past, or occurring outside the play, which must be introduced so that the audience can understand the characters or plot.

Flashback In a narrative or story, movement back to a time in the past to show a scene or an event before the narrative resumes at the point at which it was interrupted.

Flat Single piece of flat, rectangular scenery, used with other similar units to create a set.

Flood, floodlight Lighting instrument without lenses which is used for general or large-area lighting.

Fly loft, or flies Space above the stage where scenery may be lifted out of sight by ropes and pulleys.

Follow spot Large, powerful spotlight with a sharp focus and narrow beam which is used by an operator to follow principal performers as they move about the stage.

Footlights Row of lights in the floor along the front edge of the stage or apron. Almost never used in contemporary theatre.

Forestage See *Apron.*

Found space Space not originally intended for theatre, which is used for theatrical productions. Avant-garde artists often produce in found spaces.

Fourth wall Convention, in a proscenium-arch theatre, that the audience is looking into a room through an invisible fourth wall.

Freeze To remain motionless onstage, especially for laughs or in a tableau.

Fresnel ("fruh-NEL") Type of spotlight used over relatively short distances with a soft beam edge, which allows the light to blend easily with light from other sources; *also,* the type of lenses used in such spotlights.

Front of the house Portion of a theatre reserved for the audience; sometimes called simply the *house.*

Futurism Art movement, begun in Italy about 1905, which idealized mechanization and machinery.

Gallery In traditional proscenium-arch theatres, the undivided seating area cut into the walls of the building.

Gauze See *Scrim.*

Gel Thin, flexible color medium used in lighting instruments to give color to a light beam.

Genre A French word meaning type or category. In theatre, genre denotes the category into which a play falls: for example, tragedy, comedy, or tragicomedy.

Grid Metal framework above the stage from which lights and scenery are suspended.

Groove system System in which tracks on the stage floor and above the stage allowed for the smooth movement of flat wings on and off the stage; usually there were a series of grooves at each stage position.

Ground plan A blueprint or floor plan of the stage indicating the placement of scenery, furniture, doors and windows, and the various levels of the stage, as well as the walls of rooms, platforms, etc.

Hamartia ("hah-MARH-tee-ah") Ancient Greek term usually translated as "tragic flaw." The literal translation is "missing the mark," which may suggest that hamartia is not so much a character flaw as an error in judgment.

Hanamichi ("hah-nah-MEE-chee") In kabuki theatre, a bridge running from behind the audience (toward the left side of the audience) to the stage. Performers can enter on the hanamichi; important scenes may also be played on it.

Hand props Small props carried on- or offstage by actors and actresses during a performance, such as

canes, umbrellas, or briefcases. See also *Props.*

Hashigakari ("ha-shee-gah-KAH-ree") Bridge in nō theatre on which the actors make their entrance from the dressing area to the platform stage.

Hireling Member of an Elizabethan acting troupe who was paid a set salary and was not a shareholder.

House See *Front of the house.*

Hubris ("HEW-brihs") Ancient Greek term usually defined as "excessive pride" and cited as a common tragic character flaw.

Inner stage Area at the rear of the stage that can be cut off from the rest by means of curtains or scenery and revealed for special scenes.

Irony A condition the reverse of what we have expected or an expression whose intended implication is the opposite of its literal sense.

Kill To eliminate or suppress; for example, to remove unwanted light or to ruin an effect through improper execution.

Lazzi ("LAHT-zee") Comic pieces of business repeatedly used by characters in Italian commedia dell'arte.

Left stage Left side of the stage from the point of view of a performer facing the audience.

Living newspapers In the United States, the Federal Theatre Project's dramatizations of newsworthy events in the 1930s.

Long run Term used in commercial theatre when a drama is performed for as long as it is popular.

Magic if Stanislavsky's acting exercise, which requires the performer to ask, "How would I react *if* I were in this character's position?"

Mask (1) To conceal backstage areas or technical equipment from the audience by means of scenery. (2) Face or head covering for a

performer, in the image of the character portrayed.

Masking Scenery or draperies used to hide or cover.

Minstrelsy Type of nineteenth-century production usually featuring white performers made up in blackface.

Mise-en-scène ("miz-on-SEHN") Arrangement of all the elements in a stage picture at a given moment or throughout a performance.

Multimedia Use of electronic media, such as slides, film, and videotape, in live theatrical presentations.

Multimedia theatre Presentations in which theatrical elements are combined with other art forms, such as film, video, art, or dance. Frequently, several media are combined in a single production.

Multiple setting Form of stage setting, common in the Middle Ages, in which several locations are represented at the same time; also called *simultaneous setting.* Used also in various forms of contemporary theatre.

Objective Stanislavsky's term for that which is urgently desired and sought by a character, the long-range goal that propels a character to action.

Obstacle That which delays or prevents the achieving of a goal by a character. An obstacle creates complication and conflict.

Offstage Areas of the stage, usually in the wings or backstage, that are not in view of the audience.

Onstage Area of the stage that is in view of the audience.

Open To turn or face more toward the audience.

Orchestra (1) In American usage, ground-floor seating in an auditorium. (2) Circular playing space in ancient Greek theatres.

Pace Rate at which a performance is played; *also,* to perform a scene or play to set its proper speed.

Paint charge artist Person in charge of the painting of the set, based on drawings and sketches created by the scenic designer.

Parabasis ("puh-RAB-uh-sihs") Scene in classical Greek Old Comedy in which the chorus directly addresses the audience members and makes fun of them.

Parados ("PAR-uh-dohs") In classical Greek drama, the scene in which the chorus enters; *also,* the entranceway for the chorus in Greek theatre.

Parterre In French neoclassical theatre, the pit in which audience members stood.

Patio In theatre of the Spanish golden age, the pit area for the audience.

Pensionnaire ("PON-see-oh-NARE") Hireling in a French acting troupe.

Periaktoi In Greek theatre, vertical three-sided column that could be rotated to show three different scenic pictures.

Period Term describing any representation onstage of a former age (e.g., *period costume, period play*).

Perspective Illusion of depth in painting, introduced into scene design during the Italian Renaissance.

Pit Floor of the house in a traditional proscenium-arch theatre. It was originally a standing area; by the end of the eighteenth century, backless benches were added.

Platform Raised surface on a stage floor serving as an elevation for parts of the stage action and allowing for a multiplicity of stage levels.

Platform stage Elevated stage with no proscenium, sometimes called a *trestle stage*.

Plot (1) As distinct from story, patterned arrangements of events and characters in a drama, with incidents selected and arranged for maximum dramatic impact. (2) In Elizabethan theatres, an outline of the play posted backstage for the actors.

Point of attack The moment in the story when a play actually begins. The dramatist chooses a point that he or she judges will best start the action and propel it forward.

Pole and chariot Giacomo Torelli's mechanized means of changing sets made up of flat wings.

Preparation (1) Previous arranging of circumstances, pointing of characters, and placing of properties in a production so that the ensuing actions will seem reasonable. (2) Actions taken by an actor or actress in getting ready for a performance.

Previews Tryout performances of a production before an audience, preceding the official "opening" performance.

Private theatres Indoor theatres in Elizabethan England.

Producer In American usage, the person responsible for the business side of a production, including raising the necessary money. (In British usage, a producer for many years was the equivalent of an American director.)

Prologue Introductory speech delivered to the audience by one of the actors or actresses before a play begins.

Prompt To furnish a performer with missed or forgotten lines or cues during a performance.

Prompt book Script of a play indicating performers' movements, light cues, sound cues, etc.

Prop (or property) designer Person who creates, secures, and executes all props; this work may include building special pieces of furniture, devising magical equipment, and selecting lamps and all other accessories.

Props Properties; objects that are used by performers onstage or are necessary to complete a set.

Proscenium ("pro-SIN-ee-um") Arch or frame surrounding the stage opening in a box or picture stage.

Protagonist Principal character in a play, the one whom the drama is about.

Public theatres Outdoor theatres in Elizabethan England.

Rake (1) To position scenery on a slant or at an angle other than parallel or perpendicular to the curtain line. (2) An upward slope of the stage floor away from the audience.

Raked stage Stage floor that slopes upward away from the audience toward the back of the stage.

Regional theatre (1) Theatre whose subject matter is specific to a particular geographic region. (2) Theatres situated in theatrical centers across the country.

Régisseur ("ray-zhee-SUHR") Continental European term for a theatre director; it sometimes denotes a dictatorial director.

Rehearsal Preparation by a cast for the performance of a play through repetition and practice.

Repertory, or repertoire Acting company that at any time can perform a number of plays alternately; *also,* the plays regularly performed by a company.

Restoration drama English drama after the restoration of the monarchy, from 1660 to 1700.

Reversal Sudden switch of circumstances or revelation of knowledge, which leads to a result contrary to expectations; called *peripeteia* ("peh-rih-puh-TEEuh") or *peripety* ("peh-RIP-uh-tee") in Greek drama.

Revolving stage Large circular turntable in a stage floor on which scenery is placed so that, as it moves, one set is brought into view while another one turns out of sight.

Right stage Right side of the stage from the point of view of a performer facing the audience.

Ritual Ceremonial event, often religious, which takes place in a specific sequence.

Satyr play One of the three types of classical Greek drama, usually a ribald takeoff on Greek mythology and history that included a chorus of satyrs (mythological creatures who were half-man and half-goat).

Scaena ("SKAY-nah") Stage house in a Roman theatre.

Scene (1) Stage setting. (2) One of a series of structural units into which a play or acts of a play are divided. (3) Location of a play's action.

Scenic charge artist Person responsible for seeing that sets are built and painted according to the specifications and requirements called for by the scenic designer.

Scrim Thin, open-weave fabric, which is nearly transparent when lit from behind and opaque when lit from the front.

Script Written or printed text—consisting of dialogue, stage directions, character descriptions, and the like.

Set Scenery, taken as a whole, for a scene or an entire production.

Set piece Piece of scenery that stands independently in a scene.

Shareholders In Elizabethan acting troupes, members who received part of the profits as payment.

Sides Script containing only a single actor's lines and cues. Elizabethan actors learned their roles from sides.

Simultaneous setting Medieval tradition of presenting more than one locale onstage at the same time.

Skene ("SKEE-nee") In ancient Greek theatre, the scene house behind the orchestra.

Slapstick Type of comedy or comic business that relies on ridiculous physical activity—often vigorous—for its humor.

Soliloquy Speech in which a character who is alone onstage speaks inner thoughts aloud.

Spill Light from stage-lighting instruments that falls outside the area for which it is intended, such as light that falls on the audience.

Spine (1) In the Stanislavsky method, a character's dominant desire or motivation; usually thought of as an action and expressed as a verb. (2) *Also,* the "through-line" or general action that runs through a play from beginning to end.

Stage convention An established theatrical technique or practice arbitrarily accepted through custom or usage.

Stage door Outside entrance to dressing rooms and stage areas that is used by performers and technicians.

Stage house Stage floor and the space around it to the side walls, as well as the space above it up to the grid.

Stage left, stage right See *Left stage, Right stage.*

Stage manager Person who coordinates all aspects of a production related to the director and actors, both during the rehearsals and during the run of the show; he or she ensures that the director's artistic choices are maintained during performances.

Standing room only (SRO) Notice that all seats for a performance have been sold but standees may be accommodated.

Stanislavsky method Konstantin Stanislavsky's techniques and theories about acting, which promote a naturalistic style stressing (among other things) psycho-physical action as opposed to conventional theatricality.

Stock set Standard setting for a locale used in every play which requires that environment.

Storm and stress Antineo-classical eighteenth-century German movement, which was a forerunner of romanticism; in German, *Sturm und Drang.*

Strike To remove pieces of scenery or props from onstage or to take down an entire set after a final performance.

Subtext Meaning and movement of a play below its surface; that which is not stated but implied.

Summer stock Theatre companies operating outside major theatrical centers during the summer, often producing a different play every week.

Symbol A sign, a visual image, an object, or an action that signifies something else; a visual embodiment of something invisible. A single image or sign stands for an entire idea or larger concept—a flag is a symbol for a nation; a logo is a symbol for a corporation.

Symbolism Movement of the late nineteenth century and early twentieth century that sought to express inner truth rather than represent life realistically.

Teaser Short horizontal curtain just beyond the proscenium, used to mask the fly loft and, in effect, to lower the height of the proscenium.

Technical Term referring to functions necessary to the production of a play other than those of the cast and the director, such as functions of the stage crew, carpenters, and lighting crew.

Technical director Staff member responsible for scheduling, construction, and installation of all equipment; he or she is responsible for guaranteeing that designs are executed according to the designer's specifications.

Tetralogy In classical Greek theatre, four plays—three tragedies and a satyr play—written by one author for a festival.

Theme Central thought of a play; the idea or ideas with which a play deals and which it expounds.

Thespian Synonym for "performer"; from Thespis (sixth century BCE), who is said to have been the first actor in ancient Greek theatre.

Thrust stage Stage space that thrusts into the audience space; a stage surrounded on three sides by audience seating.

Tragic flaw The factor that is a character's chief weakness and makes him or her most vulnerable; it often intensifies in time of stress.

Trap Opening in a stage floor, normally covered, which can be used for special effects or allows for a staircase ostensibly leading to a lower floor.

Treadmill Belt or band, usually 3 feet to 5 feet wide, that moves across the stage, on which scenery, props, or performers can move on- or offstage. Generally moves parallel to the front edge of the stage. Operated electronically today, with safety devices to avoid injuries to performers.

Trilogy In classical Greece, three tragedies written by the same playwright and presented on a single day; they were often connected by a story or thematic elements.

Unities Term referring to the preference that a play occur within one day (unity of time), in one place (unity of place), and with no action irrelevant to the plot (unity of action).

Unity A requirement of art; an element often setting art apart from life. In drama, the term refers to unity of action in structure and story and to the integrity and wholeness of a production.

Upstage At or toward the back of the stage, away from the front edge of the stage.

Wagon stage Low platform mounted on wheels or casters by means of which scenery is moved on- and offstage.

Wings (1) Left and right offstage areas. (2) Narrow standing pieces of scenery, or "legs," more or less parallel to the proscenium, which form the sides of a setting.

Work lights Lights arranged for the convenience of stage technicians, situated either in backstage areas and shaded or over the stage area for use while the curtain is down.

Yard Pit, or standing area, in Elizabethan public theatres.

Notes

Chapter 1

1 Walter Kerr, "We Call It 'Live Theater,' but Is It?" *New York Times,* 2 January 1972. Copyright 1972 by the New York Times Company. Reprinted by permission.

2 Bernard Beckerman, *Dynamics of Drama: Theory and Method of Analysis,* Knopf, New York, 1970, p. 129.

Chapter 2

1 Jean-Claude van Itallie, *The Serpent: A Ceremony,* written in collaboration with the Open Theater, Atheneum, New York, 1969, p. ix.

Chapter 3

1 Notes on *King Lear* are from G. K. Hunter's edition of Shakespeare's *King Lear,* Penguin, Baltimore, Md., 1972, pp. 243–244.

Chapter 4

1 The Performance Group, *Dionysus in 69,* Noonday, Farrar, Straus, and Giroux, New York, n.d.

2 Ibid.

3 Material on the proscenium, arena, and thrust stages was suggested by a booklet prepared by Dr. Mary Henderson for the educational division of Lincoln Center for the Performing Arts.

4 Antonin Artaud, *The Theater and Its Double,* Grove, New York, 1958, pp. 96–97.

Chapter 5

1 Richard Findlater, *The Player Kings,* Weidenfeld and Nicolson, London, 1971, p. 25.

2 Konstantin Stanislavsky, *An Actor Prepares,* Theatre Arts, New York, 1948, p. 73.

3 Mira Felner, *Free to Act: An Integrated Approach to Acting,* Harcourt Brace, Fort Worth, Tex., 1990, p. 14.

Chapter 9

1 Albert Camus, *Le Mythe de Sisyphe,* Gallimard, Paris, 1942, p. 18.

2 From the book *Waiting for Godot* by Samuel Beckett. Copyright 1954 by Grove Press; renewed copyright 1982 by Samuel Beckett. Used with the permission of Grove/Atlantic, Inc.

Chapter 10

1 Robert Edmond Jones, *The Dramatic Imagination,* Theatre Arts, New York, 1941, p. 25.

Chapter 15

1 The material on Native Voices at the Autry was based on reporting by Sarah Lemanczyk in the March 2007 issue of *American Theatre.*

2 Jacki Apple, "Art at the Barricades," *Artwork,* vol. 21, May 3, 1990, p. 21.

Index